Partners With Power

Partners With Power

*The Social Transformation of
the Large Law Firm*

Robert L. Nelson

UNIVERSITY OF CALIFORNIA PRESS
Berkeley · Los Angeles · London

University of California Press
Berkeley and Los Angeles, California

University of California Press, Ltd.
London, England

Copyright © 1988 by
The Regents of the University of California

Library of Congress Cataloging in Publication Data

Nelson, Robert L., 1952–
Partners with power.

Bibliography: p.
Includes index.
1. Law partnership—United States. 2. Law firms—
United States. 3. Practice of law—United States.
I. Title.
KF300.N45 1987   346.73'0682   87–35854
                      347.306682
ISBN 0–520–05844–5 (alk. paper)

Printed in the United States of America

1 2 3 4 5 6 7 8 9

To my parents

Contents

Preface ix

Acknowledgments xv

Introduction 1

PART I. PATTERNS OF SOCIAL CHANGE IN THE LARGE LAW FIRM

1. Social Change and Organizational Structure 37
2. Bureaucracy and Participation in Historical Perspective 86

PART II. THE STRUCTURE OF THE LARGE LAW FIRM

3. The Changing Structure of Opportunity: Recruitment and Careers 127
4. The Organization of Work 159
5. Economic Rewards 190
6. Professionalism, Bureaucracy, and Commitment: Authority in the Large Law Firm 205

PART III. THE LAW FIRM AS A SOCIAL INSTITUTION

7. Ideology, Practice, and Professional Autonomy:
   Social Values and Client Relationships   231
8. Rationalization and Power   270

Appendixes   291

Notes   335

References   347

Index   363

Preface

I became interested in patterns of organizational change in the large law firm through the conjunction of practical and intellectual experience. After clerking a summer in a large Chicago law firm in 1977, I took Arnold Feldman's course on industrialism and industrialization at Northwestern University and was exposed to the writings of E. P. Thompson, Alfred Chandler, Jr., and Reinhard Bendix on the rise of the modern industrial order. It struck me that corporate law firms constituted an important and interesting set of organizations within industrial society, for they constituted the elite strata of a professional sector that had undergone explosive growth in recent years and were themselves in the midst of an apparent transformation in the size, structure, and functioning of the organization. Yet no one writing on the professions or the sociology of law had attempted an analysis linking processes of structural change in the corporate law firm with the changing role of law and lawyers in the United States.

Erwin Smigel's book *The Wall Street Lawyer* (1969), for which the primary data were collected in the late 1950s and which had been given only a minor update in 1969, remained virtually the only serious scholarly work on large law firms. In the decade following the publication of the last edition of Smigel's book, large firms had experienced dramatic growth. While only twenty firms had more than one hundred lawyers in 1968, by 1984 more than two hundred firms had surpassed the one hundred mark and sixty firms had more than two hundred lawyers. The striking pace of change in firms not only emphasized the dated character of Smigel's research but also called attention to other problems of theoretical emphasis and analysis. Most glaring was the absence of any theory of growth or structural change that might explain the increasing size of firms or the implications of growth for the governance of the organization and the role the large firm plays in the legal system.

Indeed I soon learned that the limitations of Smigel's work were characteristic of the professions literature in general. Scholars of the professions largely had ignored the economic structure of professional organizations and the relationship between the structure of the professional firm and the market for professional services. Although the sociology of the professions frequently had examined the relationships between professionals and bureaucratic organizations of various types (universities, hospitals, social welfare agencies), much less attention had been given to hierarchical relationships among professional colleagues in autonomous professional organizations or to changes in the nature of these relationships under the force of increasing organizational size and complexity.

To understand the large law firm and the changes it was exhibiting, research needed to focus on these less studied aspects of the professional organization. I have done so by developing what I call the organizational dominance framework, a framework that attempts to explain how large law firms have achieved and maintained a dominant position in the market for corporate legal services, as well as how the leading partners of firms have gained and legitimated a dominant position within the organization.

This book, however, is not intended only as an organizational analysis. It also aspires to a contribution to the sociology of law. Although the large law firm contains only a relatively small percentage of American lawyers (some 7.3 percent of private practitioners work in firms of more than fifty lawyers [Curran 1985, p. 13]) and in that sense is an atypical element of the American legal profession, it is an institution that has had a much greater impact on the American legal system than mere numbers indicate. It has been described as the pinnacle of the status hierarchy of the legal profession in that it recruits the top graduates of the top law schools, it represents the most resourceful of clients in the most intellectually challenging and rapidly changing fields of substantive law, and its members often occupy positions of leadership in bar associations, law reform commissions, and civic and political organizations (Auerbach 1976). The large law firm has therefore been a central institution in the development of the distinctive norms and cultural understandings that define the ideal of professionalism for American lawyers, including autonomy from clients, an orientation to public service, and a commitment to the practice of law as something more than a business.

The fate of professionalism within the American legal profession is very much connected to the changes taking place in large firms. Despite almost a century of public doubts about the autonomy and social responsibility of large law firms, Talcott Parsons (1962) and Erwin Smigel (1969) expressed optimism about the role that lawyers and large firms play in society. Both argued that the elite of the legal profession could perform a mediating role in legal and social change by convincing their powerful clientele to follow the dictates of legal rules and to abide by policies that served the public interest rather than the client's narrow purposes. Thus the independence of corporate law firms and their commitment to civic and professional values were asserted to be potent forces for the normative integration of society.

All these elements—the historical legacy of professionalism in large law firms, the functionalist conviction that large firms contribute to the development of legal outcomes and legal rules that are rational and just, and the dramatic but largely unexplained expansion of firms in the last decade—suggested that the study of social change in the large law firm was significant to theories of the role that law plays in American society.

Indeed there is perhaps more anxiety now within the elite of the legal profession over what that role is than ever before, and much of this concern centers on the large law firm. The same lawyers who built large law firms into the kinds of organizations they are today openly express the fear that economic pressures have become so intense that partners and associates are driven to specialize narrowly, bill "too many" hours, and forgo activities in bar associations, civic institutions, and pro bono litigation that would serve the public interest. Such public figures as the Chief Justice of the United States (Rehnquist 1986) and the president (and former law school dean) of Harvard University (Bok 1983) voice similar concerns about the impact of the changes taking place in firms on the ethics and public service orientations of lawyers. The sense of malaise that grips the corporate elite of the profession reflects broader questions about the legal system. The whole edifice of American law and the prominent part law has come to play in American life is attacked from both the right and the left. Politically conservative critics allege that the law has gone too far, that it has become too costly, that it has begun to undermine the moral fabric of the community (see the references in Galanter 1983b). Critics on the left, who have come to occupy a significant portion of the faculty positions in the elite law schools from which large firms recruit, argue that the law has not gone far enough, that any system of rights and rules that legitimates the current structure of inequality and domination is itself unjust and subject to internal contradictions (see the readings in Kairys 1982, especially Mensch 1982). The increasing bitterness of divisions within the legal academy over the nature and proper function of law may have contributed to the loss of self-confidence among the leaders of the profession, for the debates make clear that there is no consensus on the intellectual content of law.

So it is that the large law firm, as the leading private institution in the legal profession, has come to embody the central paradox confronting American lawyers today. Why, at the height of their economic success, are lawyers and law firms subject to unprecedented doubts about the social value of their activities and their privileged position in society? This book attempts to explain the conditions that produced the success but that at the same time have contributed to the sense of impending decline which now pervades the corporate elite of the profession.

One of the perils of systematic empirical research and academic writing is that it takes a long time. When I began studying firms in 1979 the most significant question concerning the practicality of the research was whether I could gain access to information. Corporate law firms took pride in their function as the repository of the confidences of clients and studiously avoided publicity about firm operations, fearing that they would appear unprofessional or, worse, that clients might not feel comfortable divulging secrets to their law firm counsel. My dissertation committee thought I would be lucky to get access to one large firm, much less the four that my research design called for. Obtaining permission to gather comprehensive historical and behavioral data from four firms was at that time a significant accomplishment. Shortly after I began my research, however, the norms about the public disclosure of information by law firms changed rapidly, largely because of the rise of legal journalism. The *American Lawyer*, the *National Law Journal*, and the *Legal Times of Washington* bathed law firms in a new spotlight, reporting on such matters as who was coming and going in firms, which firms were growing and which were declining, what associates thought of different law firms based on their experiences in summer clerkships, and, eventually, financial information about the earnings of partners and associates. The law firms, confronted with the prospect of potentially damaging and inaccurate information, reversed their traditional practice of avoiding public comment and began to cooperate with and cultivate the new legal press. Firms hired public relations consultants and began to provide the press with information on their economic and managerial practices.

In a sense I had been scooped by the very process of change I was studying. While I am not sure whether large firms today are appreciably more open to the kind of in-depth empirical investigation reported here than when I began my research, the volume of press reports about the changing managerial practices of firms has created the widespread perception that all large firms have become bureaucratic organizations. Indeed I am commonly asked by audiences of lawyers and legal scholars whether there are any large firms today that are not bureaucratically organized. The implication of the question is that six- or seven-year-old data concerning firms already are outdated.

My first response is that I doubt it. The analysis presented here goes into aspects of the structure of law firms that, at least in part, lie below the surface of press reports and public relations material. The structural tendencies I have identified here, although certainly subject to change, are not likely to be transitory in character. My reading of the continuous stream of information about law firms in the legal press has, if anything, increased my confidence in the theory of organizational change presented here. Nonetheless, I would welcome attempts to replicate my analysis with more recent data. My second response is that social research, particularly that concerned with processes of social change, is always aiming at a moving target. To more fully understand what is happening now, we must look to the analysis of data that may seem a bit stale from a popular standpoint.

I have tried to write this book so that it can be read by a broad audience, including the lawyers and law students involved with large law firms, and yet address the methodological and theoretical concerns of social scientists. Much of the data contained here are qualitative in nature and are therefore readily interpretable. The statistical analyses presented are quite straightforward, mostly involving simple cross-tabulations and analyses of variance, and should with application be understood by nonspecialists. The reader inclined to avoid statistical analyses, however, may choose to skim chapters four and five because they rely more heavily on sophisticated statistical techniques.

The overall argument of the book, the theoretical literature I address, and the nature of the research design are discussed in the introductory chapter. The remainder of the book is organized in three parts. The first part develops the theory of social change in the large law firm. Chapter 1 draws on historical data on firms nationwide, as well as on interviews with firm elites, to develop a general theory of structural change in law firms that relates changes in the market for corporate legal services to changes in the organization of the law firm. Chapter 2 examines how these general patterns have taken concrete form in the four firms that are studied in depth throughout the rest of the book. This chapter presents historical narratives tracing the political-economic development of each firm. The second part consists of a series of chapters on particular aspects of the structure of the large law firm. Successive chapters present analyses of the survey data collected in the four firms which examine the changing nature of careers in firms, the organization of work, the income structure, and the authority system of firms. The third part analyzes the large law firm as a social institution. Chapter 7 examines the client relationships, behavior, and social and legal attitudes of the sample of large-firm attorneys to assess their autonomy from clients and their orientation toward legal and social change. Chapter 8 summarizes the results of the study and presents a general theory of the relationship between patterns of legal change and patterns of social change in the large law firm.

Earlier versions of chapters 1 and 3 appeared as articles in the *American Bar Foundation Research Journal* (1981: 95; 1983: 109); chapter 7 was published in article form by the *Stanford Law Review* [37:503].

Acknowledgments

This book evolved from my dissertation research. My list of debts begins therefore with the people who advised me on this project while I was still struggling to finish law school and graduate school. The student who finds one good teacher to work with during his or her graduate career is fortunate. I consider myself twice blessed in that regard, having had the intellectual and institutional support of Arnold S. Feldman and John P. Heinz. I owe a great intellectual debt to Ackie, first, for instilling a sense of excitement in doing sociological work and, second, for artfully combining the role of demanding supervisor and reassuring adviser during the course of the dissertation research. I hope this book reflects some measure of what I've learned from Ackie over these years. Jack Heinz has been the ultimate mentor, colleague, and friend from the very inception of the research. Jack's own work on the legal profession inspired my interest in the field and proved to be an essential backdrop to my research. And it was largely through Jack's efforts that this project enjoyed such extraordinary institutional support. I look forward to continued colleagueship with Ackie and Jack.

I also owe a debt of thanks to several institutions and the persons who make them work. The research could not have been conducted in the fashion it was without the support of the American Bar Foundation. Spencer L. Kimball, who was then the executive director of the foundation, extended himself personally to help arrange access to the firms studied. A doctoral dissertation grant from the National Science Foundation's Program in Law and the Social Sciences (Grant no. SOC 79-20246) also provided helpful support. Four other institutions must be thanked anonymously. To the four firms who opened their doors to an unprecedented degree to a young sociologist, I owe an immense debt of gratitude. They had the courage to look at themselves from a new and potentially disturbing perspective. I am especially thankful to the lawyers who acted as my contacts within the firms. Had it not been for the respect they commanded in their organizations and their commitment to the worth of the project, the study would not have been possible.

The list of colleagues who helped in various ways runs to embarrassing length. The other members of my dissertation committee, Bob Bell, Howie Becker, and Kent Smith, provided useful comments and encouragement throughout the project. Other friends at Northwestern University and the American Bar Foundation made helpful suggestions at various stages of the research and writing, including Ray Solomon, Michael Powell, Errol Meidinger, Tom Davies, Janet Gilboy, Charlie Cappell, Terry Halliday, Ted Schneyer, Bette Sikes, Whit Soule, Sam Gilmore, William Finlay, Allan Schnaiberg, and Art Stinchcombe. Thanks as well to Edward Laumann, Robert Salisbury, Eliot Friedson, William Simon, Sam Krislov, Richard Abel, Richard Lempert, and an anonymous reviewer for further encouragement and constructive criticism. Marc Galanter deserves special mention for the advice and support he gave at both the beginning and end of the research. Amanda Clark Frost provided skillful editing of the manuscript, effectively curbing the penchant for jargon which afflicts both sociologists and lawyers.

Many research assistants played an integral role in gathering and analyzing the data, including Janis Lane, Darlene Conley, Gia Interlandi, Brian Frankl, Alfred Darnell, Leah Feldman, Sunita Parikh, and Jim Curtin. Their efforts were complemented by other members of the professional staff at the ABF, Clara Carson, Marge Troha, and Kathy Rosich. Kristin Nelson did the printing and drawing for several figures. Thanks also go to the best of secretaries, Eddie Maria Clark and Jan Atkins, who ably typed every word in every draft, and to Hazel Vines, who supplied the pencils and a little bit of faith.

My parents deserve thanks for the moral and material support they have given all these years, even though they could never really understand the madness that would inspire a son to study lawyers rather than to become one.

The greatest debt is saved for last. To Kris, Hannah, Ben, and Willy. You have given all the patience, love, humor, understanding, and distraction that any man could ask for. I know you are as happy as I am that "the book" is finished.

Introduction

The large law firm sits atop the pyramid of prestige and power within the American legal profession. Although comprising but a small fraction of lawyers, through its impact upon patterns of recruitment, styles of practice, and the collective institutions of the bar, the large firm has a significance that far exceeds the number of lawyers it employs (J. Auerbach 1976, pp. 22–23). It regularly recruits the best graduates of the most prestigious law schools and pays the highest financial rewards of any broad category of practitioners; its members dominate positions of status within the legal communities of major cities and many professional associations (see Carlin 1962, 1966; Ladinsky 1963; Heinz and Laumann 1982; Grossman 1965; Halliday and Cappell 1979; Powell 1982). If any group of lawyers in the increasingly complex and specialized system of American law approximates Weber's conception of the legal *honoratiore* (Weber 1978), it is those based in the large law firm. For the specialist practicing in the large firm has the incentives and resources to write new laws, either through participation in legislative drafting or through membership in court-appointed law revision committees and the like. Important as these public functions are, they may be dwarfed in significance by the functions the large law firm performs in its representation of private clients. As legal counsel to major corporations, the large law firm participates in transactions and disputes that have enormous economic consequences for society. And if some large-firm lawyers are busy writing new laws, many more are busy devising how their clients can avoid them (McBarnett 1986). Judging by the growth of firms in recent years, the importance of their activities has increased dramatically. The nation's 50 largest firms increased some sixfold since 1960, by 70 percent in the first half of this decade alone (*Legal Times* 1984; *American Lawyer* 1979). In 1968, when Erwin Smigel wrote the last edition of his classic study of Wall Street firms, there were only 20 firms that employed as many as 100 lawyers (1969, pp. 358–359). Today 200 firms employ 100 lawyers or more; the largest contains over 700 lawyers scattered in some 32 locations throughout the world (*National Law Journal* 1982).

Ironically, it has become clear during this recent period of dramatic success that the large law firm is an organization of profound contradictions, both with respect to its internal organization and its role in society. The very forces that provided the impetus for the economic success of the large law firm have begun to undermine the traditional basis for its privileged position within the legal profession. The transformation in size and complexity of the organization itself and the development of intense competition between firms in the market for corporate legal services has challenged the organizational arrangements by which firms were traditionally governed. Direct, ad hoc control of day-to-day operations by a few leading partners has been replaced by management structures that include long-range planning groups, professional administrators, and the division of managerial functions among department heads. As the stability of relationships between corporate clients and firms has broken down and as the demand for particular fields of expertise has undergone rapid change, the power of the generation of elites who presided over the rise of the firm has become more vulnerable. The pages of the *American Lawyer,* the *National Law Journal,* and the *Legal Times of Washington* carry a steady flow of reports of bloodletting within the once staid corridors of large firms: palace coups by younger partners, conspiracies to oust other partners, defections by whole departments, and even the dissolution of long-established partnerships. Institutional loyalty is no longer strong enough to hold firms together. With growing frequency partners bolt from one firm to another. Faced with increased competition and a constant need for additional clients, the new generation of managerial partners has sometimes cut the shares of partners who do not bring in business, reducing many to the status of well-paid employees who are partners in name only. At the same time that firms have mounted massive recruiting programs for new associates, lavishing high starting salaries and signing bonuses on fresh law graduates, they have raised the threshold for full partnership by lengthening the number of years required before admission to partnership, inserting intermediate levels of partnership, and conferring partnership status on only a small percentage of any entering cohort.

These changes in the organization of firms have provoked a crescendo of rhetoric from leaders of the bar about the loss of professionalism in law practice. While this is hardly a new theme (see Gordon 1984), there is clearly heightened anxiety that big-time law practice is becoming little more than big-time business. Two recent past presidents of the American Bar Association, both partners in prominent firms, voiced these concerns on the President's Page of the *ABA Journal* (Harrell 1983; Shepherd 1984). The establishment of the ABA's Commission on Professionalism in 1984 was inspired in part by the fear that the commercialization of practice may have gone too far (American Bar Association 1986). The ethic of professionalism is hardly a hollow concern for the large law firm. Despite manifest changes in the relationships between firms and clients, the justification for the high cost of large-firm counsel is tied to the ideology of professionalism. The large firm must maintain its image as the ultimate professional organization whose command of knowledge and customized style of practice produces legal services of a quality not readily purchased elsewhere. If lawyers' services are seen as an interchangeable commodity, corporations are far more likely to shop for the lowest price or to internalize legal representation.

The privileged position of the large firm in the legal profession also rests on the ethic of professionalism. The inequities inherent in a legal system in which representation is allocated by a private market can be justified in part by the professional status of lawyers. A distinguishing characteristic of professional occupations, which justifies self-regulation by the professional group, is that they are committed not just to profits but to public service as well. Lawyers, as officers of the court, are obligated to serve the public interest even as they advocate the interests of their clients. Hence, although large-firm attorneys represent the most powerful interests in American society and thus enjoy a tremendous advantage in the adversarial process over lesser foes, they represent themselves as independent professionals who can check the narrow self-interest of clients. Almost from the inception of the large law firm, critics have challenged its claim to professional autonomy, arguing that firms are the captives of client interests and that their commitment to procedural fairness masks the attempt to maximize the substantive interests of corporate clients through superior representational resources. These long-standing questions have been underscored by recent scholarship, which suggests that corporate lawyers may be substantially less autonomous from clients than are those lawyers representing individuals (Heinz and Laumann 1982).

The turmoil generated by the changes taking place in the large law firm suggests that this organization is trapped in a conflict between bureaucracy and professionalism. This book focuses on the sources, dimensions, and potential implications of that conflict both for the law firm as an organization and for the legal system in which it is such an influential actor.

Many of the tensions confronting the large law firm in the course of social change show up explicitly as issues concerning the bureaucratization of a professional organization. The structural changes that mark the bureaucratization of firms—specialization, departmentalization, and increasing stratification in the earnings and authority of partners—run counter to traditional conceptions of the professional partnership in which all partners are in some sense peers, "a company of equals," to use Freidson and Rhea's term (1972). To encourage the enthusiastic commitment of lower level partners to their work, leaders of firms must maintain this sense of collegiality. As a result, traditional norms about relationships between partners continue to shape the style, if not the substance, of managerial practices. Similarly, effective recruitment of top law students must at least pay lip-service to the traditional (and idealized) conception of the professional career held by most law students in which the individual professional chooses the type of work he or she does. The reality is that firms increasingly assign associates to high-demand fields, even if this runs counter to individual preferences. Nonetheless, the image of free choice projected by firms in the interviewing rooms of law schools, while not often honored in practice, tends to drive assignment and departmentalization systems underground.

These conflicting tendencies produce a collegial hierarchy in which processes of organizational rationalization are modified or cloaked in traditional professional terms and in which the dynamics of hierarchical relationships between lawyers are denied or left unstated. The professional media that have grown up around large firms invariably focus on the latest trends in organizational innovation and change. But the more interesting problem may be why firms have been so slow to change in view of the transformation of their environment. Why has the bureaucratization of the law firm been a conflictual and partial process? In short, why has the law firm changed so much while claiming to have changed so little?

No doubt part of the answer lies in the traditional professional values of large-firm attorneys and the constraints those values impose on the managerial practices of firm leaders. But I will argue that there is a more fundamental source for the contradictory character of social change in the large law firm: the lack of autonomy from clients. Despite mounting pressures for the development of rational managerial structures, power in the firm remains inextricably tied to "control of clients." The ability to plan strategically for a changing environment and to establish efficient internal administrative systems depends (1) on the political balance of power within the firm—a power alignment that is increasingly subject to rapid shifts because of the collapse of particular fields or client accounts or because of the departure of leading partners—and (2) on the ideology of the client-responsible elite. Managerial authority in the law firm can never achieve autonomy from those partners with client responsibility. As this book's title suggests, the organizational rationalization of the firm will be controlled by the partners with power.

Dependence on clients is also the source of the contradictions in the social role of the large law firm, for this dependence undermines the large firm's claim to professional autonomy. Although scholars have suggested that the diversification of the client base of firms in recent years has enhanced the autonomy of large-firm practitioners from corporate clients by making firms less dependent on any given account, a closer examination of the structure of firms and the attitudes and activities of their members casts doubt on the assertion. Not only does the large firm remain an organization dominated by those partners most closely associated with clients but the evolving division of labor in corporate legal services appears to have the effect of limiting the participation of large-firm lawyers in the decision-making processes of clients. Even if law firm counsel were inclined to act as the conscience of their clients, their opportunity to do so has diminished as a result of the rise of internal counsel inside the corporation and the changing nature of relationships with corporate clients. Moreover, my research indicates that through the process of advocating the interests of clients, large-firm attorneys come to strongly identify with them. It is highly unlikely, therefore, that lawyers in large law firms will act as an independent voice that checks the self-interest of clients. It is far more likely that the

6   Introduction

large law firm will be the enthusiastic voice for the interests of clients. This is the second sense in which the title of the book describes the theme of the analysis. As dedicated advocates for the corporation and the power it commands in the American legal system, large law firms themselves are partners with power.

The analysis presented here is novel in several respects. First, I present a conception of the law firm which departs significantly from the optimistic portrait painted by Erwin Smigel in his study of Wall Street firms (1969). If Smigel was correct in his interpretation of New York firms in the 1950s, his work is seriously out of date now. Given the frequent references to Smigel's work in the literature on professional organizations (see, e.g., Ouchi 1980), it is important to offer an alternative analysis of the strengths and weaknesses of this organizational form. Second, relatively few studies in the professions literature have attempted a political-economic analysis of the professional organization in which changes in the market for professional services are related to the changing structure of the organization. Indeed this lack may be impeding the development of more powerful theories of social change in the professions. In recent years, as more and more professionals are employed in organizational settings, it has become increasingly clear that the work organization is the vortex of professional power. Here the power of the profession as a collectivity is converted into an economic value. By focusing primarily on the efforts of professional groups to gain a monopoly over the services they provide or on the control of applied knowledge in the dyadic relationships between professional and client, the literature on the professions has given inadequate attention to one of the main engines of change in the professions: the efforts of professionals to reproduce themselves economically in the professional work organization. The perspective adopted here, which I refer to as the model of organizational dominance, explictly attempts to examine the interrelationships between changes in the market for corporate legal services, the changing structure of firms, and the role of the law firm in the legal system. This approach may provide a more comprehensive understanding of patterns of social change in the corporate sphere of the legal profession.

Third, the analysis of the social organization of the law firm represents a particular approach to the sociology of law. Like other research on the legal profession, the study of the organization of the law firm is removed from the behavior of public legal authorities, such as arrests, judicial decisions, and sentences, which is the more common focus of sociolegal studies. But as Abel (1982), Galanter (1974), Macaulay (1979), and others have noted in various ways, the functioning of formal legal institutions is heavily dependent on the social organization of the legal profession. The incentives, resources, and political, social, and cultural orientations of lawyers often determine the relationship between law and society. It is in this light that the analysis of social change in the large law firm becomes significant to the sociology of law. Patterns of social change in the large law firm—the dominant organization in the private sphere of the legal profession—both reflect and shape the changing functions of law in American society.

THE TRANSFORMATION OF THE LARGE LAW FIRM

The halting transformation of the large law firm from a traditional to a bureaucratic organization has its roots in the changing functions of law in modern American society. The sixties and seventies were a watershed in American law. During this period significant expansion in the scope of federal law and regulation produced new and sweeping regulatory structures in such diverse areas as the environment, food safety, occupational safety and health, product safety, the public financing of medical care, the production of energy, and the establishment and control of pension funds. One measure that reflects the rapid growth of federal regulatory activity is the number of pages in the *Federal Register,* where federal agencies are required to publish proposed actions. From 1960 to 1980 the *Federal Register* grew some fourfold (Bibby, Mann, and Ornstein 1982). The creation of new legal entitlements for minorities and other groups, the liberalization of rules on class-action litigation and on the standing necessary to initiate litigation, the expansion of statutory provisions for citizens' participation in regulatory proceedings, and the increase in government support for the representation of individual claims through legal services programs and the development of enforcement capacities of such agencies as the Equal Employment Opportunity Commission all led to a qualitative shift in the scope and character of the involvement of legal authorities in the affairs of public and private organizations (Reich 1964; R. Stewart 1978; Katz 1982; Burstein 1986; Friedman 1985). In addition to massive changes in public law, private law functions also underwent dramatic expansion. Private parties invoked the law with increasing frequency and intensity in the form of protracted and complex litigation between major corporate actors (Galanter 1983b), the development of new forms of corporate finance, innovative applications of the tax code, and the creation and widespread use of new tactics for acquiring other corporations and blocking takeover attempts. The consequences of such changes in the law for business corporations were enormous. The result was a sharp increase in the demand for the specialized legal knowledge offered by large law firms as well as for the capacity of such firms to mobilize groups of legal experts on short notice for uncertain and unpredictable periods of time.

The transformation in the legal needs of the corporation transformed the market for large-firm services. The emergence of new functions for the corporate law firm was also associated with the decline of its traditional practice base. Routine corporate matters were taken over by inside counsel, meaning that law firms were left with more novel and rapidly changing practice fields. Moreover, the firm's relationships with corporate clients underwent a discernible change. Continuous broad-ranging relationships between firms and corporate clients were increasingly displaced by a series of ad hoc, case-by-case, field-by-field relationships between a corporation and many law firms. This shift itself can be attributed to the rise of internal counsel in corporations, who asserted their control over legal affairs by distributing work among several firms. But it also reflected the shift to a more specialized practice in which the reputation of a firm (and often the reputation of a particular partner) for a *specific* type of service became more important for attracting business than the general institutional reputation of the firm. As traditional client ties have begun to change, firms have adopted a more openly entrepreneurial approach to practice: opening branch offices as a means of defending their client base or entering a new market, merging with boutique specialty firms to diversify the client base and gain instant recognition in a new field, hiring partners (even whole work groups) away from other firms to compete in a new specialty, attracting notable government officials to achieve higher levels of visibility in a particular field or locale, holding seminars for the clients of other firms.

The changing environment has produced significant tensions in many firms. Relationships between partners have become strained as firms have grown and as the governing elite has assumed a significantly different relationship to the rest of the firm. The fundamental principle of the partnership as a legal form is that all partners share in profits and governance. For law partnerships this has seldom meant equal participation. In their earlier periods large firms exhibited paternalistic patterns of authority in which the founding partners ran the firm with a minimum of input from other partners and took home the largest share of the profits. Although the hierarchical nature of the relationships was clear, they had the force of custom. In an organization of such size there was some realistic prospect that the other partners would eventually inherit the role of patriarch (see McCurdy 1984). Moreover, the direct, personal nature of the relationships imparted a stronger sense of shared identity to the group of partners. This close personal order has been replaced by a more differentiated hierarchy in which relationships between the strata—"the finders, the minders, and the grinders"—are mediated by the structures of committees and departments.

Heightened uncertainty over business and economic difficulties has led the managerial elite of some firms to divest some partners of their property rights by creating new categories of nonequity partners at the bottom of the partnership pyramid or "superpartners" at the top. These efforts add new incentives for bringing in business but also create greater inequality among partners. This has proven a particularly wrenching phenomenon, leading to an increased number of defections from major firms. Similarly, the career prospects of associates in large firms have changed dramatically. In the early seventies a job with a big firm seemed a reasonably sure route to financial success and professional esteem. But increasing numbers of firms have gravitated toward the "New York system," promoting only a small proportion of associates to partnership and prolonging the time required to gain partnership status. The type of work associates do is increasingly dictated by the firm either directly or indirectly, with the result that many associates are assigned to work they find unrewarding. The high levels of turnover and alienation in many firms demonstrate this dissatisfaction.

The emerging managerial order clashes with the ideology by which firms have historically justified the structure of the organization and its functions in society. The elite of the legal profession has consistently insisted that the practice of law is not a mere business, that it entails a commitment to professional values more than the pursuit of profit (see Gordon 1984). The claim of professionalism has had special importance in the large law firm both internally and externally. The status hierarchy of the firm is justified in terms of professionalism. Even though the managerial role is increasingly important to the firm, managerial skills per se are not the criteria by which leaders are chosen. Those at the top are "the strongest lawyers." The middle-level partners may have much less input into governance and a smaller share in the profits than leading partners, but their status in the profession and the community largely rests on their membership in "a leading firm." Firms appeal to law students in terms of professionalism as well. A career in the large firm is represented as offering the opportunity to practice at the highest level of professional quality on matters of social and economic significance. The financial incentives for beginning associates have been substantial, of course. But even the economic performance of the firm depends on deference to its professional status. As corporations develop a larger capacity to do legal work internally, large firms must maintain the image of unique competence in certain types of legal work. Hence, even though clients are a major force in the bureaucratization of the firm because of their demand for services provided in a more rationalized fashion, those same clients are still attracted by the traditional mystique of the professional organization.

The process of bureaucratization in the law firm has, therefore, been problematic. A dramatic change in organizational policies risks alienating the traditional values of partners, associates, even clients. Yet failing to adopt structural innovations to improve strategic planning and internal coordination risks inefficiency, overworking of the professional staff, the departure of partners who do not see adequate return for their efforts and the business they bring in, and eventual economic decline. The failure of some firms to adopt new managerial policies results from structural factors. In firms in which client responsibility is divided among a number of partners, a coherent managerial approach is more difficult to develop. The result is a series of ad hoc responses to organizational needs which do not intrude on the baronial domains of important partners. The lack of managerial innovation is often justified on the basis that organizational change would be inconsistent with professional values, although the content of these values is extremely vague. I will assert that the conflict between bureaucratization and professionalism is not inherent. The meaning of professionalism is socially constructed. The managerial elite in some firms have succeeded in redefining professionalism to sanction a bureaucratic structure. Bureaucratically organized firms have material advantages over their traditionally organized counterparts which enhance their attractiveness to members. But only a few firms consciously embrace a bureaucratic ideology. More often the leaders of firms have sought a compromise between bureaucratization and tradition by attempting to maintain the image of professional tradition while pursuing managerial policies that produce a more bureaucratic structure. This dual aim accounts for the frequent divergence between ideology and practice inside the organization.

Reshaping the meaning of professionalism inside the law firm has broader implications for the legitimacy of the large law firm as a social institution. The traditional view of the lawyer's professional role holds that legal services are not merely a commodity to be bought and sold in the marketplace; this perspective implies a special tripartite relationship between lawyer, client, and the law. The lawyer is to act both as the representative of the law—as an officer of the court—as well as the representative of the client. When Brandeis criticized the corporate bar at the turn of the century for its lack of independence from client interests, he was stating the Progressive ideal of the professional role (1933). Even in a private market economy lawyers could act as "counsel for the situation," that is, in the public interest, not just in their own or their client's economic interest. This characterization is strikingly similar to the functionalist model of the profession that Talcott Parsons would present years later when he argued that lawyers served the function of normative integration, mediating between the narrow, self-interested claims of clients and a broader set of social values (1954; see also Simon 1985).

The Progressive ideal that formed the basis for Brandeis's famous critique constitutes a critical element in the professional ideology justifying the role of the large law firm in society. The elite corporate bar has been active in law reform (see, e.g., Gordon 1983, 1984). Although its efforts could be seen as mere hobbies, as a way of generating business, or as a means of keeping control of the profession (Carlin 1966; J. Auerbach 1976), at least in part these efforts have been informed by the Progressive conception of the corporate bar's professional obligation. A leading practitioner in a large Chicago law firm described such public service as a means of "repaying the public for the privilege to practice law." This professional ideology extends to the law firm's role in private practice as well. The lawyers I interviewed often hastened to claim that the highest ethical standards were a tradition of the firm. On one occasion a prominent partner told me what was obviously an important war story, about the time he faced a client down over how a securities prospectus would read. Other members of the elite forthrightly asserted that inside counsel could not be as independent as outside counsel and that this significant virtue of the large law firm served both the client and the general good.

The realities of practice and ideology diverge with respect to the social role of the large firm, just as they do with respect to its internal organization. The large-firm lawyers interviewed in my sample, for example, are politically more liberal than the business clients they represent. The majority agree that lawyers should act as the conscience of their clients. Lawyers in large firms see themselves as an autonomous, progressive group. Despite this ideology, large-firm lawyers are above all committed advocates. Almost never do they seriously disagree with a client's proposed course of conduct (see chap. 7). On questions of law and policy specifically related to their own practice they strongly identify with positions favorable to clients.

The ideology of professional autonomy remains remarkably resilient in spite of periodic attacks by critics (see, e.g., Berle 1948; Mills 1956; Nader 1970; Green 1975) and its relative irrelevance to practice. In the late sixties and early seventies firms were forced to increase commitments to pro bono work to accommodate the concerns of politically active associates and law students. As the social movements of the time lost their momentum, however, such concerns inside firms and among recruits waned. Whether the structural changes in the firm documented here will signal a more fundamental challenge to the ideal of professional autonomy remains to be seen. There is at least a possibility that if legal expertise is treated as just another commodity, with the traditional relationships between lawyers themselves and between lawyers and clients being replaced by an increasingly impersonal bureaucratic order, the claim of the law firm to professional autonomy will be weakened. As the marketization of law firm practice becomes more apparent, the legitimacy of the system in which such an organization is so powerful may be questioned.

The model of the large law firm presented here reveals an organization experiencing a conflict between its past and its future both with respect to its internal workings and its role in society. This model differs substantially from the optimistic reading offered in Smigel's landmark study of Wall Street firms (1969). It is appropriate therefore to introduce the theoretical framework of this study by considering Smigel's classic account.

THE WALL STREET LAWYER

Erwin Smigel began studying Wall Street law firms in the late 1950s and first published his findings in 1964 (second edition, 1969). This work remains one of the few accounts of the internal organization of an autonomous professional organization (see also Montagna 1968). Smigel conceived his study as a general inquiry into the impact of bureaucratization on a professional organization, and accordingly he provides rich description of several organizational dimensions: recruitment, patterns of promotion, the organization of work, internal hierarchies of status and power, and the rationale for the success of the organization. Despite pervasive attention to organizational characteristics, Smigel devoted relatively little analysis to an organizational theory of law firm structure as such. Instead, he began with the almost casual supposition that large firms are bureaucratic organizations (1969, pp. vii–viii). The issue that then interested Smigel was the extent of the lawyer's personal freedom in a bureaucratic structure (1969, p. 14). Borrowing William H. Whyte, Jr.'s, term, Smigel subtitled his book with a question: Has the Wall Street lawyer become a "Professional Organization Man"? The question led to Smigel's preoccupation with the law-firm-as-culture in which the individual dramas of success and failure, independence and conformity are acted out: Which prep schools and social clubs are favored by the large firms? How does law review breed the personality that can thrive in the large-firm setting? How is failure defined and assuaged? What leads a lawyer to lose imagination and "overconform"?

While all these are interesting issues, Smigel's fascination with how individuals play the law firm game made him gloss over fundamental questions about the game itself: Who makes the rules of the game? What are the interests of the rule makers and within what constraints do they operate? What are the economics of the firm? What are the consequences of different approaches to the organization of practice, both in terms of organizational success and of the relationships between lawyers within the firm? In short, Smigel left us without a theory of social change in the law firm.

Smigel's organizational analysis—his attempt to define and explain the organizational structure of firms—is relegated to a secondary role. The core of this analysis is the argument that the large law firm is a "professional bureaucracy" (1969, pp. 275–286). Contrary to other types of bureaucratic organizations (he refers explicitly to Gouldner's typology of mock, representative, and punishment-centered bureaucracies [1954]), the professional bureaucracy functions with fewer rules than otherwise expected for an organization of such size and complexity. A host of factors takes the place of rules in holding the firm together and making it work efficiently, including homogeneity of social and

14   Introduction

educational background, "esprit de corps," controlled competition, and
norms of debate and discussion (1969, pp. 249–250). The most important of these according to Smigel was the external professional controls
codified in the canons of professional ethics. Because the profession was
composed of individuals who had internalized common standards of
practice, there was little need to define the division of labor or to
articulate the powers attached to different positions in the firm's hierarchy. In Smigel's conception everyone knows his or her place; there is
little conflict, little need to justify the distribution of power and profits.

It is no accident that Smigel's argument concerning professional
bureaucracy comes in a chapter entitled "The Success of the Organization: Rationale." In maintaining that firms are held together by ex-
traorganizational factors, Smigel largely dissolves the conflict between
bureaucracy and the autonomy of individual practitioners with which
he began. Although he continues to characterize the organization of the
firms as bureaucratic and more formal than even the members like to
admit, he concludes that with the exception of a few aberrant individuals bureaucratization has not transformed practitioners into "organization men" (Smigel 1969, pp. 337–338). Professional bureaucracy seems
to provide the best of both worlds. Professional traditions, integrity,
and imagination are preserved while increased demands for specialization and efficiency are met.

Smigel's interpretation of the social role of the Wall Street firm is
based on the analysis of its internal organization. In his conclusion he
argues that as a result of the increasing complexity of law, corporations
are more dependent on the kind of expertise large law firms offer. And
he suggests that the client base of firms has become more diverse. As a
result he claims that large firms are now more autonomous from their
clients than in the past. These developments reinforce his view that
professional norms control the internal operation of firms. Smigel specu-
lates that the triumph of professional norms inside the organization
validates its role in society.

> Primarily [lawyers in large firms] are advisors to big business and in this
> capacity they also serve as its conscience. They provide, as Parsons remarks,
> "a kind of buffer between the illegitimate desires of . . . clients and the social
> interests." Their main function is to maintain the status quo for their large
> corporate clients . . . [They] do it in an efficient, quiet, creative, and knowl-
> edgeable manner: observers enough to know they are fighting the tides of a
> shifting economic system, artists enough to advise and provide for cautious
> change (a position, incidentally, to which many clients object). Thus these
> lawyers help give our society continuity. Their cautious use of societal brakes

provides the liberal with time and opportunity to seek change in a relatively stable society. (Smigel 1969, p. 342)

This is the realization of the Progressive ideal of the professional role. The large law firm thus embodies the autonomy of modern law, significantly affecting social outcomes by curbing the rapacious appetites of clients.

Smigel's theory of the professional bureaucracy cannot be dismissed as a naive relic. Not only has the model been applied to other autonomous professional organizations (see Montagna 1968), but Smigel's findings have been rediscovered in recent developments in the organizations literature. Based on Smigel's characterization of the law firm, professional firms have been cited as exemplars of nonbureaucratic organizations that achieve high levels of commitment to the organization through a minimum of formal structure (Satow 1975; Ouchi and Johnson 1978). Some scholars suggest that this organizational form will become increasingly important in the high-technology, high-innovation sectors of the postindustrial economy because nonbureaucratic structures are more adaptive to changing circumstances and more conducive to individual creativity than bureaucratic ones (Swanson 1980; Scott 1981, pp. 286–289).

Both the earlier empirical studies by Smigel and Montagna and the more recent interpretations in the organizations literature present an idealized and incomplete model of the social structure of the professional firm. First, the literature underestimates the tendencies toward bureaucratization in professional firms. Law firms are under considerable pressure to develop centrally coordinated managerial, administrative, and work-group structures to cope with greater organizational size and complexity and to deal with rapidly changing market conditions. That they have been slow to do so is not by design, nor does it reflect professional values. Instead the relative lack of bureaucratization results from constraints on managerial authority resulting from the primacy of authority based on client control. Without an autonomous managerial stratum, managerial policies depend on the ideology of the client-responsible elite and must compromise with different sources of client production within the firm. Second, prior research fails to adequately explain the relationship between professional values and organizational structure. The assertion that shared professional norms embodied in the profession's code of ethics substitute for organizational controls is highly implausible given the extremely general character of ethical provisions and their almost total silence on the organization of professional practice. More likely, prior research has it backward: professional norms relating to organizational policies are largely determined by the firms themselves and reflect the interpretation that the leaders of firms give professional values. Moreover, beneath the surface of consensus are differences of opinion about firm organization and these differences stem from the positions that individual lawyers occupy in the organization. Third, while recognizing the importance of the commitment of professionals to their work, prior research minimizes the problematic nature of commitment both at the top and at the bottom of the organization. With increasing frequency the consensus over who will run the organization and how it breaks down, resulting in managerial shake-ups and the departure of important partners. Associates often disagree with firm policies, exhibit high levels of turnover, and express low levels of career commitment to the firm. Finally, prior literature fails to recognize the significance of client interests to the stratification system of the firm. This literature thus draws unwarranted inferences about the degree to which the diversification of the client base results in greater autonomy from clients.

Either firms have become less like social clubs and thus more heterogeneous in membership or firms were never so consensual as Smigel suggests, for I propose a different explanation for the relative lack of rules in firms. The law partnership traditionally has been and continues to be a system of collegial domination. In such a hierarchy leadership operates in direct, personal fashion—as a form of personal influence rather than vested power. A favorite cliché used in placement office résumés and law firm directories to describe law firm governance is "policies are arrived at by consensus." Indeed, collegial norms and working relationships are more important to firm operations than formal rules. But organizational policies and the division of power and profits are not simply the product of consensus among partners and associates. Instead, they reflect the collegial hierarchy of the firm, a hierarchy structured by the distribution of client responsibility and the managerial ideology of the governing elite (both past and present). Smigel mistakenly read this form of domination as a lack of domination. Hierarchical relationships were thus only a secondary issue in his analysis.

Domination is a central issue in this book: how have different structures of domination emerged within the law firm in different historical eras and in different organizations? More particularly, why have some firms developed bureaucratic structures while others have not? And what do these patterns of structural change suggest about the institutional order in which the law firm is a prominent actor? The kind of political-economic analysis of law firm organization that the focus on domination implies is quite different from the typical analysis of the relationship between bureaucracy and professionalism. Much of the professions literature, including Smigel's work, treats bureaucratization as problematic in its consequences for professionals (see Johnson 1972; Cain 1983). I will treat bureaucratization in the professional organization as a process that is problematic in itself. Bureaucratization in the law firm involves a contest between competing ideologies about how to run a professional organization and increasingly results in sharp conflicts between competing groups of partners and associates. We are witnessing increasing levels of competition between firms which results in the dramatic success of some firms, the collapse of others. This competition takes place at least in part between bureaucratic and traditional law firms, and the results are likely to determine which organizational form will dominate the market for corporate legal services.

My attempt to analyze the determinants of bureaucratization in the law firm, rather than taking the structure of the firm for granted, addresses a set of questions prior to those Smigel emphasized. In addition, the structural analysis of law firm organization has implications that go beyond those Smigel offered. By examining more directly how the law firm is organized and by probing the values and activities of its members with respect to legal change, the study of the law firm becomes a study of the role of law in modern American society. The large law firm has been a leading instrument by which the modern business corporation has dealt with a changing social environment, first through the development of new legal forms for transacting business and shaping control of the corporation itself and second through the representation of business in its increasingly broad set of dealings with government. The bureaucratization of the law firm reflects the increasingly specialized, technocratic function that law has assumed in the modern era. But the particular character of bureaucratization in firms reveals that the preeminent function of the law firm remains the advocacy of client interests. Given the link between the organizational form of the law firm and its functions in society, sociological theories of the law firm as an organization take on significance for the sociology of law.

THEORETICAL PERSPECTIVE

Organizational Dominance and the
Market for Professional Services

As Eliot Freidson (1970a, *xvii*) observed, the word *profession* has a double meaning. It is both an avowal, a promise to uphold high standards of competence and public service, and a job, an activity that entails economic exchange. This definition captures the dualism inherent in the professional organization in capitalist society. On the one hand, such an organization is structured by the norms through which the professional group justifies its privileged position in society and which dictate how members of the professional group relate to one another. On the other hand, despite the monopoly position enjoyed by the profession as a whole, the organization is confronted with the exigencies of the marketplace and the necessity to produce services in a fashion that makes it economically viable.

Neither the professions nor the organizations literature has devoted much attention to this economic dimension of the professional organization. Researchers have largely ignored the potential implications of changes in the market for professional services for the structure of the organization, for the system of professional norms operating within the organization, and for the role of the professional group in society. The scholarship on the professions has enlightened our understanding on a number of important questions: the conditions for achieving professional status and a monopoly over professional services (Wilensky 1964; Larson 1977), the position of the professions in the class structure (Larson 1977), the role of the professions in politics (Gilb 1967; Halliday 1987), the nature of professionalism as a cultural system for aspiring groups (Bledstein 1976), the increasing demand for professional services in postindustrial society (Bell 1976), and the power of professionals in interactions with their clients (Freidson 1970a; Rosenthal 1974). Much of the professions literature focuses on professionals in organizations, seeking to determine how they relate to administrators (Goss 1963; Scott 1965) and to other elements of the organization (Kornhauser 1962; Marcson 1960) as well as the degree to which they are satisfied with or alienated from their working conditions (see, e.g., Hall 1968; Miller 1968). Only rarely, however, have studies of the professional organization examined hierarchical relationships among professionals (but see Bosk 1979, Bucher 1970, Goss 1961) or the nexus between this organizational hierarchy and the market for professional services.

This leaves a serious gap in theories of structural change in the professional organization and indeed in theories of social change in the professions generally. The limitations of the existing literature are illustrated in Eliot Freidson's recent and significant book on the professions, *Professional Powers* (1986). Freidson's central concern is the character of power exercised by the professions in American society, in particular the extent to which the professions' control of formal knowledge allows them to influence human activities. An impressive and thorough review of the literature leads Freidson to conclude that organized institutions are critical mediating structures between the formal knowledge the professions possess and the impact of their knowledge on society. In his words, to understand the power of the professions it is necessary to understand "how the institutions are put together, how they work, how the people participating in them are differentiated by position and perspective, and how those institutional positions influence their work of creating, transmitting, and applying their knowledge" (Freidson, 1986, p. xi).

Freidson clearly is sensitive to the importance of the economic circumstances of professional practice. For example, he discusses how economic insecurity frequently vitiates the celebrated independence of self-employed professionals (1986, pp. 123–125). Yet the literature Freidson synthesizes so effectively in his book tells us relatively little about a fundamental aspect of how professional organizations "are put together" and "work": the relationship between organizational structure and the market for the organization's services. Many of the questions Freidson identifies as critical to the power of professionals must be addressed through a political-economic analysis of the professional organization. The power of management to control the work of professionals, for example, depends on management's position in the economic exchanges involved in the delivery of professional services. Does the organization control the flow of clients to professionals, such as with group health plans, or does it primarily internalize preexisting professional-client relationships, as hospitals have traditionally done? Similarly, the autonomy of professional organizations and individual practitioners from clients is determined by the structure of the market and the degree to which the organization or its practitioners are economically dependent on any given client. Without attention to the forces that structure these relationships and cause them to change, we cannot assess the trends in the power of professional groups.

Freidson's analysis also treats the problem of professional power in a limited way. His primary concern is the power of professionals as distinguished from individuals in other occupations. As a result, he is not very interested in power relationships within the professional group, such as those between partners and associates in law firms. In his review of the position of professionals in various kinds of large organizations, for example, Freidson focuses solely on whether the organizational hierarchy constrains the exercise of technical expertise by individual practitioners (1986, pp. 160–166). He concludes that employed professionals retain substantial autonomy in how they perform their work. The amount of discretion exercised by subordinates in the professional hierarchy is, of course, an important issue in its own right. In emphasizing it Freidson clearly is attempting to respond to recent arguments that professionals are being proletarianized, that is, reduced to the equivalent of unskilled and alienated factory labor (see, e.g., Derber 1982), or that the employment of professionals in organizations necessarily marks the decline of professional status (see, e.g., Rothman 1984).

Freidson effectively counters the proletarianization argument. My findings on the organization of work in law firms support his position. But the refutation of one theory of domination in the professional firm does not eliminate the need to develop another. Granting the technical autonomy of professional subordinates, it also is critical to explain how the organization harnesses the energies and knowledge of professional workers as well as to clarify who benefits from their efforts. Without attention to these issues we cannot understand how professional organizations function and change. Nor can we predict how future changes in the structure of the organization might affect the technical autonomy of professional workers.

The limitations of the major paradigms in the professions literature for explaining patterns of change in professional organizations become apparent when we attempt to explain patterns of growth and structural change in the large law firm. Functionalist theories of the professions suggest that the status and organization of professional groups derive primarily from the nature of the important social functions they perform (Parsons 1951, 1960; Carr-Saunders and Wilson 1933; Shils 1975). It follows that the structure of a professional organization derives both from the functions it performs and the consensus among practitioners on the professional values the organization serves. The core function of an organization is, of course, an important determinant of its structure. But one major difficulty with the functionalist explanation is that it does not readily account for variations in the organization of professional activities even within one profession in one society, much less the kinds of dramatic differences we observe across societies. Another challenge to this explanation is the presence of conflict within professional firms over organizational policies. If the structure of professional organizations is rooted in its core values, why do we find such strident differences of organizational philosophy both within and across professional firms? Moreover, the functionalist perspective has a largely benign view of professional groups and the effects of professional knowledge and thus fails to consider the degree to which professionals pursue their self-interest in the development and application of professional knowledge.

These limitations have led to the rejection of functionalist conceptions of the professions in favor of theories stressing professional power. Freidson's theory of professional dominance is among the most important in this line (1970a, b). Freidson asserts that the power of the professions at the institutional level (as in state licensing, control of professional education, control of practice organizations) stems from support from other powerful elites in society (1970b, pp. 23–46). At the individual level of relationships with clients, the professional enjoys both technical authority, which is based on knowledge about technical issues, and moral authority, which is essentially normative in nature and is connected to the profession's status in the community and its position of "objectivity" in dealing with the difficulties of clients. Freidson's analysis poses a critical challenge to orthodox conceptions of the professions, for he questions the legitimacy of the power professions exert over human lives. In this perspective even the most personal of conditions, illness, becomes a struggle between doctor and patient, with the doctor attempting to impose his interpretation on the patient (1970a, pp. 203–331). Especially troubling to Freidson is the tendency of professionals to couch essentially normative prescriptions in technical terms (1970a, p. 335–338).

Significant as the professional dominance paradigm is, it provides little assistance here. Although Freidson attributes great importance to the institutional arrangements between the state, professional schools, and practice organizations in establishing and maintaining professional dominance, the ultimate focus is at the dyadic level of relationships between professionals and clients. The analysis of organizational struc-

22   Introduction

tures provides a backdrop to Freidson's principal concern with how well the professions regulate themselves. Thus, while Freidson argues that the organizational structures governing work are perhaps the most important determinants of the quality of professional performance, the theory of professional dominance does not develop a theory of change in the professional work organization. Moreover, as Freidson notes in his new book (1986, pp. 174, 218), the large law firm does not fit the general model of professional dominance. The imbalance of knowledge between individuals and professionals is not repeated in the relationship between law firms and corporate clients. Corporations are often aided in their relationships with law firms by their own internal legal counsel, who can monitor, if not control, the nature of the exchange.

Another related theory of the professions within the conflict framework gives greater emphasis to institutional structure: the theory of professional monopoly, given the most recent and articulate expression by Magali Larson (1977). The centerpiece of Larson's analysis is the professional project, the process through which a professional group establishes the primacy of its paradigm of knowledge and practice against other potential competitors and then solidifies its position through state licensing, the standardization of training for entry, and the control of the organizational contexts in which members provide their services. According to Larson, the most successful projects have been carried out by the classic professions, medicine and law. Other professions, such as engineering and social work, never have achieved the same level of control over participation in a profession's domain or over the organization of the workplace.

The monopoly perspective also does not provide a satisfactory explanation of social change in the large law firm. As Larson herself notes (1977, pp. 166–177), the American legal profession is hardly a unified set of practitioners. Different segments of the bar often take conflicting positions on questions of professional regulation, such as those involving lawyer advertising and the profession's ethical code (see Powell 1985; Heinz and Laumann 1982). Moreover, the period of greatest economic success for large firms has come during the period when the organized bar was losing many of its traditional powers to control competition by limiting advertising and setting fees. (Somewhat ironically it was the profession's leading public institution, the Supreme Court, that struck down these restrictions [see Bates v. State Bar 1977; Goldfarb v. Virginia State Bar 1975]). It is therefore doubtful that the profession's power as a collectivity is responsible for the growth of large firms. Indeed, the law firm may be an example of a much larger problem in Larson's theory of the rise of professionalism. Her emphasis on the professions' efforts to control the market, which may have been critical in the formative phase of professional groups, led her to ignore the market as the primary source for the increasing demand for professional services. Professionalism provided not only a new ideological justification for the class system of advanced industrial society, as Larson suggests, but also itself became a site for capitalist economic production. Larson fails to develop a theory of the professional organization as capitalist enterprise.

While the professions literature offers theories that are not sufficiently general to explain patterns of change in the professional organization, the organizations literature primarily offers theories that are too general to have explanatory power. Theories based on the formal characteristics of organizations and their environments—such as size, level of administrative intensity, or niche width—presume an underlying similarity in processes of organizational change which is unwarranted or so abstract as to be uninteresting. Qualitative differences in professional organizations which derive from their legal status, the character of professional norms shared by members, or the expectations of clients fall outside most organization theories.

I suggest that a more useful perspective is to treat the problem of change in the professional organization as a problem of organizational dominance, both in terms of the organization's ability to reproduce itself economically and in terms of the ability of the leaders of the firm to exercise their authority. The central questions this framework poses are then: What are the conditions that produce different organizational structures? What is the basis for the legitimacy of relationships between the various strata of professionals within the organization and between the organization and its social environment? And what determines the success or failure of different organizational structures? In a sense this is a traditional approach to social organization which originated with Weber's theory of legitimate domination (1978). The same questions motivated Weber's complex typology of forms of domination (see especially 1978, pp. 941–955). My approach differs from that in most of the organizations literature, which, emphasizing the more formalistic treatment of bureaucracy that appears elsewhere in *Economy and Society,* attempts to explain variations in organizations solely in terms of

24   Introduction

structural properties (see, e.g., Blau 1956). Important as these analyses are, they fail to specify the historical conditions that give rise to organizational structures and cause them to change, and they largely ignore the ideological variables that shape and mediate structural change.

My emphasis on organizational domination attempts to provide a more comprehensive view of social change in the professional organization by examining the relationship between organizational structure, the market for professional services, and professional ideology. Such a perspective informs many of the important studies of industrial organizations (see, e.g., Bendix 1974; Chandler 1962) but is novel with respect to professional organizations (but see Katz 1982). Consideration of both economic and ideological elements is critical to understanding social change in the law firm. The relationships between the law firm and its environment (clients, professional institutions, and law students) are predicated on a particular view of the law and the role of lawyers. Relationships between lawyers within the firm also are rationalized in terms of what is necessary for the proper representation of clients and the maintenance of professionalism. Thus the market in which the firm competes, the nature of its product, its internal organization, and its role in society are heavily influenced by professional ideology.

Analysis of dominance in organizations may make a distinct contribution to theories of the professions and social change. Increasingly we have come to recognize that the power of the professions and the quality of the work life of professionals are tied to the processes of social change in the professional organization. The professional work organization is the site where market forces converge with professional authority. This is the context in which we can examine the material factors that have led to the dramatic growth of the professional organization but which also may pose serious conflicts with professional ideals and ultimately produce the same economic uncertainties that befall any industry in capitalism. This is the context in which as we observe how professionals work and how they relate to clients and to each other we can test broader social theories concerning the role of the professions in modern society. Does the professional work organization reflect Durkheim's (1958) hope that the professions could transcend the dictates of economic interest to provide the intellectual and institutional basis for a new moral order in industrial society? Or does the professional organization reflect and perpetuate the dynamics of hierarchy, inequality, and alienation that characterize the broader society?

Introduction

PRACTICE AND PRIVILEGE: SOCIAL CHANGE
IN THE LARGE LAW FIRM

The structure of any organization reveals both its special purpose and the special interests of its constituent groups. Automobile assembly lines, organized to produce cars as efficiently as possible, display common characteristics across firms and cultures. Yet the relations of production vary in certain critical respects depending on management's theory of efficiency, the relative power of labor vis-à-vis management, and available technology among other factors (Cole 1979). Hospital surgeries everywhere are similarly organized because of the diffusion of standard medical procedures, yet relationships between attending physicians and interns and patterns of social control vary significantly depending on the predominant interests of the attending physicians (research or clinical?) and patterns of patient admission (Bosk 1979). Legal-aid clinics provide similar services to similar kinds of clients. Yet legal services organizations have evolved dramatically different functions in the legal system, with different ideologies concerning social reform, different ways of appealing to the professional aspirations of staff attorneys, and different organizational structures (Katz 1982). Thus, to explain variation in the structure of an organization we must consider not only the functions it performs but also the relationships between various strata within the organization and the ideology that legitimates the internal hierarchy and the activities of the organization as a whole.

The structure of the law firm is the historical product of the material conditions of corporate law practice and the professional ideology that defines both the relationship between the large law firm and the broader institutional order and the relationships between lawyers within the organization. I refer to these respectively as the forces of *practice* and *privilege*. Many elements of the practices and ideologies of firms have not changed over time, and many do not vary by firm. This produces a basic similarity in the structure of firms. Yet as the pace of change in firms has quickened, structural differences have become more apparent.

The organization of law firms reflects the nature of their law practice. First, no matter how large, law firms are relatively small organizations involved in various specialized forms of information processing and client service. As a result, they have relatively simple organizational structures compared to other organizations. Second, the matters that large firms handle are in some respects extraordinary for their clients:

they involve complex or uncertain questions of law or fact and thus are not easily solved by internal counsel; they entail questions that raise difficult political questions internal to the client, that is, they are "hot potatoes" (Rosen 1984); or they involve massive risks for which the client seeks assistance in avoiding mistakes. Some of the work performed involves highly uncertain processes of gathering information and developing a plan of action. This work genuinely requires a craftlike division of labor which is closely monitored by senior attorneys (Perrow 1970). Even in large litigated matters work groups are small, typically comprising fewer than ten lawyers. Very often tasks are accomplished in pairs of a more senior and a less senior attorney.

This does not mean there is no "routine" work. Kritzer's characterization of much of the work of large-firm lawyers as "very pricey paper pushing" is correct but misses the more fundamental point (1984). What gets defined as a "routine" legal matter depends more on the significance that various parties attach to the transaction than on the intrinsic nature of the matter. The legal problems of poor persons are labeled "routine" because the stake does not merit detailed legal effort, whereas the corporation's legal affairs are of greater economic significance and are treated with considerable care (Katz 1982, pp. 17–33). Large firms are organized to make the extraordinary routine. Specialization is the primary means for achieving greater efficiency. Given a sufficient volume of demand for a particular service, a large firm will develop standard forms and standardized processing. The fields in which large firms have developed rationalized procedures, however, are not the "mass market" fields involving individual clients. Instead, large firms primarily work in corporate fields that can support a high overhead. Despite some potential for rationalizing the work process, firms rely on the skill and commitment of specialists. There is a clear status-based division of labor in firms, both between more senior attorneys and their juniors and between "client-intake fields" and "service fields" (which primarily service clients brought in by other fields). But little evidence exists to support the argument that large law firms have proletarianized or "deskilled" their professional labor force (for law, see Rothman 1984 and Spangler 1986; more generally see Oppenheimer 1973; Haug 1973a, b). The conflict between associates and firms is not over reduction of skills so much as over resistance to choosing a particular skill right out of school with little control over the choice. It may be true that firms attempt to exploit their associates by exacting a large number of hours worked and by charging substantially more for their services than they are paid, but proletarianization hardly seems an appropriate characterization when starting associates earn over $60,000 a year and appear to retain substantial discretion in how they perform work tasks (see Freidson 1984).

Third, practice shapes patterns of leadership and participation. Simply, the leadership of the firm is dictated by those who control the largest clients. The leaders of a firm will therefore be drawn from its leading economic fields. Any change in the client base will thus generate change in the leadership. Hence, the managerial elite can become a group of producers *manqué* who may be challenged by emergent client producers. The manner in which the managerial elite governs will also reflect the configuration of client interests. If client responsibility is divided among a group of partners, there will be more openness at the top than if client responsibility is concentrated in just a few. But the dilution of client authority may result in a lack of coherent management.

While practical factors are important determinants in the structure of firms, the social organization of the large law firm reflects its privileged status in the legal profession as well as a hierarchy inside the firm based on an ideology of professional privilege. The law firm is an institution of privilege in the first instance because it is an organization of professionals. The hallmark of the professions is the privilege of enclosing a set of activities through a licensed monopoly from the state in exchange for the observance of high standards and a commitment to public service. The professional organization will therefore be shaped by the norms and traditions by which the professional group has established its position in society. Large firms have developed their own distinctive professional cultures, drafting attorneys from only the best law schools, and in some cases only the best prep schools, refusing to do the "dishonorable work" of divorce law or criminal defense, and maintaining links with civic and cultural elites (Smigel 1969, pp. 36–140, 150). This professional style has had a broad impact on legal education, on the content and enforcement of professional ethics (Carlin 1966), and on the status hierarchy of fields of practice (Heinz and Laumann 1982, pp. 52–83). Corporate clients certainly have deferred to the intraprofessional status of the large firms. By relying on large law firms to solve uncommon legal problems without questioning how such firms organize their work, corporations have fostered an organizational style with less than rigorous management and cost control which can be justified under the mantle of high professionalism. Whether status translates into influence in the courts or regulatory agencies is more difficult to determine, although there is at least some suggestion that large firms gain better access to government decision makers than other representatives (Kagan 1978).

The authority system of the firm is a hierarchy based on professional privilege. In bureaucratic organizations power and status are established by position itself, but in the law firm power and status depend on the personal domain that the individual attorney builds throughout his or her career and generally is identified by the size of the clients for which he or she is responsible. Managerial authority thus derives from professional success. It is a privilege won by "being a good lawyer," not an office with defined duties and responsibilities. Recognition of professional privilege pervades relationships between lawyers in the firm. The leadership of the firm is constrained by norms of collegiality; partners and associates are given certain perquisites in recognition of their status, even when not merited on economic grounds. Associates defer to the seniority and experience of the partner they work for in exchange for respect for the younger lawyer's professional status, the promise of receiving "significant" work, and support in the organization. The ability of partners to attract talented associates is based on their standing in the firm and their reputation as effective sponsors. While these aspects of professionalism are common across firms, professional norms relating to important organizational policies vary by firm and by stratum within firms. The meaning of professionalism is established by the early leadership of firms and will reflect their theory of effective organizations. Associates often enter firms with a more traditional orientation toward questions of law firm organization than that possessed by partners. The divergence between partners and associates is attributable in part to their conflicting interests: associates will oppose the rationalization[1] of the firm to the extent that it means the rationalization of their activities; partners will favor measures aimed at improving the profitability of the partnership. The divergence may also result from processes of self-selection and socialization. Associates who disagree with organizational policies leave the firm or are eventually convinced that the policies are appropriate. The conflict in values is continually renewed, however, as each year's crop of new associates begins with an idealized conception of big firm practice.

The dictates of practice and privilege were roughly consistent in the traditional era of the law firm. In a smaller office with a relatively stable set of clients, there was no need to establish a formal departmental infrastructure or to develop a strategy for attracting and securing clients.

But the exigencies of modern practice, requiring intense specialization, internal coordination, and strategic planning, have forced firms to alter professional traditions. Nonetheless, traditional arrangements, because they are embedded in the structure of the organization and have continuing appeal to partners, associates, and clients, have a continuing impact on the ideology if not the managerial practices of firms. Thus practice and privilege have become partially antagonistic social forces affecting the structure of the law firm.

RESEARCH DESIGN

Typology and Sampling Frame

Every research design must make certain trade-offs between depth and breadth. To address the dynamics of change in the structure and ideology of an organization it is necessary to collect a variety of historical and cross-sectional data from individual firms. In contrast to Smigel, who conducted a small number of interviews in each of several Wall Street firms, I concentrated on four large law firms in Chicago. After extensive preliminary fieldwork, I selected firms to represent variations in two structural variables: scope of practice (ranging from general service firms to specialty firms) and bureaucratization (ranging from traditional to bureaucratic firms). This typology, with pseudonyms provided for the four firms, can be illustrated thus:

	Organizational Structure	
Scope of Practice	*Traditional*	*Bureaucratic*
General Service	Aaron, Smith & Kimball	Becker, Solomon & Jones
Specialty	Curran, Geller & Heinz	Duncan, Martin & Levy

Bureaucratization and specialization are the principal directions of change in the large law firm. Choosing firms that vary on these two dimensions serves a dual purpose. First, the analysis of these organizations directly addresses the major patterns of social change in firms. By examining how four firms arrived at different combinations of these fundamental variables, it is possible to develop a more powerful theory of social change. What elements were present in some firms but not others that led to a more bureaucratic form? Moreover, the consequences of different organizational structures for the success of the firm and the career prospects of individual lawyers can be evaluated. Second, even though four firms is too small a sample from which to make sweeping generalizations, to the extent that the firms represent significant structural variations between law firms in general, the results have broader significance.

Chapter 1 introduces a theory of structural change in the law firm which makes explicit the theoretical significance of the two variables. Chapter 2 introduces each of the four firms in detail and describes the pattern of historical development that resulted in their current organizational structure. For this reason only a brief definition of the variables underlying the design is necessary here. Scope of practice denotes whether a firm has a reputation for and a concentration of lawyers in a particular field as opposed to a set of clients for whom it provides virtually all legal needs. Chapter 1 argues that there is a distinct movement toward special representation as the dominant form of law firm growth, such that specialty firms have been among the fastest growing in the profession, and the high growth fields in many traditionally general service firms involve the special representation of clients on a case-by-case or functionally specific basis.

The use of bureaucratization as a variable requires somewhat more explanation. A bureaucracy is an organization with a well-defined hierarchy of officials, an authority system defined by office rather than by personal characteristics, governance by written rules, fixed jurisdictions, specialization of function, and hiring and promotion based on merit and performance (see Blau 1963, pp. 1–2). Very few organizations conform perfectly to these characteristics. Informal processes inevitably produce departures from formal bureaucratic structure. Such departures are so profound in professional organizations that scholars inevitably are driven to characterize professional organizations as a special form of bureaucracy (Freidson 1986, p. 160). Hence, Goss (1961, 1963) described an outpatient clinic as an "advisory bureaucracy"; Smigel (1969) developed the term "professional bureaucracy" for law firms; Montagna (1968), Bucher and Stelling (1969), and Scott (1965) in their respective studies of accounting firms, hospitals, and social agencies used the term "professional organizations."

From these prior studies and my own research we can conclude that the term *bureaucracy* must be used carefully and with qualification when applied to professional organizations. Indeed, an important element of my argument is that the bureaucratization of the law firm is a conflictual and partial process. But given the systemic pressures on both the internal administration of law firms and the management of their relationships with a changing environment, we cannot abandon the terminology of bureaucratization without also retreating from an appropriate level of analysis. When I speak of the bureaucratization of the law firm I refer to a process of structural change within an essentially collegial organization. Three structural levels are involved: management, administration, and work group. In terms of my four case studies, the two bureaucratic firms have developed specialized managerial, administrative, and work-group structures; the traditional firms have done so only to a limited degree. This does not necessarily mean that management has self-consciously pursued policies that create a bureaucratic structure. For a striking example of the potential for divergence between ideology and structure, in one of the bureaucratic firms the ideology of the governing elite and their partners remains traditional in many respects.

The Data Collected

Analysis of the contradictory tendencies in law firm organization required two types of data collection: in-depth interviews with members of each firm's elite and topical interviews with a random cross section of other lawyers, stratified proportionally by seniority. I personally conducted sixty-one interviews with the elite in the four firms, choosing individuals who had been current or past members of the governing committee or who were heads of a department or work group. Some lawyers who qualified as elite members were not interviewed, but at least one leading attorney from the major field and virtually all currently on governing committees were interviewed. Interviews were conducted with a dozen elite members in other firms that were not studied in depth. The in-depth interviews covered aspects of personal career development but focused on the history, current practice, and managerial policies of the law firm as well as the lawyer's views on his or her field of responsibility and the future of the firm. The topics considered in the interview are outlined in appendix A. These interviews were taped and transcribed or transcribed from notes. The cross-sectional sample of 224 attorneys was administered a standardized personal interview that contained closed- and open-ended items. A substantial proportion of the lawyers in each firm were interviewed, with the proportions varying by no more than 10 percent across firms. These interviews were conducted by nonlawyers and taped for purposes of cross-checking responses recorded on the protocols and to aid in the coding of ambiguous responses. The interview schedule, reproduced in appendix B, sought information on personal background, career, work, community and professional activities, and attitudes on the organization of the firm and social and legal issues. Thirteen lawyers from the elite also answered portions of this standardized instrument, giving a total of 237 responses on some items.

The two forms of data collected combine in a useful manner. This combination proved feasible given the nature of the organization under study. Norms of confidentiality in firms virtually preclude participant observation. Because time is in fact money to the organization, we limited the amount of time each lawyer was asked to devote to answering questions. The two kinds of interviewing succeeded in efficiently obtaining valuable information from top to bottom in the organization. Only two attorneys refused to be interviewed. A small number of other attorneys were not available because of scheduling problems and were replaced at random. Given the presumption at the outset that lawyers' perceptions might be colored by professional or organizational ideology, the mix of methods was invaluable. The convergence of findings from different methods enhances the validity of the observations. The sheer volume of detailed behavioral data collected minimized the overall threat to validity from response bias. Much of these data, when analyzed in the aggregate, such as that collected on networks of working relationships, provide a far more comprehensive analysis of organizational structure than any single individual could. Because the nature of authority was an important concern, gathering data from all levels of the firm enabled us to compare the attitudes and activities of various groups in the organization.

GENERALIZABILITY OF RESULTS

The generalizability of results is a special concern for a study that concentrates primarily on four law firms in one city in a given period. To a certain extent this is an inevitable problem in research. One cannot gain more than a superficial understanding of organizational dynamics without concentrating considerable time and resources on any given organization. While the four firms were selected to meet the theoretical needs of the study by maximizing the variation by type of practice and organizational structure, I must concede that the sample cannot be defended on purely statistical grounds. It is therefore important to comment generally on the nature of the firms studied and the terms under which access was gained.

The four firms are not pure types to the extent the analytical categories might suggest. But they are sufficiently representative of the variations the typology was intended to capture that typological categories (general service versus specialty and traditional versus bureaucratic) will be used throughout the presentation of results. In other respects, the firms were chosen to control for the effects of size. All four firms contained over fifty lawyers at the time they were chosen, and the smallest firm was at least two-thirds the size of the largest firm. Unfortunately, there is a confounding in the choice of firms between organization size and organization structure, in that the two traditional firms were also the two smallest firms. As a result we cannot statistically separate the effects of size and structure. While this raises an alternative explanation for differences between firms based on size alone, size quite clearly is not a sufficient explanation for many of the differences in the organizational structures of the firms. As the historical analysis of the firms will indicate (see chap. 2), differences in the organizational structures of firms emerged early in their histories when the relative sizes of the firms were much different than they are today. These histories demonstrate that at times when the firms were of comparable size significant differences in organizational structure still existed. The relationship between size and structure, however, is not necessarily spurious. It may be that although size does not produce structure, certain structures promote more rapid growth. Indeed, I will present considerable evidence that bureaucratically organized firms have significant material advantages over traditionally structured firms (see chaps. 2, 4, and 6).

The extraordinary access that the firms permitted for the conduct of this study also may lead some to wonder if these firms are peculiar in some way—whether they are particularly peaceful or particularly open. Although all law firms are in some sense unique, I do not believe these four firms are any more peculiar than any other four that might have been selected to meet the needs of the research design. All four firms were approached with great care; all proceeded judiciously to consider access. Two of the firms granted access in stages, although the same amount and kind of data collection was eventually allowed. A condition for the research was that the firms be guaranteed anonymity. While this limits some of the detail in my account, the analysis has been reviewed by readers who know the identities of the firms and are sufficiently familiar with their organization to provide a check on my analysis. Moreover, members of the firms themselves have read the findings reported here without registering objections about accuracy or bias.

The first four firms I approached in a formal way agreed to participate in the study. A fifth firm balked at the notion of allowing widespread random sampling. I concluded that the range of variation provided by the other four firms was adequate and that the additional expenditure of resources on an organization that had not granted comparable access was not justified. The four firms studied are all significant actors in the Chicago legal scene and clearly would be included in any list of major Chicago law firms. I mention this at the outset to preclude the suggestion that some of the problems I identify could be attributed to the unusual nature of the firms selected, or that the firms constituted a kind of backwater of the profession. On the contrary, from talking informally to lawyers in numerous other firms and from extensive reading of journalistic accounts, I believe that the strengths and weaknesses of the sampled firms reflect the general conditions of change in the large law firm. The four firms that participated in the study have all been success stories. None has suffered the serious setbacks that have plagued a few large Chicago firms during the last decade. But the sample firms have not been without turmoil either. Three of the four have experienced some conflict over how their firms are to be governed. Some have experienced the departure of prominent partners and even whole work groups. All these events might well have been considered sensitive. Each firm might have felt that it had something to hide, or at least to lose, by participating in the research. But all became convinced that the research was asking serious questions about processes of change they themselves did not understand well.

The fieldwork and surveys were conducted from 1979 to 1981. In the years since then, patterns of change in firms have, if anything, accelerated. There also have been some major changes in the four firms studied. These events, both in law firms in general and in these four firms in particular, have not led me to alter my interpretation of the results. Indeed, many of the trends I identified in earlier research have become more apparent in recent years. The situation in large law firms is far from static. My theory of the law firm will no doubt be challenged by the very patterns of social change I have attempted to explain.

PART I
Patterns of Social Change in the Large Law Firm

1
Social Change and Organizational Structure

The large law firm dominates the market for private legal services in the United States. Such firms, having made dramatic gains in absolute size,[1] encompass a growing proportion of lawyers[2] and command an increasingly disproportionate share of the gross receipts for private legal services.[3] Their position of leadership in the legal profession is nothing new. Virtually all scholarship on stratification among lawyers locates large firms at the top of the legal profession's status hierarchy (see, e.g., Carlin 1962, 1966; Ladinsky 1963; Auerbach 1976; Heinz and Laumann 1982). Nor is there any doubt that the success of firms has rested on their representation of wealthy corporate clients (see, e.g., Heinz and Laumann 1978). But there is surprisingly little analysis of *why* large firms have gained dominance in the market for corporate legal services (as against smaller firms or inside counsel), how their organizational structure has developed, or what the consequences of such an organizational form might be for sociolegal change (see Galanter 1983a). These questions take on new urgency given the current wave of entrepreneurial activity by large firms which promises to expand further the economic and professional power of these organizations. As firms vie for new clients and geographic markets, smaller firms are increasingly forced to choose between becoming a branch of a larger firm or competing with it directly. Moreover, these trends may lead to a fundamental redefinition of the professional authority of America's legal elite in which the power of lawyers is measured less by their social and political ties in the community than by their positions in the technically sophisticated bureaucracy of the large law firm.

This chapter applies the perspective of organizational dominance that I argued for in the introductory chapter in that it attempts to explain the link between position of the professional organization in the market for its services and the patterns of authority among the professionals working in the organization. Thus my analysis focuses on the relationship between changes in the market for corporate legal services, changes in the internal structure of firms, and changes in the functions law firms serve in the legal system. My premise is that these three dimensions can only be understood in terms of their interrelationships. Moreover, I suggest that the political-economic analysis of the large law firm has significant implications for the sociology of law.

My argument is that a fundamental shift in the market for corporate legal services has resulted from the expanding functions of law in the affairs of major corporate actors. While this expansion has stimulated the growth of large law firms, it also has undermined the traditional relationships between law firms and corporate clients, thus creating new tensions in the traditional law firm structure. The resulting "new structure" of firms is marked by the emergence of a distinctive managerial elite and increasing disparities in the status and income of partners. Also apparent is a new managerial ideology, which sanctions efforts to attract clients and notable attorneys, actions that would have been thought "unprofessional" only a few years ago, and which seeks to reorganize the firm internally by improving efficiency and providing additional rewards for those lawyers bringing business to the firm.

Such changes in law firms have captured the headlines of the *American Lawyer* and the *National Law Journal*. But the structural transformation underlying press reports has been partial and conflictual. In many firms the governing elite has resisted change. In others initiatives by new leaders have met sharp resistance from other partners and have produced bitter divisions and breakups. Even the most radically changed firms have attempted to justify the new structure in traditional professional terms so as to minimize conflicts with lesser partners and associates and to maintain the image of professionalism that has been so important in attracting business. Hence, even though firms have experienced enormous changes in their environment and their internal organization, they retain their traditional organizational form—the partnership—and much of the ideology of the independent professional that partnership implies. This contradiction raises the central question examined here and underlying much of the remainder of this book: How has the law firm changed so much by changing so little?

THE HISTORICAL CONSTRUCTION OF THE LARGE LAW FIRM

GENERAL PATTERNS

The historical literature on the development of large law firms is sparse. There are some general descriptive accounts in surveys of American legal history (Hurst 1950; Friedman 1973) and numerous hagiographies of law firms written by partners of firms or commissioned historians, but nothing exists approaching a comprehensive analysis of the life cycles of firms. An examination of the origins of today's leading firms reveals that most were established firms before World War II, indeed, many have roots in the nineteenth century. The oldest firms typically began as an extension of the practice of a prominent individual lawyer. Cravath, Swaine, and Moore, for example, was created by William Seward, senator from New York and secretary of state under Lincoln (Swaine 1946). David Dudley Field, the distinguished author of the *Field Codes,* was the central figure in the predecessor to Shearman & Sterling (Earle 1963). Mayer, Brown & Platt began as the personal practice of Levy Mayer and his family, and Mayer descendants have played a prominent role in the firm throughout its history (Masters 1927).

The sense of continuity conveyed by the histories of these firms suggests that status as a leading firm at the turn of the century guaranteed the continued success of a firm in the modern era. Hobson's analysis of early volumes of the *Hubbell Legal Directory* shows that this is not the case (Hobson 1984, p. 5). Less than 47 percent of the firms with five or more lawyers in the 1893 directory survived until 1904; between 1904 and 1915 the survival rate was 54 percent. Not until the period 1915–1924 did the odds of survival become appreciably better than even: some 71 percent of the firms persisted throughout this period. Hobson's statistics tend to confirm the reports of elder lawyers I have interviewed who suggested that many firms notable in the Chicago legal community in the 1920s had either disappeared or had dropped from the ranks of leading firms. Some firms were casualties of the shift of money and power in the profession away from the advocate as a public personality in the courtroom and legislature to the less visible,

40   Patterns of Social Change

more technical lawyer operating in the financial market and the corporate boardroom (Hurst 1950; Friedman 1973, p. 549). In the absence
of an institutional client base, many firms could not survive the death
or retirement of their leading partner. Other firms represented clients
that did not survive; others specialized in fields that did not expand.
Hence, fifty years ago it would have been difficult to predict which firms
would be the largest or most successful today.

    This record suggests that the first step in the study of organizational
change in law firms should be a systematic analysis of which firms have
succeeded and which have failed. To gain some insight into these patterns I have culled information from lawyers' directories, sources compiled for purposes other than research, and examined how firms have
grown over time. I consider historical data on Chicago law firms first,
then more limited historical data on the leading firms nationally.

    To examine the relative standings of Chicago law firms since the
Great Depression, I compiled information on the size and rank of the
ten largest firms in Chicago for the years 1935, 1950, 1965, 1979, and
1984 (see table 1).[4]

    Of the ten largest firms in 1935 five did not rank among the largest
ten in 1984. Two of these remain large, well-established firms. Scott,
MacLeish & Falk is the predecessor of Keck, Cushman, Mahin, & Cate,
a firm with 100 attorneys. The Sonnenschein firm, which employed 145
lawyers in 1984, has remained just below the ten largest firms since
1965. The other three firms are more telling cases. Sims, Stransky &
Brewer is the predecessor of a series of smaller firms that failed to
maintain a client base. Charles W. Hills and Jones, Addington, Ames
& Seibold, both patent firms, represent the fate of the patent practice.
In 1935 they were among the largest firms in the city. Although maintaining a consistent practice, they have not matched the growth rate of
other firms. The nature of patent practice has not led to the kind of
broad-based client ties that support expansion. Instead, patent firms
have been limited to their specialty. And even in that field their potential for growth has been restricted by the development of large in-house
staffs of patent lawyers in enterprises generating a steady stream of
patent work.

    Other firms make brief appearances in the table but have not main-
tained the rate of growth achieved by other firms. Isham, Lincoln &
Beale, who served as counsel to Commonwealth Edison (Comed), was
among the largest ten in 1950 and remains among the twenty largest
firms in 1984. Its growth has been limited by the internalization of some

TABLE 1. TEN LARGEST LAW FIRMS IN CHICAGO: 1935, 1950, 1965, 1979, 1984[a]

Rank	1935 Firm Name	1935 Size	1950 Firm Name	1950 Size	1965 Firm Name	1965 Size	1979 Firm Name	1979 Size	1984 Firm Name	1984 Size
1	Winston, Strawn & Shaw (a)[a]	43	Kirkland, Fleming, Green, Martin & Ellis (g)	54	Mayer, Friedlich, Spiess, Tierney, Brown & Platt (h)	81	Baker & McKenzie	512	Baker & McKenzie	697
2	Sonnenschein, Berkson, Lautman, Levinson & Morse (b)	29	Winston, Strawn, Shaw & Black (a)	43	Kirkland, Ellis, Hudson, Chaffetz & Masters (g)	79	Sidley & Austin (j)	231	Sidley & Austin (j)	441
3	Chapman & Cutler (c)	25	Mayer, Meyer, Austrian & Platt (h)	40	Baker & McKenzie (j)	61	Kirkland & Ellis (g)	205	Mayer, Brown & Platt (h)	301
4	Fisher, Boyden, Bell, Boyd, & Marshall (d)	25	Chapman & Cutler (c)	35	Sidley, Austin, Burgess & Smith (j)	60	Mayer, Brown & Platt (h)	193	Kirkland & Ellis (g)	267
5	Sims, Stransky & Brewer	19	Lord, Bissell & Kadyk (i)	33	Winston, Strawn, Smith & Patterson (a)	53	McDermott, Will & Emery (k)	167	McDermott, Will & Emery (k)	237
6	Poppenhusen, Johnston, Thompson & Cole (e)	19	Sonnenschein, Berkson, Lautman, Levinson & Morse (b)	31	McDermott, Will & Emery (k)	52	Lord, Bissell & Brook (i)	137	Lord, Bissell & Brook (i)	215
7	Charles W. Hills	18	Pope & Ballard	30	Chapman & Cutler (c)	50	Winston & Strawn (a)	126	Winston & Strawn (a)	206
8	Scott, MacLeish & Falk (f)	18	Bell, Boyd, Marshall & Lloyd (d)	27	Raymond, Mayer, Jenner & Block (e)	46	Chapman & Cutler (c)	115	Chapman and Cutler (c)	195
9	Kirkland, Fleming, Green & Martin (g)	17	Isham, Lincoln & Beale	26	Ross, Hardies, O'Keefe, Babcock, McDugald & Parsons	45	Seyfarth, Shaw, Fairweather & Geraldson	111	Seyfarth, Shaw, Fairweather & Geraldson	194
10	Jones, Addington, Ames & Seibald	16	MacLeish, Spray, Price & Underwood (f)	16	Sonnenschein, Levinson, Carlin, Nath & Rosenthal (b)	45	Jenner & Block (e)	98	Jenner & Block (e)	188

SOURCES: *Martindale-Hubbell Law Directory*: 1935, 1950, 1965, 1979; *National Law Journal*, Aug. 1979, for the six largest firms in 1979. *Legal Times of Washington*, Sept. 1984, for all ten firms in 1984. The *Martindale-Hubbell Directory* often does not include the cohort of attorneys passing the bar just prior to the compilation of lists from firms. Therefore, firm sizes based on the directory will be slightly understated.

[a] The letter in parentheses following some of the firm names enables the reader to trace these firms from year to year despite changes in firm name.

of Comed's legal work. Indeed Comed hired a partner from the firm to head its internal legal unit; he in turn recruited other lawyers from the firm. Ross-Hardies was among the ten largest in 1965, but as a result of slow growth in the 1970s and the recent departure of partners holding managerial positions in the firm it has fallen to thirtieth in size with sixty-five lawyers. Pope & Ballard appears in the table in 1950 and remained among the twenty largest firms until the late seventies, when a series of significant defections reduced its size. In 1984 it ranked thirty-fourth in the city with fifty-five lawyers. Three firms with established reputations for a particular specialty joined the ranks of the ten largest firms more recently. Baker & McKenzie first joined the list in 1965. Starting from a base in insurance defense work, the firm now is known primarily for its specialty in international trade. By establishing a network of foreign offices, it has become the largest law firm in the world. McDermott, Will & Emery, with a reputation for tax work (including employee benefits, estate planning, and general tax), also first appears in the table in 1965. Seyfarth, Shaw, Fairweather & Geraldson, predominantly a labor law firm, first appears in 1979 and almost doubled in size from 1979 to 1984.

Four firms in table 1 are present throughout the period shown, but there are some interesting shifts in their relative sizes. Winston & Strawn, counsel for the First National Bank of Chicago, was considerably larger than other firms in 1935 but has gradually moved to the middle of the top ten. Chapman & Cutler has experienced some decline in size relative to others as well. The Kirkland firm jumped to the largest firm in 1950 and has remained close to the top since then, although its growth has been reduced by the departure of a number of partners and specialty groups over the years (including Don Reuben and Richard Wiley among others). The Sidley firm grew rapidly from 1965 to the present, aided by mergers with medium-sized firms in 1972 and 1980. It opened a substantial gap between itself and other Chicago firms from 1979 to 1984. The firm was not listed in earlier years because it did not list associates. Mayer, Brown & Platt has been a leading firm throughout the period, but no 1935 listing could be found for the firm. Known for its close relationship with the Continental Bank, it was the city's largest firm in 1965 and ranked third in 1984. Whether it can maintain its position is unclear, given the economic difficulties encountered by Continental Bank and the recent departure of six middle-level partners to start the Chicago office of Skadden-Arps, a New York firm.

These data demonstrate considerable stability in those firms among the largest in Chicago, but the fortunes of particular firms can change dramatically within a few years. The pace of change has quickened in recent years as a result of both the increasing fragmentation of firms and the rise in merger activity among law firms. This, as well as other trends, is more apparent if we consider patterns of change in the largest firms nationwide.

Table 2 lists the size and rank of each of the fifty largest firms in the United States in 1984 and 1979, also reporting the sizes of these firms at ten-year intervals back to 1950. Although it would have been preferable to provide true national rankings in these earlier years as well, that would have required scanning the entire directory for the nation for each year of interest. For these earlier years, therefore, I only rank the firms within the list itself. Despite this limitation the table reveals some interesting trends.

New York City has been and continues to be the leading legal center in the nation. Half of the fifty largest firms are located there. The table does show, however, that the predominance of New York firms has receded in recent years. Until 1970 at least eight of the ten largest firms were located in New York City. By 1979 only one New York firm (Shearman & Sterling) ranked in the top ten. The surging growth of Finley-Kumble and Skadden-Arps put two more New York firms in the top ten by 1984, but much of their growth took place in branch offices. (More than half of Finley-Kumble's lawyers are located outside New York, as are a quarter of Skadden-Arps' lawyers.)

A significant portion of large-firm practice is now established outside New York City. Chicago, Houston, and Cleveland each have three firms among the twenty largest nationally; three other Chicago firms rank in the top fifty. Two Los Angeles firms appear among the twenty largest; another appears among the top fifty. One San Francisco firm ranks in the top twenty, two more in the top fifty. Philadelphia, Pittsburgh, Washington, Richmond (Virginia), Minneapolis, Dallas, and Boston each have one firm among the fifty largest in the country. Table 3 reports the number of firms with fifty or more lawyers in 1984 in cities with at least ten firms of such size. New York City has more than twice the number of fifty-person firms than any other city, but there are at least thirteen other cities that qualify as major legal centers according to the criteria used in the table. Moreover, several firms located elsewhere (fourteen of the top one hundred) maintain New York City branches, creating direct competition on the New York firms' home turf. The relative decline in the predominance of New York firms

TABLE 2. SIZE AND RANK OF 50 LARGEST LAW FIRMS IN 1979 AND 1984 FOR 1970, 1960, AND 1950[a]

Firm Name	Principal Office	Size in 1984				Size in 1979				Size in 1970				Size in 1960				Size in 1950[a]			
		Rank	Total	Partners	Associates	Rank	Total	Partners	Associates	Rank	Total	Partners	Associates	Rank	Total	Partners	Associates	Rank	Total	Partners	Associates
Baker & McKenzie	Chicago	1	697	276	421	1	512	186	326	17	116	81	35	47	27	18	9	—	—	—	—
Sidley & Austin	Chicago	2	441	174	257	7	231	113	118	31	79	46	33	30	51	27	24	28	34[c]	17	18[c]
Finley, Kumble, Wagner, Heine, Underberg, Manley & Casey	New York[b]	3	433	136	271	*	63	30	33	56	23	6	17	—	—	—	—	—	—	—	—
Skadden, Arps, Slate, Meagher & Flom	New York	4	426	106	317	22	189	47	142	54	32	10	19	54	14	5	8	52	6	4	2
Gibson, Dunn & Crutcher	Los Angeles	5	410	139	261	17	193	97	96	28	91	43	45	25	55	26	29	31	33	17	16
Shearman & Sterling	New York	6	409	104	294	2	288	98	190	3	164	56	104	4	106[c]	36	70[c]	1	91[c]	31	60[c]
Jones, Day, Reavis & Pogue	Cleveland	7	402	156	237	15	194	90	104	16	117	73	43	28	52	40	12	16	52	34	18
Pillsbury, Madison & Sutro	San Francisco	8	385	142	240	6	237	98	139	14	125	54	68	10	87[c]	36	51[c]	29	34[c]	14	20[c]
Morgan, Lewis & Bockius	Philadelphia	9	381	148	222	5	257	116	141	15	122	60	52	22	61	38	28	24	41	17	24
O'Melveny & Myers	Los Angeles	10	376	113	256	9	223	79	144	19	108	40	65	18	69	24	43	21	44	15	29
Fullbright & Jaworski	Houston	11	363	153	200	4	260	125	135	12	129	45	81	16	77	30	47	23	42	16	76
Vinson & Elkins	Houston	12	352	146	195	3	279	118	161	7	142	58	76	9	91	25	66	10	65	20	45
Squire, Sanders & Dempsey	Cleveland	13	308	137	164	8	227	100	127	10	130	60	64	19	65	33	31	18	50	31	19
Simpson, Thacher & Bartlett	New York	14	307	72	231	19	193	52	141	4	160[c]	43	117[c]	8	93[c]	25	68[c]	5	79[c]	21	57[c]
Davis, Polk & Wardwell	New York	15	304	70	227	16	193	57	136	2	166[c]	49	117[c]	6	95[c]	28	67[c]	2	85[c]	25	60[c]
Mayer, Brown & Platt	Chicago	16	301	125	174	18	193	100	93	23	100	65	35	26	55	28	27	25	40	22	18
Weil, Gotshal & Manges	New York	17	299	63	228	34	164	48	116	49	52	16	34	55	28	12	13	45	19	9	10
Baker & Hostetler	Cleveland	18	286	139	134	41	138	80	58	42	64	35	28	26	43	27	16	33	32	14	17
Baker & Botts	Houston	19	270	115	144	10	216	86	130	11	129	46	83	15	79	25	54	13	53	16	37

Firm	City																				
Cravath, Swaine & Moore	New York	20	269	56	212	25	183	47	136	1	172	44	127	1	117c	30	87c	4	82c	21	61c
Kaye, Scholar, Fierman, Hays & Handler	New York	21	269	72	187	31	168	64	104	20	102	43	57	38	38	16	22	116	18	10	8
Fried, Frank, Harris, Shriver & Jacobson	New York	22	268	78	180	21	191	57	134	33	79	26	51	39	38	16	21	26	40c	12	28c
Kirkland & Ellis	Chicago	23	267	114	150	11	205	70	135	25	97	55	40	17	71	38	33	12	54	25	29
Sullivan & Cromwell	New York	23	267	75	192	13	196	65	131	6	148c	49	99c	7	93c	31	62c	38	24	22	2
Milbank, Tweed, Hadley & McCloy	New York	25	254	63	185	23	187	57	130	5	158c	48	110c	5	98c	30	68c	7	70c	21	48c
Paul, Weiss, Rifkind, Wharton & Garrison	New York	25	254	73	177	27	178	59	119	24	97	37	58	20	64c	21	42c	20	46c	15	30c
Cleary, Gottlieb, Steen & Hamilton	New York	27	253	86	160	24	185	65	120	21	101	35	65	27	53c	18	33c	44	20c	7	13c
Latham & Watkins	Los Angeles	27	253	91	158	49	132	58	74	50	48	24	24	52	19	10	9	48	10	6	4
Reed, Smith, Shaw & McClay	Pittsburgh	29	250	94	132	28	177	70	107	30	79	62	17	23	59	37	22	17	51	22	29
White & Case	New York	30	246	72	172	20	192	61	131	8	139	56	83	2	110c	35	75c	3	85c	27	58c
Hunton & Williams	Richmond, VA	31	241	99	133	55	129	55	74	48	57	24	33	45	29	17	12	—	—	—	—
Dorsey & Whitney	Minneapolis	32	240	122	113	43	137	90	47	35	77	49	25	40	38	24	13	39	24	13	11
Wilkie, Farr & Gallagher	New York	33	239	65	170	50	131	40	82	22	101c	32	66c	21	62c	20	41c	14	53c	17	35c
McDermott, Will & Emery	Chicago	34	237	131	101	32	167	94	73	38	74	43	30	37	39	20	18	42	22	7	15
Debevoise & Plimpton	New York	35	234	64	169	45	135	48	87	29	84	35	47	31	50	20	29	35	30	12	17
Stroock, Stroock & Lavan	New York	35	234	69	155	58	127	44	83	44	61	21	40	51	21	12	9	47	14	8	6
Brobeck, Phleger & Harrison	San Francisco	37	231	77	151	42	138	54	84	41	66	33	33	42	36	17	19	36	26c	10	16c
Morrison & Foerster	San Francisco	38	230	96	132	37	153	47	106	51	42	21	20	46	28	15	12	43	21	10	11
Cahill, Gordon & Reindel	New York	39	229	57	165	30	169	48	121	26	95	39	52	3	107c	30	76c	8	67c	19	48c
Rogers & Wells	New York	39	229	72	151	40	139	58	81	40	68	39	29	29	52	24	28	22	43c	18	25c
Akin, Gump, Strauss, Hauer & Feld	Dallas	40	228	97	128	67	116	51	65	57	14	7	7	—	—	—	—	—	—	—	—

TABLE 2 (continued)

Firm Name	Principal Office	Size in 1984				Size in 1979				Size in 1970				Size in 1960				Size in 1950			
		Rank	Total	Part-ners	Asso-ciates	Rank	Total	Part-ners	Asso-ciates	Rank	Total	Part-ners	Asso-ciates	Rank	Total	Part-ners	Asso-ciates	Rank	Total	Part-ners	Asso-ciates
Hale & Dorr	Boston	40	228	101	125	64	117	72	45	47	59	36	22	41	38	30	7	31	23	8
LeBoeuf, Lamb, Leiby & MacRae	New York	43	227	78	140	71	114	52	62	52	45	24	21	50	22	12	10	49	10	6	4
Rosenman, Colin, Freund, Lewis & Cohen	New York	44	226	73	148	68	115	45	70	55	24	9	15	55	12	5	7	51	7	3	4
Dewey, Ballantine, Bushby, Palmer & Wood	New York	45	222	61	151	14	194	63	131	9	135ᶜ	44	91ᶜ	11	86ᶜ	28	58ᶜ	19	49ᶜ	16	33ᶜ
Covington & Burling	Washington, D.C.	46	220	87	125	12	196	77	119	18	111	51	60	12	83	32	51	15	53	22	31
Mudge, Rose, Guthrie, Alexander & Ferdon	New York	46	220	60	153	33	164	45	119	13	126ᶜ	34	90ᶜ	14	80ᶜ	22	58ᶜ	9	66ᶜ	18	48ᶜ
Cadwalader, Wickersham & Taft	New York	48	219	63	149	38	152	46	106	27	95ᶜ	28	64ᶜ	24	59	20	39	11	56ᶜ	17	39ᶜ
Kelley, Drye & Warren	New York	49	217	59	151	90	99	34	65	53	33	11	22	49	23	8	15	—	—	—	—
Lord, Bissell & Brook	Chicago	50	215	78	132	47	134	56	78	32	79	38	39	33	49	22	27	31	32	16	17
Firms in top 50 during 1979 which do not appear in top 50 in 1984																					
Donovan, Leisure, Newton & Irvine	New York	137	126	46	79	26	180	50	130	37	75	35	40	13	83ᶜ	23	60ᶜ	6	73ᶜ	20	52ᶜ
Coudert Brothers	New York	57	204	68	125	29	170	58	114	46	60	33	23	32	50ᶜ	17	33ᶜ	30	34ᶜ	11	22ᶜ
Foley & Lardner	Milwaukee	51	212	108	96	35	156	77	79	39	69	34	35	38	38	17	20	37	25	11	14
Pepper, Hamilton & Scheetz	Philadelphia	63	197	92	105	36	156	67	89	36	75	42	29	35	44	25	19	40	24	17	7
Kutak, Rock & Huie	Omaha, NB	63	197	100	89	39	141	72	69	58	7	5	2	—	—	—	—	—	—	—	—

Proskauer, Rose, Goetz & Mendelsohn	New York	55	205	73	131	44	137	56	81	34	78	34	44	34	44[c]	18	26[c]	27	35[c]	14	20[c]
Hogan & Hartson	Washington, D.C.	70	189	73	113	46	134	67	67	45	60	33	25	43	36	20	16	41	24	15	7
Arnold & Porter	Washington, D.C.	61	202	93	105	48	133	57	76	43	61	33	28	53	18	9	9	50	9	3	6

SOURCES: *Legal Times of Washington*, 1984; *National Law Journal*, Aug. 1979; *Martindale-Hubbell Law Directory*: 1950, 1960, 1970. Note: Rank in 1984 and 1979 is based on national law firm surveys. Rankings in 1970, 1960, and 1950 are based on size among the 58 firms listed here.

[a] Discrepancies between total size and the sum of partners and associates is a result of attorneys of counsel.
[b] Estimates of the size of New York firms based on current partner-associate ratios may be slightly inflated for earlier years.
[c] Estimated associates and estimated total size.
* Not included in lists of largest firms in 1979.

48   Patterns of Social Change

TABLE 3.   NUMBER OF FIRMS WITH FIFTY OR MORE
LAWYERS BY CITY*

City	Number
New York	87
Chicago	36
Los Angeles	30
Washington, D.C.	29
Philadelphia	23
Boston	21
San Francisco	20
Dallas	16
Minneapolis/St. Paul	12
Atlanta	11
Houston	11
Pittsburgh	10
Baltimore	10
Kansas City	10

SOURCE: *Legal Times of Washington,* Sept. 24, 1984, p. A6

* Only includes cities with ten or more firms of fifty or more lawyers.

reflects the ability of firms in other regions to capitalize on regional economic growth. Whereas New York firms previously had a distinctive advantage in legal work concerning the national financial markets located there, that advantage has waned.

Table 2 provides more testimony to the age of leading firms. Only six firms listed in the table have had their inception since 1950. Thus it is clearly difficult to crack the ranks of the nation's largest firms without a historical base. A comparison of the rankings for 1979 and 1984 shows that, as was the case for Chicago firms, the cast of characters among the fifty largest firms nationally has not changed much. From 1979 to 1984 only eight firms dropped from the top fifty. Even so, there is considerable movement within the rankings. Thirty-two of the firms in the table shifted ten places or more in the rankings in the five years from 1979 to 1984; fifteen firms moved twenty places or more. Among the most dramatic cases are firms that have grown very rapidly, often through extensive mergers. Finley-Kumble grew more than sixfold from 1979 to 1984, jumping from an unranked position, with 63 lawyers, to the third largest firm in the country, with some 433 lawyers. Skadden-Arps, Gibson-Dunn, Jones-Day, Baker-Hostetler, and LeBoeuf-Lamb are firms that doubled in size during the same five-year period and thus moved up dramatically in the national rankings.

Firms that grew at a modest pace amidst this surge fell significantly. For example, such extremely prestigious firms as Sullivan & Cromwell, Dewey-Ballantine, White & Case, Covington & Burling, Hogan & Hartson, while averaging better than 30 percent growth since 1979, dropped significantly in the rankings. Firms that experienced economic difficulties and significant defections declined even more precipitously. Donovan-Leisure fell from twenty-sixth to one hundred thirty-seventh, shrinking in size by 20 percent over the period because of a drop in demand for antitrust work and because of the defection of important partners (see *Wall Street Journal,* November 18, 1983, p. 1, col. 6). Kutak, Rock & Campbell fell from thirty-ninth to sixty-third as they closed branch offices in Minneapolis and Los Angeles (see Martindale-Hubbell Directories 1979–1984). Coudert Brothers dropped from ninth to forty-seventh amidst reports of dissension and defections resulting from too rapid expansion and mismanagement (*American Lawyer* 1983). Similar reports surfaced concerning Pepper, Hamilton & Scheetz, which declined from thirty-sixth to sixty-third. When we look beyond the fifty largest firms numerous other examples of rapid decline appear. For example, Howrey & Simon, an antitrust firm that had grown to a size of 125 in 1982, declined by almost 40 percent from 1982 to 1984 as the demand for defense against government antitrust suits fell off under the Reagan administration. Similarly Wald-Harkrader, a major Washington law firm, has suffered from economic difficulties resulting from the drop in antitrust work (*Legal Times,* June 30, 1986).

The historical tables on firms in Chicago and nationwide tell a similar tale. Law firms have experienced an explosive rate of growth in recent years. While the principal beneficiaries have been the same firms that traditionally ranked as the largest firms in major legal centers, this period of expansion has been accompanied by unprecedented volatility in the absolute size and relative standing of firms. The increasing instability in law firms is symptomatic of a broader shift in the market for corporate legal services.

THE THEORY OF LAW FIRM GROWTH

Two Paths to Growth: General Service and Special Representation. In the era of traditional practice the strategy of law firms was simple, if

50   Patterns of Social Change

unarticulated: add enough good men to handle client demands (Earle 1963, pp. 204–207). Some economies of scale could be realized by small increases in size, and there was little need for internal organizational control beyond the observance of professional ethics and a loose set of master-apprentice relationships between partners and associates. But as the law increased in complexity, growth by volume alone was no longer feasible. Growth and specialization became interdependent. In order to grow, a firm followed one of two paths. It could develop a "stable of clients" for whom the firm provided a full range of general counseling and specialized services; this development constitutes expansion through a concept of general service to existing clients. Or it could develop a stable network for securing referrals, with the firm providing specialized services to various clients on a case-by-case basis or providing continuing service to some clients but only for one particular function (such as labor law). This expansion through special representation aims at serving the needs of a specialized market rather than the general needs of regular clients. Most firms rotated between these two modes of growth, attempting to expand in a specialized field and then to consolidate the remainder of the client's legal business. Other firms attempted the converse, capitalizing on specialties developed for regular clients by offering services in those specialties to other clients on a case-by-case basis. Such a strategy, however, was often limited by potential conflicts of interest with existing clients.

The uncertainties of the large-firm marketplace contributed to the push-me-pull-me character of growth. While regular clients could provide a steady flow of work to firms, there was no guaranteed flow. There was always the possibility of losing a client, either through its acquisition by a corporation with its own counsel or as a consequence of the death, retirement, or departure of the lawyer chiefly responsible for the client. More recently, the development of corporate house counsel has eaten into much of the old bread and butter of corporate practice. The same is true in other fields that have become sufficiently routine to allow deployment of in-house counsel. And even stable clients have unexpected shifts in the demands they make on law firms: clients (and, therefore, their attorneys) frequently face unusual or unexpected litigation or new developments in the law (such as the imposition of wage-price controls). Firms relying more on client referrals to their specialty fields than on providing general service to a stable clientele have the mixed blessing of "certain uncertainty." They may staff in a way that is more sensitive to fluctuations in the demand for specialized services, a demand that may be more predictable in the aggregate than the demand of any one client. But they lack the steady flow of business to make up for fluctuations in the market for their special services and they constantly face competition from the expansion of general service firms into their specialty fields.

The two paths of growth I have suggested here represent distinctive strategies pursued by large law firms, strategies that are in part shaped by circumstance and in part by conscious design. It may be useful therefore to label the two paths of growth more formally. Growth of the first type—what I call *general service growth*—begins with the firm's acting as general counsel to stable clients and continues as the firm develops the specialties necessary to provide enhanced general service to clients. Hence one partner in such a *general service firm* commented: "We haven't really done anything but keep up with the growth of our clients."

Growth of the second kind is more directly conditioned by changes in specialized markets for legal services. If potential competitors do not find it economical to develop particular specialties or to staff matters that generate less than a certain volume of work, such matters are likely to be left to specialty firms. Some fields of law can be seen as unique marketplaces better served by a highly specialized staff, such as in the patent or labor law area. Or there may be new types of clientele not currently represented or new demands for a specific type of work which

Fields of Law by Type of Growth

General Service Growth	*Growth by Special Representation*
Banking	Litigation
General corporate	Labor
General securities	Securities/takeovers
Public utilities	Antitrust, trade associations
Regulated industries (railroad, etc.)	Criminal defense
	Divorce
	Real estate
	Trusts/probate/estate planning
	Patents
	Municipal law (including bond issues)
	Admiralty
	Bankruptcy

afford growth opportunities for a firm. I call this second form *growth by special representation*; this type of firm is clearly a *specialty firm*.

I distinguish between these two forms of growth principally for analytical purposes. Few law firms present a pure case of one form of growth, in part because firms seize those opportunities for expansion which do not conflict with their concept of professionalism or pose direct conflicts with existing clients. Hence the distinction between the two forms of development is most clearly visible in the fields of law. The general service fields are identified with particular types of clients with broad-ranging legal needs: banks, corporations, utilities. Special representation fields may also correspond to client types: municipalities, labor unions, real estate concerns, and individuals, for example. But most of the specialty fields are defined by function more so than by client and historically have been organized as specialized practices provided to numerous clients, often on a case-by-case basis. There is an obvious asymmetry in the list. Firms organized around general service fields are far more likely to develop the specialty fields listed in the right-hand column than are specialty firms likely to develop the general service fields in the left-hand column. As a result, the distinction between types of growth also shows up concretely at the level of the firm. The prototypical case of the general service law firm is a firm representing a large bank, for example, Shearman & Sterling in New York or Mayer, Brown & Platt in Chicago. The prototypical cases of specialty firms are those organized around a particular field, such as labor law (e.g., Vedder-Price; Seyfarth-Shaw), tax (e.g., Hopkins-Sutter; McDermott-Will), or litigation (e.g., Howrey & Simon; Jenner and Block).

The combination of fields developed by a law firm is partly a matter of chance. As one partner put it: "Law firms inevitably grow up like Swiss cheese. Due to a number of factors—personal contacts, history, accident—firms develop certain strengths in their practice, but there are always gaps." Nonetheless, it is clear that a number of structural factors dictate the fields in which the firms will grow. Many of these factors differentiate between general service and specialty firms. As has been observed of organizations in general (see Stinchcombe 1965, pp. 153–164), the time of origin has a pronounced effect. Older firms are more likely to have grown through general service relationships with long-standing clients, whereas newer firms, typically lacking an institutional client base, must attract clients based on a particular specialty or an innovative legal technique.

Once a firm has established a client base or a reputation in a particular specialty, it cannot arbitrarily change strategies for growth. One constraint is the formal one of conflict of interest, which prohibits firms from representing clients with conflicting positions in transactions or litigation. But perhaps more important are "moral" conflicts of interest over what is proper work for the firm. The leadership of a firm may discourage work it sees as potentially offensive to existing clients, even if the work does not pose a direct conflict. As a leading partner in one firm suggested:

> Another thing to realize is we do work primarily for defendants. Probably 99 percent of our work is for defendants. So if a plaintiff comes into the firm, even if it is a good solid client—and there are an increasing number of cases where good, solid, major companies are suing other solid companies—even if there are no direct conflicts of interest, we will turn down the business. Because there are times when you want to make sure you are not engaged in making law that may hurt you in other areas with other clients and embarrass positions you may have to take in future cases.

As a result, some special representation fields can develop more freely in a firm that is not dominated by general service fields. Conflict with general service fields, however, is less likely for some special representation fields. Labor, tax, and some corporate work, areas concerned primarily with problems internal to clients or with the relationship between the government and clients, can attract a diversified client base and complement a firm's established general service practice. Fields of law serving individuals—estate planning, probate, divorce, criminal defense—do not pose a conflict with the domains of general service fields. Hence, these special representation fields can readily develop within a general service firm. Indeed, because the clientele of general service firms may include a significant number of corporate executives, special representation fields serving individuals may have better growth potential in that context.

Another self-imposed set of constraints on the fields a firm can accommodate is the attitudes of firm leaders about what constitutes "dishonorable work." For many years, and even now to some extent, large firms would not allow divorce or criminal defense work in the firm. The same was once true of labor law. The head of a labor department in a large firm reflected on the reluctance of his firm to allow the labor practice to develop.

> At that time there was no such thing as a labor department as such. There was one man who, among other things, did some labor work. And the extent

of our labor practice consisted of negotiations of a union contract once every three years and that was about all.

Q. Was that a reflection of the state of labor law in those days or just this firm's practice?

A. Oh no, the labor field was already quite developed in those days. [X] and [Y] were both already established labor firms doing a substantial amount of labor work. But—I don't want to apply labels—in those days, how should I say it, labor law was not considered the kind of practice that was completely respectable. It was one of the things that we didn't do back in those days, it was something like divorce work. And so there was that kind of traditional resistance to getting into that field.

My distinction between general service and special representation addresses more than forms of growth in firms. The differentiation also corresponds to two quite different roles that large firms and their lawyers play with respect to clients. One role, which typifies general service, is the fiduciary. The fiduciary relationship is characterized by mutual trust, continuity, an ongoing flow of information, an identification with the interests of the other party, and mutual dependence (Stinchcombe 1980). The client depends on his attorney's knowledge of the corporate structure and history as well as on the sheer quality of trust and reliability. The attorney relies on the continuous flow of benefits (work, revenue, prestige) from the client. As a leading partner in one firm describes such a relationship: "I became in charge of the [X] account because I had done a substantial amount of work with the lawyer who originally represented [X]. And I had extensive contact with the younger executives in [X]. So to a large extent, we all grew up together, and we are now in a position of mutual understanding and trust based on a long relationship."

The other role, which frequently characterizes special representation fields, is the agent for special purposes. Rather than establishing an ongoing, broad relationship, the lawyer serves his client for a single case, transaction, or function. Knowledge of the client's structure and personnel is less important than mastery of certain skills (negotiation, advocacy) or familiarity with certain environments (courts, legislatures, agencies). In short, the special representatives are the hired guns of the profession. A litigator expressed the function of his firm in the following terms: "People come to us when they are in trouble, when it's their last alternative. They come to us when there's no hope. We are experts at pulling people out of the fire."

Lawyers (and law firms) serving as special representatives differ from general service specialists in more than their relationship to clients. They are also likely to have a more external orientation that is reflected in higher levels of activity in bar associations, community organizations, civic affairs, and government. These forums are part of the marketplace in which information about and contacts with lawyers and clients are exchanged. The careers of special representatives are more likely to originate outside the firm. They are the criminal prosecutors turned defense attorneys, the tax officials turned tax counsel, and, in some cases, the chief of a division in a corporate counsel's office turned substantive specialist. Not infrequently, then, they join partnerships by lateral entry, with the partnership offer extended to them because of their established notability. This departs from the traditional pattern of steady progression in careers by lawyers who serve a large, long-standing client in a firm. It can be a source of tension in firms because it violates the expectations of younger partners about the pathway to success. A partner in the litigation section of a large, general service firm cited an illustration.

> One thing that jolted all of us was when [X] [an attorney who had gained some notability in government service] was interviewing firms. [The head of the litigation department] came around and said, "We really have a need for a person with a public personality who will attract litigation business." A lot of us said, "We do?" There were groups that would congregate. And one guy would say, "You know for years they told us just keep our nose to the grindstone. Just do our work, and not worry about new business. Third chair, second chair, first chair, right? Wrong! That's the new message." ... The market is changing. We have to have people who attract business.

This quotation illustrates more than the differences in the career paths of lawyers acting as special representatives versus those acting as general counsel to clients. The comment shows how profoundly the shift to special representation has affected the market for large law firm services. In order to gain highly visible individual lawyers who can attract business, general service firms have been forced to recruit partners laterally, a departure from the traditional pattern of expanding the partnership exclusively from the ranks of associates. A firm's institutional ties and reputation are no longer enough. As another partner in a general service firm suggested, there is a new urgency in the established firms to expand the client base:

56   Patterns of Social Change

Now that the firm is bigger, I think there is more concern about getting
clients; there is much more concern about generating new business. In the
old days when the firm was smaller, we had an old line of existing clients
who had been with the firm for years. The firm was not worried about the
flow of business coming in. It was generally assumed that there was plenty
of work to be done and that bringing new business in was not important;
clients were house clients, not the clients of individuals. And so the chief
consideration in the earlier days was how well someone performed to keep
the clients that we had happy, and that was by far the most important thing
in succeeding in the law firm.

The Rise of Internal Counsel. In the latter half of the nineteenth century
the relative status of lawyers working in law firms and inside corporations was not so clear as it has become in the modern era. Certainly
one of the most prestigious and powerful roles in private practice in
the post-Civil War period was the railroad general counsel, a position
that lured lawyers away from the federal and state supreme court bench
(Hurst 1950, pp. 297–298). By the early twentieth century, however,
large law firms had clearly captured the leading position in the profession in terms of money and status (Hurst 1950, pp. 303–308). The
historical record does not explain the victory of independent professional firms in the legal profession; in some professions (such as engineering), in contrast, professionals were primarily employed internally
(see Larson 1977, pp. 19–39). Ideological and practical factors seem to
have been at work. Leaders of the bar (themselves law firm practitioners) argued that house counsel could not function independently and
that such employment relationships threatened "to destroy the possibility of securing popular confidence" in the profession (Hobson 1984,
p. 4, nn. 2–8). The prevalence of this ethic among lawyers and law
students made internal corporate positions a less preferred career path,
giving law firms a significant advantage in recruiting law graduates.
Prior to the establishment of regulated financial markets, law firms may
have served an important function as reputational intermediaries in
the sale of securities as well as in other types of commercial transactions (see, e.g., Hurst 1950, p. 348; Gordon 1983, p. 79). Independent
counsel enjoyed other practical advantages. In litigation they could
present themselves more effectively as objective advocates for clients
than could corporation employees. Lawyers in law firms also could
claim greater knowledge of the local conditions in the courts within a
jurisdiction than could a corporation's centralized legal staff.
    Internal counsel have nevertheless enjoyed a significant resurgence

in recent years in large part because the cost of legal services has led corporations to attempt to economize by internalizing as much legal work as possible. Cost pressures became so significant that Ralph Nader, for years a bitter opponent of corporations, organized a conference on the high cost of corporate legal services (*New York Times*, May 19, 1981, p. 29, cols. 7–8). The movement to internalize legal work has made corporate legal departments, not law firms, the fastest growing segment of the legal profession in the last twenty years. The proportion of the profession working as house counsel has grown from 5.5 percent in 1951 to 12.9 percent in 1980 (Sikes, Carson, Gorai 1971, pp. 10–11; Curran 1982, p. 12). Some of the largest groups of lawyers are now assembled inside corporations. Before its divestiture AT&T employed more than nine hundred lawyers (*New York Times*, April 2, 1982, pp. 32, 33).

Traditionally, internal counsel have confined their practice to relatively routine, small-scale matters (Johnstone and Hopson 1967, pp. 199–242). This pattern appears to persist, with corporations consistently seeking outside counsel for certain kinds of matters. General Motors, for instance, refers all trial work to law firms for strategic reasons, the theory being that outside counsel can be more effective advocates because they are removed from the client (personal communication, May 1982). As the volume and regularity of certain legal problems increase, internal counsel will often take over. Airline companies, for example, internalized much of the Civil Aeronautics Board practice, which formerly had been handled by specialists in outside firms. The tendency for inside counsel to move into routine areas of practice led the elites in the general service firms I interviewed to suggest that traditional corporate law practice (contracts, licensing, proxy statements) will not grow as rapidly as in the past.

The role of the corporate counsel in delegating legal work to outside law firms and monitoring its execution is also on the rise. Corporations have succeeded in attracting some distinguished attorneys as general counsel, such as Nicholas Katzenbach, former U.S. attorney general, now chief counsel at IBM. There is even a trend for corporations to formalize the relationship with their lead outside counsel by making them officers of the corporation but allowing them to retain a partnership in an outside firm. Howard Treinens, for example, is vice president for legal affairs at AT&T but retains his position as a leading partner in Sidley & Austin. Such joint positions may work to cement a relationship between corporation and law firm. The more pervasive effect of

58   Patterns of Social Change

the rising stature of internal counsel, however, is that relationships between corporate clients and law firms are brokered through a legally
trained intermediary. This has undercut the fiduciary relationship between firms and corporations. As a leading partner in a general service
firm suggested:

> Inside corporate counsel has had an effect on the extent to which a strong
> direct personal relationship between a lawyer in a firm and the corporate
> leadership can have an impact on distributing legal work. . . . More and
> more these days, communications from outside law firms into corporations
> are to be channeled through corporate counsel. . . . Old relationships are
> beginning to fragment. In some cases I think work is being sent out to
> individuals more than it is to firms. . . . And I think corporate counsel plays
> an important part in deciding to distribute work among a number of different
> firms.

This represents a fundamental shift away from the strategy of growth
that created most large firms, expansion from a stable client base. A
number of factors, however, will continue to favor growth based on
the general service model. Many firms continue to enjoy wide-ranging
relationships with institutional clients and will do all they can to maintain them. Much of the new entrepreneurial activity by firms is aimed at
keeping such relationships intact. Emulating the general service model,
firms constantly attempt to turn one-shot clients into general service
clients. Certain types of clients are less affected by the growth of house
counsel. "Mom and pop" corporations, for example, do not have a sufficient volume of legal work to warrant a full-time legal staff and will
continue to turn to law firms for general service representation. Even
in the more competitive market, the reputation and institutional ties of
general service firms will attract some specialty work. But the decline
in the general service model already has had significant effects on the
landscape of law firm organization and promises to have a more dramatic impact as the pace of change accelerates.

The Changed Market for Large Law Firms. The shift toward special
representation and the rise of internal counsel has led to the commercialization of relationships between corporate clients and large law
firms. Certainly there has always been a "market" for corporate legal
services in which information about the cost of services has been exchanged. But this information is far more actively monitored today than
previously for a number of reasons. First, the increased absolute cost

of legal services warrants careful search and selection by consumers. Second, the expanded presence and role of internal counsel in the corporation have increased the sophistication of corporate consumers. Third, the normative climate of lawyer-client relationships and relationships between firms has changed significantly. The traditional understandings that communal ties existed between clients and law firms and that competition between firms would be limited and "tasteful" have given way to comparative shopping by clients and entrepreneurial behavior by law firms. The result has been greater competition between firms and more uncertainty within firms.

We need only look at the pronouncements in the press to find suggestions that law firms have entered "the competitive era" (*Legal Times Advertising Letter,* August 1984, on file with author; *New York Times,* January 16, 1983, pp. 1F, 10F). Of course, the legal media may tend to exaggerate these trends, for they stand to profit from increased anxiety about economic trends through the sale of newspapers and subscriptions to seminars for coping with the new difficulties. But there are undeniable indications of increased competition. Only a few years ago it was virtually unknown for corporations to ask for bids on major pieces of litigation or on major transactions. Corporate counsel now ask for such bids with increasing frequency (personal interviews, 1979, 1982). Concern over the projection of their image to potential clients has led most large law firms to retain public relations firms (*New York Times,* January 16, 1983, p. 1F).

Perhaps the surest indicator of the rise in entrepreneurial activity in the legal arena has been the opening of branch offices in other cities and mergers with smaller firms. Ninety-five of the 100 largest law firms have at least one branch office, most of which have opened in the last decade (*Legal Times,* September 24, 1984). The pace of this trend can be seen in Washington, D.C., the favorite location for branch offices. Between 1965 and 1983 over 200 out-of-town law firms opened Washington branches, bringing the total there to 247 (*Martindale-Hubbell Law Directory* 1965; *Legal Times* 1983). Los Angeles is the site of branch offices for 21 out-of-town firms, followed by New York City (14), Miami (10), Houston (5), Denver (4), Chicago (4), and Dallas (3) (*Legal Times,* September 24, 1984).

One consequence of the trend toward branching is increased pressure on smaller firms to join a larger firm. Smaller law firms risk losing referrals from larger firms and eventually face direct competition from

60   Patterns of Social Change

the specialty departments of larger firms. Thus, as a partner who led
his medium-sized specialty firm into a merger with a larger firm suggests, smaller firms may have limited options for growth.

> We had a middle-sized firm, which put us in something of a peculiar situa-
> tion. We were neither a boutique nor a giant ourselves. So we were neither
> large enough to guarantee sophisticated clients everything they wanted nor
> small enough to pose no threat to other firms. Many smaller firms do
> specialty work that is referred to them from larger firms, and the difference
> in size alone is enough to ensure that the smaller firm poses no threat. Now,
> very often—and this was the case for us—when a firm makes a referral, they
> do it to a lawyer in another firm they trust, so that the referral is based on
> personal trust among lawyers. Even in the position we were in, perhaps
> because it was a fairly specialized practice, we were at the point of having
> to turn down business. And you hate to do that.

Another consequence of intensified efforts to expand through
branches and mergers is the increasing volatility of relationships between lawyers within firms. Firms have begun to "raid" other law firms,
hiring away individual partners, even whole work groups. Kirkland &
Ellis, for example, hired four pension specialists away from McDermott,
Will & Emery in order to establish its own pension group (*American
Lawyer,* September 15, 1981, p. 15). Skadden-Arps recently hired six
partners away from Mayer, Brown & Platt in order to start a Chicago
branch office (*American Lawyer,* June 1984, p. 30). Indeed, reports
circulated that another firm was bidding for the departing Mayer-Brown
attorneys. These sorts of defections have become increasingly common.
Of the twenty-one Chicago firms listed in the *American Lawyers Guide
to Law Firms* (1984), fifteen were reported adding or losing partners
from other law firms or the legal departments of corporations from
1979 to 1984. The "Bar Talk" column of the *American Lawyer* reported some 340 accounts of departures from firms of fifty or more
lawyers from 1979 to 1984 (1979 to 1984). The majority of instances
involve lawyers' moving to other established firms. These departures
most often involve middle-level partners who seize the opportunity to
head a specialty group at another firm rather than wait for the chance
to succeed the more senior attorneys in their present firm. But a number
of defections involve the departure of leading partners with demonstrated ability to attract business. Just as institutional reputation is not
enough to ensure a growing client base, the institutional bonds between
partners are no longer sufficient to ensure continuity from one genera-

Social Change and Structure

tion of lawyers to the next or to maintain the loyalty of particular specialty groups to the firm as a whole.

Changes in the market have also made the content of work subject to rapid change. As internal counsel have taken over the routine aspects of corporate legal work, a growing proportion of corporate practice now involves either litigation, which often makes unpredictable and intensive time demands, or rapidly changing and complex technical areas, which require constant monitoring of new developments. The boundaries of large-firm practice are thus moving away from predictable, more readily scheduled work toward the more uncertain and unpredictable areas of practice. This poses a considerable organizational problem for firms, forcing them to maintain a more flexible work-group structure.

> Q. Does [the fact that your practice consists mostly of very large litigation and whatever else is changing most quickly in the law] create a problem for you in terms of planning your organization?
>
> A. Well, sure it is a problem. But I think it is less of a problem for this firm than perhaps for others. We don't have a rigid set of specialties. And in fact most of the more senior people around here are capable of practicing in a variety of fields and usually do. So they are able to react rather flexibly.

Despite this informant's optimism about the adaptability of senior partners, it is clear that the rapidly changing content of the work makes it difficult to develop an efficient internal structure.

The changes in the market for corporate legal services have had a discernible effect on the economic performance of firms. The dramatic shifts in the relative standing of firms from 1979 to 1984 (see table 2) show that the firms that have gained the most in recent years—Baker & McKenzie, Finley-Kumble, Skadden-Arps, Seyforth-Shaw, Memmel-Jacobs, Sidley & Austin, to name a few—are precisely those firms that have developed self-conscious strategies for growth in new specialties and growth through mergers and branching. The firms that have declined are those that have failed to diversify into new fields and new geographic markets.

As this pattern continues it will have serious consequences for the internal organization of firms. Firms that suffer from shrinking profits because of loss of business will no doubt make efforts to divest unproductive partners of their partnership interests. Moreover, in order to maintain economic viability firms will be forced to develop strategies

62 Patterns of Social Change

to expand their clientele. Both tendencies will serve to reinforce distinctions between the strata of lawyers in the firm, with some partners forming an entrepreneurial elite to control the greatest share of power and profits and other partners assuming de facto status as salaried employees.

Economic Theories of Law Firm Growth: Efficiency, Risk, and Information. Neoclassical economic theory suggests that firms grow toward the size at which goods and services can be produced most efficiently. Accordingly, a number of factors favor the production of legal services in larger units (see Gilson and Mnookin 1985).

1. *Requirements of minimum scale.* Very simply, only firms of a certain minimum size can handle certain projects or accounts.

2. *Economies of scale.* Larger firms can spread some fixed costs (such as for office equipment, the library, or recruiting) over a greater number of services, resulting in lower average costs.

3. *Economies of scope.* Larger, diversified firms can gain the advantages of the joint production of different services. For example, as the demand for particular fields fluctuates, these firms can move productive resources between fields, thus maximizing their utilization.

4. *Greater quality.* It has been suggested that larger firms produce more valuable services than smaller firms. Most arguments do not rely on size per se as an explanation but treat size as a proxy for status. Hence, a brief written by a large firm will be taken more seriously by courts and other public decision makers or a prospectus for a securities offering will instill more confidence in potential investors when signed by a major firm. Some authors propose that size itself improves quality. DeAngelo argues that Big Eight accounting firms produce more objective, accurate audits than smaller firms because they receive a smaller proportion of their revenues from any one client (1981). The same logic can be applied to some aspects of law practice. In instances where lawyers vouch for the good faith and reliability of a client, the representation of a larger firm can mean more to the second party because of the independence of the firm from the client. Gilson and Mnookin (1985) offer a variation on the same theme. They posit that the large firm can be considered a quality assurance mechanism. Because large firms have a lot to lose from shoddy work (in terms of lost clients or malpractice claims), the argument runs, they set higher standards for

the professional work product and monitor the performance of their lawyers more closely than do smaller firms.

But such explanations of law firm growth based on efficiency prove inadequate. They are indeterminate with respect to optimal firm size. How big is big enough? Why haven't law firms grown to the same proportions as major accounting firms? Without specifying the conditions that make a particular organizational form more efficient than another, efficiency explanations reduce to tautologies. Moreover, the four factors cited above do not clearly militate for larger firm size. The flexibility of computerized research and word-processing systems suggests that law firms can achieve economies of scale at a modest size, certainly at a more modest size than current levels. Minimum scale requirements also do not explain firm size. Rarely do the constituent work groups inside firms exceed thirty lawyers; most work is performed by much smaller work teams, generally two to six lawyers. It might be argued that several large specialty groups offer economies of specialization and meet demands for minimum scale in several different fields. But this argument moves beyond an explanation based on efficiency of production. In the absence of transaction costs it would be possible for clients to choose among a number of smaller specialty firms on a case-by-case, transaction-by-transaction basis. On similar grounds economies of scope appear insignificant. An increasing proportion of large-firm practice involves discrete transactions that can be handled within specialized work groups, without requiring joint efforts by different specialty groups. And, in the absence of information costs or opportunistic behavior by different law firms, it would be possible to assemble teams of specialists from more than one firm to meet the demand for the coordinated use of specialists (Williamson 1975).

Neither is the argument persuasive that size is a proxy for quality. If status is thought to be the underlying explanation for the success of larger firms, why speak of size advantages? As the ages of the largest firms clearly indicate, size is a consequence of status, not a determinant of it. Hyatt Legal Services, for example, by a body count of the professional staff would rank among the top firms in the country. But because the firm is oriented toward the mass market of individual consumers, it is not considered seriously by corporate clients.

The notion that larger firms assure quality because they have more to lose from a mistake is equally fatuous. Smaller firms have as much or more to lose in proportionate total revenues by alienating a client.

64   Patterns of Social Change

Indeed, some economists argue that professional service firms must remain relatively small because of the difficulty of monitoring worker
performance in larger firms (see Alchian and Demsetz 1972; Leibowitz
and Tollison 1980; but see McChesney 1982). The suggestion that
larger firms are more independent from any particular client, and thus
can more effectively vouch for the integrity of their clients, is based on
the untested assumption that the diversity of a firm's client base makes
individual partners more independent. (See chapters 6 and 7 below for
evidence contradicting this premise.)

The limitations of the efficiency explanations have led Gilson and
Mnookin (1985) to argue that law firm growth is better explained by
efforts to minimize risk by diversifying across several fields. They predict, for example, that securities lawyers will merge with bankruptcy
lawyers on the theory that when the economy is strong the firm would
capitalize on its securities practice and when the economy is weak the
bankruptcy practice would thrive. By splitting the profits the two specialty groups would minimize fluctuations in revenues resulting from
economic cycles. Gilson and Mnookin recognize that three forms of
opportunistic behavior by lawyers threaten the *ex ante* contract to share
profits: shirking, when a partner's input falls below expectations; grab-
bing, when a partner insists on revising the *ex ante* agreement in periods
when his input to profits exceeds his share of profits; and leaving, when
a partner takes his clients and leaves the firm to avoid sharing profits
as set forth in the *ex ante* bargain. Accordingly, they argue that to
maximize the prospects for diversification, firms must have developed
sufficient "firm-specific capital," meaning institutional clients that no
individual partner can claim responsibility for or take away from the
firm.

Valuable as this analysis is in articulating several economic aspects
of the law firm, it is fundamentally wrong both in the treatment of
the relationship between risk avoidance and diversification and the impact of profit sharing on organizational success. First, risk avoidance is
scarcely an adequate explanation for diversification and growth by the
law firm or by any economic enterprise. The primary concern of economic actors is to maximize return within a range of acceptable risks;
the value of investments is thus discounted according to risk. A group
of profit-maximizing securities lawyers would not necessarily seek out
a group of bankruptcy lawyers but would attempt to combine with the
specialists who would produce the highest average return. In my inter-

views with firm leaders concerning mergers and branching, risk avoidance was never mentioned as a motivating factor. Instead, the prime considerations were the opportunities for tapping new client sources and providing additional services to existing clients. Punnett's (1986) research into some eleven mergers among Chicago law firms yields similar findings. Punnett found that risk avoidance was never the most important motivation for a merger. It was unmentioned in all but two of the mergers he examined (Punnett 1986, p. 40). Goldberg's (1985) analysis of contractual relationships between corporations similarly suggests that the role of risk avoidance in planning economic activity has been greatly exaggerated.

Second, Gilson and Mnookin's model of the social structure of the firm and in particular of the relationships between specialty groups is unrealistic. The constellation of specialties that firms develop is a historical product of early client ties, norms about what constitutes acceptable work, formal rules concerning conflicts of interest, and the opportunities for developing new fields of expertise. Firms do not have unlimited possibilities for diversification and indeed often face serious constraints on expansion. While Gilson and Mnookin tend to conceive of specialty groups as equal parties to a contract, typically there is a hierarchy of specialties within a firm. The fields bringing in the largest clients get the largest share of profits. Central to Gilson and Mnookin's model of sharing among specialties is the argument that the best means to maximize diversification is a system of compensation based on lock step seniority in which lawyers of equal seniority receive equal financial rewards. But the clear trend in compensation systems in law firms is away from pure seniority systems. Strict lockstep income systems are now limited to a small set of exceptional law firms. Moreover, there is no evidence that seniority-based profit sharing has led to enhanced diversification or improved economic performance. Some of the exemplars of lockstep systems—Covington & Burling, Sullivan & Cromwell, Cleary-Gottlieb—have lost considerable ground in terms of firm size, having grown at less than the average rate for the fifty largest firms from 1979 to 1984. Part of the reason for this relative decline is that they have been slow to open new offices or merge with other firms, two avenues for rapid diversification. If Gilson and Mnookin's thesis were correct, we would expect lockstep firms to diversify more rapidly than others. While older, more established firms such as Cravath or Sullivan & Cromwell are among the most profitable in the profession (*American*

Lawyer, July/August 1986, pp. 54–55), it is not clear that their profitability is attributable to the nature of their compensation systems as distinct from any number of other characteristics.

Theories of law firm expansion based on efficiency and risk avoidance are hopelessly incomplete because they fail to consider the distinctive structure of the market for corporate legal services. It is not a free market in a neoclassical sense, but one that is defined by the professional status of the producing organizations. The status hierarchy of the American legal profession is jointly defined by the status of law schools and the types of clients represented. The leading position of large firms is historically linked to their ability to recruit the best graduates from the best law schools. Law firms enthusiastically promoted the growth of professional schools as gatekeepers for entry into the profession (Gordon 1978), in part perhaps for reasons of nativism (see J. Auerbach 1976), but more fundamentally to certify their claim to professional status. Firms thus simultaneously established themselves as the major consumers of high-status law schools and the representatives of leading business organizations.

Firms in different locales pursued different strategies for exploiting their position of status within the profession. The early predominance of New York City firms derived from proximity to the national financial markets and especially strong connections with elite law schools. Washington law firms capitalized on superior access to and knowledge of the federal government. Leading firms in other cities grew primarily through their ties to the local business and political establishments; as regional economies accelerated, the local legal elites prospered. As these patterns suggest, the market for large firms is highly segmented in that it continues to be organized around specific institutional, regional, and political structures. This is because lawyer-client relationships are still "relationships." The principal function of legal counsel is to advocate client interests. Personal relationships between corporate management and law firm partners work to ensure that the lawyer acts as a zealous advocate. It is informative to compare the segmentation of the corporate sector of legal services to the highly concentrated structure of corporate accounting. The Big Eight accounting firms perform roughly 90 percent of the auditing services for major industrial and financial enterprises and are many times larger than the next stratum of accounting firms (see Montagna 1971). The principal function of an audit is to provide independent verification of financial information used in national financial markets. The stark dominance of the Big Eight thus reflects the preference of the financial markets for audits performed by leading firms and suggests the relative unimportance of personal relationships between corporate management and their auditors. The adversarial character of legal representation, however, leads to much stronger identification between corporate clients and law firms.

The importance of personal relationships in corporate law is reinforced by the difficulty of defining the quality of services rendered. Even in litigation, where there are seemingly straightforward outcomes, how do clients assess the performance of counsel? If lawyers win a case there is the question of whether the expenditure on legal costs was worth the results or whether a less costly settlement could have been reached. If they lose, the question is whether different tactics could have changed the result. Given the uncertainties, clients often must live with their choices, trusting that counsel will perform competently. Inside legal officers may provide a more sophisticated evaluation of the performance of outside lawyers, but ultimately they too must make a leap of faith and rely on the judgment of the chosen external counsel. Clients attempt to minimize this uncertainty by selecting lawyers they know personally or to whom they have been referred by a trusted source.

The market for corporate legal services is thus a highly textured set of networks connecting law firms to corporate clients. A more useful economic theory for attempting to explain patterns of organizational change in this kind of market is Williamson's (1975) transaction-costs approach, which relaxes many of the neoclassical economic assumptions about information, the potential for opportunistic behavior, and the impact of norms on economic behavior. Williamson's concern is the conditions under which firms rely on the market for goods and services and when they internalize production. Transaction costs—that is, costs associated with gaining information about the market, monitoring the performance of contracts, and enforcing contracts—are the critical variables in this analysis.

The transaction-costs framework suggests an economic theory for the rise and fall of the general service law firm which is entirely consistent with my theory of law firm growth. In the general service model the law firm acts as a specialized extension of the corporation. Although client and law firm formally remain separate entities, for many practical purposes they operate as a coordinated unit. In the prototypical case, such as the relationship between a major bank and a law firm, it is not uncommon for the firm to maintain its offices within the

68   Patterns of Social Change

client's building and to bill the client at a fixed hourly rate no matter how senior the lawyer handling the client. In these circumstances the firm is the functional equivalent of the law department in the corporation, the only difference being that the firm has other clients as well. Even in less extreme forms the boundary between general service firms and clients is highly permeable. Partners frequently move into managerial positions in the client corporation and even more frequently sit on its board of directors. The relationship between organizations becomes entrenched, not only because of personal ties between members of both organizations but as a result of the client-specific knowledge the law firm accumulates. Other law firms are therefore at a competitive disadvantage in bidding for the corporation's legal work because they would have to absorb the cost of acquiring the client-specific knowledge possessed by existing counsel. This arrangement limits bargaining between firm and client, for unless the client is willing to pay higher prices to another firm or to develop an in-house capacity, it is dependent on its chosen law firm. Only when a corporate client perceives the prospect of significant savings or improved service does it develop an internal legal staff. Once formed, however, the internal staff is in a position to replace outside counsel as the principal source of client-specific knowledge and thus destroy the outside law firm's competitive advantage. Although the displaced external counsel may retain some elements of its portfolio with the client, it must compete with other firms for ad hoc assignments. The law firm's relationship with the corporation's inside counsel then becomes critical to the flow of business.

The transaction-costs approach also illuminates the reasons for the acceleration of merger activity among law firms. In a market in which business is channeled through personal referral networks, one way to cast a broader net is to hire lawyers who possess their own referral networks. The acquisition of new partners and the opening of branch offices is like the acquisition of additional lightning rods who can attract business to their own field as well as to other areas of the firm's practice. The operating assumption, of course, is that the revenues generated by the merger will increase the average return for the members of both organizations. Members of the legal elite repeatedly cited the rule governing a favorable merger: "2 + 2 must equal 5"; that is, both parties must benefit. In the absence of information problems and opportunism, mergers would not be necessary. If access to new client sources were not controlled through referral networks, firms could freely compete for new business simply by developing expertise in a field, without having to penetrate a new network. Moreover, two firms could garner the same benefits without a merger by agreeing to exchange referrals. The chief problem in such an arrangement is monitoring compliance. Ultimately, considerations of gaining access to new clients and gaining control over referrals have led firms to pursue mergers.

The virtue of the transaction-costs framework is its sensitivity to the complexities of information exchange, opportunistic behavior, and normative orientations in economic behavior, both within and between organizations. The explanatory power of this approach with respect to recent changes in the market for large law firms suggests the essential complementarity between economic and sociological analyses of organizational change. It underscores the importance of examining the relationship between markets and organizational structures, even in the case of professional organizations, organizations whose structures often are explained primarily in noneconomic terms.

THE STRUCTURE OF THE FIRM

The Roles: Finders, Minders, and Grinders. All organizations of size and complexity consist of a set of structured relationships, a set of roles defining the power of participants and the functions they perform. In contrast to the structures of other professional organizations, such as the hospital or the university, and despite dramatic growth and internal differentiation, the structure of roles in the law firm arises from ambiguous origins and operates with considerable informality. The hierarchy of the firm can therefore best be understood by an examination of the traditional distinctions between the various strata of lawyers. A senior partner provided an eloquent definition of the roles lawyers play in the large firm:

> Q. There are so many different lawyers here.... Some people have suggested that now there are really different kinds of partners in a firm of this size.
>
> A. There is what we call—and you have probably heard this—the finders, the minders, and the grinders.
>
> Q. That's an interesting set of distinctions.
>
> A. Well, they mean there are lawyers who seem to bring in substantial clients, there are lawyers who take care of the clients who are already

70   Patterns of Social Change

here, and there are the grinders who do the work. And there's some
truth to the saying.

Q. How would you consider yourself in that?

A. I guess I'm something of a minder. I am pretty much concerned with
answering the questions and problems of clients we already have.

The Entrepreneurial Role: The Finders. Alfred Chandler (1962), in his
comparative history of the American business enterprise, draws a distinction between executives who develop strategies for the long-term
health of their enterprises and those who deal with short-term, tactical
administrative decisions. The former, the "entrepreneurs," set the basic
organizational framework or structure within which the activities of
other managers and employees take place. A similar distinction is useful
in studying the government of large firms. As firms have grown larger,
as law has become more complex and more specialized, as the market
for legal services has grown more unpredictable, firm leaders have increasingly had to deal with long-term strategic issues. The governing
group of the firm, its entrepreneurs, whether they are conscious of this
role or not, indeed, even if they are ambivalent about growth, have
been forced to focus on how the firm can reproduce itself in a continually expanding manner.

Most entrepreneurs of the large firm sit on the relatively small governing committee of the firm.[5] With few exceptions these are partners
who bear the greatest responsibility for clients. Their governing authority is not as formal as that of their corporate analogues. Only rarely
are their powers defined in the written partnership agreement (Smigel
1969, pp. 211–215; confirmed in several interviews, 1979–1980). Instead directives are reached by a form of gentlemen's agreement. This
attitude of collegiality, what one might call the ideology of partnership, may obscure the dynamics of leadership in the firm. As a result,
the entrepreneurial role, which includes responsibility for strategies for
the future and an organizational structure for monitoring developments in the firm, has a "now you see it, now you don't" character.
After spending an hour discussing details of changes in the demand
for legal services and the approaches his firm was taking in response,
a leading partner seemed to deny any long-range policymaking.

Q. What is the firm's strategy for growth? Will it stop? Is there a size you
don't want to exceed?

A. I don't think there is any theory. We are just reacting to the needs of the clients. I don't think firms have a ten-year plan; we certainly don't. We're just trying to deal with a greater volume of practice and the increasing complexity of the law.

Nonetheless, another partner who had previously led the firm expressed a greater awareness of his role in the expansion of the firm. He commented on his involvement in designing a merger substantially expanding the size of his firm: "I was betting there was going to be an explosion in the demand for law, the way the bureaucracy of government regulation was going, its intervention into business. . . . I had a strong idea about institutionalizing the firm. . . . I wanted to develop something that would last . . . to institutionalize things."

New York City firms have preceded law firms in other cities in developing distinctive strategies for growth. In addition to having a considerable head start in the market for legal services as a result of their location in the largest money center in the nation, New York firms could follow the example of Paul D. Cravath, who introduced the "Cravath system" to the Seward firm in 1900 and became to New York law firms what Alfred P. Sloan, Jr., would become to the multidivisional corporation twenty years later (Swaine 1946; Chandler 1962, p. 130). Because many of the organizational issues that Cravath addressed are issues of concern to modern legal entrepreneurs, he deserves special attention.

Paul Cravath was the prototypical law firm entrepreneur. He joined the firm of Seward, Guthrie & Steele as a partner on May 1, 1899 (Swaine 1946, p. 573), after a long period of exchanging client referrals and collaborating with Guthrie. From the beginning of Cravath's career his domain was the private one of the law firm office and the corporate conference room rather than the public forum of the courtroom and the legislature. One of his early partners described his emphasis on organizational structure as a "passion for organization":

> His first great object was to organize his firm and its staff [so] as to make it competent to do, as nearly perfectly as it could be done, any acceptable work which might be offered. He sensed that a big law firm which attempted to cover the whole field of general practice could not attain the best results for its clients or for itself unless, in addition to men with broad experience in various fields, it contained specialists in those narrower fields which, with the passing years, become more and more important and more and more complicated. Prior to the time when Cravath took control as the active head of the firm there had been little attempt at scientific organization in the

72   Patterns of Social Change

office. There had been many good men and not a few distinguished members
of the firm, but for the most part each of them worked independently by
and for himself, with his own assistants, seeking to cover all the varied
problems of the particular clients with which he dealt. Cravath's organizing
genius gradually transformed the firm into a cohesive team containing men
both with training and experience designed to give them a comprehensive
view of the problems of the office clients as well as specialists highly trained
through concentration in particular fields. (Swaine 1946, p. 575)

Cravath had a clear sense of the evolving market for corporate
practice. He considered the scope of the firm's practice to be whatever
was necessary "to serve corporate and banking clients in many of their
legal problems" (Swain 1946, p. 10). Rather than rewarding business-
getting ability based on family and social connections, his system aimed
at rewarding business-getting ability that "arises out of competence in
doing law work" (Swain 1946, p. 11). Hence, at Cravath, in contrast
to many law partnerships in which there were explicit arrangements
for dividing fees between the lawyer who brought a client to the firm
and the lawyer(s) who did the work for the client, there was no fixed
division of fees between the firm and individual members who introduced clients to the firm.

Cravath was an apostle of merit, inside the firm and out. By repudiat-
ing representations that his firm had political "influence," he distanced
his firm from other firms (and indeed from the history of his own firm
during the era of Richard Blatchford) who claimed the advantages of
knowing the right people (Swaine 1946, pp. 11, 12). He consciously
organized the structure of the firm to provide opportunity and incentives
for associates to steadily increase their responsibilities. He instituted an
"up or out" rule, mandating that associates leave the firm as soon as
it became clear they could not make partner. He avoided the lateral
hiring of partners, preferring instead to advance lawyers from within
the ranks (Swain 1946, p. 5).

Cravath's organizational theory has become institutionalized in most
large firms. They have moved toward hiring and promotion based on
merit principles, although questions concerning sex, race, and religious
discrimination remain.[6] Permanent associates, a familiar aspect of firms
early in the century, have largely disappeared, making most firms up-or-
out hierarchies. While it is a testament to Cravath's vision that the
organization of firms reflects his organizational philosophy, the modern entrepreneurial agenda is drastically changed from Cravath's era.
At that time the leading firms in New York as well as in other major

Social Change and Structure   73

cities occupied a relatively secure niche based on long-standing social and commercial ties. To retain that position today firms must develop strategies to diversify their client base and deal with an increasingly unpredictable demand for their services. The Cravath firm itself experienced a dramatic organizational challenge in assembling a legal staff capable of handling the massive IBM antitrust litigation and then dealing with the sudden drop in demand for their services after the suit was settled (*New York Times,* January 18, 1982). These changes point to the need for self-conscious management in firms, but the degree to which the governing elite has developed an entrepreneurial role remains highly variable across firms (see chap. 2).

The Managerial Role: The Minders. In addition to the problems posed by a more complex and uncertain market, the governing elite of firms must develop an administrative infrastructure to coordinate diverse practice areas and promote an efficient organization of work. This entails the relationship between the elite and other senior partners—the minders, or, in Chandler's terminology, the relationship between entrepreneurs and managers. The managerial role in the large firm arises from the necessity of decentralizing control over a large professional staff working on highly specialized matters. Thus most managerial issues revolve around policies of departmentalization.

Q. What are the toughest things involved in managing the law firm?

A. I would say that communications is the most difficult. With a small firm you knew everybody and knew what was going on; it was easy to keep things coordinated. But now that is no longer possible, so you have to try and develop a line of communication that makes everybody in the firm feel like a member, like they are contributing something.

How are lines of communication developed? Again, organization in the large firm exhibits a chimerical quality. The same interview continues:

Q. Beyond setting up a committee on standards, have you done anything in terms of structure in the firm, for example, in terms of departments or teams, that would contribute to checking on quality?

A. No, we do not have any formal mechanism for doing those things. Of course, there are about twenty to thirty attorneys who have substantial supervisory roles in the firm. And we make an extra effort to consult and communicate to those lawyers what the standards of the firm are. We realize that it is very important that those men who are actively involved in coordinating and supervising the work maintain very high standards. And we really aim our effort at them.

74   Patterns of Social Change

Managers in law firms do not occupy offices in the formal sense that corporate managers do. Rather, they are an intermediate stratum of partners with various combinations of client and supervisory responsibility but who do not play a central role in policy-making. With varying degrees of formality, they have jurisdiction over a field of practice and a group of specialists in the field. They are called on to perform certain administrative tasks, such as providing information on staffing needs for recruitment purposes or evaluating associates with whom they have worked. More important, they are the specialists to whom other lawyers will turn when a client has a problem in their field. The referral networks among partners often do not follow formal channels. Which partner in a particular field will get an assignment often depends on chance factors and on interpersonal links. Where there is a regular flow of matters from a subdivision of a major client, the referral pattern will develop more stability and give rise to a more fully developed supervisory role.

The difference between the managerial role in the law firm and in industrial enterprise runs deep. Partner-managers in firms have tenure in the firm; the industrial managers serve at the discretion of upper-level management. More important, partner-managers have access to the lifeblood of the firm: clients. Industrial managers have no control over the capital necessary for the operation of their units. As a result, the managerial stratum in law firms is less dependent and more volatile than in the industrial enterprise. With increasing frequency partners who head specialty groups have departed firms as a consequence of disagreements with the governing elite (see, e.g., *American Lawyer,* August 11, 1978, p. 1; *Legal Times of Washington,* May 28, 1979, p. 1). The less a department's clientele derives from the long-term "unmovable" clients of the firm, the more autonomous it is from the rest of the firm. As competition between firms has increased, specialty groups have more opportunity to leave one firm for another. Such a move has proved especially attractive to the younger lieutenants in work groups who may be offered the opportunity to head a specialty group in another firm, whereas it might take years for them to rise to the top of the department in their current firm.

Conflict between the finders and the minders can lead to the departure of the finders as well. At Donovan-Leisure a group of dissident partners demanded the resignation of the firm's "all powerful executive committee," insisting that five nonproducing partners be expelled from the firm and that another fifteen be demoted to salaried status (*Wall*

Street Journal, November 11, 1983, p. 1, col. 6). The governing committee resigned and its chair left the firm. At the Chicago firm of Ross & Hardies a new governing committee insisted that nonequity partners had to bring in business or leave the firm. A majority of the equity partners then rebelled, prompting the new governing committee to leave and establish its own firm (*Crain's Chicago Business,* November 14–20, 1983, p. 29).

The relationships between finders and minders have clearly become problematic in recent years. Defections from large firms are no longer isolated incidents. This pattern is very different from what Smigel found. He thought it remarkable that so few firms had suffered serious rifts (1969, p. 258). But as firms have encountered economic difficulties and as they have begun to raid each other for established specialists, significantly increased levels of conflict and fragmentation within the ranks of partners have resulted.

The Grinders. At the base of the law firm's professional pyramid are the young partners and associates. For the most part these are the most successful graduates of the most prestigious law schools (Smigel 1969, pp. 36–69). Much has changed from the old days of apprenticeship in the firm. A named partner in one firm recounted the story of how in the thirties, after he was so audacious as to ask for more than $40 a month, the leading partner of the firm showed him a stack of one hundred letters from men begging to work for free in his office. The rising demand for large-firm services has created staffing needs that firms must meet primarily through recruiting law school graduates. All major firms have highly organized recruiting and summer internship programs. This has contributed to greater heterogeneity in the ethnic and law school backgrounds of the newer partners and associates.[7] The demand for top legal talent has also generated dramatic inflation in the starting salaries of associates. In 1968 Cravath, Swaine, & Moore startled the world of corporate law firms by raising starting salaries from $8,000 a year to $15,000 (*National Law Journal,* May 26, 1986, p. 8, col. 1). More recently it again jarred its competitors for top legal talent, setting starting salaries at $65,000 a year and giving $12,000-a-year increases to all associates (*National Law Journal,* May 26, 1986, p. 8, col. 1). Although New York firms define the top of the market, they exert pressure on the salary structures of firms in other cities. Starting salaries among large Chicago firms range from $38,000 to $42,000 a year. The salary competition between leading firms has become so intense that many New York City firms offer "signing bonuses" as an additional enticement to law graduates to locate there. The competitive market for law school graduates has given recruits a surprising degree of influence over the image, if not the organization of the large firm. This is most evident in how firms approach the topics of departmentalization and specialization during the recruitment of law school students. Stevens (1971) suggests that law school prepares a generalist lawyer who values the image of the omnicompetent professional. This view is widely shared by firm leaders. One managing partner asserted that law schools preach against specialization. Recognizing these preferences among recruits, law firms often disclaim the existence of departments and promise entering associates a free choice of specialty.[8] Practices inside firms, however, depart from the claims of the interviewing room. Many firms require a close-to-binding choice of substantive specialty within a few years after entering the firm (Rosenberg 1978). The apparent paradox is resolved by the rationalization that the choice of field is determined by the individual rather than by the organization. Consider the following comments by a managing partner:

> Here we have always handled things somewhat informally. An attorney comes into the firm out of law school; some have an idea of what they want to practice. You try to let them work in that field as much as possible, then you evaluate how they're doing. If it appears to be going well, [if] they like it and are doing good work, that's fine. But, if they don't do well, or find they don't like [the field], you make a change that you think will be to their liking and good for the firm. You put him in a different kind of work.

Perhaps without acknowledging its part, firm management guides the distribution of manpower into needed areas. Informality can be an advantage for recruiting in an environment dominated by traditional professional values.

Policies on the admission of associates to the partnership have traditionally varied by firm in different cities. While all firms represent that they hire only people of partnership caliber, that is not the case. Large law firms in New York City and to a lesser extent in Philadelphia, Houston, and Washington have maintained a high ratio of associates to partners. New York firms frequently have three times as many associates as partners. Large firms in Chicago, Los Angeles, and other cities have traditionally aimed for an equal number of partners and associates, but the recent spurt in growth at the associate level has begun to alter the ratio of partners to associates. The ratio for the fifty largest firms nationally declined from 1 to 1 in 1975 to .63 to 1 in 1979 (*National Law Journal,* Oct. 1, 1979, p. 1). Large firms still must choose between the New York model of a relatively closed partnership and an open one. Each form has its disadvantages. A partner in a Chicago firm suggests: "The firms in New York have a problem hiring people when they hire thirty associates a year and make two partners a year. That requires them to pay much higher salaries and they must also charge higher fees." Problems of cost can also affect the open partnership. As another partner noted:

> One of the great problems is that—and this is true of any service industry—you cannot get leverage on your capital cost. As you combine services that bring increased revenues, the cost of providing those services increases just as quickly. So costs escalate directly with revenues.... The way you really make money in a law firm is by having junior partners and associates who bill 1,800 to 2,000 hours a year. Now you can make possibly $100,000 in revenue on those people, and we pay them some $35,000. For a long time firms in Chicago have had pretty much a one-to-one ratio of partners to associates, so the problem is that if you continue to add partners so that [the ratio] stays the same, you can never really gain a profit. So I think in the future we will strive to make that ratio better by being somewhat more restrictive in terms of granting membership to the partnership.

This discussion of strategies for dealing with associates underlines the economic role associates play in the large firm. Leaders of firms readily admit that they buy associates' time "wholesale and sell it retail," making the work of associates an important source of surplus for the partnership. Assuming conservatively that Chicago firms bill their associates' time at $60/hour and that associates bill 1,700 hours/year, the firm generates $102,000 in revenue. If the firm pays its associates $50,000 a year and spends another $30,000 per associate in overhead, it nets $22,000/year per associate. One survey of medium and large firms found that partners bill at twice the rate of starting associates but earn more than five times as much while working somewhat fewer hours than associates (Darby 1985, pp. 66–67). It is therefore no surprise that the recruitment and organization of associates is a critical function in every large firm.

VALUE RATIONALITY, COLLEGIAL
DOMINATION, AND BUREAUCRACY

The traditional structure of the law firm has undergone only a limited transformation to a bureaucratic form. In many firms the finders deny

78   Patterns of Social Change

their distinct status in the organization and continue to react to policy
questions on an ad hoc basis. Even in firms in which the managerial
elite has adopted a self-conscious policy-making role, organizational
policies often defer to partners' and associates' traditional expectations. Given the mounting pressure on firms to plan strategically and
increase the efficiency of production, what explains the resilience of
traditional roles?

One recent line of argument in the organizations literature (Satow
1975: Ouchi and Johnson 1978; Ouchi 1980) suggests that autonomous
professional organizations, such as the law firm, are "value rational"
organizations, meaning that relationships within the organization are
primarily determined by core professional values rather than formal
rules. As Satow explains:

> It is possible to construct a . . . type of authority based on "faith in the
> absolute value of a rationalized set of norms" (Willer 1967, p. 235).
> . . . Obedience is given to an ideology, that is, to ideological norms rather
> than formal laws or rules. Those in authority are therefore also obliged to
> obey the norms in giving orders and the content of orders are legitimized
> by their relationship to the goals of the ideology. . . . The ideological com-
> mitment to the profession and professional norms override the commitment
> to the organization. (Satow 1975, pp. 527, 539)

Professional ideology has pervasive effects on the law firm, just as it
does in other professional organizations (see Bosk 1979, p. 189; Katz
1982). It affects recruitment, office decoration, the regulation of lawyers' work, the search for business, among other elements. My interviews with elite partners elicited numerous testimonials that professional values take priority over economic considerations in organization
policies. One partner spoke of the perceived antagonism between professional values and the administration of a law firm according to an
economic calculus.

> Q. In at least two of the firms that I have talked to, partners said that
>   although it would be easy to compile [information on] the profitability
>   of different kinds of practices in the firms, that they have never done
>   that kind of thing. One thought it was primarily because they were
>   afraid to actually take a look at the information . . . [for fear] that it
>   [would] begin to control decisions.
>
> A. Yes, well, that's right. But really, if you are a professional organization
>   and don't think of yourself as really trying to maximize profit, there
>   isn't a reason to do that. In fact, I think there has been some self-
>   conscious rejection of [calculating the profitability of different fields]

in our firm at least. . . . And really, if you think about what a professional organization is, it does seem inconsistent with it. For instance, what if a hospital began to look at what different kinds of operations were profitable and those that were not profitable. How well do you think that would be accepted? . . . Things should be cross-subsidized in a professional organization, otherwise, you are no longer professional.

Hence certain organizational practices are dismissed as "unprofessional." But the critical question becomes What is the source of norms that define what is 'professional' or 'unprofessional?' To what extent do professional norms exercise an independent effect on organization structure? Many scholars argue that the professional values that shape the professional organization originate outside the firm, in the profession's collective institutions—the professional association and the professional school (see Montagna 1968; Halliday 1983). Smigel adopted this interpretation for the law firm. To describe the firm's professional norms he simply listed the canons of ethics (1969, pp. 268–270).

If the key elements of professional norms originate outside the law firm, however, why do managerial practices vary significantly by firm? The reason is that professional codes provide almost no specific guidance on how a law firm should be organized. The governing committee of the firm of the partner just quoted, for example, collects and analyzes computerized time-utilization records for all attorneys. Why is this practice seen as professional while others are not? Indeed, there is no consensus among firms on the role business judgments should play in governing the organization. As the leading partner in another firm commented: "Some people like to say that law isn't a business. But whatever they say, believe it or not, it is. Unless a firm is run like a business, you would have everyone contributing to a loss at the end of the year."

Professional ideology cannot be treated as a structural determinant that is wholly, or even primarily, independent of the politics of the organization. In chapter 6, I argue that professional ideology is largely created inside the law firm and reflects the efforts of the governing elite to rationalize the organization of the firm and their position in it. The relative absence of rules and the prominent role that professional norms play in governing firms is better explained as a structural characteristic of the authority system of the law firm rather than as a direct reflection of professional values. The law firm represents a system of collegial domination in which the leading client-responsible partners act as *primus inter pares* (Weber 1978, pp. 271–282). The dominant colleagues, the "finders," typically can dictate the ideology by which the organization is governed. But their positions of authority are inherently fragile. They depend fundamentally on their ability to generate business. If they lose their client bases, they will suffer a loss of power in policy-making. Their positions also depend on their ability to reach a consensus among themselves on how to run the firm. If there are significant differences in the managerial ideologies of different groups of client-producers, it is unlikely that any cohesive managerial regime will emerge. Finally, the authority of firm leaders is contingent on maintaining the enthusiastic commitment of partners and associates. Without the dedicated support of the professional staff, the leading partners cannot deliver the high quality legal services clients demand. The "weak" nature of authority in the law firm is not dissimilar to that found in other collegial organizations. The dean of a law school or the chairperson of an academic department may formally possess unlimited powers over recruitment and promotion. But to rule effectively he or she must gain a consensus, or at least a working compromise, among the various members or groups in the faculty.

My interpretation of the resilience of traditional structures in firms has very different implications from the explanation based on the value-rational character of the organization. First, I suggest that there may not be an inherent conflict between bureaucratization and professional values. Given a cohesive managerial elite, a bureaucratic managerial ideology could become the dominant professional ideology in a law firm (see chap. 2). I also suggest, however, that the development of bureaucratic structures will not alter the collegial underpinnings of managerial authority. Even in a bureaucratically organized firm the bureaucratic apparatus will be subject to the dominant colleagues. Second, my analysis suggests that firms are subject to higher levels of conflict than Smigel or other theorists of autonomous professional organizations acknowledge. While the literature may have been correct in arguing that professional firms are organized around a consensus on core professional values, research has not addressed the issue of what happens when that consensus breaks down. The recent record of widespread dissension and defections in firms suggests that the law firm's collegial structure is indeed vulnerable to fragmentation in periods of economic or political turmoil.

The prospects for structural change in the law firm may ultimately depend on its role in the American legal system, which raises the question of change in the law firm as an aspect of sociolegal change.

FROM A SOCIOLOGY OF THE FIRM TO A SOCIOLOGY OF LAW

Max Weber concludes his sociology of law with the supposition:

> Whatever form law and legal practice may come to assume under the impact of these various influences, it will be inevitable that, as a result of technical and economic developments, the legal ignorance of the layman will increase. The use of jurors and similar lay judges will not suffice to stop the continuous growth of the technical elements in the law and hence of its character as a specialists' domain. Inevitably the notion must expand that the law is a rational technical apparatus, which is continually transformable in the light of expediential considerations and devoid of all sacredness of content. (Weber 1978, p. 895)

The emergence of law as a rational technical apparatus in modern America is linked to the development of the large law firm. Weber observed that the rationalization of law is associated with the rise of legal specialists (1978, pp. 775–776), and the large firms have provided the client base and thus the reliable volume of legal work that have made possible the great increase in specialization over the past half century (Christensen 1967; Zehnle 1975). Following Weber's logic, the specialists in large firms are more likely than other members of their profession to have the incentives and resources necessary to develop new legal doctrines in any particular field of the law (Laumann and Heinz 1977). It is frequently the expert from the large law firm who drafts new laws, through participation in legislative drafting or as a member of bar association committees (Halliday 1976). Partners at major Chicago firms have recently played significant roles drafting state constitutional amendments, as well as new laws on property settlements in divorce, condominiums, and civil procedure. Moreover, research on the values of lawyers in large law firms indicates their support for the selection of judges by merit and for other efforts to rationalize law.[9]

Why have large law firms, despite all the pressures toward and manifestations of bureaucratization, retained so much of their traditional organizational structure and failed to develop more fully bureaucratized systems of work and authority? Is the structure of the large firm an aberration that will in time be transformed into a "rational technical apparatus"? I think not. Instead, the answer may lie in the role of lawyers in large firms, who function much as they always have, even though their role has become more specialized and technical. An examination of the issue leads us back to the same question with which we

82   Patterns of Social Change

began this chapter: How have firms changed so much by changing so little?

The rationalization of law, as defined by Weber, does not necessarily imply the bureaucratization of the professional organization that promotes rational law. Weber's rationalization hypothesis is based on a fourfold typology in which legal institutions can be categorized according to whether they follow substantive principles that are rational or irrational and formal (or procedural) principles that are rational or irrational (1978, pp. 334–337, 813–814).[10] As Weber's quotation indicates, he argued that in advanced capitalist society, in which the secular concerns of the marketplace and modern bureaucracies (both private and governmental) displace the concerns of traditional segments of society, legal institutions would themselves become technically rational organizations that would adapt to those secular concerns. Hence, traditional legal doctrines, such as the just-price theory of contracts, would be altered to accommodate the growth of economic enterprise (see Horwitz 1977).

Weber's macrolevel theory about developments in the legal system, however, cannot be transplanted to explain organizational dynamics within the legal profession. Bureaucracy, as Stinchcombe has pointed out (1959), is a subtype of rational organization. Depending on the market for an organization's services and the interplay between persons in positions of power within an organization, a nonbureaucratic organizational form may be more viable. The large law firm is such a modern, nonbureaucratic organization. I argued above that methods of control that may be effective in a corporation, including government by rules and the centralized administration of capital, are not effective in the large law firm. This is true in part because the law firm has a fragile authority system in which a number of lawyers may have significant client relationships and consequently an economic base that gives them a voice in the firm. The dependence of firm leaders on the commitment of the attorney staff strengthens norms of collegiality and enhances the impact of professional traditions on organizational policies. But the structure of the firm also derives from the role large-firm lawyers play in society. It is at this point that the convergence between the sociology of the firm and the sociology of law becomes clear.

The practice of law in the large law firm is the highest form of legal craft. Such a suggestion may seem baldly elitist, but it seems to be supported by evidence presented here and elsewhere. Large-firm lawyers deal with the most complex legal issues, the most controvertible kinds of litigation, the most creative forms of financial transactions, the most rapidly changing bodies of law. The continued expansion of the American business enterprise and the progressive efforts by government to bring aspects of social life within legal strictures put large firms, as representatives of corporations, on the frontiers of legal and economic developments. This role requires lawyers in the large-firm practice to constantly adjust their activities to the changing needs of clients. As a result, even though firms develop groups of specialists, work is organized on the basis of mutual adjustments among lawyers rather than by standard procedures.

The continuing importance of this progressive role in social change is the foundation for the future of the large law firm. When the leading partner of a firm told me that his firm did not have a plan for the future, I asked whether that meant that the firm was vulnerable to the uncertainties of the market for large-firm services. He replied with this view of the history of large firms:

> Lawyers are an aspect of their society. We don't make the policies. If . . . President [Reagan] has his way, as suggested in the speech he made Sunday, if he had the power to do it, he would substantially reduce the regulation of business. If that would happen there would be much less work for lawyers. The volume of lawyer's work depends on the extent to which government regulates business. We can't control that. We are reactive. . . . You know the greatest factor in the rise of large firms in America was when Franklin Roosevelt built the New Deal. And all those Republican lawyers who spent their careers fighting the New Deal made a fortune from it. They told their clients how awful it was, and their clients loved to hear it, but that built the large law firm in America.
>
> If we put an end to EPA, if we repeal the antitrust laws, it would put us out of business. If those things can happen, I guess we're vulnerable.

The wry smile on his face reflected his confidence that such eventualities were hardly possible.

Hence, even the threat from the expansion of house counsel is modified by the specialized nature of large-firm practice. That observation was made explicitly by a senior attorney in one firm. I asked him to describe what kind of law practice the firm would engage in during future years. He replied:

> The kind of cases that are bigger than the law offices inside corporations can handle. That can involve anything from the large piece of litigation that is simply too large for in-house staff to deal with it. It also involves new fields of law. You and I can go through a list of areas such as OSHA, environmental stuff, etc., all of which are so specialized that at least for a

84   Patterns of Social Change

few years in-house counsel are not going to be in a position to handle that.
So we are going to continue to handle that kind of unique work.

Q. That's very interesting. So it sounds like you have a business that is
largely based on existing clients, all of whom tend to develop in-house
counsel. The in-house counsel take over the routine work and you are
left with the very large litigation and with whatever is changing most
quickly in the law.

A. That's about right. . . . Unlike other firms, we don't dislike law departments in corporations. In fact, we like them. This firm gets more work
than it can possibly do, and there is a lot of work that this firm turns
down. Very often the house counsel of a client is much more capable
of dealing with certain kinds of problems, and they really aren't the
kinds of problems we want to devote a lot of time to. . . . In fact, you
know I've set up several corporate law departments.

These interpretations begin to suggest the answer to the riddle with
which we began. The large law firm is a creature of law and social
change. The business of the large law firm is the business of changing law. While it may be argued that the work of all lawyers requires
keeping up with the law, certainly there are qualitative differences between lawyers in that respect. Laumann and Heinz (1979) concluded,
after reviewing the distribution of lawyers' time in different fields of
law, that those fields characterizing large-firm practice required the
highest levels of specialization, in part because mastery of those fields
required continuous training after law school. It is ironic in a sense that
those fields of law dealing with the most traditional kinds of legal
problems, the problems of individuals (divorces, wills, residential real
estate), are precisely those fields most likely to be offered in coming
years in the most rationalized form of legal services organization, the
large law clinic. It is through the economies of scale obtained through
computerized forms, centralized administration, advertising, and rou-
tinized procedures that the practice serving individuals can expand in
scope and profitability. In contrast, the exercise of professional craft in
the large firm has been underwritten by a corporate clientele that demands custom work and can pay for it. (This is similar to the concept of slippage in organizations suggested by Hirschman [1970].) The
class of sophisticated lawyers concentrated in large law firms has been
able to devote more time to rationalizing law than to rationalizing
their firms. Because of the unique character of its practice and its organizational structure, the large firm may have been less efficient and
less profitable than it could have been, but it has retained the flexi-

Social Change and Structure

bility to adapt to the changing needs of its clients. Although increased competition and organizational growth will continue to press the large firm to develop bureaucratic structures, the nature of its practice, the privileged status it traditionally has enjoyed in the legal profession, and the weakness of managerial authority in the firm will preserve some of the nonbureaucratic characteristics of the organization.

This general analysis of the changing market and organizational structure of firms defines the issues to be pursued in greater depth by examination of the historical development and current organization of four specific firms. To what extent have these firms developed a bureaucratic structure? What factors explain differences in bureaucratization by firm? And what are the consequences of these patterns for the careers of lawyers in firms and for the role firms play in legal and social change?

2
Bureaucracy and Participation in Historical Perspective

The law firms Aaron, Becker, Curran, and Duncan are all success stories. From two- and three-man firms early in the century these firms have grown to large professional organizations today. Their recent success has been particularly dramatic. As figure 1 demonstrates, each firm doubled in size during the 30-year period 1940–1970 and then doubled again in less than half the time (1970–1984). This record of achievement makes the historical analyses in this chapter especially poignant, for at different times even these successsful firms have experienced economic uncertainties, political turmoil, and internal disorganization. Such problems are not unique to these firms. On the contrary, they reflect inherent tensions between what I have labeled the forces of practice and privilege. As the large law firm has confronted an increasingly uncertain environment and the rapid transformation in the size and complexity of its organizational dimensions, there has appeared a growing disjuncture between the economic and political realities of law-firm governance and the traditional conception of the partnership, in which all partners are peers entitled to participate in managerial decisions. I now turn to the examination of how the tensions between bureaucracy and participation, that is, between the mounting pressures to develop rational managerial structures and the demands of partners for a voice in firm governance, have been worked out historically in these four firms. The central question is why the interaction of these

86

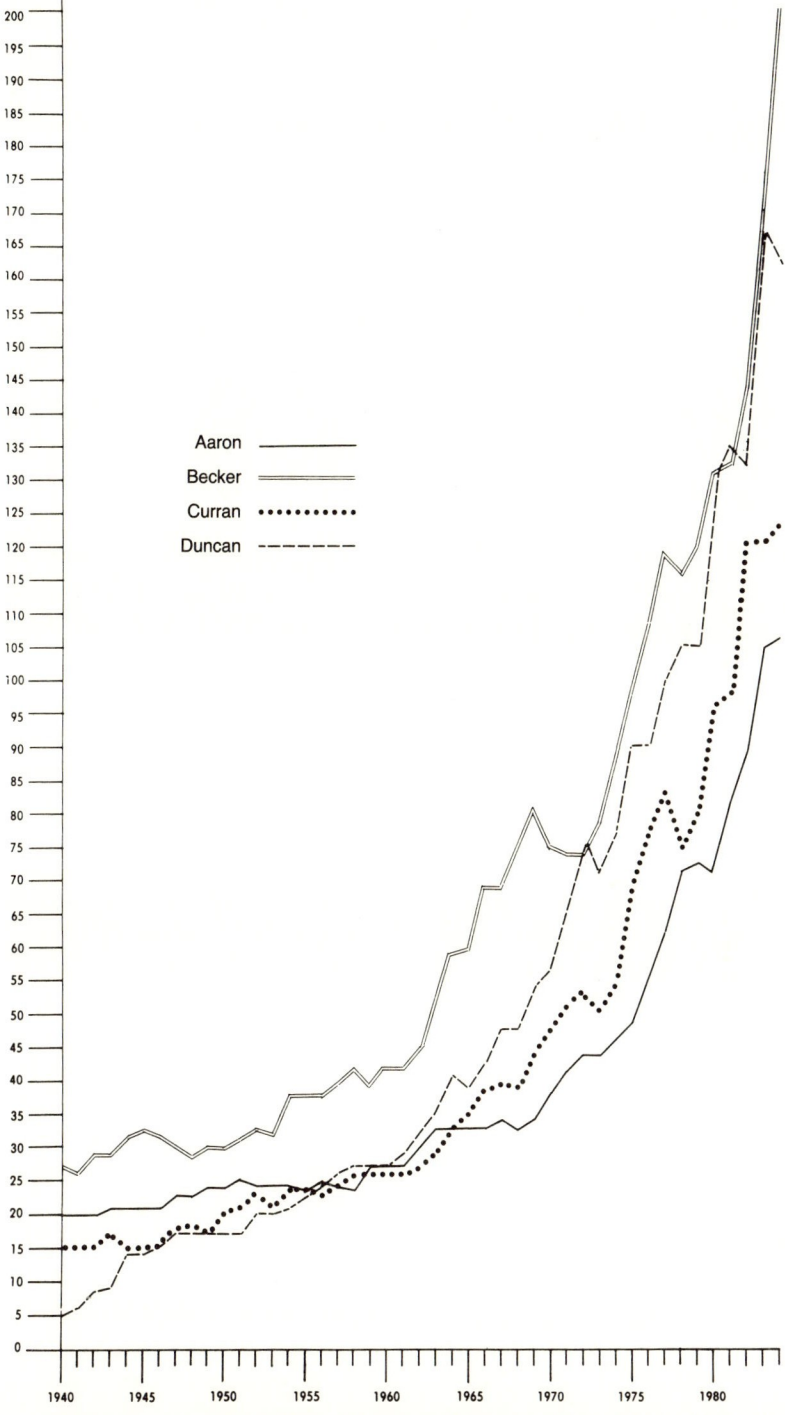

Figure 1. Aaron, Becker, Curran, and Duncan: Firm Size by Year

88   Patterns of Social Change

forces led to the development of bureaucratic structures in two firms but not in the other two.

My argument is that the histories of the firms demonstrate that differences in bureaucratization are the product of professional ideology and client relationships. The development of bureaucratic structures in Duncan is the result of self-conscious efforts at rational management dating to the firm's founding partners. In contrast, bureaucratization in Becker has occurred in the context of traditional managerial values as a result of client relationships that produced parallel work groups and a cohesive client-responsible elite. Such structures have never developed in Aaron or Curran, where influential partners have rejected deviations from traditional, ad hoc managerial practices as a threat to professional independence and participatory governance. Hence, the conflict between bureaucracy and participation is explicit in the traditionally governed firms but takes a different form in the bureaucratic firms. In Becker the conflict has been muted, in part because of powerful, centralized leadership, in part because bureaucratization has occurred tacitly, without an articulated managerial policy. In Duncan the conflict has never been over how to manage the firm but over who should run the bureaucracy.

The historical analysis of the conflict between bureaucracy and participation in the law firm has considerable theoretical and practical importance. Research on professional organizations generally has not attempted to examine patterns of structural change over time but rather has been confined to making inferences based on cross-sectional data (but see Perrow 1961; Katz 1982). Without longitudinal data, however, it is difficult to disentangle the causes of organizational change from their consequences. A classic example of the problem is the relationship between size and bureaucratization. Does growth determine bureaucratization or does bureaucratization cause growth (Meyer 1972)? Moreover, without engaging in a broad consideration of the political economy of an organization, it is impossible to consider the relationship between various aspects of organizational change (Zald 1970). To what extent do changes in the nature of governance in firms reflect the shifting economic power of different groups of practitioners? To what extent does the ideology of the governing elite respond to political pressures inside the organization or to developments in the organization's environment? By tracing the evolution of the client base, the patterns of governance, and the managerial ideology in four law firms that have developed significantly different organizational structures, I examine the relationship between these dimensions and assess their impact on organizational change.

The historical narratives provide important insights into the determinants and consequences of bureaucratization in the professional organization. First, the histories underscore the argument that although professional ideology plays an important role in shaping the structure of the law firm, it alone is not a sufficient explanation of organizational structure. What emerges quite clearly is that the ideology by which firms are governed is itself a complex outcome of the conditions under which the governing elite came to power, the nature of the relationships between members of the elite and their interactions with other partners, the historical position of the firm in the legal community, and the firm's economic performance. We must therefore examine professional ideology in an organizational context and consider how professional norms reflect the political and economic power of different groups in the organization.

Second, the histories suggest how structural differences between firms affect organizational effectiveness. Although all four firms have enjoyed success as a result of tremendous growth by clients or of dramatically expanded demand for their leading specialty, the limits of traditional managerial structures become apparent in these narratives. The two traditionally organized firms, Aaron and Curran, show signs of a lack of internal coordination. These difficulties result in lower rates of profitability and greater stress on the professional work force (see chaps. 5 and 7). While such organizational differences may not have appeared important to the survival of firms a few years ago, they take on added significance in the current climate of uncertainty and change among law firms. If traditionally organized firms become the losers in the increasingly competitive market for corporate legal services, if they are literally forced from the field or constrained to adopt the same managerial policies as their bureaucratic competitors, we will probably see a further shift toward bureaucratization of large-firm practice.

Third, the histories demonstrate the peculiarities of the law partnership as an organizational structure. In the axiomatic conception organizations consist of three levels (Thompson 1967; Parsons 1960). At the core of the organization is its technology, the central function it performs, whether it be providing legal services or making cars. At the opposite extreme is the institutional level, which interacts with the organization's environment. Between the technical core and the institutional environment is the managerial level, which functions to mediate between the technical core's demand for certainty and the institutional level's demands for change. Under norms of rationality management buffers the technical core to achieve efficient production while interacting with the organizational environment to ensure that productive processes do not become obsolete.

This conception implies autonomy of management as a critical aspect of structural variation in organizations. In the modern industrial enterprise management has emerged as an autonomous stratum, removed from direct divisional responsibility and controlling overall operations through decisions on how to allocate capital among operating divisions (Chandler 1962). In large professional organizations, such as the hospital or the university, the managerial level is constrained both by the degree of financial control exerted by the board of directors and by the norms of the professional groups regulated. But a university administration has control over a vast array of policies affecting the operation of subunits, which includes considerable discretion in allocating funds to different fields. Hospital administration enjoys its own professional identity and has recognized jurisdiction over housekeeping functions. Moreover, the increasing intrusiveness of third-party payment systems into matters of professional judgment and the corporatization of medical services is giving management additional control over matters previously left to the exclusive jurisdiction of medical professionals (Starr 1982).

Management in the law firm, in contrast, suffers an almost total lack of autonomy from the technological and institutional levels. Who sets managerial policies and the degree to which managerial policies attempt to control the activities of other lawyers are both contingent on the distribution of client responsibility. Unlike the ideal of autonomous management, in which managers develop plans to maximize organizational goals without regard to their self-interest, it is difficult for the leaders of law firms to plan objectively about the firm's practice because they are themselves so strongly identified with certain fields or clients. The efforts of the client-responsible elite to diversify the client base could threaten to dilute their power in the organization. This has retarded the development of rational managerial techniques in many firms and is a continuing source of uncertainty for partnerships in general. The histories of Aaron, Becker, Curran, and Duncan dramatically demonstrate this characteristic of the partnership form and the problems it can foster.

Detail in the narratives presented here is limited by the nature of material available and by the necessity of preserving the anonymity of the four firms. I have developed these histories from interviews with members of the elite and firm elders, from published obituaries and historical works written by retired firm members, and from other published accounts. Forced to stand alone, these histories might not sustain my argument about the differences in ideology and structure or their implications. But the comprehensive quantitative data on the current organization of the firms presented in following chapters provide a strong anchor for the historical sketches. Together, the historical and cross-sectional data offer a consistent portrait of the organization of these four law firms and the changes they have experienced in this century.

AN OVERVIEW OF STRUCTURAL DIFFERENCES

What follows is a political-economic analysis of organizational change. Bureaucratization in the law firm can only be understood in terms of the relationship between the economic structure of the firm (its client base), patterns of participation in governance, and managerial policies (Zald 1970). Because I refer to these analytic variables throughout the historical narratives, some preliminary definitions may be useful.

Client base simply refers to the fields or clients that are the sources of revenue for a firm. Client responsibility refers to the control of a client account by a particular lawyer. Patterns of participation relate to the political aspects of the organization: who runs the firm, how are these leaders selected, what powers do they possess? Firms vary in the nature and degree to which they are governed democratically. Managerial policy refers both to the ideology by which the governing elite rules as well as the administrative and work-group structures into which the firm is organized. The firms fall on a continuum between traditional and bureaucratic managerial policy. I define traditional management as that characterized by (1) ad hoc and reactive policy-making, with little long-range planning; (2) direct administration by leading lawyers, aided only by a part-time managing partner, with no regular monitoring of internal performance measures or financial information; and (3) informally defined and shifting work groups. Bureaucratic management is defined by (1) a specialized policy-making group that actively engages in strategic planning; (2) a developed administrative component consisting of a managing partner and a mechanism for collecting and analyzing data on the financial performance of individual lawyers and work groups; and (3) well-defined work groups (usually taking the form of departments) with recognized heads who supervise the group and report to the central policy-making group.

Table 4 provides an overview of the structural differences between the four firms and facilitates the interpretation of the historical narratives in this chapter as well as some of the cross-sectional results reported in later chapters. The first two rows locate the firms in the typology that guided their selection. Aaron and Becker are general service firms, meaning that their practice primarily is organized around a set of clients and their needs. Curran and Duncan are specialty firms, with notable reputations for a particular field. Cross-cutting scope of practice is organizational structure. Aaron and Curran are traditionally organized; Becker and Duncan are bureaucratically organized.

The firms each contain several specialties, but particular fields predominate in each. The leading fields in Aaron and Becker correspond to major clients. Thus the core of their practice is in the corporate and commercial fields. Both also have reputations for representing types of business organizations identified with particular fields of law. To preserve the anonymity of these firms I must use only general labels for these specialties. Aaron's client-based specialty primarily concerns a particular form of corporate finance and is denoted "special finance." Becker's specialty is defined by a type of business organization and so is denoted "business specialty." Because litigation is also among the most significant elements of Aaron's practice, it is listed here as well. By far the largest field in Curran is "litigation." I put the term in quotes because it does not refer solely to civil litigation but to a broader range of fields that primarily involve contests between parties. Duncan is best known for its work in a field involving a particular kind of financial transaction that I will label "finance." This field has contributed to the development of a significant general corporate practice.

There are significant differences in firm governance. Aaron and Becker are the least "democratic," although it might not be apparent in formal descriptions of their structure. Becker is the clearest case of closed governance. Its eight-partner governing committee selects its own replacements, who serve without a fixed term; its members have generally sat for an average of ten years. This committee polls the partnership only on the question of who will be admitted as a partner. Compensation is determined by a subcommittee of the governing committee. Aaron has a similar structure, but a monthly meeting of the partnership supposedly votes on all major policy issues. This democratic forum is largely an exercise in symbolic politics, however, for it consistently ratifies the major policy decisions reached by the governing committee.

Curran is the most democratic firm in ethos and practical effect. The governing committee selects its own replacements, but the size of the committee—twenty-two partners, or about a quarter of the partners in the firm—and the three-year limit on terms ensures wide participation in management. It should be noted, however, that these rotation rules are violated for a small number of leading partners, who have been on the committee throughout its history.

Duncan is governed by a dual committee structure. Members of the larger committee are elected to three-year terms by a vote of partnership shares. This committee in turn elects a four-partner policy committee and nominates its chair. The policy committee exercises the active leadership role and its decisions are consistently ratified by the larger committee.

The managerial ideology of all but Duncan's governing elite is traditional. In Aaron and Curran this ideology is reflected in the administrative and work-group structure, which is underdeveloped and only informally defined. Becker is an anomaly. The elite articulate a traditional orientation, in the sense that associates are not required to choose a specialty immediately, departments are not formally defined, and the firm does not aggressively seek new markets or clients. Nonetheless, the firm has developed a centralized administrative structure, de facto departmentalization, and a cohesive entrepreneurial core that performs active economic planning. Duncan's organizational policies are informed by a self-conscious commitment to norms of efficiency and rapid economic growth.

THE HISTORICAL DEVELOPMENT OF FOUR FIRMS

Aaron, Smith & Kimball

The Aaron firm traces its roots to three lawyers in general practice in turn-of-the-century Chicago. The firm's founding partners established relationships with real-estate, retailing, and manufacturing interests that, though small at the time, developed into significant enterprises later in the century. Indeed, relationships with two of the firm's leading clients today date to the firm's earliest years. In addition to

TABLE 4. MAJOR STRUCTURAL CHARACTERISTICS OF THE FOUR FIRMS

	Aaron	Becker	Curran	Duncan
Scope of practice				
1. Organization structure	General	General	Specialty	Specialty
2. Leading fields	Traditional	Bureaucratic	Traditional	Bureaucratic
3.	Corporate/special finance/litigation	Corporate and commercial/business specialty	Litigation	Finance/corporate
Governance structure				
Governing committee(s)				
4. composition	6 partners	8 partners	22 partners	20-partner committee/ 4-partner policy sub-committee
5. Selection	Self-selected	Self-selected	Elected by vote of governing committee	Vote of shares by equity partners/vote of 20-partner governing committee
6. Term/median years on committee	No fixed term/ 10 years	No fixed term/ 10 years	3-year term (with a few permanent members)	3-year term/1-year term
Partnership participation				
7. Meetings	Monthly meetings	No regular meetings	No regular meetings	No regular meetings
8. Votes	All major policies/ 1 partner-1 vote	Admission to partnership/1 partner-1 vote	Admission to partnership/1 partner-1 vote	Election of governing committee/vote of equity partners by shares, admission to partnership/1 partner = 1 vote

Who decides compensation	9. Subcommittee of governing committee, ratified by partnership	9. Subcommittee of governing committee	9. Subcommittee of governing committee, ratified by full governing committee	9. Subcommittee of governing committee, ratified by governing committee
Managerial ideology	10. Traditional	10. Traditional	10. Traditional	10. Bureaucratic
Administrative structure	11. None; direct command by governing committee	11. Permanent managing partner/professional office manager	11. Rotating managing partners	11. Chair of policy committee acts as managing partner/professional office manager
Work group structures	12. With the exception of litigation, informal client and specialty groups	12. Departments	12. Informal teams in litigation; small specialty departments	12. Departments

96   Patterns of Social Change

general practice, the firm developed a reputation in a particular kind of corporate financing that became highly significant to business development in Chicago and throughout the United States. As a result, the firm grew quickly in the years preceding the Great Depression. When these financial structures collapsed during the depression, the firm retained its prominent role by reorganizing defaulted financial arrangements. Roughly half the time and fees of the firm during the thirties came from such reorganization work.

The founders were in their twenties when they started the firm and so exercised a leading role in the firm until the 1950s. The second generation of leaders joined the firm during the 1920s. These lawyers gradually took responsibility for the existing client base, adding other clients in the real-estate, securities, and corporate fields. The longevity of leading partners, combined with distinctive changes in the volume of business, produced a skipped-generation cohort structure that has always marked the firm. To meet the demand generated by the boom in reorganizations, the firm added several lawyers in a three-year period beginning in 1930, increasing the size of the firm by fifty percent. But within a few years the reorganization work had climaxed. By 1935 the firm was encouraging new associates to seek better opportunities elsewhere if they could find them. As figure 1 demonstrates, the firm did not regain the size of the early thirties for thirty years. Only one lawyer joining the firm between 1932 and 1942 became a partner. Therefore, at the beginning of the fifties the hierarchy was quite top-heavy: partners outnumbered associates two to one; 90 percent of the partners had been with the firm for twenty years or more; one-half had thirty or more years seniority.

During the fifties several senior members, including the founding partners, died, retired, left to establish other offices, or left to become executives in major client corporations. The generation of lawyers who had joined the firm in the 1920s assumed command, changing the firm's name to reflect the new composition. The transition was smooth for the most part. Although some partners left in a dispute over control following the death of a founding partner, the firm was extremely well positioned for the post–World War II economic expansion. The financial markets in which the firm specialized again flourished. The new wave of capital expansion proved especially demanding of legal expertise, in that it required the creation of new legal instruments. The innovations devised by the firm reaffirmed its reputation for specialized financial transactions. In addition, many of the closely held corporations that formed the long-standing client base of the firm experienced rapid expansion. Their growth thus generated new levels of demand for corporate, securities, commercial, and antitrust representation.

Tremendous growth in the traditional areas of expertise and the long-standing client base threatened to overtax the senior partners of the firm. The firm was clearly out of balance because of the absence of a middle stratum—the cohort lost because of the downturn in the financial markets during the Depression. After adding several new associates between 1953 and 1970 the firm was still significantly unbalanced. Partners outnumbered associates by a ratio of more than 3:2. In 1957 all of the associates who would become partners were under thirty; all but two partners were over forty-five. Although the lack of junior partners who could succeed to clients represented a threat to the continuity of the firm, it also represented an unusual opportunity for the associates who had joined during the fifties. They took full advantage of the opportunity, making the status of partner in an average of less than six years, taking over major responsibility for the firm's traditional client base, and in the last half of the sixties beginning to add significant new business in the specialized financial areas for which the firm was traditionally known. In recognition of this transition the second generation of leaders, by now in their seventies, drafted and passed amendments to the partnership agreement requiring retirement from administrative positions at age seventy and establishing a retirement program. The third and current generation of leaders achieved their status at an extremely young age for law firms, assuming leadership in their late thirties and early forties. Their youth gave the firm positive prospects for growth. Client succession would not be an issue for several years. The leading partners were at an age at which they could be expected to develop new clients aggressively.

The Aaron firm thus began the seventies in an extraordinary position. It was a firm of modest size, with a young elite and a burgeoning client base. The firm's governing committee met for a weekend planning conference and concluded that the firm should try to grow as quickly as possible while still integrating new lawyers. As a leading partner recounts:

> I would say that the decision was made in the early 1970s that we would grow as quickly as we could. We made the decision that we would hire as many people as fast as possible. It was at that point that we concluded that even though we were growing at a steady pace, we were always swamped with work, so it really did not make any sense to agonize over what three

or four people to extend offers to, but [we] decided to extend offers to [twelve][1] and then something like [twenty] people. And we still are stretched tightly.

Having grown slowly from 1965 to 1970, the firm tripled the number of new associates it hired from 1971 to 1975 and tripled yet again the number of associates hired from 1975 to 1982. The firm's economic base has strengthened considerably over the years. The expansion of corporate clients and the growth of the litigation practice has reduced the firm's dependence on financial work, which is particularly subject to economic fluctuation.

The chief difficulties the firm faces relate to internal governance. Since the early fifties Aaron has been governed through a combination of closed-committee rule and direct democracy. Questions of admission to partnership and other firmwide policies are subject to direct vote at monthly partnership meetings. But most fundamental economic and managerial decisions are formally or de facto controlled by a self-perpetuating governing committee. This committee, composed of a small group of lawyers, decides the division of points, the rate of growth, the opening of branch offices, and similar matters. Its decisions have never been reviewed by the partnership.

The youth of the governing elite has generated some concern among younger partners that they might never have an opportunity to have a significant voice in firm governance. A member of the governing committee described the background to this complaint about lack of participation, which resulted in the addition of a younger partner to the governing committee.

> I think there was quite a bit of pressure which was brought by younger members of the firm for change in the [governing] committee. The format for election to the [governing] committee was basically: when the [governing] committee felt like appointing someone they would do so, and then somebody would basically go off, because he would retire. And there was a feeling among a number of younger partners that what had happened was that there had been one transition, the old guard had moved out, our very senior people had moved off the committee, basically brought on a new guard, and that the new guard had pulled up the gangplank . . . [A]nd there was a feeling that now they were entrenched, and they would just stay for twenty years maybe.
>
> Q. Because they were so young?
>
> A. Yes, because they were so young, and, oh, a lot of people felt that there had to be succession.

Ironically, this is the problem of hierarchical balance showing up in a different way. With the accession of a young client-responsible elite, the question now became how to offer younger partners an opportunity to develop increased client responsibility and increased participation. The formally democratic aspects of governance clearly do not satisfy these interests. One partner interviewed as a member of the cross section indicated that he would leave the firm unless he was made a member of the governing committee. Unless Aaron expands its governing body, tension will likely mount.

Despite the centralization of the governing committee and the emergence of a conscious growth policy, the governing committee has not established administrative or work-group structures. The firm never has had a professional manager and recently lost its senior accounting officer to another firm, leaving financial administration temporarily in the hands of a member of the governing committee. The work-group structure is avowedly informal. Although de facto work groups have emerged in some areas of litigation and around some partners, the firm explicitly rejects departmentalization. Only recently was a centralized assignments system instituted—and that only to regulate first- and second-year associates. The lack of formal structure leaves much of the day-to-day administration in the hands of the governing committee. Three of the eight elite partners I interviewed voiced dissatisfaction at the amount of time they devote to administrative detail. A substantial segment of the cross section in Aaron (41.0 percent), more than in any other firm (the next highest was 29.5 percent), favored the introduction of more structure into firm organization.

Why has the firm been slow to introduce more structure, even though a majority of the partners feel it is desirable? The answer is that such innovations are inconsistent with the traditional managerial ideology of the governing elite. A member of the governing committee spoke of a perceived trade-off between the rationalization of the firm and collegiality:

> My general attitude is that the collegiality and the harmony of the partnership is the critical factor in making it a success. And therefore, I think it should be run on as democratic a basis as possible, and with as much voice in affairs for individual partners as possible, and perhaps run closer to [a] confederation than a federal system. And that there may—and I'm not even sure—there may be a price of some inefficiency because of that. Maybe every partner doesn't need a secretary. . . . The factors on the other side make that a price I'm willing to pay, what I would think is the increased productivity,

the increased loyalty, the increased sense of self-worth. I think those far outweigh the inefficiency.

This quotation is telling in two respects. First, it identifies the structure of the firm through a normative statement: the firm should be "run closer to [a] confederation than a federal system." Aaron is a confederation of partners with largely independent, unrelated client bases. The polycentric nature of its elite requires that governance decisions be made through collegial consensus (Weber 1978, pp. 272–273). A dominant client or a single dominant lawyer lacking, administration must be negotiated piecemeal. Administrative decision making cannot be delegated to a professional manager or department heads, for that raises the potential for decisions that do not satisfy the relevant elite partners.

Second, the statement suggests that Aaron has not yet faced the kinds of economic scarcities that force cost cutting. Only as the firm begins to encounter serious threats to profitability or internal performance will the elite be forced to impose a new administrative structure. Third, the comment expresses the managerial ideology of Aaron's elite, that despite economic incentives to develop an administrative structure, they see their traditional managerial style as intrinsically valuable. Again the issue is posed as a potential trade-off between collegiality and efficiency. While we have little direct data on the firm's economic condition which would directly test the question, several members of the elite interviewed expressed the view that tighter cost control and more rigorous management could increase profits. But the economic incentives are probably not overwhelming. The privileged nature of these organizations is reflected here. As one elite member suggested, he earns more than he ever expected to earn when he began practicing law and thus cannot worry about small changes in his earnings. Another partner on the governing committee saw this as a general sentiment among the elite: "There is something akin to love for this institution. . . . There is a loyalty that transcends dollars. For the most part at one point or another I think that every one of the people that are really critical to this place have said . . . 'I could probably make more on my own or . . . by having a group of people or what have you. But I don't want to.'"

As long as the elites see their common values in other than economic terms, as long as they identify their common bond with the traditional style of managing their firm, Aaron will not develop a more bureaucratic structure. While Aaron's elite are correct in viewing their collegiality as critical to maintaining a stable client base, they would probably be surprised at the level of support among their colleagues for a more rational managerial structure. And it is dubious that the adoption of a more rational managerial structure could in itself disrupt the links between members of the elite. It may be that Aaron's leadership has not yet discovered what is in their best interest.

BECKER, SOLOMON & JONES

The Becker firm developed a bureaucratic organizational structure without ever defining such a structure as an organizational imperative. Its policy-making group has self-consciously identified opportunities for expanding the client base and for developing new fields of technical expertise. Internal affairs are managed through a permanent firm-wide administrative apparatus and a set of stable, well-recognized (if informally defined) work groups. This structure has emerged with a minimum of internal conflict in the light of a consensus among members that the firm should be organized traditionally—without formal departments, without mandated specialization, without an emphasis on businesslike management or aggressive market behavior. An informant in another firm characterized Becker's style as uniquely genteel among modern firms.

Becker presents a very interesting study in the relative effects of managerial traditions and the client base on organization structure. Bureaucratization in Becker derived from its client base, both through the development of work groups paralleling the major units of the firm's clients and through the investment of control over managerial policy in a relatively small, mutually dependent group of elite partners who shared responsibility for the major clients. The dialectical aspect to this great strength is that the firm is dependent on these core accounts and therefore vulnerable to any fundamental change in these relationships.

The Becker firm's institutional success began with the success of its founding partners, who were generally recognized as among the most prominent of Chicago's lawyers at the turn of the century. The founding partners fit the contemporary classic mold of effective attorneys. They were active and famous litigators but also involved in organizing the major corporations of the day, including granaries, meat packers, railroads, breweries, and banks. So successful was their practice that the most important item on the firm's agenda has always been to maintain this established client base. The leading client of the firm today is only

102   Patterns of Social Change

one of many corporations organized by the founding partners. But not until after a series of acquisitions (for which Becker served as legal counsel) did this client emerge as regionally dominant in its industry and therefore Becker's principal client.

Historical accounts reflect the concern that this major client might abandon the firm upon the death of the partner identified with the client. Responsibility for the client in fact passed to one of the founding partner's close personal associates, who had specialized in the fields concerning the client. This lawyer assumed an authoritative position in the firm, acting as both lead counsel for the major client and managing partner for thirty years. Under his leadership the firm developed a coordinated set of specialty fields to meet the demands of the firm's corporate clients. The lateral admission of two experienced litigators buttressed the firm's litigation practice. These partners enhanced their own reputations and the firm's name for litigation through a series of successful defenses of Chicago-area industries. The cohort of attorneys joining the firm in the 1930s, many of whom returned after the war as partners, assumed greater responsibility for the expanding business of the firm's major clients and began to add new corporate clients. Tax, real-estate, probate, and labor fields developed separate identities but primarily served the core of the firm's corporate and commercial clients.

By the mid-fifties, after the lawyer who succeeded the founding partners had retired, authority for major fields and clients became more dispersed. Committee rule replaced one-man rule, although one of the leading figures in governance was again the lead counsel for the firm's largest client. Responsibility for this client had passed once more to a close personal associate of the former leader, another specialist in the commercial area of particular interest to the client.

An important innovation in the administration of the firm took place at this time. The governing committee appointed a full-time managing partner who participated in the governing committee and ran the day-to-day affairs of the firm. The managing partner represented a fundamentally new role. General administration and general policy-making assumed distinct roles, in contrast to the managerial approach heretofore followed by Becker and by most firms in which the client-responsible group administered the firm directly. The goal was to improve performance of both functions. The change, however, derived not so much from insightful managerial theory as from historical happenstance. The first managing partner fell into the position because his principal client internalized a substantial portion of its legal work. Left with little to do in his specialty, this partner was asked to take on some administrative duties. Having practiced in New York City at the beginning of his career, he was familiar with administrative techniques used in New York firms. These administrative duties, although originally envisioned as part-time work, rapidly expanded into a full-time job. The partner held the position of manager for twenty years, until his retirement. Not only did he have the powers of his position but he also had strong personal ties with the firm's leading partners dating from law school. One partner credited this unique combination of official power and informal influence with "holding the firm together for twenty years." A current member of the governing committee commented on the significance of his role:

> You know I believe that he was the best managing partner in any law firm in the United States. Part of it was a matter of the unique circumstances that he had in the firm. He came here as a close personal friend of . . . I think it was [X] and [Y] [two leading members of the governing committee]. That in combination with the position that he held allowed him to operate this firm and accomplish certain things better than any other lawyer could have. The tremendous thing about it was that he had not only the position but the strong friendship connections behind it.

By chance Becker developed an administrative infrastructure that was "kept among friends" and thus was seen as pursuing the traditional goals of the firm. Because the role was fashioned by a lawyer who did not have a client base of his own, this innovation was never viewed as a power play by one group over another. Yet personal ties to the client-responsible elite increased the managing partner's influence. None of the other three firms has yet developed a permanent, full-time managing partner.

During the 1960s the governing committee persuaded two attorneys with established reputations and client affiliations to join the firm. As anticipated, both brought a substantial amount of new corporate business and were quickly integrated into the policy-making group. Shortly thereafter, the principal counsel to the firm's leading client died unexpectedly. The client's senior management group, which included a former partner from Becker, selected the replacement for this traditionally important position. Instead of choosing a specialist in the field, the client's executives selected a lawyer with a broad corporate background who was responsible for a variety of smaller corporate accounts but who had also done considerable work for the client (as many partners had). The new lead counsel was to emerge as the central figure in firm governance but not until after a shift in managerial structure.

By the beginning of the seventies the governing committee comprised more than twenty lawyers, including not only the leading client-producers but also a dozen more senior attorneys who supervised various work groups. The chairman of this committee proposed a new structure in which a smaller executive committee would make policy and plan for the future of the firm while the larger committee would be broken into functional subcommittees to handle the library, paralegals, interior decoration, and other aspects of general administration. The plan was adopted unanimously. The new executive committee included the chairman of the former governing committee, the managing partner, the lead counsel for the principal client, four attorneys with responsibility for major corporate clients, the head of litigation, and the head of the labor-law group. The chair of the larger committee served as chair of the new committee for a brief period, after which the lead counsel for the principal client assumed the chairmanship. He has held the position ever since.

Becker has continued its pattern of steady growth under this structure. The traditional areas of corporate practice have grown more slowly than in the past largely as a result of increased use of house counsel for routine corporate and commercial matters. Litigation has expanded dramatically, mostly through an influx of major cases from the firm's long-standing clients in antitrust, bankruptcy, commercial disputes, mergers and acquisitions, employment discrimination, energy law, and environmental proceedings. To meet the expanded demand for litigation the firm has begun to hire larger cohorts of new associates and has added laterally several partners with eight to fifteen years litigation experience. In the new fields of law required by corporate clients, notably employee compensation and energy law, the firm has made lateral additions with established experience who have built their own work groups in the firm. The executive committee has also allowed partners to pursue new areas of practice, such as municipal bonds and antitrust counseling. In response to client interest, the firm has opened branch offices in other cities. As this pattern suggests, Becker has responded principally to the demands of existing clients rather than initiating practices to tap new opportunities. Yet through the successful maintenance of its client base, the firm has continued to grow.

Becker continues to rationalize its administrative and work-group structure, despite the resilience of traditional sentiments about firm organization. Following the retirement of the first managing partner in the late seventies, a middle-aged partner was asked to take the position. In the three years he has held the post, the firm has hired a professional manager and developed information systems that gather and summarize financial data as well as data on professional time utilization. Both innovations had been resisted in the past by senior members of the firm who considered the change unprofessional. After the retirement of the more senior lawyers, the new managing partners proposed the innovations and they were adopted.

Nonetheless, Becker continues to adhere to traditional policies on departmentalization and specialization. When I began interviewing, the partner I first contacted proudly suggested that I would discover how unstructured the firm was. Indeed, the lawyers who work on the problems of the firm's major corporate clients have something of a general corporate and commercial practice. And associates have the option of trying different fields before choosing a particular specialty. Interviews with the leading partners in various fields, however, began to suggest that underneath the affirmations of informality a stable set of structures was set up by the work-group and they both coordinated work and reported to the firm's management. Work-group leaders could readily list the members of their groups. They also told of performing basic administrative functions: evaluating associates, forecasting personnel needs, developing routine procedures and quality-control mechanisms, holding regular meetings to monitor developments in the field and within the work group. What became apparent was that work groups had become defined in practice rather than through administrative fiat. Much of the work-group structure paralleled the operating divisions of major clients. Other work groups had developed to provide specialized services to these major clients.

The conflict between bureaucracy and participation has never surfaced in Becker, in part because the process of bureaucratization was never articulated as policy and in part because the question of who should participate and how was dictated by the clear dominance of the partners responsible for the firm's major clients. Unlike Aaron, in which leading members of the elite had semiautonomous client bases, the institutional nature of Becker's leading clients made its elite mutually dependent. As a result, Becker has been governed by benign dictatorships and oligarchies. The only deviation from this pattern took place in the 1960s when the governing committee expanded to virtually all finders and minders. The 1970s shift to a smaller policy-making committee composed almost exclusively of finders restored the legacy of centralized managerial authority.

Becker's economic and managerial success is then largely a result of the positive effects of its relationship with its leading clients. The chairman of the governing committee described one of these as "the best client you could possibly have. Not only has it grown tremendously all by itself, but it also acts as a tremendous feeder, whereby we continue to get a substantial amount of new business." Moreover, the predictable volume of work from the leading clients allows the firm to perform more efficiently, at higher levels of profit than it might otherwise. The chairman of the governing committee spoke candidly of these structural advantages.

> You know there is also a lot of talk these days about firms not being dependent on any given client. In fact, I heard of one fellow who said that his firm had a rule that no one client should . . . contribute more than 10 percent of the revenue of the firm, which seems to me to be something of a curious suggestion. It seems to me if you want to be very successful, if you have a highly lucrative practice from one client, . . . it is ridiculous to impose any upper limits on how much work you will do for a client for that reason.
>
> Q. Yes, but I have heard of one New York firm that does not have any one client that contributes more than 5 percent of its revenue.
>
> A. Well, I don't know how you can afford to be so diffused.

Becker's relationships with its leading clients are those of lucrative dependence. While the firm has significant advantages so long as its relationships with its major clients remain stable, the relative lack of client balance puts pressure on the firm to resist the growth of in-house counsel in the leading clients and to ensure that there are steady lines of succession to responsibility for major clients. The recent introduction of an in-house staff in one of the firm's major clients has been received somewhat anxiously by Becker's senior partners, even though the amount of work from the client has continued to increase since the in-house staff was formed. The impact of house counsel, however, is mostly out of the hands of Becker's leadership; they can do little to control it. More curious is the suggestion by some partners that the firm has not dealt with an issue over which they might have more control, the question of succession to major clients. As one partner pointed out:

> I think there's a lot of uncertainty in the firm about just how the relationship [with the leading client] would be handled with [X] [the partner in charge

of the account] gone. I don't think anyone has quite figured it out . . . and to some extent you can't figure it out, which is part of the problem with all client relationships. I think in all the relationships, there are two people . . . [Y]ou can sit down and work out a plan, but personalities come into play.

Nothing suggests that Becker's characteristic pattern of stable succession from one generation of leadership to another will be interrupted. Yet other firms have experienced the departure of major clients in equally unlikely circumstances. The preceding quotation points out the inherent instability of large-firm practice, even for firms with longstanding, institutional client relationships. In this greatest strength lies the firm's greatest weakness.

CURRAN, GELLER & HEINZ

The Curran firm is strongly identified with a field of practice that has become increasingly important in the American legal system since the Great Depression. The prominence Curran has achieved in this field has contributed to rapid growth of the firm in recent years, despite a lack of balance in fields and a lack of strong, firmwide administration. To preserve the confidentiality of the Curran firm I shall refer to this leading field as "litigation," a category I define very broadly to contain all controversy-oriented fields, including labor law, administrative law, utilities regulation, bankruptcies, and civil litigation. Although this category includes disparate fields, their common features are a set of functionally specific or predominantly case-by-case client relationships and work that primarily involves contested matters rather than transactions.

The firm began as a combination of three small partnerships engaged in general practice in corporate and litigation fields. Curran then started to develop a specialized focus after the depression, when many of the firm's general service clients went bankrupt. As corporate practice declined, the litigation fields began to grow. From the depression to World War II the firm gained a reputation in litigation as the result of the successful defense of highly visible cases against corporate defendants and the lateral entry of well-known government officials who also had established reputations in the field. Through their participation in lecturing, publishing, and bar association work, these partners played a prominent public role in the field, further adding to the firm's national repute. One of the leading partners of the firm commented on the importance of such public activities in producing business for the firm.

108   Patterns of Social Change

I'm not bragging, but [a lawyer must] do what I did in my field—become
acquainted with everybody, get active within the various sections [of the
organized bar]. . . . That's where the business comes from, from other lawyers, really, as they recommend their corporate officers to us and that's what
has happened to this firm, not merely to me but others. So, as I tell [the
other lawyers in the firm], you can kill two birds with one stone. You can
respond to your obligation to the public at the same time [as] you advance
yourself.

During the early postwar period one lawyer was the unquestioned
ruler on matters of firm governance. Although he informally consulted
with partners, he administered the firm single-handedly throughout the
fifties, deciding when and where the firm should relocate, what branches
to open, whom the firm should hire, even such details as the kind of
stationery to use. During this decade the firm roughly doubled in size.
This lawyer presided over the development of the next generation of
firm leaders. Most important of the new cohort were two lawyers who
joined the firm prior to World War II. They followed in the footsteps
of their mentor, participating in bar associations and community activities. In part through these activities they established their own reputation in litigation, eventually emerging as the central figures in the firm
through its most recent period.

Throughout the sixties the firm grew steadily, but unevenly between
litigation and the office fields. The lawyers who had joined the firm in
the forties began to cultivate their own reputations and clients. Probate
and estate planning, commercial law, and real estate developed as
relatively independent practice groups. The corporate practice was only
slightly larger than these. The firm had only a few Fortune 500 clients
for which it acted as general counsel. Again the main growth took place
in litigation. A significant group of the attorneys who had joined the
firm in the forties and fifties and who had worked with the firm's
leading attorneys had established their own reputations in litigation and
began attracting a significant clientele of their own. By 1970 the firm
had a dozen established specialists in litigation who could generate their
own business. Related fields of law, such as trade regulation and bankruptcy, which often generate litigation, benefited from the drawing
power of the firm's stature in litigation. When the demand for litigation
increased dramatically in the late sixties and seventies, the firm was well
positioned. Its rate of growth accelerated, increasing in overall size by
more than 150 percent from 1970 to 1982. Demand was sufficient
throughout the period for the firm to make significant lateral additions

to the litigation area at the partnership level, again hiring prominent former government officials.

The Curran firm will live or die by its field of specialty. If the trend of the last fifteen years continues in which the litigation fields have absorbed an increasing share of large-firm practice, Curran will prosper. In some respects the litigation fields have offered more consistent overall growth potential than other fields. They are less subject to general economic cycles than other fields, such as real estate, municipal bonds, and securities. But they also pose intractable organizational problems, particularly for large contested matters. To effectively represent clients requires sufficient staff to meet deadlines that are not controlled solely by lawyers in the firm but are subject to pressures from opposing counsel, judges, and other interested government parties. Hence, firms either must build up staffs that would be excessively large if a matter were settled quickly or must work a smaller staff harder to meet demands as they arise. In this sense Curran's practice reflects the problems facing any firm involved in controversy work. Donovan-Leisure, Howrey-Simon, and Wald-Harkrader are three litigation firms that suffered a dramatic decline in the demand for their services as a result of shifts in prosecutorial policies in antitrust (*Wall Street Journal*, November 18, 1983; *Legal Times*, June 30, 1986). Their fate illustrates some of the dangers litigation firms face. Confronted with a drop in demand, a firm must attract new matters or reduce its size. Although Curran's practice in the litigation field is sufficiently diverse to avoid dramatic boom-and-bust cycles, the difficulty must exist to a degree.

The dominance of litigation poses problems for Curran's other fields, deepening the firm's dependence on litigation. Except for fields that border on litigation and can make use of similar skills, the litigation fields are not effective "feeders" to other fields. Unlike tax or even real-estate law, the litigation fields bring case-by-case or specialized business that is relatively independent from the general legal needs of a client. Indeed, Curran's reputation as a litigation firm may adversely affect the prospects for getting corporate work; as one corporate practitioner suggested, clients "think of us as a [litigation] firm first." While lawyers in the office fields describe their speaking, writing, and teaching as a means of generating business, these public activities are less effective in attracting corporate business than in attracting business in the litigation fields. Moreover, the corporate practice has generally lower visibility. As one corporate executive described: "It's awfully hard, I think, during the first twenty years of practice . . . to establish a reputation in the corporate area. It's not like [litigation] where you can get a publicized [case], and that helps to establish your position as a [litigator]. A lot of work that goes on in the corporate world never gets published. . . . One of your efforts is to keep a low profile." In corporate work the client base begets a larger client base. Curran's corporate practice is thus at a disadvantage.

The nonlitigation fields also are at a disadvantage in competing for firm resources, the most precious of which is associates. Elite partners in office fields spoke of the necessity of recruiting laterally to fill manpower needs because the office fields could not compete with litigation for new associates. A leader of an office field attributed the difficulty in part to attitudes about what work was most valued:

> Even when you get somebody here, who comes to our firm not sure of what they want to do, they get sort of allured by [the litigation practice] because the [litigators] are handling exciting [cases] and doing exciting things. And I do think among the associates here . . . and to a slight extent among the partners there is a feeling . . . that the . . . true lawyer is a [litigator]. . . . And so it makes it difficult to have balanced growth because . . . it [is] difficult to interest people in the office practice area.

But the difficulty is also structural. Lawyers in the firm's leading field control the assignment system for associates. The same group leader quoted above described the system and its tendency to favor assignments in litigation fields.

> Over the last several years . . . we've had a [litigation] committee. There's no comparable office practice committee. . . . And the [litigation] committee was responsible and is responsible for assignments of work to new lawyers and for conducting evaluations for all [associates].
>
> Q. Even if they were not in [litigation]?
>
> A. Yes, that's right. Now that's an anomaly and it doesn't make any sense. Particularly the assignment part of it, because . . . it means that people . . . tend to get [litigation] assignments. In fact, the [litigation] committee was loath to take on office practice assignments.

The allocation of associates may well limit the ability of nonlitigation fields to provide the level of service that might foster additional business. Nonetheless, the strength of the litigation fields has given the firm a solid, if unbalanced, economic base. One member of the firm's corporate elite confided that he used to be concerned about the firm's dependence on litigation but that the steadily increasing demand in the area over the last fifteen years had persuaded him that there was no problem.

While the economic history of Curran reflects an increasing concentration in its major field of practice, its political history reveals a diffusion of power through the implementation of democratic governance. Like other firms, Curran was ruled in its earlier period by an autocrat or at most a small oligarchy of leading partners. Hence, the most prominent partners in the leading field ran the firm, consulting other lawyers on an informal basis. The most recent group of leaders played a similar role until the present era. This group functioned less as autocrats and more as a group of the *primus inter pares,* in part because the firm was larger, more diverse, and therefore less familylike, in part because they believed democratic principles should apply inside organizations. While these leaders influenced decisions, they preferred that decisions be made by the group.

These lawyers' concepts of governance became institutionalized in new procedures adopted in the early seventies. The details of who wrote the new constitution and the factors contributing to its adoption are unclear. But by this time a number of partners in addition to the firm's two leading partners had established reputations and demonstrated client-attracting ability. The new administrative governance structure allowed for broad participation by leading partners while informally allowing the most prominent partners to continue to play an influential role. Under the new rules a governing committee, whose members serve rotating terms, makes key policy decisions. Upon the expiration of a term, the committee votes for a replacement. Hence, a number of partners have at one time served on the governing committee. The standing exceptions to the rotation rule have been the firm's elder statesmen. Day-to-day administration is handled by a managing partner, a member of the committee elected for a one-year term. The firm has no other professional administrator but only an accountant and an administrator who manages secretarial support.

While the leading partners continue to play an important role through the committee, they do not control its decisions and they occasionally lose a vote. Hence the rule by committee is quite genuine. Policy-making is much debated in an ongoing way by a changing cast of partners. The managing partner described the openness of this system.

> We don't have an elected [governing] committee, but we have a committee that is sort of quasi-elected, in the sense that we solicit suggestions, which are really votes, from people. And in my experience there is an effort to put people on the committee who receive substantial support and also

112   Patterns of Social Change

give some balance in terms of age, fields of specialty . . . [S]o the hope is that
. . . [through] partners' meetings and otherwise . . . there is some feedback
and consensus in terms of what's done. Generally, the [governing] committee
acts on matters of administration, and their leadership is accepted . . . by
other people.

One of the leading partners suggested that the key to the success of
the organization was an esprit de corps among members. But given such
a basis for organizational cohesion, this lawyer saw size as a threat to
the organization. Indeed he had set notions of just how large the firm
could become.

> I don't think we will ever be larger than say about [75] to [80] lawyers,
> because I think this firm will lose its esprit de corps if it gets up to that point.
> The administration probably will become unmanageable. We will be spend-
> ing more time administering this damn thing than we can afford to, the firm
> will become less attractive to law students because of the erosion of [personal
> relationships between attorneys] . . . you won't be able to know each other.

But he laughingly admitted that he had been wrong before about how
large the firm would become.

This partner's observation emphasizes the difficulties of democratic
governance. As firms grow larger and deal with more complex managerial issues, democratic governance may not produce a coherent managerial approach and may increase the time required to reach decisions.
Some members of the elite pointed to major problems in firm administration. Although they did not connect the problems to democracy
per se, they emphasized the difficulty of insulating and protecting managerial innovations from the objections of partners. The question arose
in a discussion of the kind of internal financial information the firm
collected. The partner I was interviewing had just received preliminary
figures from a study of the firm's nonchargeable time, including pro
bono work, uncollectable bills, bar association work, and time spent
on administration. Over the course of the preceding fourteen months
the money equivalent of uncharged time was estimated to equal a
substantial portion of the firm's gross annual revenues. This same
partner indicated problems in the firm's financial accounting system.
When asked if the firm had data measuring the profitability of different
fields, he responded that the firm did not possess that information.
When asked if the firm consciously decided not to gather that information, he replied: "No . . . we have a big problem with our computer
system. We can't get the information we need to function on a daily

basis. So while it would certainly be lovely to know what areas are more profitable, we are lucky to get our bills out every month."

Such problems result from a collegial authority system in which attempts at rational management conflict with the prerogatives of partners, thus being subverted. The same interview continued:

> I would like to see us hire a professional manager to run the whole operation. We tried that several times, never successfully, because we haven't gone about it in the right way. . . .
>
> Q. Why hasn't it worked for your firm?
>
> A. Because the lawyers have been unwilling to give the people in that position any responsibility. And the lawyers continually second-guessed what the person was doing, so that was an impossible position to fill, because the person runs around trying to please everybody, and pleases nobody, and . . . [has no] authority to make any decisions.

The partners in Curran resemble barons in a feudal system. Unlike Becker, where the elite are integrated because of a concentrated client core, no coalition at Curran has developed which would cede control over certain aspects of the firm to a professional manager. The elite at Curran are quite aware of this. Most of the partners I interviewed spoke of the need for more coherent administrative systems, but no one articulated what such a structure might look like. To a large extent the governors were willing to trade off administrative efficiency for the continuation of baronial privileges and independence. The managing partner addressed the question, first arguing that there was no inherent conflict between more effective management and the independence of partners and then adding that he would choose independence over efficiency.

> I believe strongly that we should have a general partnership, and we should consult and keep people informed and attempt to make important decisions in that way. So I don't think that there is . . . necessarily a strong conflict between the two. I think there ought to be more efficient management, that lawyers are probably not generally very good administrators, and . . . there's a lot more that we could do in many areas. I think that most of those things are not in any way inherently or necessarily at war with professional independence. . . . We have a lot of professionally independent-minded people who are proud of being independent professionals with their own views. We're informal. People state their views strongly, and I'm proud of that and wouldn't want to change it in any way. So the question is in part, would I like to adopt or change over everybody's mentality to that which you might find in a normal business, where there is perhaps no ideology of indepen-

dence and the feeling is that everybody should be part of the group and following instructions. I would not want to see that and would be willing to make considerable sacrifice of efficiency if necessary to [avoid] that.

The managing partner may be correct that there is no inherent conflict between rational management and professional independence, but in the case of the Curran firm it appears that baronial autonomy has frustrated efforts to develop some basic administrative structures. Future planning is also underdeveloped. Although ad hoc committees on growth and on strategies for diversification have been formed at various times, they have disbanded without reaching any conclusions.

This history begins to suggest that Aaron and Curran have similar strengths and weaknesses. With relatively diffused client bases, these firms have not developed coherent managerial practices. As a result of doubt over who is in control, there is doubt and confusion over how the firms should be managed. This is far different from the pattern in Duncan, the final firm I will examine. Duncan also has a relatively diffuse client base but has a tradition of bureaucratic administration. As a result the conflict between bureaucracy and participation is not over how the firm should be administered but who should "play the central managerial role.

Duncan, Martin & Levy

If managerial coordination has been a weakness of Aaron and Curran, it has been the strength of Duncan. From its origin the Duncan firm has been organized according to a theory of cost-effective specialization and departmentalization. More than any other firm studied it has been built around a businesslike approach to law practice in which a small group of partners have planned the growth and expansion of the firm and in which work is organized through a departmental structure, complete with recognized department heads. Ironically, what has been the consistent strength of the firm gave rise to a near-crisis in the organization, precipitating a major revision of firm governance, even though the departmental structure of the firm was left largely intact. In this respect, Duncan is a particularly apt reflection of the nature of power in the law firm and its relationship to bureaucratization.

Duncan was founded at a later date than the other firms we have studied, and not coincidentally it began with a more specialized focus. The firm's specialty from its earliest days was a field I will call "finance," for it deals primarily with financial transactions by large corporate and institutional actors. The firm's founding partners were specialists in finance and its related corporate legal work. The distinct specialties these lawyers practiced gave rise to an informal departmental structure that quickly became institutionalized. A lawyer who joined the firm shortly after its inception described how the founding partners built the firm through this philosophy of departmentalization:

Q. Can you tell me how the departmental system evolved?

A. Well, it evolved because initially this firm did nothing but finance work.... And [then] we started bringing in and developing people in different specialties, and it just stayed that way. We felt it was important from the standpoint of better service to clients to have groups of specialists in their own areas [who were] not try[ing] to cover three or four areas of law.... [I]t was just about the time that I joined that we began building a corporate presence.... [X] had come with the firm, and [Y] was basically a trusts and estates lawyer.... Real estate and litigation were also conscious efforts to go out and find somebody who would head up and build this department simply because we perceived the need if we were going to be a full-service law firm to provide a full service to our clients.

All members of the elite interviewed agreed that this organizational approach was critical to the firm's success. One department head went so far as to suggest that the firm's founding partners were geniuses for devising a firm based on early and intensive specialization, which gave individuals satisfaction by making them experts early in their careers and which also "gave [the firm] high productivity," allowing it to provide many legal services "for a reasonable price." Duncan's strategy derived in part from the circumstances of the firm's origins. As one leading partner pointed out: "We attracted a lot of clients outside the Chicago area in the earlier years, and we're still doing so, principally because the largest and most stable of the Chicago institutional clients had relationships with other law firms that went back far beyond the founding of this firm." The firm was left to exploit its expertise in finance, a field that, as the chairman of the executive committee suggested, "most people weren't interested in . . . the average lawyer didn't want to do finance—beneath their dignity or something, I don't know." Moreover, because the intellectual content of the finance practice was organized around different types of organizations and logically gave rise to specialization by organization type, the firm's leading field carried its own blueprint for organization. As one department head

116   Patterns of Social Change

explained: "The complexity of finance and the detailed knowledge that is required lends itself to a fairly differentiated structure within the firm. So it is fairly easy to establish an organization structure that corresponds in some way to the different areas of finance."

Departments are more active at Duncan than in any of the other firms studied: associates immediately join a department; departments broker admissions to the partnership, each making the pitch for its members (or choosing not to put forth a candidate); the evaluation of associates is organized by departments, which channel lawyers into areas of subspecialization; and departments receive weekly reports on the availability of their associates' time.

The management of the firm has been concentrated in a small group throughout most of its history. One of the founding partners managed the firm from its inception to 1964, although he consulted with an executive committee consisting of three to five members during that time. In 1964 the committee was renamed the management committee, but, in the words of a member, "as a practical matter, most of the management in those days was handled by two people, [X] and [Y]. So forget who was on the committee and who wasn't." After the death or retirement of these lawyers, a different senior department head assumed the chairmanship of the management committee. During his tenure as chairman the management committee grew large and the role of the chairman changed. Previously, the chair had run the firm, with the committee acting as an advisory council; under the new regime, rule by committee prevailed, with several of the planning and administrative functions delegated to members of the committee on an ad hoc basis. This group actively engaged in planning and expansion. During the seventies the firm added branches in other cities and added new fields of expertise while continuing to anticipate emergent subspecialties in various finance-related fields. Particular client demands encouraged some of these innovations, but others were based on opportunities that practice groups perceived and then pursued with encouragement from the management group. A colloquy with a member of the management committee during the period demonstrated the mixture of planning and response in the firm's expansion:

> Q. The theory that I'm wrestling with is how the firms have developed in different patterns, and whether they move into a field of practice in order to serve clients they already have or move into a field of practice because they can see a market for it.

Bureaucracy and Participation

A. Could be both. We moved into [X] law because we saw a market. In the [Y] work [another field], we went into it because . . . it sort of grew out of what we were doing. So, I don't think you can necessarily say it's one way or the other. I think that maybe it just depends on which [pattern] you're talking about. Now [our branch office], we went there, which isn't an area of practice, well, maybe it is, but we went there because we felt that our clients . . . felt that was a desirable [move], . . .

Q. Let me ask about the dynamics by which decisions are made . . .

A. It could be any number of ways. The trouble is that no law firm is structured that formally, so you don't get that always it comes from a given spot. Now we . . . I think [a branch office] was decided by the management committee. The estate planning department, several people thought [X] [a new field] was a good item. So, "it all depends" is the answer. I don't think there is a single pattern. If you're looking for a universal answer, I don't think it's there. And the [Y] area [another field] that we went into because we had somebody, knew of somebody that we felt was very capable that was looking for a connection and said, well, how about coming over here. Well, fine. So that got us into there. . . . [I]t was an opportunity and we grabbed hold of it. . . . [In another new field] we [ran into] two people [who] fit in pretty well and we felt that we . . . had a lot of connections that might be useful to them and, frankly, they could provide service to our clients and conversely they had some things that they couldn't handle because they just really were in those two areas. And they were in the process of sending everything out that didn't fit their patterns. And it was stuff that we could do, so we felt that we could supplement one another and therefore, that's how we got into those. But it's, truthfully, it's more accident than it is really good careful planning. . . . We ran into it and grabbed hold of it and it worked.

This dialogue is revealing in two respects. First, it indicates active policy-making during the last decade. Duncan has continually explored and not infrequently implemented significant innovations. But, second, the quotation indicates market planning is very difficult for law firms, both because there are few systematic sources of information about potential demand and because firms cannot always assemble an appropriate group of specialists to service a new field. Without an explosion in regulation—such as occurred in the pension or energy areas—information comes in the form of a client request, an individual member's entrepreneurial efforts, or the situation sense of department or firm leaders. Even if an individual or firm recognizes an opportunity, acting on the opportunity depends on finding the "right people," of suitable background and expertise, whose practice will be compatible with the core of the firm's practice. Even at Duncan, which manifests an active entrepreneurial philosophy, expansion most often occurs by "happening upon" an opportunity.

In ten years of committee rule Duncan doubled in size. Despite the visible success of the organization, there was growing unrest about the management of the firm. During the period of expansion, a set of middle-aged partners had built considerable client bases. By the late seventies, they were bringing more revenue to the firm than some of the members of the management committee—most of whom held a dual position as department head and management committee member. The newly emerged client-responsible stratum called for more participation in firm governance. At the insistence of some partners, who in retrospect spoke of "what might have happened"—a reference to the possible departure of some leading client-producers—firm governance was restructured. The smaller management committee was replaced by a management committee almost three times as large, selected by voting weighted by partnership shares. Members of the committee were to serve for a set term, with a set proportion of terms expiring annually. Hence, a significant number of the seats were to come up for election each year. The management committee then elected a small executive committee and selected an individual to chair both the larger and smaller committees. Most of the former members of the management committee were elected to the new management committee, but only one was elected to the executive committee. They did, however, retain their posts as department heads. The one holdover from the former management group was instrumental in drafting the new structure and building consensus for its adoption. He served as the first chairman of the executive committee and stepped down from the post after two years. He recounted the process by which the change took place:

Q. What led up to the change? Why did it take place?

A. The main reason it took place was that you can't run a large organization of lawyers in these days with a self-perpetuating group of attorneys. It used to be that the firm was managed by a self-perpetuating group that was in power and tried to run things on their own, but many more lawyers are much more interested in having some say in how the organization in which they work is run. And I think that's the way it ought to be. It was a change which I knew was going to be coming sometime. I could see it very clearly, but to tell you the truth I didn't think it would happen quite so soon. And let me tell you, after all, I was the one that was really in charge of saying, hey, we've got a situation that we've got to deal with. So I went about trying to set up a new system which we thought could work.... And the new system reflects that.... We allow people to vote by partnership shares, which reflects how much is being produced [by different partners].

Thus the changing distribution of client responsibility forced a redefinition of firm leadership, giving greater voice to a younger set of client-responsible partners.

The new governing structure introduced a new group of leaders even more committed to businesslike administration and strategic planning. Shortly after taking office they hired a professional manager, a C.P.A. with a background in office management, to take over the nonprofessional staff and to modernize office systems. My impression from the interviews was that the new elite has begun to develop a self-image as modern management, that they conceive of their role in the firm as dealing with long-range planning and major policy-making. The new elite exhibits a managerial consciousness that is distinct from that expressed at other firms. Duncan's elite routinely articulated its managerial agenda, with little prompting on my part, whereas the elite in other firms were less forthcoming with issues or problems.

The new elite at Duncan continues to pursue the businesslike approach to firm organization initiated by its founding partners. The managerial ideology of the firm has therefore remained remarkably continuous—although some new issues have developed for management to resolve. The departmental organization of work has been left undisturbed. Indeed, the former leaders of the firm have remained in control of their former jurisdictions. In adopting quasi-democratic procedures for selecting management—the election of leadership through voting partnership shares—Duncan has expanded participation in governance but given "producers" greater input. Through centralizing policy-making in a small committee, it has built into the system a strong managerial role that is accountable to a broader collegial group. Duncan's structural innovation may show the path by which other large firms can accommodate the continual emergence of new client-responsible lawyers—who must be allowed to participate in governance—while concentrating managerial control in a small group.

Duncan's history demonstrates the advantages of coherent managerial policy, but it also reveals the role of good fortune, in Duncan's case specializing in a field that became immensely more important over time. Moreover, finance is an effective "feeder" for general corporate practice. Duncan's success derives in some measure from this advantageous position in the large-firm marketplace. Because Duncan had been successful and was governed by a group of senior department heads whose leadership role was based in part on departmental authority (although they also had significant client responsibility), the change in its governing structure is enlightening for the dilemma between participation and bureaucracy. The change meant that despite success, the bureaucratic elite could not achieve independence from changes in the client base of the firm. In the words of Duncan's transitional chair, lawyers with major client responsibility had to run the firm. It was the wisdom of Duncan's elite to recognize that the necessary change was not a fundamental alteration in *how* the firm was run but in *who* ran it. The limited democratization of governance introduced a mechanism that would reflect the economic role of partners, in effect giving control of the bureaucratic apparatus to the leading producers. It thus resolved the conflict between bureaucracy and participation by putting the leading participants in charge of the bureaucracy.

Historians of law firms uniformly attribute the success of firms to the professional skill and foresight of their leading partners. The historical script is predictable: a listing of the personal and professional accomplishments of generations of partners, including the great cases, the innovations in legal forms and practice techniques, the acts of government and community service. Intermixed is the catalog of name changes and comments on the distinctive styles and traditions of the firm; the result is what one law professor colleague labeled the "tribal customs" of firms. This emphasis on the personal triumphs of individuals is a natural tendency, of course, one that we apply often, whether we are evaluating the success of a football team, a political administration, or an academic department. A strain of this search for a prime mover appears in organizational theory as well. Management scholars are constantly searching for the secret ingredient in managerial theory which sets certain firms apart; the popular version of this perspective is embodied in the best-seller, *The Search for Excellence* (Peters and Waterman 1982). Chandler's classic analysis of structural change in major industrial enterprises also treats managerial strategy as the critical determinant of organizational success, although it carefully lays out the historical conditions leading to different strategies (1962).

I have developed a different perspective on organizational change in these historical narratives. The difference from law firm historiography is obvious, but the departure from some of the organizations and professions literature should be emphasized. First, without minimizing the heroic acts of individual partners, the success of these firms is attributable more to the growth of existing clients or specialty fields than to any other factor. Aaron and Becker flourished because their clients flourished; Curran and Duncan, respectively, grew because litigation and finance have undergone explosive growth in the last two decades. The leading partners of these firms are responsible for positioning their firms with respect to these clients and fields, but, with the possible exception of Duncan, managerial acumen did not generate the tremendous expansion of these firms. Expansion of the client base has been the predominant pattern of growth among law firms, although there is now a heightened consciousness concerning the necessity for strategic planning and a number of firms that exemplify a managerial commitment to rapid growth. Baker & Mackenzie, Finley-Kumble, Skadden-Arps, and Kutak-Rock are cases in which the client-responsible elite have pursued a specific theory of law-firm expansion, relying heavily on mergers with smaller firms and lateral hiring, and have thus accomplished rapid growth without a long-standing presence in a given field or established client relationships. While other firms have begun to emulate these strategies, most firms are similar to Aaron, Becker, Curran, and Duncan in that their growth has resulted from the expansion of their historical client base. The links of firms to clients and specialties is so enormously important that these environmental influences may well overwhelm the effects of managerial theories.

A second and related conclusion we can draw from the historical development of these firms is that the organizational structure of the law firm derives less from the professional ideology of its members than from the material conditions under which it was formed and the distribution of economic and political power among leading partners. The clearest example of the slippage between ideology and structure is Becker, where a bureaucratic structure emerged despite adherence to traditional managerial practices and the widespread belief among partners and associates that the firm continues to embody traditional professional values about firm organization. In the other firms professional ideology seems to have a more immediate reflection in organizational structure. But in each case the managerial ideology can be explained largely in terms of antecedent structural conditions. In Curran the commitment to participatory decision making may stem from the ideology of democracy and independence fostered by its leading partners, but it also demonstrates the diffusion of power among a number of partners. Even modest attempts at introducing administrative procedures have met with baronial resistance by various lawyers, leading to the demise of managerial initiatives. In Aaron the governing elite's reluctance to develop any administrative or work-group structures results from its own refusal to assume an explicitly managerial role. A cross section of lawyers in the firm was positively disposed to the introduction of additional administrative and work-group structures. On closer scrutiny, in neither Aaron nor Curran does the resistance to new internal structures flow from deeply felt professional values but results instead from the inability to forge a consensus among leading partners to develop and implement rational managerial policies. Duncan is the only firm to self-consciously pursue a bureaucratic managerial theory. This too derives from structural contingencies. Because the firm was established considerably later than the other three, during a time in which most Chicago-based corporations already had established ties with law firms, it was forced to pursue a distinctive approach. To attract business in its specialty field Duncan presented itself as more cost efficient than other firms and developed a highly specialized, highly departmentalized form of internal organization. This structure was particularly well-adapted to the intellectual content of its leading specialty, which was organized according to different categories of organizations and which was subject to revision on a regular cycle.

These patterns reveal that change in professional organizations involves a dialectical relationship between structure and managerial policy. The managerial policy of any given generation of leadership will reflect the conditions under which it came to power. It will be shaped by the critical issues of the day, will resist changes that are inconsistent with its theory of the organization and its environment, and will not change until confronted by a crisis with which it cannot deal. In this respect professional organizations are no different from other organizations. Theories of professional organizations which argue that structure is determined by the commitment of members to professional norms (see Satow 1975; Platt and Parsons 1968, p. 139–141) cannot explain the differences in structure and ideology that are observable across firms or over time within firms. To develop a theory of social change in professional organizations, we would do better to examine the relationship between professional ideology and the political-economic structure of the professional firm.

Third, in contrast to the optimistic image of professional firms offered in law firm histories or in the literature, in which professional norms are said to form the basis for participatory decision making and organizational consensus, these four case studies show the tensions between bureaucracy and participation in law firms experiencing rapid growth in a dramatically changing organizational environment. In some respects the most remarkably successful of the four firms is Duncan, which propelled itself into the ranks of the leading firms in Chicago without benefit of institutional ties to major corporations and whose success is attributable in part to self-conscious efforts at achieving an efficient organizational structure. Even though there was never serious disagreement over the advantages of a bureaucratic structure, the firm recently survived a political crisis over who would control the bureaucracy and averted the threat of rupturing the partnership. If the group of senior department heads had not acceded to demands from the emergent client-producers for a new organizational format, the younger partners might well have defected.

A similar scenario began to unfold in Becker after I completed fieldwork there. Changes in the client base and resentment on the part of some younger partners about their lack of voice in the governance of the firm produced calls for changes in governance. After a period of political agitation and some reshuffling of lawyers on the governing committee, a small group of lawyers who had developed a modest but significant clientele in their respective fields left the firm. The changes in governance and the departure of these lawyers did not change Becker's political or economic structure in a fundamental way, but they underscore the volatility of law firm governance. Even in firms with histories of strong centralized leadership and well-developed administrative and work-group structures, a shift in the client base will have serious ramifications for the firm's political system.

Aaron and Curran represent crises of a different sort. Because of the absence of cohesive managerial policies, the firms suffer from poor internal coordination. The interviews cited in this chapter have presented some qualitative evidence concerning these difficulties. Curran has tried to develop administrative structures but has consistently failed; as a result, problems of monitoring costs and performance in different fields persist. The problems in Aaron seem less dramatic, but a substantial segment of the attorneys supports the introduction of some kind of administrative apparatus. Succeeding chapters will quantify some serious consequences of the failure of Aaron and Curran to develop an administrative infrastructure. Lawyers in these two firms report working substantially more hours per year than their counterparts in the two bureaucratic firms. This appears to result in significantly lower levels of career commitment to the firms among associates than is the case for the bureaucratic firms. Obviously, these findings must be tested in a wider range of organizational settings, but certainly they suggest that traditionally organized firms suffer material disadvantages relative to bureaucratically organized competitors. If in the long run bureaucratic firms are able to achieve higher levels of profitability and higher levels of commitment to work, traditionally organized firms will come under increasing pressure to adopt bureaucratic managerial techniques or lose their ability to compete.

Aaron, Becker, Curran, and Duncan represent different aspects of the tension between bureaucracy and participation and are thus a promising set of cases through which to examine the causes and consequences of bureaucratization in the law firm. The next four chapters demonstrate how the development of different organizational structures and distinctive professional ideologies affect the career opportunities offered by firms, the organization of work, the distribution of economic rewards, and the nature of authority relationships between partners and associates.

PART II
The Structure of the Large Law Firm

3
The Changing Structure of Opportunity: Recruitment and Careers

Recruitment and career development in the large law firm have long been recognized as significant processes in the social organization of the legal profession. Because a partnership in a major firm is a position of wealth and influence, who "makes it" into large firms has been examined as a measure of the relative effects of social background versus individual achievement (J. Auerbach 1976). The consensus in research has been that large firms display patterns of ethnic and gender segmentation characteristic of the profession as a whole (Smigel 1969; Heinz and Laumann 1982). Growth and bureaucratization in large law firms may have begun to weaken these traditional patterns. To meet the rapidly expanding demand for their services in the late sixties and seventies, large firms doubled and tripled the size of new cohorts of associates. At the same time, the social composition of law school graduates began to change, most markedly with respect to gender (Epstein 1981) but also in terms of ethnicity (American Bar Association 1972–1983). As a result, new social groups—women, traditionally lower status ethnic groups, and the graduates of less prestigious law schools—entered firms in unprecedented numbers.

While some may celebrate the new diversity in the social composition of firms, serious questions remain about the underlying causes of change in recruitment patterns and their implications for the careers of associates entering firms. Will the change in the social composition of firms last? Or is it only a temporary adjustment to a shortage in the traditionally credentialed labor supply brought on by unusually rapid growth? Have the same forces of growth and bureaucratization that have ushered new groups into firms also begun to transform the nature of career options in firms, making work more narrowly specialized and alienating, reducing the freedom of individuals to choose the type of practice they pursue, or reducing the chances for promotion to partnership?

The patterns of recruitment and career development at Aaron, Becker, Curran, and Duncan provide some answers to these questions. In addition, data for recruitment and turnover in the twenty largest firms in Chicago from 1971 to 1984 help to track the changing prospects of women and lower status law school graduates in large firms. I began by analyzing the social background of lawyers joining firms in different periods to test the proposition that growth and bureaucratization have made firms more heterogeneous. Then I studied general patterns of entry, exit, and promotion in firms, including the rate at which lawyers leave firms, the timing of their departures, and their career destinations. I examined major events in the careers of members for evidence of differences in the organizational structure of firms and changes over time. Finally, I analyzed data on changes in lawyers' work throughout their careers and their reasons for choosing particular kinds of work in order to determine the impact of growth and bureaucratization on the freedom of lawyers to control their careers inside firms.

My approach differs from that used in other studies of the careers of lawyers. I do not focus on the social biographies of different groups, which would imply an analysis of the career stages of individuals with different social characteristics (see Heinz and Laumann 1982). Nor do I emphasize the strategies individuals pursue for advancement or career satisfaction, which would involve studying the perspectives of lawyers in different stages of their careers (see Katz 1982; Spector 1971). Rather, I examine careers as a structural dimension of law firm organization. This approach has a number of theoretical and methodological virtues. First, it strengthens the treatment of the professional career by locating the analysis in the terrain of the organization. The career alternatives open to lawyers in a given locale are shaped by the market positions, law school ties, and community associations of law firms. Moreover, careers inside a law firm are determined by such factors as the nature of the firm's practice, its growth rate, and policies on admission to partnership. The career choices available to lawyers, indeed, what they perceive as matters of choice, are an outcome of organizational processes. The significance of organizational structures for the construction and interpretation of professional career opportunities has important implications for sociological conceptions of professional occupations. One of the attributes that traditionally sets the professions apart from other occupations and that continues as an important element in the ideology of modern professionalism is professionals' ability to control their careers and to choose the work they do (Hughes 1958; Larson 1977, pp. 190–199). To address this aspect of "professional freedom" it is increasingly necessary to take the inquiry inside the professional organization and to consider the structure of career options it affords.

Second, career patterns provide critical insights into the social organization of firms. Professional labor costs account for an enormous portion of the operating expenses of the law firm. Yet the critical function of distributing professional labor is typically not achieved through direct techniques of personnel or work assignment but through the manipulation of "careers," whereby lawyers are persuaded to pursue a particular specialty. Such indirection reflects a tension between bureaucracy and professional tradition, for although it is increasingly necessary to assign lawyers to specific projects or highly specialized types of work, professional norms constrain how firms allocate manpower. This tension, however, takes different forms according to the firm, depending on the ideology of the governing elite and the nature of the firm's practice. The comparison of career patterns by firm thus presents another dimension of the conflict between bureaucracy and professionalism.

Changes in careers over time also provide an important index of the changing division of labor in the firm. In an organization marked by the relative absence of formal work regulation and by a professional ideology that cloaks structural changes, analysis of the major events in the work histories of lawyers is a unique means of determining any perceptible shifts in the organization of work and the nature of any such changes.

PATTERNS OF RECRUITMENT

The current general model of status attainment in the legal profession presents certain ethnic and class groups as less likely to gain admission to prestigious law schools and therefore less likely to gain admission to

130   Structure of the Large Law Firm

large law firms (Ladinsky 1963; Heinz and Laumann 1982, pp. 182–
198). Smigel's study of Wall Street firms found such a pattern more
than twenty years ago (1969, pp. 36–47, 72–74). Of the partners in
the twenty largest firms in New York in 1962, 71.8 percent had
graduated from Harvard, Yale, or Columbia law schools; 30 percent
were listed in the Social Register (1969, p. 39). Although Smigel
suggested that discrimination was on the wane in the fifties, a history
of ethnic segmentation had produced "Irish," "Jewish," and "Anglo-
Saxon" firms (1969, p. 173). Most large firms had begun to hire Jewish
associates by the late fifties, but Smigel suggested that "the Jewish
student must qualify twice," showing an exemplary law school record
and a proper social background (1969, p. 45; see also pp. 65–67).
Catholics were not directly discriminated against but tended to be
barred on grounds of "lower class" origins, foreign-born parentage, or
lack of proper education (1969, p. 45). Very few blacks were "qualified" for large firms, lacking Ivy League credentials (1969, p. 45).
Women were especially subject to discrimination by New York firms.
Smigel found that only 18 of the 1,755 female attorneys listed in the
New York City directory were listed with large firms (1969, p. 46).
Women in large firms generally were concentrated in particular areas
of the office practice—probate, estate planning, and tax (1969, p. 47).
The general pattern in Chicago firms was apparently similar (Carlin
1962). Heinz and Laumann's study of Chicago lawyers makes clear
that the profession is still segmented on ethnic grounds, with the odds
of reaching a position in a large firm varying considerably according to
social background (1982).

    Even among higher status law firms, patterns of ethnic segmentation
persist. Like New York firms, many Chicago law firms discriminated
against Jews as late as the mid-1950s. A leading partner in a Chicago
firm, now in his forties, recounted that he was the first Jewish lawyer
hired by the firm. He was conscious that he was breaking a barrier,
and he told of turning down offers from predominantly Jewish firms
to do so. The four firms in this case study were also identified at their
origins with distinctive ethnic and religious groups, and the ethnoreligious composition of the four firms is still significantly different.[1] Social
and business ties within ethnic groups continue to play a role in client
relationships and recruitment patterns. But the current differences between firms result primarily from the legacy of past ethnoreligious
divisions. These have become less important as client relationships have

become more ad hoc, specialized, and subject to market forces and as firms have begun to recruit large numbers of associates through a broad set of channels. The most recently hired cohorts do not manifest the ethnic or religious homogeneity that marked earlier ones. Interviews of the elite in one of the firms indicated a conscious effort to recruit associates from more diverse social backgrounds than in the past. In other firms that had previously hired very few Jewish lawyers, the proportion of Jews hired has risen substantially since 1970.

The major exception to the effective integration of large firms is race. Only three (1.3 percent) of the lawyers drawn in the four-firm sample were Black, Hispanic, or Asian. This is typical of the pattern in other large firms throughout the nation (see McHugh 1983). When we examine the racial composition of the leading law schools from which large firms recruit, minorities are substantially underrepresented. Minority enrollment in twenty major law schools[2] rose only modestly from 11.4 percent in 1973 to 12.6 percent in 1981 (American Bar Association 1972–1983), but the proportion of minorities in law schools is considerably higher than the proportion of minorities among even the youngest cohorts of lawyers in firms. Further research will be required to determine why minorities are not entering major firms. Is it because they fail to meet the standards firms set for law school grades? Do they choose not to pursue careers in large firms? Do firms discriminate against them? Whatever the additional research may indicate, it is clear that changes in the admission policies of law schools have not been sufficient to produce racial diversity in leading firms.

Law school is nonetheless the gatekeeper for a career in a large law firm. A comparison of the law school background of Chicago lawyers overall to that of lawyers in large firms underlines the importance of law school status. Among active practitioners in Heinz and Laumann's 1975 sample of Chicago lawyers, close to one-half (46.6 percent) were graduates of low-status "local" law schools (1983, p. 193).[3] A little more than one-fifth (22.1 percent) of the sample had graduated from "elite" law schools. The remainder divided between prestige schools (17.6 percent) and regional schools (13.7 percent). Within firms of thirty or more lawyers, the relative proportions of categories are reversed. Almost one-half (49.4 percent) of the lawyers in larger firms graduated from elite law schools, and another quarter (27.2 percent) received degrees from prestige law schools. Regional law school graduates occupy about one-sixth (16.9 percent) of the positions in larger

132   Structure of the Large Law Firm

firms. Local law school graduates rarely break into the ranks of larger firms. Only 6.5 percent of the lawyers in larger firms graduated from a local law school.

The upper panel of table 5 demonstrates the predominance of elite and prestige law school graduates in my four-firm sample as well. Close to half the sample (44 percent) graduated from elite law schools, another quarter (28 percent) from prestige schools, but only a little more

TABLE 5.   LAW SCHOOL REPRESENTATION BY FIRM,
            YEAR HIRED (PERCENTAGE)

Law School	Firm				
	Aaron	Becker	Curran	Duncan	Total
Elite	44.7	52.2	29.8	44.1	43.7 (N = 97)
Prestige	34.2	23.2	34.0	26.0	28.4 (N = 63)
Regional	15.8	21.7	25.5	16.2	19.8 (N = 44)
Local	5.3	2.9	10.6	13.2	8.1 (N = 18)
Total	100.0 (N = 38)	100.0 (N = 69)	99.9 (N = 47)	100.0 (N = 68)	100.0 (N = 222)[a]

Chi-square = 11.891, p = .220.

Law School	Year Hired			
	Before 1970	1970–74	1975–80	Total
Elite	56.9	46.9	35.7	43.8 (N = 56)
Prestige	25.9	34.7	26.8	28.3 (N = 62)
Regional	12.1	14.3	25.9	19.6 (N = 43)
Local	5.2	4.1	11.6	8.2 (N = 18)
Total	100.1 (N = 58)	100.0 (N = 49)	100.0 (N = 112)	99.9 (N = 219)[b]

Chi-square = 12.849, p = .046.

[a] Information was missing for 2 cases.
[b] Information was missing for 5 cases.

than a quarter from regional (19.8 percent) and local (8.1 percent) schools. The lower panel of table 5, showing patterns of hiring over time, indicates a significant shift in law school recruitment in recent years. Only 17.3 percent of the lawyers entering the firms before 1970 and 18.4 percent of the cohort hired between 1970 and 1974 graduated from local or regional schools. But the proportion of lower status graduates doubled (to 37.5 percent) for the cohort hired since 1975.[4]

The sharp rise in the proportion of local and regional law school graduates cannot be attributed to changing professional norms or the democratization of firms. Instead, it reflects a labor shortage in the large firm's traditional recruitment pool. From 1972 to 1981 the four firms in this sample grew by an average of 74 percent. During the same period enrollment at twenty leading law schools rose only 7.1 percent (American Bar Association 1972–1983). Even assuming that the firms dipped down farther into the ranks of the graduating classes of those schools and that some portion of the firms' growth came through mergers and lateral hiring, an enormous gap remained. The firms had no alternative but to begin to recruit from a broader range of law schools.[5]

The shift in recruitment practices has particular significance for some social groups. Women and Catholics are more likely than other groups to have graduated from local and regional schools. Almost half (42.9 percent) of the women in the sample graduated from regional or local law schools compared to only a quarter (25.2 percent) of the male respondents (chi-square = 5.737, p = .1252). The gap in law school status between men and women is particularly interesting given the relatively higher status social origins of the women. A majority of women (52.8 percent) had fathers with professional or technical occupations; 36.1 percent had fathers who were managers or administrators; and only 11.1 percent had fathers from lower status occupations. The comparable proportions for men were 36.2 percent professional and technical; 34.1 percent managers and administrators; and 29.7 percent in lower status occupations. The statistically significant difference (chi-square = 6.074, p = .048) reflects the difficulties women have in converting social status into the single most important determinant of professional status, status of law school attended.[6] The result confirms previous findings. Epstein found that 90 percent of the women lawyers she interviewed in New York City in 1965–1966 chose a law school based on nonprofessional criteria, primarily location near the family (1981, p. 35). Because women are more often tied to a locality than men, they have limited options for gaining admission to elite or prestige

134   Structure of the Large Law Firm

schools. Even though family relationships continue to work to the
disadvantage of women's professional careers, increased demand for
associates has improved their prospects. Moreover, to the extent that
higher social class background may in itself benefit a career inside a
large firm by creating an affinity with upper class clients or with socially
privileged senior partners, women may enjoy some advantages relative
to male counterparts.

Roman Catholics are twice as likely to have graduated from regional
or local law schools than any other ethnic or religious group (48.1
percent versus 18 percent for Jews, 20.4 percent for Northern or Western Europeans, and 23 percent for others) (chi-square = 18.545,
p = .0294). This may result in part from lower status origins. More
than a third (34.5 percent) of the Catholic respondents reported fathers
with occupations in the lowest of my status categories, compared to a
range of 20.7 percent to 22.4 percent for the other ethnoreligious
groups (chi-square = 9.226, p = .1612). Hence, in Chicago the two local law schools affiliated with Catholic universities have provided a
small window of opportunity into large firms for lower class Catholics.
In contrast, Jews have gained entry to Chicago firms by duplicating the
high status social origins and high status law school credentials of the
Protestant and nonidentifying groups. (For an extended discussion of
the status-class dynamics of Chicago lawyers, see Cappell 1980.)

The most striking change in the social composition of major law
firms and the legal profession as a whole is the increasing proportion
of women. In 1970 women made up just 2.8 percent of all lawyers
(Curran 1983). By 1983 the proportion had quadrupled to some 12
percent. The proportion is much higher among younger lawyers, where
some 23 percent of lawyers admitted to practice from 1975 to 1980
were women. The rapid influx of women began, of course, in the law
schools (see Epstein 1981) where they established a significant presence
during the seventies. In 1970 only 8.6 percent of law students were
women; the percentage of women has risen steadily since: 15.6 percent
in 1973, 33.6 percent in 1980, and 37.7 percent in 1983 (C. Auerbach,
forthcoming). As table 6 indicates, the firms reflect these changes.
Women fill 16.1 percent of the places in the cross sections of firms,
ranging from a low of 10.5 percent women in Aaron to a high of 26.5
percent women in Curran. The lower panel of table 6 documents how
recent the change is. Of those lawyers hired before 1970, 5.1 percent
were women. The group entering in 1970–1974 contained 10.2 percent women. The most recent cohort reveals 23.9 percent women.

TABLE 6. GENDER BY FIRM, YEAR HIRED (PERCENTAGE)

Gender	Firm				
	Aaron	Becker	Curran	Duncan	Total
Male	89.5	88.4	73.5	83.8	83.9 (N = 188)
Female	10.5	11.6	26.5	16.2	16.1 (N = 36)
Total	100.0 (N = 38)	100.0 (N = 69)	100.0 (N = 49)	100.0 (N = 68)	100.0 (N = 224)

Chi-square = 5.866, p = .118.

Gender	Year Hired			
	Before 1970	1970–74	1975–80	Total
Male	94.9	89.8	76.1	84.2 (N = 186)
Female	5.1	10.2	23.9	15.8 (N = 35)
Total	100.0 (N = 59)	100.0 (N = 49)	100.0 (N = 113)	100.0 (N = 221)[a]

Chi-square = 11.787, p = .0023.

[a] Information was missing for 3 cases.

The proportion of women has continued to grow since the interview data were collected. Of those lawyers listed in the four firms in the *Martindale-Hubbell Directory* in 1984, 26.1 percent are women; 30.6 percent of the associates and 16.6 percent of the partners are women.

Despite these advances, however, women do not appear to be fully integrated into firms. Their work roles continue to be concentrated in the office fields that have been their traditional niche (Smigel 1969; Epstein 1981). If one drops from the analysis Curran, the firm specializing in a litigation field, women are significantly less likely to practice in litigation than men (13.0 percent versus 40.1 percent, chi-square = 7.718, p = .052). It seems doubly ironic that the firm specializing in work outside the office practice fields has attracted a greater proportion of women than have other firms. This difference may be explained by idiosyncrasies in Curran's recruitment policies or by the appeal that

Curran has to women law students. Its members overall have somewhat more liberal political attitudes than their colleagues in the other firms. Women preparing for a professional career may be more liberal politically than their fellow law students and may well seek a politically liberal organization environment. But the greater proportion of women in Curran also may highlight an important difference between general service and specialty firms.

A review of tables 5 and 6 shows that Curran and Duncan, the two specialty firms, employ a higher proportion of lower status law school graduates and a higher proportion of women than do Aaron and Becker, the two general service firms. The differences are not large; nor do they achieve statistical significance. Nevertheless, the direction of the effects is quite interpretable. We would expect that firms oriented toward highly specialized markets would be less status conscious than those organized around continuous client relationships. Clients may not subject ad hoc representatives to the same criteria in terms of social background characteristics that they apply to general counsel. This orientation may be reinforced by recruiting demands. Given the rapid and recent growth of specialty firms, their manpower needs may be more urgent and their social connections may be less developed than those of general service firms.

The explosive growth of large firms, the shift toward special representation, and the changing social composition of law school graduates have produced greater social and educational diversity in the ranks of large-firm practitioners. But to what extent have these changes altered the nature of career opportunities offered by large firms?

ENTRY, EXIT, AND PROMOTION

Career patterns in the law firm are still modeled after the Cravath system (see chapter 1, pp. 71–73). With few exceptions firms are "up or out" hierarchies in which lawyers who fail to make partner in six to nine years must seek employment elsewhere. A majority of lawyers enter firms directly out of law school. Of the lawyers in my four-firm sample, sixty-one percent had held no previous position; another 11 percent had held nothing more than a judicial clerkship between graduation and entering the firm. The remainder came from other law firms (11 percent), government (5 percent), business organizations (4 percent), and various other positions, such as the military (8 percent). Although hiring lawyers away from other firms or from government has become more important in recent years, these data indicate that this is still quite exceptional.

To map changes in recruitment and turnover in the recent period of rapid growth by firms, I coded the Martindale-Hubbell listings in nineteen of the twenty largest firms in Chicago for the years 1971 to 1983.[7] Table 7 reports the total number of associates hired into firms for each year and the number and percentage who had left by 1984. Panel A is for all associates. Panels B and C single out women and the graduates of "local" law schools (Chicago Kent, Marshall, Loyola, and DePaul). The pattern is dramatic. The table clearly reflects the take-off in law firm hiring, from 110 associates in 1971 to 405 in 1983. As the results from the four-firm sample indicated, the numbers are even more impressive for women. Only 2 women associates were hired in 1971. By 1983 the number had increased to 146. Thus, at the beginning of the time period less than 2 percent of associate hires were females, whereas 36 percent were females in 1983. The hiring of local law school graduates also increases substantially in absolute numbers, from 24 in 1971 to 86 in 1983. But they constitute a stable proportion of associate hires over the period, from 21.8 percent in 1971 to 21.2 percent in 1983. The four-firm sample appears to exaggerate the change in recruitment policies for local law graduates.

The turnover rates of these cohorts also present interesting and interpretable patterns. A substantial proportion of associates leave firms before making partner. For the cohorts from 1971 through 1976, who presumably would have come up for partnership decision by 1984, the percentage who had left firms varies from 45 percent to 51 percent. Roughly the same proportion of departures is registered for the more recent cohorts who had not necessarily reached the "up or out" point in their careers with firms. Over half the associates joining firms in 1980, for example, had left by 1984. Fully 30 percent of associates hired in 1982 were gone within two years; and almost one in five (18 percent) of the 1983 cohort stayed less than a year.

These rates are characteristic of large firms nationally. *The American Lawyer's Guide to Law Firms* reported that between 1980 and 1982 an average of 12 percent of the associates in Chicago's largest firms left (1982, 1983). This figure is lower than the averages for the associates of large firms in New York (16 percent), Washington (13 percent), San Francisco (19 percent), and Los Angeles (17 percent) during 1981–1982 (*American Lawyer's Guide* 1981–1982). Given that lawyers typically spend six years with a firm before making partner, if we project current

TABLE 7. ASSOCIATE HIRING AND TURNOVER AT NINETEEN LARGE LAW FIRMS IN CHICAGO: 1971–83[a]

	1971	1972	1973	1974	1975	1976	1977	1978	1979[b]	1980[b]	1981[b]	1982[b]	1983	Total
A. All Associates														
Number hired	110	108	114	135	220	185	214	163	208	241	315	263	405	2,681
Number departed by 1984	49	48	55	63	115	89	103	90	94	122	130	80	71	1,109
% departed by 1984	45%	44%	48%	47%	51%	48%	48%	55%	45%	51%	41%	30%	18%	41%
B. Women Associates[c]														
Number hired	2	6	7	14	19	28	45	28	56	69	94	67	146	581
Number departed by 1984	1	4	6	10	11	15	25	19	29	44	44	21	26	256
% departed by 1984	50%	67%	86%	71%	58%	54%	56%	69%	52%	64%	47%	31%	18%	44%
C. Graduates of Local Law Schools[d]														
Number hired	24	29	19	29	48	43	41	52	47	71	82	78	80	643
Number departed by 1984	18	23	15	21	38	31	32	33	31	44	54	26	34	400
% departed by 1984	75%	79%	79%	72%	79%	72%	78%	64%	66%	62%	66%	33%	43%	62%

[a] The law firms included were Bell, Boyd & Lloyd; Chapman & Cutler; Friedman & Koven; Hinshaw, Culbertson, Moelmann, Hoban & Fuller; Isham, Lincoln & Beale; Jenner & Block; Katten, Muchin, Zavis, Pearl & Galler; Keck, Mahin & Cate; Kirkland & Ellis; Lord, Bissell & Brook; Mayer, Brown & Platt; McDermott, Will & Emery; Ross & Hardies; Schiff, Hardin & Waite; Seyfarth, Shaw, Fairweather & Geraldson; Sidley & Austin; Sonnenschein, Carlin, Nath & Rosenthal; Vedder, Price, Kaufman & Kammholz; Winston & Strawn. Baker and McKenzie, the nation's largest firm, was not included because of the difficulties of tracking associates in different branch offices. Listings for 1970 and 1984 were used in calculating figures for the intermediate years.

[b] Listings for three firms are missing for this year, resulting in a reduced base for the year.

[c] Gender was identified by name. Ambiguous cases were dropped.

[d] Local schools were Chicago Kent, John Marshall, DePaul, and Loyola.

annual rates over a six-year period, little more than one-quarter of the lawyers starting with firms would be expected to make partner. Such straight-line predictions are exaggerated, of course. More recent cohorts have been larger, and most turnover occurs within the first three years after joining a firm. In an earlier analysis of the Martindale-Hubbell listings for 1970 to 1979 I found that the average tenure of associates who left their firm was 2.3 years (Nelson 1980). Nonetheless, it is clear that firms experience high levels of turnover by associates. And it is likely that turnover is increasing.

In addition to the sheer magnitude of turnover, does the departure of associates have differential effects on any particular groups? Although women and lower status law school graduates have gained entry to firms, what has been their record in achieving partnership? Smigel's analysis of the "selecting-out process" in New York firms found that the law school and social background characteristics of incoming cohorts were far more heterogeneous than those of the group of lawyers who made partner (1969, pp. 116–127). In selecting this latter group firms reverted to a narrow set of law school and social class credentials. This tendency was particularly pronounced in the so-called "social firm," which Smigel chose to analyze because of its reputation for valuing the social connections of its lawyers. What does the recent experience of large Chicago firms indicate about the career prospects of women and graduates of low status law schools after entry?

Women and lower status graduates are far more likely to leave firms before making partner than are other associates. The turnover rate for women has increasingly converged with that of associates overall but remains appreciably higher for cohorts with enough tenure, so we can begin to detect a pattern.[8] In the early years reported in table 7 the number of women is very small, making the percentages unstable. But very few women in the earlier cohorts survived to 1984. Of women associates hired from 1971 to 1975, only 35 percent remain in 1984 compared to 48 percent of all associates. The differential in turnover declines for the next set of cohorts, those entering from 1976 to 1980: 42 percent of women remain versus 51 percent for the total group. Despite some improvement over time, the differential is substantial throughout the period. It is only for the two most recent cohorts, which do not yet show much turnover, that the differences disappear.

This pattern lends some credence to Kanter's hypothesis about the career difficulties of token women, that is, those who are isolated within predominantly male work environments (1977; see also Spangler, Gordon, and Pipkin 1978 on women in law schools). Turnover of women was highest among the earliest cohorts, when there were virtually no women in firms. As greater numbers of women were hired and retained in firms, lessening their isolation, turnover rates have declined. Nonetheless, the differential between men and women shows no signs of disappearing completely. This may result in part from voluntary choices to pursue family responsibilities. Although most law firms have developed maternity-leave policies, there are continuing tensions for women who seek both a family and a large-firm career and these conflicts tend to drive women out of firms (see Epstein 1981; Abramson and Franklin 1986; *Stanford Law Review* 1982). Women continue to bear primary responsibility for child rearing, and many find they cannot meet the pressures of large-firm practice as well as meet family commitments. Unless large firms become more flexible in their policies on part-time employment, the problem will persist (see Menkel-Meadow, forthcoming).

Local law school graduates fare much worse than women as a group, with little sign of improvement. Over the time span of table 7, 62 percent of local law school graduates had departed from firms compared to 41 percent for associates overall and 44 percent for women. The turnover rate of local graduates exceeds 70 percent before 1977 and remains above 60 percent until the two most recent cohorts. Even the most recent graduates already appear different from their higher status counterparts. Some 33 percent of the 1982 class and 43 percent of the 1983 class had departed firms by 1984, compared to 30 percent and 18 percent of the total group for the two years, respectively. The results suggest that even though some firms have experimented with hiring from lower status schools, only a very small proportion of such graduates will make partner in big firms. For whatever reason, law school status continues to affect career prospects in large firms, placing the graduates of lower status schools at a distinct disadvantage.

At the same time that women and other social groups are beginning to enter firms in greater numbers, firms are considering policy changes in recruitment and promotion that will reduce opportunities for making partner for all associates. During my interviews with members of the elite, respondents frequently suggested that partnership policies will become more restrictive for newer, larger cohorts, either by limiting the proportion of associates made partner or by increasing the number of years required before admission to full partnership. This could be a significant change; the cohort data from the cross-sectional sample as a whole indicate that, controlling for years in practice prior to joining the firm, the average number of years to make partner has declined steadily since 1950. Respondents admitted to partnership between 1950 and 1959 spent an average of 7.5 years with the firm before admission. Those admitted between 1960 and 1969 averaged 7.21 years; those admitted between 1970 and 1975 averaged 6.19 years; and those admitted between 1976 and 1980 averaged 5.64 years. Senior partners indicated that this trend will have to be reversed to preserve an economically favorable ratio of partners to associates. Associates are a critical source of revenue for the partnership (see chap. 1, pp. 75–77), so the ratio of partners to associates is an important dimension of firm economics. New York City firms strictly adhere to set partner-associate ratios. A partner in a New York firm suggested that any time an associate makes partner, the firm must hire four new associates, one to replace the lost associate and three to work for the new partner (personal communication, 1980). Until recently the promotion decisions of Chicago firms have not been controlled by considerations of partner-associate ratio. A large number of Chicago firms, more so than the law firms of any other major city, have responded to concerns about the partner-associate ratio by adopting a dual partnership structure (*American Lawyer's Guide* 1981–1982). In the new system lawyers must first be admitted to the partnership on a nonequity basis. After an additional two or three years, the decision on full partnership is made. This effectively delays the division of partnership shares for two or three years and allows firms another opportunity to evaluate a lawyer before granting tenure in the organization.[9]

Turnover among partners is much lower than for associates. Only 10.4 percent of partners in the listings for these nineteen firms had left, died, or retired by 1979. If we drop from the analysis two firms that suffered major defections during the period, the departure rate for partners falls to 7.6 percent, at least some portion of which is a result of death or retirement. Traditionally, lawyers have seldom left their firms once they made partner. Recent press reports on firms indicate that the stability of partnerships has changed significantly since 1979. With much greater frequency than in the past partners are moving from firm to firm as the result of intramural conflicts or in response to an attractive offer guaranteeing more money, more responsibility, or better growth potential in the lawyer's specialty (see chap. 1, pp. 61–62, 74–75).

Where do departing lawyers go? While it was beyond the resources

142   Structure of the Large Law Firm

of this study to pursue that question for all nineteen firms whose listings
were examined, I attempted to track those lawyers who departed Aaron,
Becker, Curran, and Duncan from 1970 to 1979 by checking for the
Chicago area in *Sullivan's Law Directory* (1982), which is somewhat
more inclusive than Martindale-Hubbell. Table 8 shows the distribution
of destinations from the four firms combined. In most cases the lawyers
simply disappeared: 55 percent are absent from later directories. Since
it is unlikely that Chicago lawyers are dying in droves, we can assume
that these attorneys left town or entered the kinds of practice less likely
to get them listed in a directory.[10] It would be interesting to know
whether these lawyers moved to other major urban centers or to smaller
towns. Although I cannot track down these departed lawyers, I do
know that more than half (thirteen of twenty-five) of the lawyers in my
sample who had previously been employed by other firms came from
cities outside Chicago. A quarter of them (six) came from New York
City. Table 8 finds little mobility between large firms within Chicago.
Only 5 percent of those leaving the four firms joined other large firms
(defined as having thirty or more lawyers). The same proportion joined
Chicago firms of ten to twenty-nine lawyers. Twice as many (10.4 percent) joined firms of two to nine lawyers; another 5 percent opened
solo practices. (By the author's tally of lawyers moving to other firms,
another sixteen lawyers, mostly in the two-to-nine-lawyer firms, had
their names in the titles of their firms. When solos are combined with
named partners, 12.9 percent of those leaving large firms could be said

TABLE 8.   CURRENT PRACTICE SETTING OF LAWYERS
           LEAVING FIRMS DURING 1970–79

Current Practice Setting	Total	
	%	N
Not Listed	54.7	110
Solo	5.0	10
2–9 lawyers	10.4	21
10–29 lawyers	5.0	10
30 + lawyers	5.0	10
Corporation or organization	14.4	29
Teaching or research	2.0	4
Government	3.5	7
Total	100.0	201

to have opened their own firms.) Thus only a quarter of the lawyers exiting firms continue in private practice in Chicago. The most frequent destination of lawyers staying in Chicago (chosen by 14.4 percent of departees) is employment in a business or other organization. Because of the incompleteness of directory descriptions, it is impossible to accurately distinguish between those in practice in a corporate legal department and those in nonlegal positions. My sense is that the majority of these positions entail law practice.

That one-third to one-half of associates leave within three or four years of joining a firm underscores the importance of the recruitment process. To replace and expand the pool of associate labor, firms expend enormous resources on recruitment, in the form of parties, airplane tickets, and lawyers' time. High associate turnover is a mixed blessing for firms. It is desirable because it reduces the number of potential partners who would share in earnings and have some formal right to participation. But because firms depend heavily on their lawyers' skills, turnover poses a significant problem. Much of the associate's work, such as research, drafting, and reviewing documents, requires general skills and intelligence. Yet there is enormous variation in the quality with which those functions are performed, which affects the amount of time a principal must devote to a project and the degree of confidence the principal can have in delegating responsibility. Assessment of an associate's capacities requires time. And to the extent that associates develop specialized skills in a particular field, specialized knowledge of particular clients, or even knowledge of the facts in ongoing litigated matters, a firm loses some of its investment when an associate leaves.

The costs of turnover are most apparent in New York City firms. Cravath's recent jump in starting salaries for beginning associates and bonuses for current associates is no doubt linked to the firm's reputation for restricting partnership offers (only four associates had been made partner in the last four years (*National Law Journal,* May 26, 1986, p. 8, col. 1). Because of the slight chance of making partner, Cravath was forced to dramatically increase financial incentives in order to maintain its staff of associates. Similar pressures have led firms to experiment with the re-creation of a permanent associate status, in which lawyers are kept on a salaried basis, with no prospect of ever making partner (*Legal Times,* February 28, 1983, p. 3; *New York Times,* May 29, 1984, pp. 27, 29). Such positions were fairly common in firms before World War II but disappeared with the complete adoption of

Cravath's philosophy of "up or out" careers as critical to motivating commitment to work. The desire to keep technical experts without diluting the ranks of the partnership has led to revived interest in such an arrangement.

How have firms resolved the dilemma of enhancing skill in the context of high turnover? And how have the firms' strategies affected the ability of individual practitioners to control their work? Detailed and systematic data on the work histories of lawyers in large firms and the degree to which they have been able to freely choose their work offer some answers.

WORK HISTORIES INSIDE THE FIRM

Major Events in Careers within Firms

The work histories of lawyers inside firms provide one means of studying the changing nature of the division of labor in the law firm and its effects on professionals' ability to control what they do. By comparing major events in the careers of different cohorts of lawyers, it should be possible to analyze changes over time in the content of practice, the degree of specialization, and departmentalization. Moreover, by comparing work histories by firm it should be possible to determine the significance of variations in the structure and ideology of firms for the careers of their members.

I attempted to collect systematic work histories of the lawyers in the four-firm sample by asking respondents to "give a brief chronological profile" of their career within the firm, "including any developments you see as important to your career here, which may include becoming specialized in a field or type of work, working on a big case, working closely with an important partner, assuming responsibility for a client or a piece of litigation, making partner, etc." The major events elicited by these questions were coded for beginning and ending date, the field the event related to (if any), the names of the partners involved, the size of cases, and the economic significance of clients for whom the respondent assumed responsibility. Additional focused questions concerning the timing and circumstances of changes in client responsibility, specialization, and working relationships with other lawyers supplemented the open-ended career narratives. The coded career narratives form the data for the analysis of career events presented in this section. The more structured questions concerning choice of work provide the data for the next section.

Although the career narratives were coded in a fashion that would allow the application of sophisticated dynamic modeling techniques (see Hannan and Tuma 1979; Tuma, Hannan, and Groenveld 1978), the distribution of events did not merit so complex a treatment. The narratives yielded only skeletal information on careers within firms. Almost half the sample (45.1 percent) reported only one event; three-quarters (72.3 percent) reported no more than two events. This pattern is attributable in part to the short career span of associates, who make up about one-half of the sample. But it is also clear that even for most lawyers with longer tenure in firms, the career narratives picked up only the most prominent aspects of career development. While the career histories do not provide the richness of detail necessary to present a subtle analysis of career changes, they reveal interpretable patterns of change over time and differences across firms.

Table 9 tabulates career events by time period. The 224 respondents reported a total of 433 events, two-thirds of which involved specialization in a particular field. Another 22.5 percent concern types of work, including working on an important case or transaction, developing a particular subspecialty within a major field of law, or doing general research. Only 11.5 percent of the events concern other aspects of career development: 4.6 percent deal with gains in client responsibility; 6.9 percent of the events are combined into the residual "other" category, including the performance of military service, working elsewhere, or handling a special assignment (such as practicing in a foreign country for the firm). The sequence of events follows a consistent pattern. General research or practice is almost always (26 of 27 times here) a first event. Similarly, involvement in a big case is far more likely as a first or second event. The development of a subspecialty within a particular field quite logically follows the development of a general specialty and thus never occurs earlier than as a second event. Gains in client responsibility also occur only later in a career, usually as a third or fourth event.

The distribution of career events, analyzed for four different time periods, reveals a subtle but perceptible shift in organizational careers. These data, however, like that analyzed in the first section of this chapter, must be interpreted cautiously because of the potential for confounding age and cohort effects. The events of the earliest period consist only of reports from survivors, who were probably the younger lawyers in their firms in the early period. There is no indication that patterns of attrition produce inflated estimates of change over time.

146   Structure of the Large Law Firm

TABLE 9.   CAREER EVENTS BY PERIOD

Period of Event

Type of Event	1901–67		1968–73		1974–76		1977–80		Total	
	%	N	%	N	%	N	%	N	%	N
Specialization[a]	71.1	54	63.3	62	64.7	75	66.4	95	66.1	286
Major case or transaction	1.3	1	4.1	4	10.3	12	11.2	16	7.6	33
Gain in client responsibility	2.6	2	10.2	10	4.3	5	2.1	3	4.6	20
Subspecialization	6.6	5	6.1	6	10.3	12	9.8	14	8.6	37
General research or practice	10.5	8	8.2	8	3.5	4	4.9	7	6.2	27
Other	7.8	6	8.2	8	6.9	8	5.6	8	6.9	30
Total	99.9	76	100.1	98	100.0	116	100.0	143	100.0	433[b]

Number of lawyers = 224

Chi-square = 25.944, p < .05. NOTE: Because individuals could report more than one event, the assumption of independent observations required for the chi-square statistic is violated. The statistic should therefore be interpreted cautiously.

[a] Specialization in tables 9 and 10 includes placement in a department.

[b] Information was missing for 2 events.

Indeed, if we had narratives from more senior practitioners for the earlier period, we would expect to find more pronounced differences in career patterns. In addition, we must consider whether senior attorneys censor (probably unconsciously) events in their later career. For example, rather than seeing themselves as working on a series of big cases, they may be more likely to see themselves as litigators. We might also consider whether lawyers think of themselves as specialists in a broad field rather than as experts in a subfield, which would lead to an underreporting of subspecialization. Here, too, however, the likely direction of censoring would tend to understate the amount of change over time. With these cautions in mind we can see in table 9 a unique summary of changes in professional work careers.

The distribution of events differs significantly over time (chi-square = 25.944, p < .05), with most of the differences suggesting an increasingly advanced division of labor.[11] Specialization remains by far the most frequently reported event. It takes up the greatest proportion of events for the earliest period, perhaps because of the failure to remember other events after several years. After the drop for the period 1968–1973, it then increases slightly over the next two periods. The incidence of involvement with a major case increases substantially across the periods, from one instance before 1968 to sixteen (11.19 percent of events) for the period 1977–1980, reflecting the rise of big-case litigation in firms. (Although respondents could have reported working on a major transaction as opposed to a litigated case, only one respondent did so. Therefore, the category of major cases can be treated as a litigation phenomenon.) Gains in client responsibility rose sharply in the 1968–1973 period, when they constituted 10.2 percent of the period's events, but dropped off for the later two periods. This may reflect expanding opportunities for client responsibility in the earlier phase of takeoff in law firm growth, opportunities that have become less general in firms in recent years. The rate of subspecialization has increased steadily but modestly over time, from 6.6 percent of the pre-1968 events to roughly 10 percent of the events since 1974. Perhaps most striking, the proportion of lawyers reporting a phase of general research or practice has declined, from 10.5 percent of reported events before 1968 to a low of 3.5 percent of the events in 1974–1976 and 4.9 percent of the events from 1977 to 1980.

None of these shifts is dramatic in itself. But considering the collapsed time frame (only 11.3 percent began before 1965) and the relatively crude nature of the career narratives, these data are certainly consistent with the model of an organization undergoing a transition to an increasingly detailed division of labor: increases in the "big case," a diminution in the proportion of lawyers experiencing a gain in client responsibility, an increase in subspecialization and a concomitant decrease in general practice. The gradual character of the changes in the work histories is consistent with the pattern of general structural change presented in previous chapters. Careers continue to reflect traditional modes of organizing work—by substantive field, case, and client. But specialization has intensified and cases have grown bigger.

While the continuity in career events over time makes for rather subtle evidence of a changing division of labor, the structural differences by firm come through the work histories more clearly. To examine differences across firms while controlling for cohort effects, I constructed dummy variables indicating the occurrence of the different events (coded "1" if they occurred, "0" if they did not). I then performed an analysis of variance, entering firm and cohort as main effects and a term for their interaction.[12] Table 10 reports the incidence of

148   Structure of the Large Law Firm

TABLE 10.   PERCENTAGE OF LAWYERS REPORTING
GIVEN TYPES OF EVENTS BY FIRM

Type of Event	Firm				
	Aaron	*Becker*	*Curran*	*Duncan*	*Total*
Specialization*	97.4	89.9	95.9	100.0	95.0
Major case or transaction**	23.7	14.5	22.4	0.0	14.0
Gain in client responsibility	10.5	7.2	8.2	3.3	6.8
Subspecialization*	2.6	18.8	4.1	19.1	13.1
General research or practice**	23.7	20.3	6.1	1.5	12.2
	(N = 38)	(N = 69)	(N = 48)	(N = 66)	(N = 221)[a]

* $p < .05$, F-statistic.[b]
** $p < .01$, F-statistic.

[a] Information was missing for 3 cases.

[b] F-tests were based on a two-way analysis of variance entering firm, period joined firm, and their interaction.

different events for the four firms and the probability levels for the effects of firm from the analysis of variance.[13]

The first row of table 10 again reflects the importance of specialization as a career event for large-firm lawyers. Even in Becker, the firm with the lowest incidence of specialization, virtually 90 percent of respondents reported concentrating on a particular field at some point in their career. Aaron and Curran have somewhat higher proportions of those reporting a specialty (97.4 percent and 95.9 percent, respectively). As a result of its system of automatic departmental assignment, 100 percent of Duncan's lawyers report having specialized at some time. The relative importance of departments as the organizing framework for Duncan compared to the other firms is also reflected in the second row of table 10. An appreciable proportion of the lawyers in the other firms (23.7 percent in Aaron, 14.5 percent in Becker, and 22.4 percent in Curran) have been involved in large cases and presumably in the case teams they involve. None of the lawyers at Duncan reported such an event. Litigators at Duncan see themselves as members of a department rather than as members of case teams.

The final two rows of table 10 indicate the differences in the division of labor in bureaucratic and traditional firms. Subspecialization is a far more common feature of careers in the two bureaucratic firms, Becker and Duncan (18.8 percent and 19.1 percent, respectively, versus only 2.6 percent and 4.1 percent for Aaron and Curran, respectively). Different organizational structures affect the detailed division of labor, with stable work-group structures encouraging subspecialization. Yet the differences in managerial approach at Becker and at Duncan also come through in table 10. Becker continues to allow lawyers to begin their careers with a period of general practice. The first row of the table reflects this custom, with one-fifth of Becker's lawyers reporting having had a period of general practice. Aaron and Curran have similar policies. The highest proportion of lawyers beginning their careers in general research is in Aaron (23.7 percent). Despite an express policy of giving associates time to choose the type of work they will pursue, the proportion in Curran is only one-third as high (6.1 percent). This reflects the dominance of the leading litigation field in Curran and the control of the assignment system for associates by practitioners from the leading field. In a specialty firm that has excess demand for its leading field, general practice does not really exist as a viable career option. By default, entering associates without strong alternative preferences will be channeled into the firm's leading field. The almost total absence of general practice in Duncan is expected, a product of the firm's program of placing associates directly into departments.

The only row of the table that does not yield statistically significant differences by firm is "gain in client responsibility." The overall incidence of such events is universally low, less than 7 percent across the firms. None of the differences are consequential.

The event-history data, although crude, allow us to make three observations about the nature of change in law firms. First, the overall shift in the careers of lawyers in large firms reflects the gradual bureaucratization in the organization. The division of labor has become more specialized, but these changes have emerged inexorably in practice rather than by fiat.

Second, the transformation to bureaucratic organization has progressed in varying degrees and shapes in various firms, depending on the nature of their practice and their managerial ideology. As expected, Duncan's official policy of departmentalization produced the highest levels of departmental identification and subspecialization and the lowest levels of identification with particular cases and periods of general practice. In the other bureaucratic firm, Becker, the relatively high incidence of general practice points up to the firm's adherence to traditional treatment of associates, but its high levels of subspecialization expose its system of de facto departmentalization. Although the data reflect traditional organizational patterns in Aaron and Curran, they also suggest how traditional patterns are shaped by practical factors. While Aaron has the highest incidence of a general practice phase, it also has the highest incidence of career events identified with large cases, largely a result of the recent expansion of large-scale litigation. To accommodate these new demands the firm has had to reverse its traditional flexibility toward associates and assign them to big cases. Despite Curran's expressed policy of allowing associates a period of general practice, the data show that associates seldom exercise the option. Instead, they overwhelmingly tend to begin working in the firm's leading field of practice.

Career histories thus betray the paradox that law firms have confronted in an era of rapid growth. They have attempted to adhere to the traditional images of professional organization, in which individual professionals exercise direct control over their careers. But to meet the exigencies of modern practice, they are increasingly forced to assign personnel to certain tasks. This paradox, and the various forms it takes in firms, becomes more apparent in patterns of job change and job choice within the law firm.

JOB CHANGE AND JOB CHOICE WITHIN THE FIRM

One of the characteristics used to distinguish professionals from other workers is their ability to choose the type of work they perform (Hughes 1958). As numerous testimonials in chapter 2 suggested, the ideal of the independent practitioner continues to appeal to lawyers in large firms. Even though lawyers play an increasingly specialized role in the division of labor, the image they project to themselves and to potential recruits is that of a professional who can freely choose his or her own work. In chapter 6, I address this issue as an aspect of the ideology of professionalism and the authority structure of the firm. Here I examine patterns of job change and job choice over the course of careers within firms to determine the degree to which attorneys are free to choose the kind of work they perform and what organizational factors expand or limit the available choices.

A meaningful analysis of the degree of "free choice" in a lawyer's career in a large law firm is difficult. We cannot simply put the question to the individual and expect an honest answer. A more successful research strategy is to broach the issue in the course of open-ended questions about changes in work and the reasons for those changes. Such an approach elicits information on the context of career development as well as information on an individual attorney's perceptions of such developments. The researcher then ascribes a meaning to the responses about career changes, even though this meaning may depart from the respondent's subjective views of the change. While this method no doubt introduces some error into the assessment of motivations, it is superior to relying on the respondent's even more subjective and unreliable interpretations when asked whether he or she had been directed to follow a certain path in the organization.

In a set of follow-up questions to the career narratives, I asked respondents to review the type of work they had concentrated on in the firm, the period during which they had done so, and their reasons for choosing the work. I then divided the responses into two sets: those revealing some kind of direct order or request by the firm or a department (labeled "channeled") and those primarily reflecting personal inclinations for pursuing a particular type of work.[14] My definition of a "channeled" choice was conservative, requiring a fairly direct statement of an assignment, a request, or a "need" by the firm. Responses that cited aspects of the organization, such as "the thrust of the firm's practice," were not considered channeling because no one had explicitly approached the respondent.

Conservative as my definition of channeling was, responses showed that choice of work in firms is often dictated by the organization. Table 11 reports the incidence of channeling for the first through the fifth fields in which lawyers worked. All 224 respondents reported at least one field of work (even if it was only general research). Channeling is most prevalent in the initial phase of an attorney's career, occurring in 41.5 percent of the cases. Slightly less than a third of the sample (72) report a second field, and only a third of these respondents gave reasons I classified as channeled. The number of lawyers reporting additional fields then drops considerably, although roughly the same proportion of changes in work are channeled in the later stages of a lawyer's career. Overall, of the 328 fields or changes in fields reported, 40 percent were pursued at the suggestion of the firm. Even though such large and complex organizations presumably attract and hire recruits interested in the types of practice found in the firm, a surprisingly large segment of career choices (some 60 percent) are based on personal inclinations. If firms are controlling career choices, they are doing so

152   Structure of the Large Law Firm

TABLE 11.   PERCENTAGE OF LAWYERS CHANNELED[a] INTO
A FIELD OF PRACTICE BY SEQUENCE OF FIELD OF WORK

Sequence of Field of Work	% Channeled	N
1st	41.5	224
2nd	37.5	72
3rd	37.5	24
4th	40.0	5
5th	33.3	3
Total	40.0	328

[a] Reasons for choosing a type of work that were not considered to be channeled by the firm were: interest prior to law school, interest from law school, liked it after exposure, liked people in the field, chose that department or type of work, related degree (CPA, MBA, etc.), happenstance, improved chances for advancement, appropriate work for a woman, thrust of firm's practice, provided broader practice. Reasons that were considered to be channeled by the firm were: assigned to it, firm asked me to, need for that work in firm, department or person in department asked me to, hired for a specialty or already specialized in field.

in a limited or indirect fashion. An analysis of channeling by field, firm, and over time suggests why explicit channeling occurs less frequently than might be expected.

Table 12 reports the percentage of changes into particular fields which were channeled by the firm. The field with the highest proportion of channeling is securities (64 percent of 14), followed by probate (55 percent of 20), real estate (45 percent of 29), litigation (44 percent of 111), banking (42.9 percent of 14), tax (39.5 percent of 43), other (the miscellaneous category) (29.9 percent of 67), and corporate (24.1 percent of 29). The high proportion of lawyers directed to do securities work results in part from the assignment of corporate practitioners to even more specialized types of corporate transactions. The high proportion of assignments to probate may reflect the relatively low status of the probate practice in some of the firms studied. For firms to meet demands in the field, they must encourage associates to take up the practice. One of the more striking findings shown in table 12 is the relative infrequency of channeling into corporate practice. Although more than one-third (37.5 percent, 6 of 16) of the lawyers whose first field is corporate work are assigned, 12 of the 13 lawyers entering the field at a later stage in their career do so by choice (as I have defined it). This may well reflect the drawing power of a field that affords greater potential for developing client responsibility.

The fields that produce the greatest volume of channeling in firms, although not the highest proportion of channeling compared with other

The Changing Structure of Opportunity

TABLE 12. PERCENTAGE OF CHANNELED CHOICES BY FIELD OF PRACTICE

Field of Practice	% Channeled	Number of Choices of Field
Securities	64.0	14
Probate	55.0	20
Real Estate	44.8	29
Litigation	44.0	111
Banking	42.9	14
Tax	39.5	43
Other (n.e.c.)	29.9	67
Corporate	24.1	29
Total	40.0	327[a]

[a] Information was missing for 1 instance of a job change.

fields, are those I have labeled litigation. Because the litigation fields are the largest practice area in these four firms and have been the leading growth fields in large firms in general, entry and exit data comparing litigation fields to other fields are particularly instructive. Table 13 reports the movement of lawyers between litigation and office fields by firm. Lawyers were assigned a starting position in their first field and then assigned an ending position based on their last field. The proportion of lawyers staying in or leaving their first field was then computed for each of the four firms and for the cohorts of lawyers entering firms during different periods. No significant differences were found by cohort; therefore, no breakdowns by cohort are presented here.

Table 13 shows that litigation and office fields have significantly different rates of departure and that firms exhibit significantly different rates of mobility in fields. Panel A of table 13 reports that almost one-third (29.5 percent) of all lawyers who began in litigation eventually left for other fields; in contrast, virtually all lawyers (96.3 percent) who began in an office specialty remained in the office sphere of practice. The departure from litigation is most pronounced at Aaron and Becker (37.0 percent and 30.8 percent, respectively). The somewhat lower rate of exit from litigation in Curran (25.6 percent reflects the dominance of a litigation specialty in the firm; there are simply fewer alternatives for work outside litigation. There was virtually no movement in Duncan (only one of sixty-five cases changed from litigation to office fields),

154   Structure of the Large Law Firm

TABLE 13.   RATES OF CHANGE FROM FIRST FIELD
OF SPECIALTY BY FIRM AND FIELD

Rate of Change	Firm									
	Aaron		Becker		Curran		Duncan		Total	
	%	N	%	N	%	N	%	N	%	N
	First Specialty in Litigation[a]									
Stay	63.0	17	69.2	18	74.4	29	92.3	12	70.5	74
Leave	37.0	10	30.8	8	25.6	10	7.7	1	29.5	31
Total	100.0	27	100.0	26	100.0	39	100.0	13	100.0	105

Chi-square = 4.002, p < .3

	First Specialty in Office Fields									
Stay	88.9	8	94.9	37	87.5	7	100.0	52	96.3	104
Leave	11.1	1	5.1	2	12.5	1	0.0	0	3.7	4
Total	100.0	9	100.0	39	100.0	8	100.0	52	100.0	108

Chi-square = 4.15, p < .3

	Specialties Combined									
Stay	69.4	25	85.1	57	76.6	36	98.5	64	83.6	178
Leave	30.6	11	14.9	10	23.4	11	1.5	1	16.4	35
Total	100.0	36	100.0	67	100.0	47	100.0	65	100.0	213

Chi-square = 17.629, p < .001

[a] Fields of specialty are divided between litigation and office fields. Litigation includes administrative law, antitrust, civil litigation, criminal defense, labor law, and utilities regulation. All other fields are coded office fields.

another testament to its departmental structure. When job change figures for litigation and office fields are combined, the differences by firm are statistically significant. Lawyers in the traditionally organized firms, Aaron and Curran, emerge as having less structured careers. Almost one-third (30.6 percent) of Aaron's attorneys and one-quarter (23.4 percent) of Curran's leave their first field. Because of the prevalence of office fields at Becker, only 15 percent of their lawyers changed fields. Duncan, the departmentalized firm, showed very little movement.

These patterns indicate that litigation presents a special case for career development in the large law firm. The general service firms must meet the need for labor in litigation by assigning associates to that work. The twenty-three instances of channeling at Aaron included nineteen channelings into litigation. After serving a mandatory stint, one-third of these lawyers not surprisingly moved to other types of work. If we had complete information for attorneys who have left firms, we might find even more lawyers leaving litigation, some by leaving the firm itself.

A number of factors make litigation an undesirable field in some firms. Analysis of the organization of work in large law firms suggests the alienating character of litigation (see chapter 4). In the litigation fields we find the greatest differences in the tasks and responsibilities of partners and associates. Moreover, litigation requires substantially more work time than other fields. Although the litigation fields have been growth areas, they may offer fewer opportunities for career advancement. In large-case litigation the proportion of associates to partners is higher than in other types of work, and it typically takes several years to work up the ladder of responsibility. In many firms the number of top positions in litigation cannot expand enough to accommodate the expectations of younger lawyers. Clients demand the most notable litigators for major litigation. Litigators working their way up the hierarchy of the firm cannot readily achieve the kind of reputation that will qualify them for such positions of authority. While lateral entry into firms is rare as a general matter, at least some of the leading litigating positions get filled by lateral recruits who have made a reputation in government. Some associates may prefer to work in litigation as a means of developing generalized (and thus transportable) skills, but there is some question as to whether associates receive any specialized training in the field. Although my data indicate that litigation associates are the most specialized lawyers in firms in terms of time allocation, they are less likely to consider themselves specialists. Little more than half (56 percent) of the associates in litigation fields reported that they consider themselves specialists, compared with more than three-quarters (78 percent) of the associates in other fields.[15] From these self-perceptions we can infer that the time spent in litigation at the start of a career is less likely to produce specialized skill.

Finally, table 14 compares channeling by firm. Because only a few lawyers changed their work more than once at the request of the firm, I computed a dummy variable measuring whether they had been channeled at any time in their career. Ironically, Duncan, the firm with formally departmentalized boundaries, has the lowest proportion of

156   Structure of the Large Law Firm

TABLE 14.   REASON FOR CHOICE OF FIELD BY FIRM

	Firm									
	Aaron		Becker		Curran		Duncan		Total	
Reason for Choice	%	N	%	N	%	N	%	N	%	N
Not channeled by firm	42.1	16	40.6	28	55.1	27	66.2	45	51.8	116
Channeled by firm	57.9	22	59.4	41	44.9	22	33.8	23	48.2	108
Total	100.0	38	100.0	69	100.0	49	100.0	68	100.0	224

Chi-square = 10.752, p = .013

NOTE: A case is coded as channeled if at any time during his or her career the respondent offered any reason for beginning a type of work which was deemed "channeled by the firm." See footnote *a* to table 11.

lawyers reporting having been channeled into a type of work (33.8 percent). Apparently, at Duncan, where lawyers enter a department from the outset, matters of choice are obviated. Joining a specific department is not seen as an assignment or as a direction from the organization but as an offer and acceptance of a specialized employment opportunity. And as we saw from the data on mobility between fields, this decision is more permanent in Duncan than in other firms. Similarly, lawyers working at Curran know the thrust of the practice from the outset and expect to do litigation. Thus Curran does not often direct lawyers into a field (44.9 percent of the lawyers at Curran were coded as having been channeled).

The general service firms, Aaron and Becker, in contrast, must more often override the personal inclinations of members. In the absence of departmental jurisdictions or a dominant specialty, many associates arrive without a clear sense of direction. The needs of the various areas of practice are thus met by the firm's steering its lawyers' careers. Hence a majority of lawyers at Aaron and Becker (57.9 percent and 59.4 percent, respectively) are channeled into particular types of work, much of it in litigation. Clearly, in the general service firm, careers must be controlled through direct, personal instructions. This pattern reveals an irony in the professional's choice of work in the large law firm. For it is precisely in the type of firm that offers the widest range of options for work, the traditionally organized, general service firm, that career choices are controlled most directly by the firm. Careers are dictated in the other firms as well, but the mechanisms are less personal and are a part of the structure of the organization. The result is that lawyers in highly bureaucratic or highly specialized firms do not see their careers as being directed by the organization.

These findings show how the careers of lawyers are shaped in various ways to suit the needs of firms. But is this a new phenomenon brought on by growth and bureaucratization? To answer this question I examined the incidence of channeling in the first five years of the respondents' careers with their firms, thus controlling for the longer exposure to career channeling for attorneys with more seniority. The proportion of lawyers reporting direction of their choice of work by the firm was the highest for the most senior cohort (54 percent) for lawyers hired before 1970 compared with 49 percent of those hired in 1970–1974 and only 42 percent for those hired after 1974). These data suggest that we should not romanticize the earlier era of law firm organization. Careers have been no more directly manipulated in recent years than in the past. If anything, firms have developed approaches to career management that have reduced the degree to which they explicitly guide an individual's work career. While bureaucratization and specialization may have affected the choices available to associates by requiring earlier specialization and even subspecialization, these changes have affected career choices indirectly.

Although the limitations of cohort data for drawing longitudinal inferences must be kept in mind, these findings are consistent with the comments of elite partners about changes in firms and in their careers. Several members of the elite from different firms spoke of starting their careers "doing what they were told to do," unlike today's ritual of asking associates what their preferences are. The leaders of law firms have always controlled the careers of their juniors. This control was exercised more bluntly in the paternalistic era of law firm organization, when a few leading partners called the shots. Today firms manage the careers of new members through the apparatus of committees, departments, and assignment partners. While the assignment process may be more bureaucratic, it does not issue direct orders to associates any more often than the previous system did. Indeed, it seems that increased competition between firms for the best law school graduates has led firms to soften their approach to career guidance in an effort to enhance the image of flexibility in career patterns. In an effort to improve recruitment appeal, even Duncan has considered revising its policy of placing associates directly into departments. The heightened concern of firms about the impressions they make on potential recruits underscores the conflicts firms confront. As the work-history data imply, firms must develop a more advanced division of labor to meet the demands of practice and use their personnel efficiently. But to attract the best legal talent and garner enthusiastic commitment to work, firms must maintain an aura of freedom and individual choice.

4
The Organization of Work

Classic and contemporary scholars have long recognized the division of labor as a fundamental aspect of social ordering in organizations, reflecting both the technical requirements of work and the ability of different groups to control the work process (Durkheim 1964; Marx 1967; Homans 1950; Burawoy 1979). Nonetheless, the organization of work in professional organizations has been relatively neglected (but see Blau 1973; Bosk 1979; Freidson and Lorber 1973; Menkel-Meadow and Meadow 1983). The large law firm is no exception, having received but cursory treatment (Johnstone and Hopson 1967; Smigel 1969). We have only a series of conflicting characterizations of its division of labor: "a bunch of little law firms" (personal interview, 1980), "the last of the cottage industries" (personal interview, 1980), "a mixture of a university, a Mayo-type clinic, a country law firm, and a big business" (Smigel 1969, p. 205), "a law factory" (Mills 1953, p. 24).

More than a measure of ignorance, these divergent images expose the conflicting demands made upon the law firm's division of labor. On one hand, to compete with inside counsel and other firms, the large law firm must become a bureaucratic work apparatus that maximizes efficiency by coordinating the activities of diverse groups of technical specialists or by assembling work teams capable of handling large-scale projects. On the other hand, it must remain a craft shop. An increasing proportion of its work is nonroutine, in the sense that it involves huge

160   Structure of the Large Law Firm

sums of money, rapidly changing or esoteric law and legal technique, or matters of political sensitivity within corporations. To give these problems the custom treatment they require, firms must depend on the skill and judgment of the experts they employ and must therefore defer to the norms of the professional group concerning the organization of work.

The organization of work is then of pivotal importance in interpreting patterns of social change in the law firm. We cannot fully understand the nature of stratification and authority in the law firm unless we know how these organizations work. But, equally, we cannot understand how firms work unless we know for whom they work. Comparison of the work structures at Aaron, Becker, Curran, and Duncan provides important insights into these relationships. By studying these firms I can assess the impact of bureaucratization on the work process. Is there evidence to suggest that bureaucratic work organization is more efficient? What is the impact of bureaucratization on the work roles of individual professionals? Do lawyers in bureaucratic firms have less autonomy in their work, either because they are confined to a more specialized set of activities or because they have less control over what they work on? The work process is a unique avenue from which to approach the political-economic structure of the firm. What are the relative positions of different groups in the division of labor? Does the economic dominance of certain specialties show up in the labor process? How does the work of associates compare to that of partners? What is the relationship between the political power of elites and their position in the division of labor?

The analysis here shows that indeed significant differences do exist in the organization of work in bureaucratic and in traditional firms, but these differences are not necessarily of the sort we might expect. The chief difference between bureaucratic and traditional firms concerns the organization of work groups, not the work roles of individual lawyers. Lawyers in bureaucratic firms are not more specialized than their counterparts in other firms, nor is the origin or scope of their assignments much different. But because lawyers in bureaucratic firms work in well-defined, tightly knit groups, demands on their time are significantly diminished. What emerges as fundamentally more important than differences between bureaucratic and traditional firms, however, is the status-based division of labor in both types of firm. Not only are associates employed in different work roles from partners but the dominant fields in any given firm occupy a distinctive position in the work hierarchy. While bureaucratization may shape the overall division of labor in firms and even alter the relationship between leading practitioners and other lawyers, the invariant aspect of the organization of work in the large law firm is the dominance of certain groups of lawyers over others.

I construct these arguments based on two broad types of data analysis. First, I develop global models of the work structures of the four firms and analyze them through techniques of network analysis. The network models allow us to represent graphically relationships between individuals and groups in firms. They provide a powerful confirmation of the qualitative analysis of organization structure presented in chapter 2. Second, I examine the responses of the lawyers in the four-firm sample to several questions concerning their work behavior. The analysis revolves around three central independent variables: firm, partnership status, and legal specialty. Comparing work activities across these categories of lawyers allows us to test several hypotheses concerning determinants of the detailed division of labor in firms. The combination of network models and quantitative measures of work behavior constitutes an unusually rich and theoretically provocative portrait of the organization of work in a professional firm.

THE SOCIAL STRUCTURE OF WORK: A NETWORK'S APPROACH

The social structure of a group consists of the relationships between its members (Homans 1950). The social structure of work in the law firm (excluding the roles of nonprofessional staff) thus consists of the working relationships between lawyers, either as individuals or groups. Techniques of network analysis allow us to examine the structure of these working relationships in unique and powerful ways. First, they provide models of the configuration of the elite and of specialty groups which are a useful overview of segmentation and stratification in firms. Hence, we can see which members of the elite and which fields are the most central to a firm's work and which are peripheral. Second, these techniques allow us to partition firms into groups on empirically defensible grounds (rather than on the basis of the organization's or its members' own labels). The density and interconnectedness of these groups then can be examined quantitatively, allowing us to compare organizations in a more exact fashion than would otherwise be possible (see Berkowitz 1982).

162   Structure of the Large Law Firm

As a measure of working relationships, the cross-sectional sample and the members of the elite were asked to indicate from an alphabetical list those firm members with whom they had worked "on several occasions" or more in the last twelve months.[1] This matrix of working ties forms the basis for the following analysis. After experimenting with several techniques, I settled on smallest space analysis, which provides a spatial representation of similarities in relationships between individuals, and blockmodeling, which partitions firms into groups with structurally equivalent relationships with other groups.

Figures 3 through 6 present smallest space models of the four firms. Each letter-number combination denotes a lawyer who responded to the question concerning his or her working relationships in the last year. The configuration of points is produced by an algorithm that derives the best fit with the matrix of ties under analysis for the number of dimensions allowed.[2] Those points closest together in the space represent lawyers who have the most similar sets of working relationships; those farthest apart represent those who have the least similar profiles. To aid the interpretation of the models the points are labeled according to a key for the lawyer's specialty, which is listed on the left side of the diagrams.[3] Lawyers among the elite, that is, the partners who were systematically selected for interview because of membership on the governing committee or identification as work-group heads, are indicated by a circle drawn around the letter-number combination. The center of the space, called the centroid, is marked by a triangle.[4] In addition to this labeling of points, I have drawn a set of boundaries between various groups of specialists. These lines are merely my attempt to focus on distinctive regions in the spatial models; they are not produced by the algorithm itself.

These conventions make possible a preliminary appraisal of the four models. Each of the models presents a highly intepretable graphic representation of the firm which is consistent with expectations based on extensive fieldwork. First, we would expect that because the elite in firms are the leading client-responsible laywers and thus a source of work as well as political power, they would occupy a central position in the work structures of firms. To a large extent this expectation is confirmed. The centroid in each model is surrounded by members of the elite, even though the firms vary somewhat in the overall configuration of elite lawyers. Second, we expect the leading specialties to occupy the central position in the work structure. This is confirmed as well. The centroid falls in the historically dominant fields: the special finance field in Aaron, the corporate and business specialties in Becker, the litigation fields in Curran, and the finance and corporate fields in Duncan. Finally, I expected the bureaucratic firms to demonstrate a departmental structure. Indeed, inspection of the letter codes for fields reveals that specialists are more distinctly clustered within regions in Becker and Duncan than in Aaron and Curran. While a few fields in Aaron and Curran do cluster, the boundaries are far more obvious for the other two firms. Given the apparent validity of these spatial representations, we can investigate each in greater detail and discuss its implications for interpreting the work structure of each firm.

In chapter 2, I argued that Aaron was a confederation of strong partners—lawyers who had clearly defined personal responsibility for major clients—rather than a firm noted for a particular specialty or one whose clients were largely institutional, passed through several generations of the leadership. Figure 2 illustrates this pattern. Aaron's lawyers are loosely organized around a group of elite partners in the corporate and special financing fields who are not themselves a cohesive unit. The fields of practice do tend to cluster in different quadrants, with corporate and tax practitioners in the lower left, litigation on the right, antitrust litigation to the far lower right, and the special financing field at the center of the space where the quadrants intersect. But the specialties are diffuse and intermixed.

The smallest space model for Becker (fig. 3) exhibits a more structured set of group relationships than does Aaron's but shows some similarities. Its elite, like Aaron's, is composed predominantly of corporate lawyers or specialists in the firm's leading business specialty. Unlike the pattern at Aaron, they are grouped densely at the center of the space around C67, the partner who serves both as chair of the governing committee and as the lawyer with chief responsibility for the largest client of the firm. The density of these members of the elite and the mixing of corporate and business specialists reflects the client-structured nature of the firm suggested in chapter 2. Outside the mass of business and corporate specialists is a set of distinctive specialty groups in probate, tax, and labor law. The litigators are distributed throughout the right-hand side of the space, with L73, the head of the litigation group, occupying a boundary position with the corporate elite. A number of other elite partners are found among their fellow specialists: P78 in probate, E65 in employee compensation, B80 and B81 in the business specialty. These are lawyers who function as department heads rather than as members of the governing committee. This con-

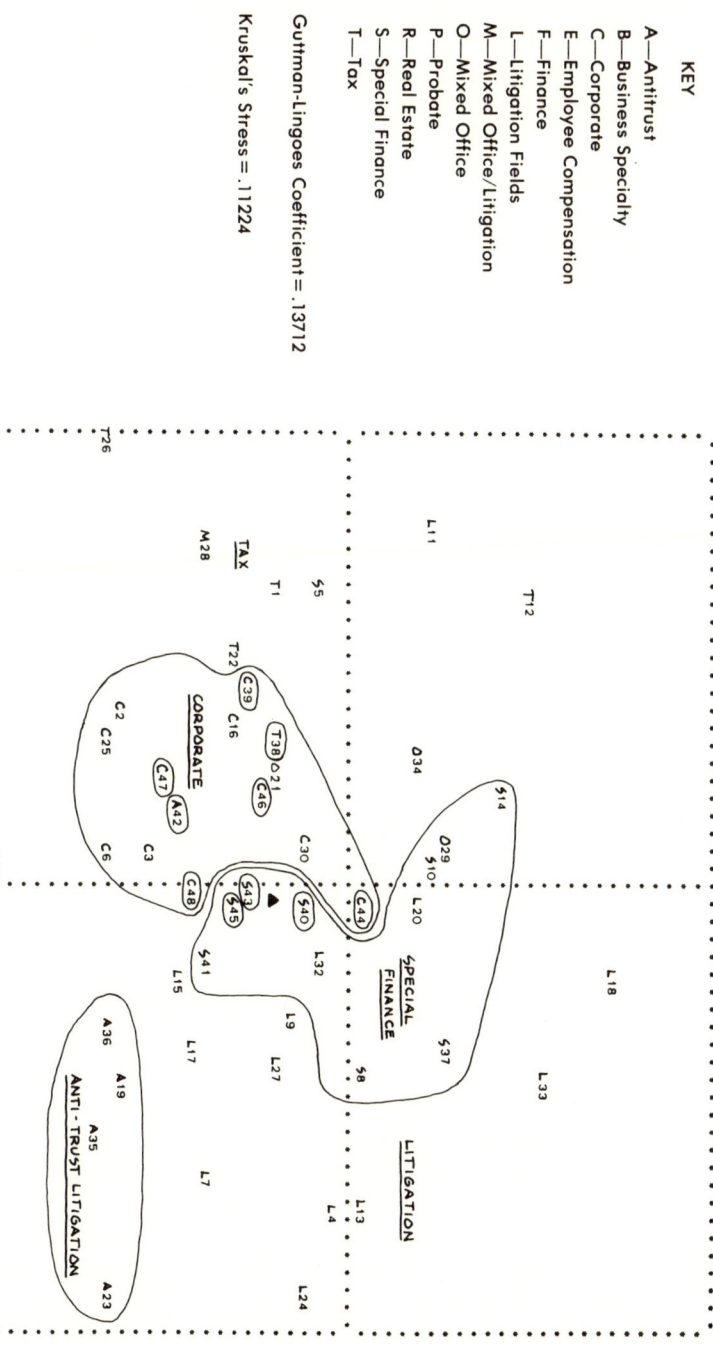

Figure 2. Smallest Space Model of Aaron, Smith & Kimball

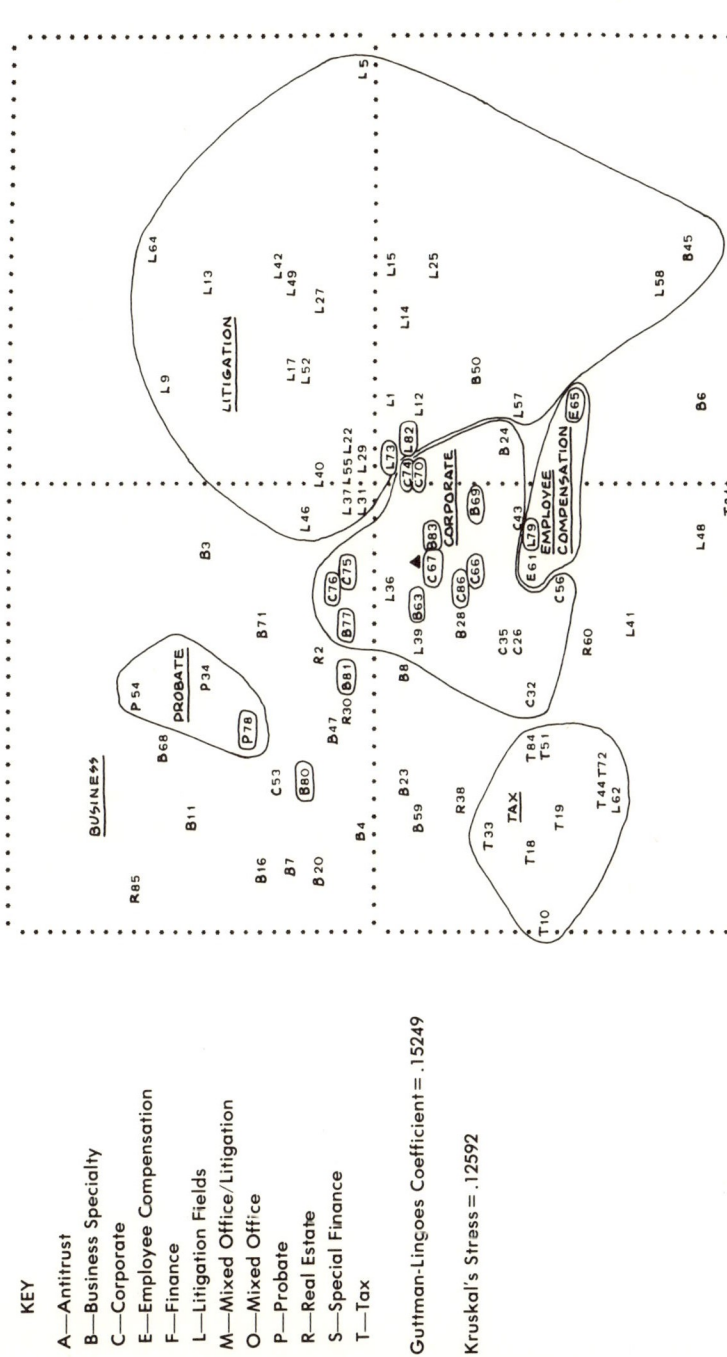

Figure 3. Smallest Space Model of Becker, Solomon & Jones

figuration is consistent with the paradoxical aspects of Becker noted in earlier chapters. Because of its traditionalism and client-centeredness, Becker affords more opportunities for general practice than other firms. But because of its client parallelism and the development of specialty groups to provide technical advice to the client core, it has more work-group cohesiveness than many firms.

Curran represents the clearest form of domination by a single field. Three-quarters of the lawyers sampled practice in the litigation fields; they cluster in the lower left quadrant of figure 4. The corporate, tax, probate, labor, and real-estate practitioners are very much on the periphery of the litigation fields. The corporate group is linked to the litigation fields through M37 and M49, the leading partners in the firm. The personal reputations of these two lawyers are strongly identified with litigation, but they are also responsible for bringing major corporate clients to the firm. While the sheer numbers of lawyers in the litigation fields may lend some cohesiveness to the firm's work structure, the configuration of elite partners and specialty groups suggests that overall working ties are relatively diffuse.

Duncan exhibits the clearest case of departmental organization. As figure 5 demonstrates, with the exception of real estate, all specialties have departmental forms. Not only do specialists cluster in the same regions but the elite partners are located within their respective specialty groups. Elite status in Duncan is exerted through departments rather than through client responsibility alone. Duncan's structure still reflects the philosophy of its founding partners. They built the firm department by department, starting from a base in finance; today the firm consists of a set of departments with finance as the central department.

The great virtue of the smallest space model is its ability to present a holistic image of social relations based on distances between points. In contrast to other techniques, this model allows us to consider the proximities between individuals as continuous variables. An important limitation of smallest space analysis for my purposes, however, is that distances between points cannot be compared by organization. Hence, although differences in the configuration of points suggest important structural differences across firms, there is no meaningful way to compare the densities of working ties based on the smallest space models. Moreover, because smallest space analysis does not classify individuals by group, characterizations of the composition of groups and of the relationships between groups are highly subjective. To compare the

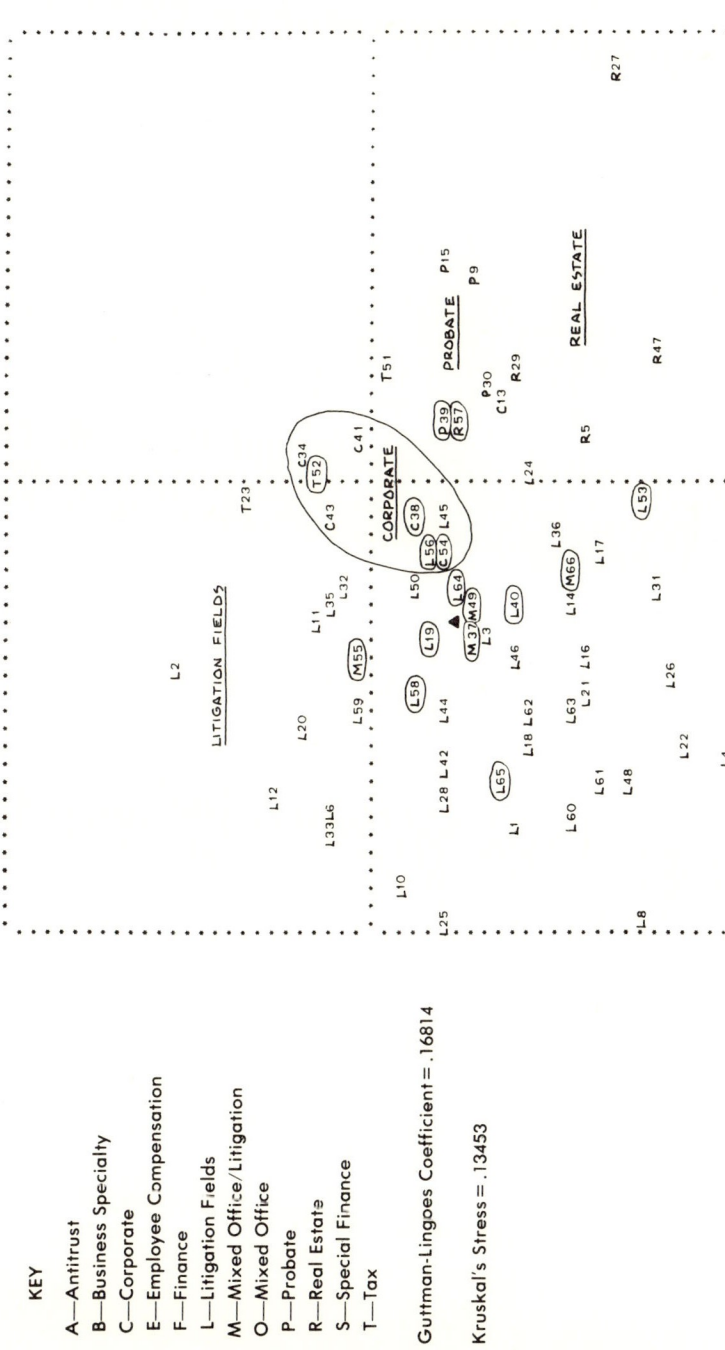

Figure 4. Smallest Space Model of Curran, Geller & Heinz

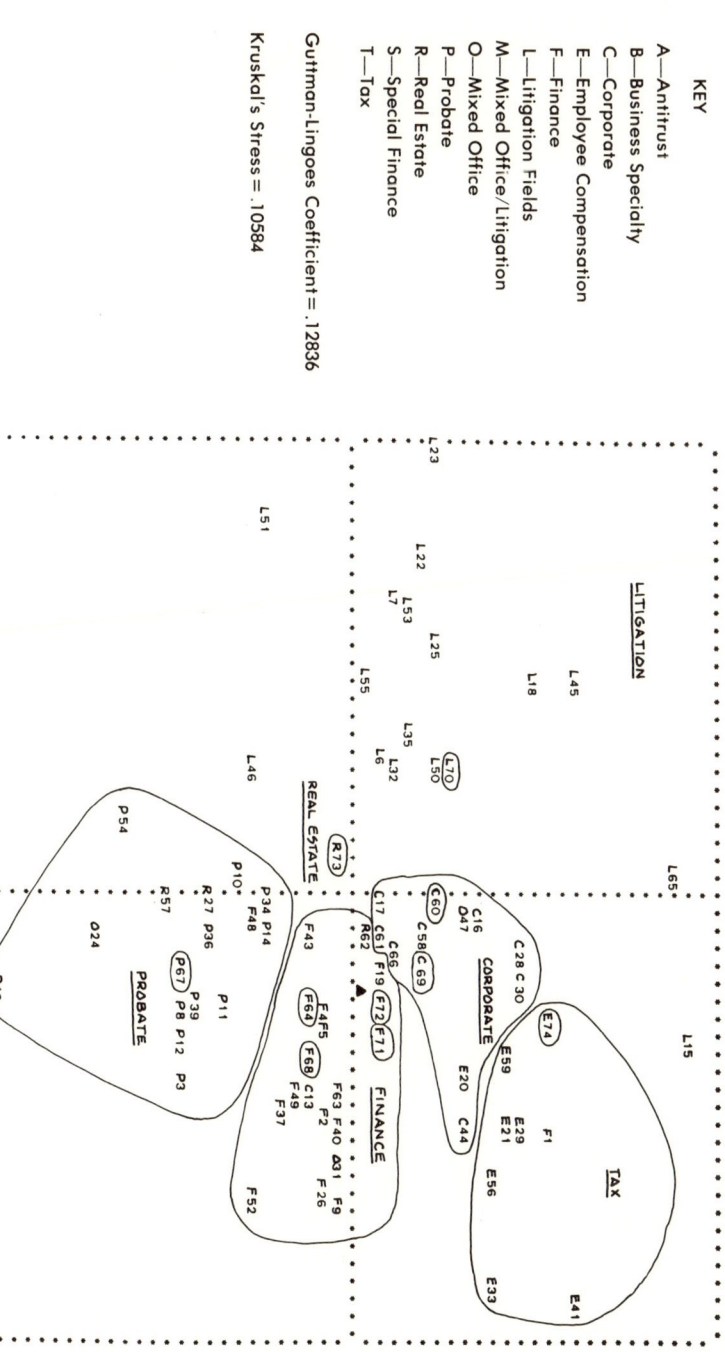

Figure 5. Smallest Space Model of Duncan, Martin & Levy

structure of work groups by firm more rigorously, I developed block models of the working relationships between lawyers within firms.

Blockmodeling is a technique that divides individuals into structurally equivalent groups, that is, groups in which individuals have relationships similar to those in other groups in the network under consideration (see White, Boorman, and Breiger 1976; Boorman and White 1976). The object is to reduce the complexity of ties between numerous individuals to a set of theoretically interpretable relationships between groups or "blocks" of individuals. I applied the technique for the specific analytical purpose of dividing lawyers into particular work groups that could then be examined for the density of within-group ties and for the nature of ties between work groups. The matrix of working ties between lawyers within each firm was submitted to the CONCOR algorithm (see Breiger, Boorman, and Arabie 1975), which partitioned lawyers into groups with similar working ties. I allowed the algorithm to continue dividing groups into smaller subgroups until the divisions failed to produce higher within-group densities. This procedure produced a meaningful set of work-group distinctions in which lawyers with similar specialties or who held elite positions were grouped together. As a simple test of how well the models fit in these terms, I counted the number of lawyers whose specialties differed from the specialty of the group to which they were assigned. By this count some 87 percent of the respondents overall, and no less than 81 percent of the respondents in any given firm, were "correctly" classified.[5] According to this criterion all four models fit the data exceptionally well.[6]

As anticipated, the blockmodels indicated that the two bureaucratic firms contain work groups that are more clearly defined and internally cohesive. The overall density of working relationships, that is, the proportion of working ties observed out of the total number of possible ties, varies from a low of .133 in Becker (meaning that 13.3 percent of all possible ties between lawyers were actually reported) to a high of .22 in Duncan. Because the two bureaucratic firms fall at the bottom and at the top of the range, it is clear that overall density does not distinguish meaningfully between bureaucratic and traditional firms. When one compares overall density to density within groups, however, the difference between the two types is apparent. Becker and Duncan have the densest intragroup ties.

The internal cohesiveness of Duncan's groups is by far the highest, with some 56.2 percent of all possible ties within groups actually observed. The absolute levels of in-group choices in the other three firms

170 Structure of the Large Law Firm

are not very different from one another. Becker's groups realize 31.9 percent of all possible ties within groups, compared to 29.6 percent in Aaron and 25.6 percent in Curran. But lawyers in Aaron and Curran are only moderately more likely to work with lawyers within their group than with other lawyers in the firm. This tendency to choose members of their own group, commonly referred to as an inbreeding bias, can be computed by simply subtracting the overall density from the in-group density and dividing the difference by the overall density. Multiplying by 100 expresses the measure in terms of a percentage increase. The inbreeding bias in Aaron and Curran is about 50 percent (48.7 percent and 52.9 percent, respectively), compared to 139.8 percent in Becker and 165.1 percent in Duncan. Thus while lawyers in the two traditional firms are only half again as likely to work with someone within their group, lawyers in the two bureaucratic firms are roughly one and a half times more likely to do so.

Network analyses of the working relationships between lawyers within these four firms reveal important aspects of their structure. It is clear that the distinction I have drawn between the two bureaucratic and two traditional firms reaches a fundamental aspect of the organizations, the organization of work. Other significant differences between firms are reflected in their work structures. These firms are not simply collections of different specialties engaged in the free exchange of referrals or the sharing of receipts. Certain fields, clients, or partners play a dominant role in the organizations; they are the source of much of the work done and are responsible for holding the firms together in particular ways.

But what are the implications of these differences for the work that individual lawyers perform? A more detailed analysis of the division of labor in each firm is necessary to address this question.

THE DIVISION OF LABOR IN THE LAW FIRM

The labor process in the large law firm warrants careful scrutiny. As early as the turn of the century, when the largest firms numbered no more than twenty lawyers, large law firms were accused of being "law factories" in which individual practitioners had lost control over their work (see Chamberlayne 1906; see also Mills 1953, p. 24). With the massive growth of professional organizations, there are new assertions that the labor process in professional firms is undergoing a fundamental transformation that mirrors the changing division of labor in industrial organizations. Hence, researchers have argued that we are witnessing a "proletarianization" of professional labor, marked by an "extensive division of labor" in which "the typical worker performs only one, or a small number, of tasks in a total process" and in which "the pace of work, the characteristics of the work place, the nature of the product," and "the uses to which it is put . . . are determined not by the worker, but by higher authorities (private or public bureaucracies) . . . " (Oppenheimer 1973, p. 213; see also Haug 1973a, b; Derber 1982, pp. 3–33). This is a supposition of considerable importance to social theory, for it implies that despite the ideology of professional autonomy and responsibility the work of professionals is subject to the same pressures of control and exploitation that more generally characterize the division of labor in capitalist society (see Larson 1977, pp. 208–244).

There is some evidence for a transformation of the work process in the large law firm. The analysis of career events in chapter 3 documented the declining incidence of general practice and client responsibility and the increasing frequency of subspecialization and big cases in recent years. Moreover, there has been a dramatic increase in the use of paralegals and in the computerization of research and document preparation. But we must be careful in interpreting these developments. I suggest that it is inappropriate to characterize the changes in the organization of work in the large law firm as a process of proletarianization or, as some have suggested, a "deskilling" of professional work. For while it is true that work is becoming more specialized, that work groups are tending toward a departmental structure, and that the work roles of the different strata of lawyers in firms are becoming more distinct, the organization of work in the law firm is fundamentally different from that in the industrial organization. The law firm retains a status-based division of labor in which the senior partners use the skill, commitment, and professionalism of junior partners and associates. Rather than seeking to reduce the level of skill in legal work, the elite of firms have actively sought to cultivate the specialized skill base necessary to attract the business of corporate clients in a rapidly changing and uncertain legal environment. This has not been accomplished by redesigning the labor process itself but by developing a set of structured relationships between specialists in different fields and with different client bases. Even in those firms that have achieved a well-defined bureaucratic structure, the labor process within operating subunits remains similar to that which exists in other firms.

Three kinds of data can be used to validate this argument: (1) mea-

172   Structure of the Large Law Firm

sures of specialization by field of law and task, (2) measures of the
source and nature of assignments, and (3) measures of total hours
worked. Analysis of the first two demonstrates the fundamental similarity of work structures in firms. Analysis of the last exposes an important
difference in the work demands lawyers face in bureaucratic and traditional firms.

SPECIALIZATION BY FIELD OF LAW

Despite the lack of formally licensed specialties (Greenwood and
Frederickson 1964; Zehnle 1975), law practice in urban areas is highly
specialized by subject matter. Laumann and Heinz found that 70 percent of Chicago lawyers considered themselves specialists in a particular
field (1977, p. 155). The proportions are even higher in large firms.
Smigel found that 86 percent of his sample of Wall Street lawyers had
a specialty (1969, p. 150). Seventy-nine percent of my cross-sectional
sample as a whole considered themselves specialists; the percentage
among partners is 98 percent. Beyond these general indications of the
prevalence of specialists in large firms and the recognition that work
groups in firms often organize around fields of law (Smigel 1969;
Johnstone and Hopson 1967), we have little data on the role that
subject-matter specialization plays in the division of labor in large firms
or the nature of relationships between specialty groups. (For a general
discussion see Heinz and Laumann 1982, pp. 36–56; Cappell 1979.)
From the outset I expected to find a more advanced division of labor
in bureaucratic firms, including higher levels of specialization by field.
The data on work-group form and density presented in the previous
section tended to support this expectation. But a more complex pattern
emerged. Overall levels of specialization do not vary by firm. Specialization does vary, however, by field of law and according to the positions
of different fields within the hierarchy of the law firm.

To examine these patterns I presented respondents with a detailed
list of fields of law and asked them to estimate the percentage of time
they had spent in each during the last twelve months.[7] From the responses I computed a specialization index, which provides a continuous
measure of the degree to which a lawyer concentrates his or her time
in particular fields of law (see Cappell 1979, pp. 12–13).[8] The index,
SI, can vary from 0, meaning equal allocations of time across all fields
(or the absence of specialization), to 1, meaning that all time is spent
in one field (or complete specialization).[9]

The Organization of Work 173

Table 15 presents frequency distributions of the specialization index by firm, followed by summary statistics. The table indicates how specialized the time allocation patterns are in the firms. On the average, the sample is 77.5 percent as specialized as possible, with almost one-fifth of the cases (18.7 percent, or 42) spending all time in one field and thus having an index of 1. The breakdowns by firm do show some differences in the distributions. There are higher proportions of lawyers practicing in one field in the two bureaucratic firms, Becker and Duncan. But there are also higher percentages of lawyers in these firms whose indices are less than .7 (33 percent and 39 percent, respectively, compared to 28 percent for Aaron and Curran). A greater proportion of lawyers in Aaron and Curran cluster around the central tendency. The bimodality of specialization in Becker and Duncan may be characteristic of firms with a more advanced division of labor. Rather than across-the-board higher levels of specialization in bureaucratic firms, we might expect greater differences in specialization among various groups than in traditionally organized firms. Moreover, it should be noted that the list of specialties presented to respondents only allows a rough measure of specialization. Lawyers developing a subspecialty within a broader field, for example, in leveraged leasing transactions within tax or in truth-in-lending law within banking, would go unmeasured here. For

TABLE 15. FREQUENCY DISTRIBUTION OF SPECIALIZATION INDEX[a] BY FIRM

	Firm				
	Aaron	Becker	Curran	Duncan	Total
.30–.39	1 (2.6%)	2 (2.9%)	0 (0)	1 (1.5%)	4 (1.8%)
.40–.49	1 (2.6%)	2 (2.9%)	4 (8.2%)	2 (3.0%)	9 (4.0%)
.50–.59	2 (5.1%)	6 (8.6%)	7 (14.3%)	9 (13.4%)	24 (10.7%)
.60–.69	7 (17.9%)	14 (20.0%)	3 (6.1%)	15 (22.4%)	39 (17.3%)
.70–.79	9 (23.1%)	11 (15.7%)	13 (26.5%)	14 (20.9%)	47 (20.9%)
.80–.89	8 (20.5%)	11 (15.7%)	12 (24.5%)	6 (9.0%)	37 (16.4%)
.90–.99	5 (12.8%)	10 (14.3%)	6 (12.3%)	2 (3.0%)	23 (10.2%)
1.00	6 (15.4%)	14 (20.0%)	4 (8.2%)	18 (26.9%)	42 (18.7%)
Total	39 (100%)	70 (100%)	49 (100%)	67 (100%)	225 (100%)

N = 225; 1 case has missing information. Two elite respondents were included by mistake in this and the remaining tables in this chapter, increasing N to 226.

[a] Summary statistics for the index are mean = .775; median = .77; mode = 1.0; standard deviation = 0.219.

174   Structure of the Large Law Firm

the list of fields used to generate the specialization index, however, no significant differences across firms were found.

An analysis of variance of the specialization index by firm, field, and partnership status confirms that firm has no direct effect on specialization, but there are significant differences by field of practice and a significant interaction effect between firm and field, meaning that differences in the level of specialization by field varied from firm to firm.[10] Associates are on the average only slightly more specialized than partners. The mean specialization index for associates is .803 versus .745 for partners, a difference that falls short of conventional standards for statistical significance (F, p = .072). It is interesting to note that although associates are more specialized in terms of behavior, they are far less likely to think of themselves as specialists. Only 71 percent of associates, compared to 98 percent of partners, perceived themselves as specialists.

Table 16 presents the breakdown of the specialization index by the two variables that significantly affect the level of specialization, field of law and firm. Inspection of the column marginals (in the row labeled "total") reveals the divergence of specialization across fields of law. By far the most specialized attorneys are litigators, who have a mean index of .836. This may in part derive from the breadth of litigation activity. Contested matters can arise in virtually all other fields of law, and there

TABLE 16.   SPECIALIZATION INDEX BY FIRM
AND FIELD OF LAW[a]

| Field | Firm | | | | |
	Aaron	Becker	Curran	Duncan	Total
Litigation	.855	.827	.785	.937	.836
	(19)	(28)	(36)	(17)	(100)
Corporate-commercial	.731	.729	.538	.594	.684
	(7)	(25)	(4)	(6)	(42)
Finance	.846	.853	.750	.745	.786
	(5)	(1)	(2)	(22)	(30)
Other office	.641	.733	.796	.723	.721
	(8)	(6)	(7)	(18)	(39)
Total	.788	.786	.765	.765	.776
	(39)	(60)	(49)	(63)	(211)

[a] In a three-way anova of the specialization index by firm, field, and partnership status, the main effect for field was found to be statistically significant (F, p < .001), as was the interaction between firm and field (F, p < .01). The numbers in parentheses are cell sizes. Fifteen cases were missing information.

are well-established subspecialties within litigation, such as antitrust, commercial, criminal defense, and personal injury litigation. It is possible that litigators spread their time among various subfields and as a result are not as specialized by subject matter as colleagues who span a small number of internally homogeneous office specialties. There is no easy solution to this analytic problem. If litigation itself is deemed a specialty, regardless of the corpus of substantive law from which a controversy arises, then it is appropriate to treat litigation as one field. This is the approach taken here. Next most specialized is the finance field, with a mean index of .786, followed by the other office fields, with a mean index of .721. Least specialized of all are corporate and commercial practitioners, with a specialization index of .684, some 15 percent lower than litigation. The relatively low level of specialization in the corporate and commercial fields reflects the client-centered nature of the practice. In contrast to other fields that are defined by particular functions (such as litigation) or particular types of clients (such as real-estate companies in the other office field), the corporate and commercial fields tend to the needs of a potentially broad range of organizations. As a consequence, the scope of their work is much less definable in terms of formal legal categories.

Client responsibility broadly affects patterns of substantive specialization, not just with respect to the corporate field. Practitioners in the central client-intake fields, and especially partners in those fields, tend to work in a wider range of fields than their colleagues. Consider the differences between specialties within firms shown in table 16. The fields in the other office category have been a traditional source of clients at Aaron. This field has the lowest level of specialization in the firm. At Becker the least specialized field is the corporate and commercial area, which is the leading client-intake field. While litigation is the most specialized field overall, the least specialized group of litigators is in the firm specializing in litigation, Curran. This reversal in the level of specialization by litigators probably derives from client ties that involve Curran's litigation partners outside litigation. In the other firms litigators play a much less central role in producing clients. The pattern in Duncan does not as clearly fit the thesis that client-intake fields are less specialized than other fields in a firm. The leading fields in Duncan are finance and the corporate-commercial practice. While the corporate lawyers behave as expected, posting the lowest mean level of specialization, lawyers in finance are roughly as equally specialized as the lawyers in other office fields; only litigators manifest a substantially higher

176   Structure of the Large Law Firm

level of specialization. Nonetheless, we should note that among the four firms Duncan's finance group is the least specialized. Compared to the finance attorneys in Becker, the other firm with an appreciable number of practitioners in the field, the finance specialists at Duncan are considerably less specialized. Finance attorneys in Becker function as specialists who provide services to the firm's major clients, whereas the finance lawyers at Duncan bring in much of their own clientele. Moreover, both the historical description of its client base and the blockmodel of its work structure suggested that the specialty fields in Duncan had developed client relationships that were less interdependent than was the case in other firms.

It is quite striking that there are no overall differences in the level of substantive specialization across firms and that the differences we find by firm reveal patterns of stratification by field. The latter finding is particularly interesting, given that the cross-sectional sample does not include the most prominent client-producers, the elites. If the time allocation patterns of these lawyers were added to the sample, it likely would differentiate the fields even more clearly. While we must recognize the limits of the data and await additional research to confirm results, the strong implication here is that there is an underlying structure to corporate legal work that does not vary by firm. Despite differences in managerial policies, firms are roughly equally specialized, with major client-intake fields playing a less specialized role in the division of labor than other fields. This finding may prove somewhat surprising to lawyers practicing in large firms. I discussed the results with three leading partners at Duncan. Two of the three expressed surprise that their firm did not turn out to be more specialized than the others; the third, the chairman of the managing committee, did not. "I told you so," the chairman said. "No matter what other firms say they do, they have to do the same things we do. I've always said that we were not that different in how we actually worked." The colloquy made clear that his had been a minority view, at least within this group of partners. In many respects his analysis is correct. It certainly applies to the next set of measures analyzed, the division of labor by task.

TASK DIFFERENTIATION

We can measure differences in the roles lawyers play in the law firm by the nature of the tasks they perform. Although I was interested in gathering some basic descriptive data on task differentiation by field of law and seniority, my central concern was to determine the extent to which task differentiation varied by firm and thus reflected differences in organizational structure. The alternative hypothesis has been suggested above, namely, that work roles vary by status within firm rather than by firm. To pursue this question I asked the cross-sectional sample to rate the frequency with which they performed a list of tasks. Table 17 reports the average frequency rating for each activity for the sample as a whole and for eight fields of practice. The left column reports the significance of F-statistics for differences by field.

With few exceptions table 17 is consistent with the common-sense view that tasks vary by field of practice. The only activities for which there are no significant differences by field are generic organizational functions—administration, conferring with lawyers outside the firm, and supervising other lawyers in the firm. The differences in mean ratings across fields largely run according to differences between the office and litigation practice. Litigators give higher ratings for taking depositions, appearing in court, writing briefs and other memoranda, preparing motions and so forth for litigation, and preparing for trial. Litigation is similar to finance in the frequency with which its lawyers do legal research and write briefs. Practitioners in office fields more frequently review documents, negotiate with lawyers outside the firm (especially high for the transactional fields of the business specialty, corporate law, and real estate), draft documents, and talk to clients.

Given such consistent differences across fields, any attempt to test for variation in task differentiation across organizations must control for type of practice. Therefore, in order to examine the relative effects of partnership status and firm on the frequency of performing activities, I ran the analyses of variance on the task variables separately for office practitioners and litigators.[11] Table 18 reports the results. The proposition tested in table 18 is that within broad types of practice task performance will vary by partnership status but not by firm. The results largely support the proposition.

First, it is clear from table 18 that tasks vary significantly by partnership status. The difference begins with the disproportionate involvement of associates in litigation, where 64 percent of the practitioners in litigation are associates. Only 42 percent of the office practitioners are associates. These proportions are significant to the relative differentiation of tasks by partnership status. Within litigation fields the frequency with which partners and associates perform various tasks is significantly different for almost every task (fourteen of sixteen F-statis-

TABLE 17. SCALED FREQUENCY[a] OF PERFORMING LEGAL TASKS BY FIELD OF LAW

	Total	Business specialty	Litigation	Corporate	Finance	Real estate	Probate	Mixed litigation	Mixed office	Significance of F-test
N	220	18	90	28	38	16	10	7	13	
Taking depositions	2.01	1.17	3.16	1.14	1.16	1.56	1.71	1.71	1.00	.001
Court appearances	2.41	1.44	3.41	1.33	1.47	1.88	2.90	2.57	1.85	.001
Legal research	3.29	2.89	3.40	2.81	3.87	2.69	2.70	3.86	3.23	.001
Administration	2.67	2.22	2.78	2.61	2.76	2.44	2.78	2.29	2.85	.710
Writing letters	4.20	4.61	3.97	4.22	4.21	4.56	4.20	4.29	4.62	.010
Negotiation[b]	3.57	4.44	3.46	4.07	2.89	4.44	3.30	3.43	3.15	.001
Conferring[b]	4.27	4.39	4.20	4.39	4.26	4.33	4.20	4.29	4.31	.937
Supervising others	3.16	3.72	3.02	3.32	3.21	3.44	3.50	2.71	3.31	.763
Writing briefs, memos	3.26	2.44	3.92	2.25	3.49	2.19	2.60	3.71	2.77	.001
Preparing motions, etc.	2.67	1.33	4.03	1.32	1.89	1.81	2.20	3.14	1.31	.001
Trial preparation	2.24	1.39	3.41	1.29	1.47	1.50	1.30	2.14	1.08	.001
Reviewing documents	3.78	4.44	3.61	3.82	3.63	4.20	4.10	3.57	3.77	.025
Drafting legal documents	3.53	4.78	2.51	4.46	4.21	4.69	4.60	3.86	4.31	.001
Talking to clients/lawyers	4.53	4.94	4.32	4.79	4.39	4.94	4.80	4.43	4.62	.001
Continuing legal education	2.54	2.33	2.53	2.25	2.34	2.93	3.30	3.43	2.69	.014
Professional activities	2.19	1.78	2.09	1.86	2.34	2.13	3.30	2.71	2.62	.045

[a] Frequency is measured on a 5-point scale: 1—Never, 2—Seldom, 3—Sometimes, 4—Frequently, 5—Very Frequently
[b] With lawyers not belonging to the firm

NOTE: N varies slightly by item. For most items, N = 220, with 6 missing cases.

TABLE 18. ANALYSIS OF THE FREQUENCY[a] OF PERFORMING LEGAL TASKS: MEAN SCALED FREQUENCIES BY PARTNERSHIP STATUS AND FIELD; F-TEST SIGNIFICANCE OF THE EFFECTS OF PARTNERSHIP STATUS AND FIRM

	Office Practitioners					Litigation Practitioners				
	Mean frequency		F-test significance of effects			Mean frequency		F-test significance of effects		
	Associates	Partners	Partnership status	Firm	Interaction	Associates	Partners	Partnership status	Firm	Interaction
Taking depositions	1.19	1.19	.796	.001	.003	2.70	3.66	.000	.372	.107
Court appearances	1.54	1.70	.442	.002	.436	3.13	3.72	.003	.224	.159
Legal research	3.42	2.99	.008	.272	.360	3.70	2.88	.000	.555	.783
Administration	2.48	2.70	.489	.004	.220	2.57	3.09	.033	.283	.330
Writing letters	4.25	4.46	.108	.863	.677	3.82	4.36	.002	.460	.028
Negotiation[b]	3.44	3.78	.055	.014	.471	3.10	4.18	.000	.189	.008
Conferring[b]	4.25	4.39	.288	.629	.067	4.18	4.24	.620	.007	.011
Supervising others	2.31	4.01	.000	.060	0.67	2.40	4.12	.000	.100	.177
Writing briefs, memos	2.85	2.62	.199	.094	.532	4.02	3.74	.091	.009	.742
Preparing motions, etc.	1.81	1.48	.045	.654	.724	3.98	3.97	.938	.473	.132
Trial preparation	1.31	1.38	.593	.578	.120	3.13	3.68	.014	.612	.034
Review documents	3.87	3.94	.695	.510	.715	3.44	3.94	.007	.899	.001
Drafting legal documents	4.23	4.29	.678	.653	.590	2.39	3.03	.004	.246	.071
Talking to clients/lawyers	4.49	4.84	.001	.510	.542	4.13	4.73	.000	.566	.083
Continuing legal education	2.34	2.64	.101	.549	.539	2.40	2.94	.002	.005	.578
Professional activities	2.04	2.38	.093	.152	.032	1.87	2.64	.000	.576	.573
	N = 53	N = 72				N = 64	N = 36			
	N = 125					N = 100				

[a] Frequency is measured on a 5-point scale: 1—Never, 2—Seldom, 3—Sometimes, 4—Frequently, 5—Very Frequently
[b] With lawyers not belonging to the firm

180   Structure of the Large Law Firm

tics have probabilities less than .1), while partner-associate differences
are much less pronounced on the office side (where six of sixteen
F-statistics have probability levels of .1 or less). Litigation associates
apparently function as staff to litigation partners, while associates in
office fields play a more collegial role. This difference may explain the
relatively higher rates of attrition in the litigation fields (see chap. 3).
Confined to legal research and brief writing, without the opportunity
to perform visible advocacy functions, litigation may well be alienating
work for associates. But whichever field they practice in, associates less
frequently perform the more "responsible" tasks of law practice. They
write fewer letters, take fewer depositions, appear in court less often,
do less negotiating, less supervising of others, less talking to clients, and
less trial preparation.

The second finding to emphasize in table 18 is the relative absence
of differences by firm. Of the sixteen tasks tested on the office side,
there are only six for which the direct effect of firm is statistically
significant at the .1 level; only two more for which the interaction effect
is significant at .1. Of the sixteen tasks on the litigation side, only four
show significant direct effects by firm; six more show significant interaction effects.

The findings again suggest more similarities than differences in the
organization of work across firms. A common and hardly surprising
feature of the division of labor in firms is that partners and associates perform very different tasks. The gap between partners and associates is far more pronounced in litigation than in the office fields.
The latter findings confirm the impression conveyed in reports about
the vagaries of associates' work on major cases. The tremendous growth
in litigation has imported new levels of alienating work into firms. This
trend no doubt contributes to the increasing rate of associate turnover
among firms and the exodus of associates from litigation. But it is
not accurate to characterize these changes in the composition of work
as the proletarianization of young professionals. The work regimen
that associates and junior partners are subjected to today is an accentu-
ation of the traditional status-defined division of labor in which elder
generalists have profited from the efforts of young specialists. While
the size of the organization may make the status hierarchy more face-
less and while the presence of computerized research and word processing may lend an aura of the law factory, what associates do and how
they are supervised remains much the same as under the system introduced by Cravath more than half a century ago.

SOURCES AND TYPES OF ASSIGNMENTS

In the traditional model of the professional labor process the professional deals directly with the client, assesses the client's situation, and handles the matter from start to finish. To what extent is this description true in the large firm and to what extent does it vary with the organizational structure of the firm? My supposition has been that despite greater specialization by field and an increase in large-scale litigation requiring larger case teams, most work in large firms is still done on a custom basis in which a group of lawyers collaborate on a matter from start to finish. A useful means of making a preliminary analysis of this question is to analyze the source and nature of assignments lawyers receive.

I asked the cross-sectional sample what proportion of their work time in the last year was spent on (1) assignments received directly from clients, (2) those received through formal assignment systems, and (3) "spot assignments" in which they were "called on to handle a specific task or a discrete aspect of a matter, as opposed to some kind of continuing involvement in a matter." Table 19 reports the analysis of these responses by firm, partnership status, and field. The results appear in the format of a multiple classification analysis, which assumes that all the significant effects in the model are additive.[12] The model explains a respectable proportion of the variance in all three dependent variables, although the model clearly works best for the proportion of time spent on assignments received directly from clients, for which 47.7 percent of the variance is explained, compared to 31 percent of time spent on formal assignments, and only 12 percent for time spent on spot assignments.

First, comparing the grand means across the dependent variables provides a preliminary sense of the relative importance of certain kinds of assignments. Most prevalent are assignments that come directly from clients, which occupy 38.2 percent of the lawyers' time, compared to 24.5 percent for assignments from formal assignment systems and only 16.4 percent for spot assignments. These differences are far more striking when one compares partners and associates across the dependent variables. Associates receive less than one-fifth of their assignments from clients (38.2% − 19.27% = 18.93%), more than one-third through formal assignment systems (34 percent), and one-fifth of their time is spent on spot assignments. Partners spend an average of almost 60 percent (58.7 percent) of their time on assignments re-

TABLE 19. SUMMARY TABLE: MULTIPLE CLASSIFICATION ANALYSIS OF PERCENTAGE OF TIME SPENT ON ASSIGNMENTS RECEIVED DIRECTLY FROM CLIENTS, FROM FORMAL ASSIGNMENT SYSTEMS, AND FROM SPOT ASSIGNMENTS BY FIRM, PARTNERSHIP STATUS, AND FIELD OF PRACTICE

	Dependent Variables		
	% Time on client assignments	% Time on assignments from formal system	% Time on spot assignments
Grand Mean	38.2%	24.5%	16.4%
Independent Variables			
Firm	*	*	
Aaron	−8.70	−10.58	−2.21
Becker	2.56	5.16	.27
Curran	−4.32	.90	−1.36
Duncan	5.55	—.—	1.89
Beta	.16	.19	.07
Partnership status	***	***	**
Associates	−19.27	9.51	4.00
Partners	20.51	−13.41	−4.22
Beta	.60	.34	.20
Field of Practice	**	***	***
Litigation	−5.10	9.96	−2.70
Corporate-commercial	6.80	−16.87	−3.79
Finance	−2.65	5.62	12.59
Other office	7.21	−10.95	−.45
Beta	.17	.35	.27
R^2	.477	.306	.122
N	225	147	218

* $p < .05$
** $p < .01$
*** $p < .001$

P-values are for three-way anovas entering firm, partnership status, and field.

ceived directly from clients, only 11 percent on assignments from formal systems, and about 12 percent on spot assignments. Hence, the lowest status class in the professional hierarchy—associates—receives relatively little work directly from clients and receives roughly twice as much through the rather more impersonal channels of formal assignment systems. Even for this group, however, most assignments entail

The Organization of Work   183

relatively continuous involvement in a matter. There may well be a response bias that leads partners to inflate reports of time spent on assignments received directly from clients and to minimize reported time on spot assignments. But if these measures are taken at face value, partnership status brings with it substantial direct contact with clients. Rarely do partners have a discontinuous relationship with the matters they work on.

The four firms differ on the three dependent variables, but not in any particularly obvious pattern. Contrary to the prediction that lawyers in bureaucratic firms would receive fewer assignments from clients, Becker's and Duncan's lawyers receive a somewhat greater proportion of their work directly from clients (40.8 percent and 43.8 percent, respectively, versus 29.5 percent in Aaron and 27.9 percent in Curran). The elite at Aaron and Curran apparently control a far greater proportion of the business coming into the firm than is the case in Becker, where parallels between work groups and clients facilitate direct client-lawyer contact, and in Duncan, where specialty fields have their own client sources. Becker's lawyers do report that a somewhat greater proportion of their time is spent on assignments received through formal assignment systems, which we would expect from a departmentally organized firm. But Duncan, the most explicitly departmental of firms, did not even allow the question of formal assignment systems to be asked in interviews, insisting that no formal assignment system existed outside the departmental structure. Differences between firms on spot assignments were not significant.

In a pattern similar to that found for specialization, practitioners in various fields of law receive assignments from different sources and play different roles in the work structure. Litigators, and especially associates in litigation, are less likely to receive assignments directly from clients (33.1 percent of litigators' time is spent on direct assignments) than are their counterparts in the more client-centered fields of corporate and commercial law and other office fields. The latter group spends almost one-half (45 percent) of their time on direct client assignments. Litigators also receive a larger proportion of their work through formal assignment systems (35 percent versus only 8 percent for corporate-commercial practitioners and 13 percent for other office practitioners). With the exception of Duncan, specialists in finance fields also are more likely to get their work through other lawyers than through direct client contact. Finance is the one field where lawyers are frequently asked to do spot assignments. Finance lawyers spend almost 30 percent of their time on spot assignments, compared to less than 15 percent of their time for their colleagues. Indeed, this appears to be an inherent aspect of the practice in the field in which planning raises specific questions about the legal implications of a proposed course of action. A substantial portion of the practice in this field is thus devoted to answering such queries.

More detailed observational studies of the labor process in firms are necessary to establish how work is initiated, divided, performed, and reviewed. Until such research is done we will only know the general contours of work organization in large law firms. But these preliminary data do not indicate that the organization of work in the large firm has been transformed into a bureaucratically regulated or highly segmented set of processes. Instead, data on assignments provide additional evidence that the division of labor in large firms remains organized as a kind of professional craft in which partners delegate more specialized and mundane tasks to associates and in which client-intake fields call on the services of other specialists as needed. The status-specified relationships between partners and associates and between fields are similar in form and function across firms, whether they are bureaucratically organized or not. Despite some differences by firm, the effects of partnership status and field are far more significant. Now, however, I turn to an aspect of the division of labor in which firms are quite different.

TOTAL HOURS WORKED

The final aspect of work behavior considered here is in some respects the most basic: How many hours do lawyers work? The total time an individual commits to work has important implications for the quality of work life, the productivity of firms, and the relationship between employee and organization. The folklore of large law firms is full of images of the extraordinary work efforts of their lawyers: Firms have boasted of maintaining cots for lawyers to sleep on. Leading partners recount times when teams of lawyers worked around the clock for days until they "had to be pulled from the field, exhausted" (personal interview, 1979). The wife of the tragic hero in Auchincloss's novel *The Great World and Timothy Colt* (1956) bemoans her husband's long hours; an associate on the threshold of partnership in a New York City firm, he works constantly from dawn to midnight. She pleads with a senior partner in the firm to get him off a particular deal, "Please,

Mr. Knox. It's killing him. Really, it is" (1956, p. 75). Smigel dwells at length on the necessity for putting in long hours to make partnership, quoting one associate that "a lot of men . . . lost their partnership on the New Haven Railroad" by choosing to spend time with the family rather than working late in the office (1969, pp. 75, 102–104).

Beyond these rather vague impressions and other anecdotes (see, e.g., Stewart 1983) we have little information on lawyers' work time or the factors influencing demands on their time. The professional folklore implies that there are significant differences in firms, in partners' time compared to associates', and in different fields of practice. Certain firms have reputations as "sweatshops." Associates are generally assumed to have to work more than lawyers who have passed the great divide into partnership status. And litigation is generally thought to demand more time than office fields. My research addressed these fundamental issues, but I was also interested in determining whether there were significant differences in the work demands made by bureaucratic and traditional firms. Do the differences in work-group structures noted in the first part of this chapter affect work time? The results of the analysis largely confirm the folklore. But more interesting is the difference I found between traditional and bureaucratic firms.

Lawyers in the cross-sectional samples in Aaron, Becker, and Curran responded to a series of questions designed to measure the total number of hours worked in the last year. The Duncan firm provided comparable information on the sample drawn in its firm based on its own computerized records.[13] Table 20 presents the results of a multiple classification analysis of total hours by firm, partnership status, and field of practice. The model explains a respectable 25 percent of the variance in hours worked and contains some interesting results. The grand mean for the sample overall is 2,097 hours per year.

As expected both firm and field of practice have statistically significant effects on total hours worked. Litigators do indeed work longer hours than other lawyers, averaging some 110 hours a year more than the grand mean and more than 250 hours more per year than practitioners in finance and other office fields. The biggest differences, however, appear across firms. The two traditional firms work substantially more hours than their bureaucratic counterparts. Curran, the litigation firm, leads the pack with an average of some 2,335 hours per year, followed by Aaron, whose lawyers average some 2,145 hours per year. The two bureaucratic firms fall below the grand mean, with Becker averaging 2,042 hours/year and Duncan averaging only 1,955 hours/year. Hence

186   Structure of the Large Law Firm

TABLE 20.   MULTIPLE CLASSIFICATION ANALYSIS:
TOTAL HOURS WORKED PER YEAR BY FIRM, PARTNERSHIP
STATUS, AND FIELD OF PRACTICE

	Dependent Variable
	Total Hours Worked
Grand Mean	2097.40
Independent Variables	
Firm	*
Aaron	47.54
Becker	−55.03
Curran	238.76
Duncan	−142.78
Beta	.33
Partnership Status	
Associates	37.21
Partners	−39.26
Beta	.09
Field of Practice	*
Litigation	109.47
Corporate-commercial	11.80
Finance	−145.17
Other office fields	−149.46
Beta	.26

R^2 = .255   N = 224   * p < .001

P-values are for three-way anovas entering firm, partnership status, and field.

the firms differ by as much as 380 hours per year, a factor of more than 15 percent. Part of the difference between firms results from the number of hours that litigators devote to pro bono cases. But even after excluding hours spent on pro bono work, the differences by firm and field remain significant. It is also clear that time spent on pro bono work does not displace the work demands made by paying clients. Lawyers who choose to do pro bono work must make the time themselves. The one prediction not confirmed by the data is that associates work significantly more than partners. After controlling for the effects of firm and field, associates average 76 hours more per year than partners, a difference not statistically significant.

What accounts for a difference of almost four hundred hours a year in total working time across firms? The difference cannot be explained on economic grounds (see chap. 5). Lawyers at comparable seniority levels receive comparable compensation across firms. One could argue that the difference is a result of organizational personality, that somehow particular firms develop idiosyncratic work norms that are then reproduced over time. While work norms are no doubt associated with work behavior, the question remains: why do certain firms and fields develop one set of work norms instead of another? I suggest that the demands of the work organization define work norms; the nature of the work produces the norms of work, rather than the reverse. This is clearest in the differences noted by field of law. Litigators work more hours, not because litigation attracts a certain kind of personality (although it probably does) but also because the work demands it. The effect of the demands of the work is also visible in differences by firm. Although research on a greater number of firms is required before we can accept a general proposition, I would argue that departmentally organized work-group structures place lesser demands on lawyers' time than do ill-defined collections of case teams and office specialties. In Aaron and Curran the absence of stable work-group structures and regular staffing procedures makes it necessary to work the professional staff longer than would otherwise be necessary. The development of structured work groups at Becker and Duncan apparently allows lawyers to meet the organization's work demands in less time.

The relative efficiency of departmental work structures suggests that bureaucratically organized firms may have a competitive advantage in the market for corporate legal services. They seem to be in a position to offer lower prices to clients than their poorly organized competitors. And, given the more attractive ratio of earnings to hours worked, they should be able to recruit more effectively. I do not want to exaggerate the implications of the findings. Bureaucratic firms may not be able to fully realize the potential material advantages. First, traditional firms continue to appeal to clients and law graduates on the basis of a professional ideology that minimizes the importance of efficiency and economic rewards (see chap. 6). The traditional ideology of these firms may be able to combat the emergence of technically efficient competitors, although the current commercialization of the corporate sector of the profession suggests that it has been a losing battle so far. Second, firms may not be able to alter their work structure to the degree necessary to achieve greater efficiency. Chapter 2 demonstrated that the development of rational managerial structures depended on the political

188   Structure of the Large Law Firm

and economic conditions of individual firms. Not all firms will be able
to generate the consensus necessary for constructing a more efficient
organization of work. Moreover, the findings here indicate that fields
of law require different amounts of time, different levels of specialization, and different sources and types of assignments. Firms will not be
able to alter the basic technical requirements of their core fields. Hence,
even if Aaron and Curran had the political will to develop a more stable
set of work-group structures, given the nature of their practices and the
organization of their client bases, they might not be able to do so.

The organization of work reveals some essential continuities in the
organizational structure of the law firm. A sophisticated analysis of the
networks of working relationships between individual lawyers and
groups of lawyers confirmed the qualitative observations (see chap. 2)
that the bureaucratic firms contain more clearly identified and internally
cohesive work groups than the traditional firms, despite the traditional
managerial ideology expressed by one of the bureaucratic firms, Becker.
With one important exception, these differences in work-group structure do not affect the work roles of individual lawyers. The firms are
equally specialized by substantive field and task and employ similar
assignment systems. The data here indicate that lawyers typically handle
matters from start to finish.

This quantitative analysis suggests that there has been no radical
reorganization of the professional labor process in which work activities
have been segmented or in which professionals have been deprived of
their skilled roles. Instead of a proletarianization of the professional
labor process, the data suggest that there has been an intensification of
the status-based division of labor which has traditionally characterized
professional organizations. Such status-based systems rely on delegation
to skilled professionals, who exercise considerable discretion and control over the work process. This is very different from the process that
seeks to reorganize labor to minimize dependence on worker skill. The
"finders" and "minders" very much rely on the skill and commitment
of the "grinders" and employ a far more subtle system of professional
norms to justify the hierarchy of working relationships than the "deskilling" concept allows. It is this status-based hierarchy that is the most
prominent feature of the organization of work. Partners delegate less
"responsible" tasks to associates. Client-intake fields delegate more
specialized work to the service specialties. The core of the organization
of work and the center of political power in the firm are one and the

The Organization of Work 189

same: the members of the elites who are responsible for the biggest clients.

While studies of other firms using other methods are necessary before we can draw firm conclusions about the impact of change on the division of labor in law firms, my findings are consistent with Spangler's analysis of five large law firms in Boston (1986). Spangler's characterization of the labor process takes on added significance because her research was part of a broader study of the work lives of professionals directed by Charles Derber, one of the leading advocates for the proletarianization thesis. Spangler writes:

> In the law firm, the transformation of a promising law student into an accomplished attorney is secured by emphasizing skill development rather than work simplification: the heart of this process is the ever more loosely structured supervision of an associate by a senior partner—a strategy that firms describe as "mentoring." While skill development includes training in the use of office routines and standard forms, there is little or no attempt in mentoring to simplify work or to de-skill workers. Mentoring therefore is the opposite of the many forms of technical control over industrial labor that seek precisely these ends. On the contrary, successful mentorships produce autonomous craftsmen. (p. 44)

Both my analysis and Spangler's converge on the argument that the maintenance of a craftlike labor process in the midst of an increasingly larger and differentiated organization is partially a result of the dictates of practice. But the analysis cannot end here. We must now explain what drives this division of labor. What motivates subordinate specialty groups and associates to work so intensively in a structure over which they exercise relatively little control and from which they receive substantially less money than leading partners?

5
Economic Rewards

The most tangible measure of position in an organization is income. Income ranks individuals within organizations by dollars and cents, thereby attaching a value to the activities of members and providing a rationale for the working of the organization. Although it is well established that lawyers in large law firms make substantially more money over the course of their careers than lawyers in other practice settings do (see, e.g., Leibowitz and Tollison 1978, pp. 74–77), we know little about the determinants of income within large firms. While economists have argued over the relative importance of training, work output, and client production (see Leibowitz and Tollison 1978, 1980; Alchian and Demsetz 1972; McChesney 1982), no systematic data on differences in income within firms have been available to evaluate these factors satisfactorily. The income data collected from Aaron, Becker, Curran, and Duncan provide a unique opportunity to examine these hypotheses as part of the more general inquiry into the reward structure of the law firm.

The primary question I addressed was whether differences in organizational structure and managerial ideology in these four firms affected distribution of economic rewards. Much of the recent literature on law firm management has emphasized the importance of rewarding lawyers according to productivity, that is, according to measures of how much they contribute economically to the partnership, instead of determining income on the basis of seniority (see, e.g., Moldenhauer 1972; Heintz

190

1981, 1983). Other commentators question the economic advantages of productivity-based compensation systems, suggesting that such systems face inherent difficulties of measuring individual contributions and that lockstep seniority systems may more effectively stimulate diversification in the client base without undermining the incentives of partners to produce (Gilson and Mnookin 1985). The debate over compensation of lawyers is remarkably uninformed by data on how firms actually do compensate. The assumption appears to be that the "traditional" system of dividing profits operates by seniority, whereas the "modern" method is to reward lawyers according to objective performance measures. Such an assumption is problematic, however, for many traditional compensation systems in industry generally work on a productivity basis (piecerate and wage labor, for example) and many bureaucratic structures reward seniority. But if we accept the distinction for purposes of argument, we would expect to see differences in the reward structures in the four firms represented here.

In fact, no such differences emerge. The distribution of income follows a strikingly common pattern across the four firms: the overwhelmingly powerful predictors of income differences are seniority and client responsibility. The results suggest that both seniority and productivity have always been fundamentally important in the reward structures of firms. Thus the debate between law firm consultants tends to exaggerate the practical effects of differences in compensation systems. This is more apparent given the strong correlation between client responsibility and seniority. Regardless of managerial ideology, the law firm is, and is likely to remain, an age-graded pyramid in which older lawyers control the clients and make the most money.

The analysis of income determination presented here suffers from one significant limitation. Because of the sensitivity of the subject, I did not attempt to gather systematic income data on the elite members of firms. Thus, what I present here is an analysis of the income structure with the top removed. The disparity between the economic rewards of elites and other lawyers in firms is an important concern, and there is a widely held perception that these disparities vary considerably by firm. If such data were available one could examine more comprehensively the determinants of income differences and assess the full economic consequences of differences in organizational structure and managerial policy. Nonetheless, the data analyzed here are important in their own right. The data arguably are representative of the income dynamics of most lawyers in large firms, that is, lawyers who are not

192   Structure of the Large Law Firm

members of the organization's most elite strata. But these data also can
be seen as a measure of how elites choose to pay their colleagues.

GENERAL PATTERNS: THE MEASURES
AND PRELIMINARY MODELS

Lawyers in the cross-sectional sample were asked to divulge their
1979 income from the practice of law within a set of income categories.
(The categories began at $10,000 per year, increased by $10,000 up to
$99,000, and then by $25,000 up to $200,000, and then by $50,000
up to $300,000.) After the start of data collection at Duncan, the firm
instructed members not to answer the income question. It later provided
a ranking of groups of partners. I will discuss the analysis of these ranks
briefly after presenting the more comprehensive analyses of the data
from Aaron, Becker, and Curran.

The income data from the first three firms were converted into a
continuous variable, taking the midpoint of each category. So computed, the average income of the lawyers in the samples at the three
firms was $54,625. The average income of associates and partners
differs by more than $50,000, being $31,717 for associates and $82,181
for partners. Typical of income distributions, the distribution of law
firm incomes is positively skewed. The median for the three firms is
$42,684; the median for associates is $29,035 and for partners $78,625.
Because the log transformation of the income variable did not produce
significant improvement in the fit of various models or introduce other
dramatic changes in the estimates of our models, I use the untrans-
formed income variable throughout.[1]

The breakdown of income by number of years in practice appears
in table 21. Differences between beginning lawyers are relatively insignificant, but differences in mean income increase substantially as lawyers gain seniority, from an average income of $25,500 for associates
with one or two years in practice to a mean of $31,694 for lawyers
with three to five years experience, $45,879 for lawyers six to eight
years out, $72,411 for lawyers in practice nine to fourteen years, and
$101,517 for lawyers with fifteen years experience or more. This pattern
is quite stable across firms. The mean income for associates varies by
no more than $2,000 in the three firms and by no more than $3,600
for partners. These findings tend to confirm the long-held view that
seniority is a critical determinant of income in the firms. But the question
remains: why do firms pay their senior ranks so much more? Is it a

TABLE 21. INCOME (DOLLARS) BY YEARS IN PRACTICE*

Years in Practice	Mean Income	Median Income	N
1–2	25,500	25,500	33
3–5	31,694	33,300	31
6–8	45,879	44,736	29
9–14	72,411	68,000	28
15 and over	101,517	95,500	30
Total	54,625	42,684	151

1 case was missing information.
* Duncan is not included because of incomplete information on income.

reflection of their measurable economic contribution to the firm, as demonstrated by their responsibility for clients, their higher levels of specialization and skill, their longer hours of work? To address these issues we must move to a multivariate model of income determination which assesses the relative effects of different factors.

I examined the effect on income of six categories of independent variables of theoretical interest. Two of the variables are of course firm and seniority. The third set of variables deals directly with work output, specialization by field, and total hours worked. According to the theory of human capital, workers are compensated for their marginal contribution to the firm, that is, the net increase in value to the firm that results from adding that employee to the work force (Becker 1975). Thus a worker's income is determined by the investments the worker has made to obtain skills that are valuable to employers. Leibowitz and Tollison (1978) apply this theory to the law firm, suggesting that income differences in the various levels of seniority in firms largely reveal differences in skill levels. One way to test this hypothesis is to examine the economic returns to specialization over the course of a lawyer's career in a firm. I analyze both the direct effect of level of substantive specialization on income and the interaction effect of specialization by seniority. I have used the total number of hours worked as a measure of the volume of effort contributed.

Another contribution that affects lawyers' income is the amount of business they bring into the firm or are responsible for. McChesney argues that theories of income determination in the law firm are inadequate because they do not account for that portion of income that compensates for efforts to produce new clients (1982). While no satisfactory index of efforts to attract clients could be developed, it is possible to rank lawyers in terms of client responsibility and determine the net benefits derived from different levels of client responsibility. This is the fourth set of variables included in the model.

The last two sets of variables are field of law and social background. Chapter 4, on the organization of work, demonstrated that fields play distinctive roles in firms. It is therefore possible that the relative status of fields might show up as differences in income by specialty within particular firms. Although the social composition of firms is relatively homogeneous, given the recent entry of lower status law school graduates and women into firms, it is possible that these new categories of lawyers might be penalized. Hence, I included law school status and gender in income models to determine if they had any significant effect net of other variables.

Most of the measures of the independent variables have been discussed in previous chapters and do not require extended comment here. Seniority is measured by years in practice, ranging from 1 to 44 years for this sample, with a mean of 8.95 years. Measures of work behavior, presented in chapter 4, are the index of specialization and total hours worked in a year. Client responsibility is measured through the subjective assessments of respondents about the amount of work their clients bring to the firm. This assessment is broken down into three separate judgments: new clients they have brought to the firm, clients for whom they have regular billing responsibility, and clients for whom they are a primary contact. Lawyers were asked if they had any such client relationships, and if they did, whether the client brought only a very minor amount of business to the firm, a small but significant amount, a medium-sized or substantial volume of business, or a major amount of the firm's business. The types of client responsibility were then coded from 0 to 4, 0 indicating no client responsibility and 4 indicating responsibility for a major client. While the client responsibility measures involve subjective judgments, the questions were posed in the course of the career history portion of the interview and lawyers were probed about the timing of assuming additional responsibilities. This served to check self-aggrandizement. The distributions of the client responsibility variables are apparently valid. Only 19.2 percent reported having brought medium-sized or major new clients; 19.9 percent reported having billing responsibility for medium-sized or major clients; and 57.8 percent reported acting as a primary contact for medium-sized or major clients.

The remaining variables are categorical and were analyzed as dummy variables. Field of practice was coded in the same fashion as in the previous chapter, dividing lawyers by field (litigation, corporate, finance, and other office fields) based on time allocation. Litigation was used as the reference category; the three variables were coded 1 if lawyers spent the majority of their time in the field, 0 if they did not. Social background was measured by sex (coded 0 for men, 1 for women) and law school status (coded 0 for regional and local schools, 1 for elite or prestige schools). The variable for firm was constructed by making Curran the reference category and by coding the variables for membership in Aaron and Becker 1 for members, 0 for nonmembers.

The explanatory power of the independent variables was first examined through a set of six equations in which income was regressed on the measures of each category of independent variable and their interactions with firm. These are presented in table 22. Comparison of the R^2 values indicates substantial differences in the variance explained by the sets of independent variables. The seniority and client-responsibility variables are by far the most powerful predictors, each explaining three times more than any other set of predictors. I reserve extended discussion of these two variables until the presentation of the final model. A brief review of the impact of the independent variables taken individually provides some insights into income differences between various groups of lawyers in large law firms. It must be noted, however, that these are only interim results. The ultimate explanatory power of each set of variables is affected by the other variables included in any given model. Indeed many of the variables with significant effects in equations 1 through 6 are found not to be significant in the full model when other variables are controlled for.

Equation 1 reflects the similarities in income structure in the three firms. Firm alone explains less than 1 percent of the total variance in income; none of the differences between firms were significant.[2] Equation 2 reports the strong effect of seniority on income. Years in practice and its interactions with firm explain 64 percent of the variance in income. In contrast, the work variables are not very powerful, explaining only 11 percent of the variance.

Equation 3 suggests that it does not pay to work long hours. Although none of the coefficients are statistically significant, the equation estimates that lawyers at Curran make $10 less for each hour they work and that lawyers at Aaron and Becker make $26 and $30 less for each hour they work. The reason for this inscrutable result is the long

TABLE 22.   INCOME (IN DOLLARS) REGRESSED
ON SETS OF INDEPENDENT VARIABLES

Equation 1: Income Regressed on Firm

	Beta	Standard error	Standardized beta	T Significance
(Constant)	50,455.56	5,087.91		.000
Aaron	3,886.55	7,519.46	.0496	.606
Becker	7,044.44	6,539.84	.1034	.283

R^2 = 0.008, Overall F significance = .560, N = 151.

Equation 2: Income Regressed on Years in Practice and Interactions with Firm*

	Beta	Standard error	Standardized beta	T Significance
(Constant)	24,636.28	2,504.40		.000
Years	3,802.67	382.80	.938	.000
A Years	−276.04	445.56	−.042	.537
B Years	−753.30	376.04	−.185	.047

R^2 = .641, Overall F significance = .000, N = 151.

Equation 3: Income Regressed on Work Variables (Specialization Index and Total Hours
Worked in Year) and Interactions with Firm*

	Beta	Standard error	Standardized beta	T Significance
(Constant)	122,220.89	19,482.67		.000
Specialization	−613.98	260.70	−.296	.020
Total hours	−10.37	8.49	−.131	.224
A Specialization index	493.30	373.52	.474	.189
A Total hours	−16.46	13.09	−.432	.208
B Specialization index	596.12	309.41	.711	.056
B Total hours	−20.02	10.92	−.612	.069

R^2 = .110, Overall F significance = .012, N = 144.

Equation 4: Income Regressed on Client Responsibility Variables (New Clients, Billing
Responsibility, and Primary Contact) and Interactions with Firm*

	Beta	Standard error	Standardized beta	T Significance
(Constant)	31,815.25	3,360.07		.000
New clients	364.58	4,575.14	.012	.937
Billing responsibility	17,040.42	4,139.06	.655	.000

TABLE 22. (continued)

	Beta	Standard error	Standardized beta	T Significance
Primary contact	−3,116.73	2,671.64	−.146	.245
A New clients	16,872.80	7,766.21	.348	.032
A Billing responsibility	−7,882.25	7,053.30	−.173	.266
A Primary contact	3,361.77	3,537.21	.109	.343
B New clients	12,713.38	5,449.45	.308	.021
B Billing responsibility	−12,588.81	5,168.98	−.268	.016
B Primary contact	8,967.43	2,795.56	.435	.002

$R^2 = .555$, Overall F significance $= .000$, N $= 143$.

Equation 5: Income Regressed on Field of Practice and Interactions with Firm*

	Beta	Standard error	Standardized beta	T Significance
(Constant)	50,292.68	3,681.75		.000
Corporate	57,040.65	19,597.60	.708	.004
Finance	54,207.32	23,860.45	.477	.025
Other	16,807.32	15,357.79	.167	.276
A Corporate	−57,690.48	23,006.54	−.356	.013
A Finance	−56,500.00	28,872.97	−.267	.052
A Other	−11,850.00	19,006.52	−.078	.534
B Corporate	−49,073.33	20,370.86	−.536	.017
B Finance	−56,000.00	26,062.79	−.390	.033
B Other	−4,528.57	19,521.69	−.028	.817

$R^2 = .098$, Overall F significance $= .092$, N $= 151$.

Equation 6: Income Regressed on Social Background Variables (Sex and Law School Status) and Interactions with Firm*

	Beta	Standard error	Standardized beta	T Significance
(Constant)	54,297.64	3,015.96		.000
Women	−9,545.57	9,862.93	−.103	.335
Elite/prestige	−14,024.86	23,156.15	−.145	.546
A Women	−21,167.41	18,827.22	−.100	.263
A Elite/prestige	60,686.21	26,201.35	.375	.022
B Women	−19,796.59	14,907.27	−.130	.186
B Elite/prestige	31,202.93	24,834.20	.257	.211

$R^2 = .152$, Overall F significance $= .001$, N $= 151$.

* A denotes interaction with Aaron; B denotes interaction with Becker.

198   Structure of the Large Law Firm

hours that associates work and their lower income, which produces
an estimate of negative returns to hours worked. Nor does it pay to
specialize. The regression coefficient for the index of specialization estimates a loss of some $600 as a lawyer moves from general practice
to specializing in one field at the Curran firm. The loss is substantially
less at the Becker firm, only $20 ($614–$596), and at Aaron, only $120
($614–$493).

Client responsibility is almost as powerful a predictor of income as
seniority, even though it is measured rather crudely through three or-
dinal scales and even though the elites, lawyers with the most client
responsibility, are not included in this sample. The client-responsibility
variables and their interactions with firm explain 55.5 percent of income
variation. Based on explanatory power alone, we can see that client
responsibility and seniority are positively correlated. Field of practice
is not a significant determinant of income, as indicated by the borderline
significance of equation 5. The social background variables (see equation 6) explain 15.2 percent of the variance in income. The only term
that is statistically significant is the interaction between membership in
Aaron and graduation from an elite law school. While the lawyers in
Curran with elite law school credentials are estimated to make $14,024
less than the graduates of regional and local schools, at Aaron they are
estimated to make over $46,000 more. It should be noted that Curran
has the largest proportion of lawyers from regional and local schools.
Aaron has the smallest proportion of low-status graduates, having begun to admit them in recent years. Hence, the differential observed at
Aaron is between the associates from regional and local schools and
partners from elite law schools, while in Curran there are a number of
partners from regional and local schools who make more than associates from higher status schools.

THE FULL MODEL

A full model of income determination was constructed by including
all statistically significant terms from the initial equations reported in
table 22 and then eliminating those that were no longer significant at
the .05 level or that did not contribute a minimum of 1 percent variance
explained (Althauser 1971). The effects of higher order interactions
between independent variables were also tested, as were terms for the
nonlinear effects of the continuous variables. The final model is pre-

sented in table 23, which achieves an excellent fit, explaining 79.3 percent of the variance in income at the three firms.

We must note immediately the variables that do not appear because they lack explanatory power net of other variables. Notably absent are differences by firm, field of specialization, hours worked, and social background. The model estimates that lawyers start out making an average of $22,214 a year and receive an additional $2,479 for each year in practice net of other variables (that is, after controlling for the effect of other variables). Hence, over the course of a thirty-year career, a lawyer's earnings are estimated to grow by almost $65,000. Moving up the ranks of responsibility for billing clients nets $4,760; thus a change from no billing responsibility to billing major clients of the firm is estimated to be worth $19,040. The coefficients for the interactions between firm and client responsibility are consistent with the analysis of the nature of the client base in the three firms presented in earlier chapters. Those lawyers at Aaron who have brought in new clients have gained a substantially larger income. The difference between lawyers who have brought no new clients to the firm and those bringing a major client is estimated to be $47,396, controlling for other variables. In Becker bringing in new clients has not netted significant rewards, but maintaining existing clients by acting as a primary contact has. Control-

TABLE 23. THE FINAL MODEL OF INCOME*

	Beta	Standard error	Standardized beta	T Significance
(Constant)	22,214.02	2,192.33		.000
Years	2,479.31	193.77	.607	.000
Billing responsibility	4,759.93	1,311.24	.183	.000
Corporate	28,757.44	10,216.73	.354	.006
Finance	33,295.81	12,029.47	.298	.007
A New clients	11,874.31	2,034.39	.244	.000
B Primary contact	4,679.25	1,163.82	.227	.000
A Corporate	−34,790.16	12,597.34	−.187	.007
A Finance	−57,044.63	14,691.02	−.275	.000
B Corporate	−38,038.63	11,506.66	−.423	.001
B Finance	−33,021.25	13,426.82	−.235	.015

R^2 = .793, Overall F significance = .000, N = 142.

* A denotes interaction with Aaron, B denotes interaction with Becker.

ling for other variables, lawyers with primary contacts for a major client are expected to receive $18,716 more than those with no responsibility as a primary contact. This is the pattern to be expected in a firm that has a large institutional client base. Although few lawyers bring in major new clients to such a firm, responsibility for keeping clients is a more prevalent source of economic benefits.

The coefficients concerning field of practice primarily reflect idiosyncrasies resulting from the small number of cases involved when interaction effects are tested. The coefficients for finance and corporate practice suggest the greater monetary rewards of working in those fields. But because the coefficients for the interactions between those fields and membership in Aaron and Becker are negative and, in all but one case, of greater magnitude than the direct effects of practicing in the finance or corporate fields, the six field variables in the equation indicate that lawyers in finance and corporate fields in Curran make substantially more than those in litigation. Even though the differences in income are statistically significant, they must be regarded as tentative because of the small number of respondents in Curran who have practices outside the litigation area.

The final model reasserts the significance of seniority as a determinant of income in the large law firm. Dropping any other term from the final model results in a reduction of explained variance of less than 5 percent. Dropping years in practice reduces the variance explained by 25 percent, meaning that almost one-third of the income variance is explained uniquely by the seniority variable. This finding holds even if associates are dropped from the analysis. For partners alone the final model explains 68.9 percent of the variance in income. If years in practice is eliminated from the equation, however, the variance explained drops to 47.2 percent. Moreover, the standardized beta for years in practice is .607, two or three times higher than most other effects.

The more limited data on Duncan exhibit a profoundly seniority-specified income structure as well. In predicting the rank of the partners by income (among a total of eight ranks), years in practice alone accounts for 78.5 percent of the variance. That such a high proportion of variance is explained is remarkable given the limitation of the variance in the dependent variable to a small number of ranks and the limitation in the range for years in practice because only partners are included. Moreover, no other variables had statistically significant effects on income when entered simultaneously with years in practice.

Below the level of the elite, the reward system of the large law firm is fundamentally a seniority system. Seniority uniquely explains five times more variance than any other variable. Moreover, it correlates significantly with other explanatory factors. The lawyers in the fields commanding higher income tend to be older than the lawyers in other fields, such as litigation, in particular, which contains a large number of associates. Client responsibility follows an age curve. Years in practice correlates positively with billing responsibility ($r = .354$), acting as a primary contact at Becker ($r = .312$), and bringing in new clients at Aaron ($r = .241$). Unlike the age-income curve for the population in general, earnings do not decline throughout the period of active practice (Mincer 1974). Despite differences in practice and organizational structure this pattern does not vary substantially across firms. The only effects of firm are through interactions with client responsibility, indicating that client responsibility takes a different form in different firms. Where firms have substantial new clients, lawyers are rewarded for attracting them to the firm; where firms predominantly rely on long-standing clients, lawyers are rewarded for maintaining those relationships.

These findings cast doubt on the theory that income differences within firms can be explained by differences in the skills that lawyers accumulate over the course of their careers in firms. Leibowitz and Tollison (1978) argue that during the first three years of practice associates learn only general skills. It is not until later in a lawyer's career that the firm is willing to invest in more specific training for an associate or that the associate is willing to invest in firm-specific skills that may be less transferable outside the firm. The result of this pattern of investment in learning is to shift the earnings curve back; as a result partners reap the return on their investment in human capital later in their careers and associates make less in their early years. Leibowitz and Tollison present no direct data for the nature of work done, the degree to which it is specialized, or the processes of skill acquisition, but they confidently conclude from data on the stream of income that contrary to popular belief associates are not "exploited" by firms.

The meaning of "exploitation" in this context is not entirely clear. Associates beginning in large firms may be making rational economic choices, in that the present value of their expected earnings (appropriately discounted for the costs of education and the probability of making partner) is at least comparable to that presented by alternative career paths. But the evidence supporting a learning model in Leibowitz and Tollison's analysis is hardly convincing. While Leibowitz and Tollison employ no direct measures of work behavior, the income patterns in the four-firm sample quite clearly demonstrate that specialization by field, even when multiplied by years in practice, does not have a statistically significant effect after controlling for the direct effect of seniority. Specialization by field of law does not tap the full range of skills that lawyers develop over the course of a career in a firm. Qualities of judgment and knowledge of the inner workings of the firm and its clients are possible dimensions of "skill" which could explain income differences based on learning. I am willing to admit that skills accumulate over time. What I dispute is the bold assertion that associates do not provide firms with specialized skills until several years have passed, which implies that associates are not an important source of surplus for the partnership. Beginning associates, especially in litigation, may not be given "responsible" tasks, but they develop all kinds of specialized knowledge. Indeed, the chief problem from the associates' point of view is that they can only develop firm-specific knowledge, such as knowledge of the working habits of a particular partner or the documents in a particular case, rather than the kinds of general skills that would allow them to work more independently.

What data we have suggests that the exchange between the firm and the associate is almost immediately profitable to the firm. Surveys of medium and large firms indicate that starting associates often bill as much as 2,000 hours per year at $75 to $80 per hour, generating between $150,000 and $160,000 (*American Bar Association Journal 1985*, pp. 42–43; Darby 1985). With starting salaries in the range of $40,000 to $65,000 a year, and allowing for overhead costs, firms extract a huge surplus from the work of associates. Whether you call it exploitation of associates, exploitation of clients, or just good business, partners net substantial profits from the labor of their associates over and above the earnings that accrue from the partners' accumulated skill.

Despite the widespread discussion of new techniques for distributing income in law partnerships, there is little evidence of change in the four law firms in my sample. In traditional and bureaucratic firms alike, economic rewards are determined on the basis of seniority and client responsibility. The number of hours lawyers work or their degree of specialization by field does not have a significant effect on earnings. Although we observe some significant differences by field of law in certain firms, these appear to be idiosyncratic to this sample and to the distribution of cases by field in one of the firms. When we consider the relationship between seniority and client responsibility, it is clear that law firms remain age-stratified organizations. The growth of firms in recent decades has worked to the advantage of the most senior members. They have reaped profits from the efforts of the growing number of lawyers in the firm who are their juniors in terms of years and client responsibility.

The most telling indication of this pattern is the sheer explanatory power of years in practice. Seniority alone explains almost two-thirds of the variance in income, whereas when all other significant variables are added to the model the variance explained only increases some 15 percent. It may be that the explanatory power of client responsibility is not accurately represented by the results from the cross-section because elites are not included in this analysis. Nonetheless, below the level of the elite, client responsibility and other variables do not add greatly to the explanatory power of seniority.

Still, the outpouring of consultants' recommendations and scattered reports in the legal press suggest a trend toward compensation systems that weigh client responsibility more heavily, or at least these reports identify increasing agitation by young client-producers about the earnings of older, less productive members of firms. The managing partner in Kirkland & Ellis described a change in the firm's compensation formula giving increased weight to client production as a response to the demands of young partners: "We're concerned about the younger people and have to take into account who is making the firm prosperous" (*Chicago Sun-Times,* January 19, 1981). This response may not be entirely altruistic. Older client-producers probably benefit from the new formula as well. Winston and Strawn announced a similar policy change, denominating the leading client-producers "capital partners" and the rest "noncapital partners" (*Crain's Chicago Business,* July 30, 1979, pp. 1, 28). Many of the reports of dissension in firms, such as that which occurred in Donovan & Leisure and Ross & Hardies (see chap. 1), were precipitated by conflicts over compensation policies and over the status of partners who did not bring in substantial amounts of business. As firms adopt a more entrepreneurial approach to management, the trend toward compensation formulas emphasizing client production will gain momentum. For firms to attract partners laterally or to negotiate mergers with smaller firms, they will necessarily move away from seniority-based systems to systems that peg partnership shares to revenue production. Indeed, one of the chief means of attracting younger specialists from established firms will be the opportunity to escape a seniority-based system that limits their access to additional client responsibility and constrains future earnings.

The resilience of the seniority-based income structure in the four firms provides more evidence that social change in the law partnership has taken place only gradually. The structure of inequality among lawyers remains much the same as in the past: we still see an age-graded pyramid in which the older lawyers control the clients and the profits. Even at Duncan, the firm with a bureaucratic managerial ideology, there is no indication that the income of the rank and file is determined by any factor other than seniority. The distribution of economic rewards may be one aspect of organizational structure which is slow to change in any organization. Bread-and-butter issues typically provoke the most active response from organization participants. Fearing the reaction, leaders of firms might well hesitate before cutting the points of older partners. In a relatively small organization that depends on interpersonal relationships between members to coordinate the work process, this hesitancy may be all the more important. But other factors are also involved in the slow pace of change.

First, the client base of firms changes only gradually, so more senior lawyers are still more likely to have greater client responsibility than younger lawyers. Second, the image of the partnership as a professional community in which all partners have rights to participation remains an important aspect of the ideology of the law firm (see chap. 6). Members take pride in belonging to "a leading firm." Its leaders invoke "the firm's" high standards of professionalism and its distinctive style of practice as a means of maintaining the enthusiastic commitment of the professional staff to their work. It would be inconsistent with this ideology to impose a purely economic criterion in distributing profits. The irony is that in such a close community the realities of economic and political power are always in danger of being made immediate when a lawyer demands more money or a seat on the governing committee. This has begun happening more frequently as a number of firms have encountered economic difficulties and as firms have begun to bid for well-known specialists in other firms. Hence, the continuing commercialization of corporate legal services may provoke a redefinition of the ideal of the firm as a professional community and the gradual decline of seniority as the principal determinant of income. That this redefinition has not yet taken place in more firms demands more than economic theory. It requires a theory of authority in the law firm.

6
Professionalism, Bureaucracy, and Commitment: Authority in the Large Law Firm

I have argued throughout this book that the large law firm is caught in a conflict between bureaucracy and professionalism. Despite pressures for bureaucratization resulting from dramatic changes in the market and in the dimensions of the organization, firms have remained creatures of professional tradition. Even though there has been significant differentiation within firms, both horizontally by department and vertically in terms of the power and earnings of the various strata of lawyers, firms retain their traditional professional form, the partnership, and many of the implied norms of collegiality and partner participation. Even though firms have become more specialized, both because the market for corporate legal services has shifted in the direction of special representation and because firms demand higher levels of specialization from lawyers as a means of increasing efficiency, work still is performed on a custom basis, according to a status-based division of labor. Thus, the quality of the work product depends on the skill, commitment, and resources of the lawyers doing the work.

The question that now arises is how firms have accommodated these conflicting tendencies and how they will do so in the future as the pressure for change mounts. The answer that Smigel (1969) and a number of organization theorists (see, e.g., Satow 1975; Ouchi 1980) propose is that law firms are structured by the values of the professional group. Because professional values predominate, firms will remain essentially nonbureaucratic in form or will at most assume a hybrid structure, what Smigel called the professional bureaucracy (1969, pp. 275–286). This interpretation has significant implications. If professional values control the course of organizational development in firms, the organization will then enhance the professional autonomy of its members. As a consequence, lawyers practicing in large law firms should be in a better position to exert a positive moral influence on the powerful corporate actors they represent.

This is an idealized and incomplete conception of the relationship between professionalism and the structure of the firm. Rather than relying on a direct relationship between professional values and the structure of the firm, we must consider the role that professionalism plays in the authority structure of the firm. Who in the organization defines what professionalism means and what are the implications of their definition for how the firm will be organized? In short, it is necessary to examine the relationship between professional ideology and what I have called patterns of organizational dominance. How does the definition of professionalism relate to the position of the large law firm as the dominant organization in the market for legal services and how do conceptions of professionalism affect relationships between lawyers inside law firms? Through the analysis of these questions we can develop a far more satisfactory explanation of the relationship between bureaucracy and professionalism in the large law firm than did Smigel. The organizational dominance perspective allows for the possibility that the elites of firms can redefine professionalism to suit their own interests, including the introduction of bureaucratic managerial practices, while at the same time attempting to appeal to partners, associates, and clients in traditional professional terms.

While this approach answers one set of questions about the relationship between bureaucracy and professionalism in law firms, it raises two others. First, if the large firm is not held together by a consensus on professional values, what explains the lawyers' commitment to their firm? And second, if the meaning of professionalism can be redefined by firm leaders, why has the bureaucratization of firms been so limited? The answers to these questions challenge some significant elements of the literature on professional organizations. Contrary to much of the earlier literature positing an antagonism between professionals and bureaucratic organization, I find that the bureaucratic firms can command higher levels of career commitment from their associates than the traditional firms. Moreover, I argue that the ultimate constraint on bureaucratization in the law firm may derive from structure rather than attitude. Because managerial authority in the firm is subject to the control of client-responsible lawyers, it is constrained by the balance of power between partners with client responsibility. The dominance of the firm by those lawyers most strongly identified with major clients also calls into question the extent to which the law firm will foster the autonomy of practitioners from clients.

AUTHORITY IN THE LAW FIRM

POWER, EXCHANGE, AND AUTHORITY

All organizations exhibit the dynamics of inequality and power. Some persons or groups have greater influence over the distribution of scarce resources than others do. The sociological question is how a pattern of domination arises, how it functions, and why. The three variables central to theories of social hierarchy are power, exchange, and authority (Weber 1978). Power refers to the ability to coerce behavior; exchange refers to the economic transactions between actors; and authority refers to the processes by which subordinates willfully obey the directives of leaders, accepting their position and commands as legitimate (see generally Wrong 1968; Lukes 1974). Debates over the nature of social organization concern what weight to attach to each of these variables in different societies, organizations, and historical periods.

The first question to consider here is whether we need be concerned with authority as an explanation of relationships between lawyers within law firms. One could argue that law firms are best understood economically. Accordingly, relationships between lawyers are determined by market forces and the contracts they freely enter into with each other. Yet many aspects of law firm organization seem inconsistent with economic models. The market for corporate legal services has a distinctive "atmosphere," to use Williamson's (1975) term, such that transactions between producers and consumers are governed by professional norms and typically are brokered through networks of mutual relationships (see chap. 1). Leaders of firms reject seemingly simple organizational innovations on grounds that they contradict professional norms. Lawyers in different firms work different hours for the same pay and exude an enthusiastic identification with work that goes beyond a rational economic calculus. Something more than economics is operating in these organizations.

One could also argue that recourse to the slippery and ephemeral concept of authority is not necessary in professional organizations. It has been suggested that relationships between professionals do not involve patterns of deference between superordinates and subordinates but merely the assertion of power by dominant groups (Bucher and Stelling 1969). The firm is a kingdom; the lords are those who control clients. While I have suggested that the distribution of client-control—the most palpable source of power in firms—is vitally important in explaining how firms are governed, it is not a full answer. The partners who control the business depend on the work of other firm members. Lawyers in firms do not grudgingly perform their tasks. On the contrary, they work diligently to serve clients and make a contribution to the organization. More than power and money are necessary to explain hierarchical relations in firms.

In order to fully understand the nature of these hierarchical relationships within law firms, we must develop a theory of authority which explains the patterns of deference, mutual obligation, and commitment we observe among the members of the law firm. A pivotal concept in my analysis is what I call the ideology of professionalism. Professionalism as a sociological concept has many dimensions and is used at several levels of analysis. Hence, it can refer to the political, institutional, and economic structure of professional occupations in society (Larson 1977), the cultural meanings society attaches to professional status (Bledstein 1976; Starr 1982, pp. 13–17), or the attributes of individuals and the way they do their work ("they are real professionals"). I use professionalism to refer to the set of norms and values that justify (to clients and recruits) the privileged position of large law firms in the market for legal services and that define the status of individuals within the organization.

In its traditional (and no doubt idealized) form the ideology of professionalism defined the practice of law in the large law firm as a craft performed by a professional elite, who, while primarily serving business clients, organized their firms to accord with their own distinctive set of professional values—including the control by individual lawyers of the work they do, deference to other partners as equals in the organization, and an orientation to public service—rather than economic norms of profit maximizing. This traditional ideology could legitimate both the higher standing of law firms in the profession as a whole and patterns of paternalistic relationships between lawyers within leading firms based on the belief that high status (both within the broader professional community and within the firm) was an appropriate reward for superior knowledge, skill, and judgment. While significant elements of the traditional model of professionalism remain, as the disparities in the earnings and functions of lawyers within firms have become more apparent and as firms have moved inexorably toward more bureaucratic organizational structures, there has been a subtle shift in the content of this professional ideology and in the relationship between professional ideology and managerial practice. Increasingly, the appeal to professionalism by the leaders of firms is being used to legitimate the rationalization of the organization. Thus at the same time the leaders of firms invoke the imagery of the traditional model of professionalism, they are moving the organization farther away from the traditional model of the law firm.

The Prior Literature and Authority in Professional Organizations

The concept of professionalism developed here differs from the treatment of professional values in much of the literature on professional organizations, notably Smigel's study of Wall Street law firms (1969). Smigel began with much the same premise as I do. He too was struck by the paradox that firms were able to orchestrate a highly specialized set of activities with a minimum of rules (1969, pp. 249–287). But instead of developing a theory of authority that addressed the nature of relationships between lawyers within firms, he limited the discussion to the power of client-responsible lawyers (1969, pp. 234–236) and the consensus among lawyers about how the organization should be run. He attributed the latter to a number of factors outside the organization itself, including "external professional controls, both formal and informal" (1969, pp. 250–287). Hence, Smigel never explicitly addressed the ideology that mediated between the power of the client-responsible elite and the asserted consensus on organization policies. And the cohesiveness that explained the relative lack of rules he determined to originate outside the firm, in the profession's code of ethics and the cultural milieu of prestigious corporate practice.

This interpretation of the social organization of professional firms has been widely cited in the professions and organizations literature. Montagna (1968) applied the same conception to Big Eight accounting firms. Studies of medical clinics (Goss 1961, 1963), hospitals (Bucher and Stelling 1969), and social agencies (Scott 1965) also find that professional organizations deviate from the ideal type of bureaucratic organization because of the presence of professionals. Satow (1975) uses these findings on professional firms as evidence of the existence of a fundamentally different organizational form, the value-rational organization, in which organization members give allegiance not to the rules of the organization but to a set of norms that supersede (and thus determine the structure of) the organization.

Ouchi and his colleagues develop a variation on this theme, arguing that nonhierarchical organizational structures that emphasize the pursuit of organization goals over adherence to rules offer distinct advantages over bureaucratic organization (Ouchi 1980; Ouchi and Johnson 1978). Ouchi's analysis differs from those of Satow, Smigel, and Montagna in that he locates the origin of goals within the organization, but he conveys the same optimism that goals can be translated into organized activities without the development of a structure of domination. The research on professional organizations has led to rather far-reaching speculation in organization theory about the relative advantages of such nonbureaucratic forms, even to the prediction that because of their greater adaptability they may become a dominant organizational form in postindustrial society (Scott 1981, pp. 286–289; Swanson 1980).

The model of the professional firm presented in this literature is consistent with many of my findings on law firms. A distinguishing characteristic of professional organizations is the relative lack of rules. Professional practice in the large law firm, in accounting firms, in hospitals depends on the discretion and judgment of the professional. Whatever rules are formulated in professional organizations attempt to control the organizational context of work but not the content of work itself (Freidson 1970a, p. 142). This in part results from the relative power of professionals vis-à-vis the organization (see Bidwell and Vreeland 1963) but also from the nature of the work itself. Given the largely nonroutine and situation-specific nature of decisions that lawyers make in corporate practice, they must exercise considerable discretion (Perrow 1970, pp. 80–85). Beyond these basic points of agreement, however, I find a number of difficulties with the model.

First, the model exaggerates the differences between the authority structures of bureaucratic and collegial organizations. Even in bureaucratic organizations, such as in industry or on the shop floor of a factory, there is an ideological system that legitimates organizational rules (see Bendix [1956] 1974; Burawoy 1979). It is not only in professional organizations that leaders must be responsive to norms that supersede the organization (see Selznick 1968). Second, the conception of the professional firm portrayed in the literature tends to minimize the degree of hierarchy in groups of professionals and the observed or potential level of conflict between these groups. The literature typically assumes that the leaders of professional organizations derive their authority from professional competence, that is, from the recognition by their peers that their knowledge and skill entitles them to command. While this accurately distinguishes professional organizations from bureaucracies, where authority derives from office, it ignores the possibility that the definition of professional competence may in part be ideological or that there might be serious conflict over what is or is not "professional." Despite the common assertions of firms that policies are made by consensus, I suggest that there are serious tensions between groups of lawyers in most firms. Indeed, I suggest that appeals to professionalism frequently are used to channel or defuse potential conflicts within the law firm.

Third, this literature incorrectly identifies the relationship between structure and professional values. Research has assumed that professional values structure the organization, without considering the possibility that the structure of the organization may tend to reproduce certain kinds of professional values. As I will demonstrate, professional values are at least in part produced inside the organization and may therefore be used to legitimate the bureaucratization of the law firm.

The Partnership: A Collegial Form

It is appropriate for an analysis of authority in the law firm to begin by considering the legal form that defines the rights and privileges of organization participants and that expresses the spirit of relationships within the organization. The partnership is an economic and legal form embodying principles of collegiality, or mutual obligation. At some level all partners in a law firm are equal: they have tenure, they have a right to share profits, their income from the practice of law goes into a common pot, they are liable as a group for the debts and misfortunes of the firm, and they have various rights spelled out in a partnership agreement.[1] Although associates are legally employees of the firm, they are prospective members of the partnership and thereby enjoy a measure of the same relationship with partners. With the exception of the large professional organizations in such fields as law, architecture, and accounting, the partnership form is usually limited to small groups. There-

212   Structure of the Large Law Firm

fore, as a matter of practical operation and legal theory, a partnership presumes close relationships between members. A retired member of the elite elaborated on the significance of this orientation for the hierarchical relationships between partners.

> When a firm is small—and this was the way it was in this firm—the lawyers are very close. In fact the whole idea of a partnership in legal theory . . . is the notion that the people who are partners are very close to one another. In fact, the next closest thing is something like a family relationship. People are members of the firm almost like they are relatives of a family. And you respect and give rights to people on the basis of an ongoing relationship, not on the basis of a document or a formal agreement. This firm certainly was sort of like a family in the old days. You never had . . . a five to one vote on different matters. You wouldn't do that. You wouldn't oppose the strong feelings of another lawyer if you thought it would result in a schism. It is almost like . . . you don't force something on your wife that she doesn't want to do.

Nonetheless, even in small partnerships, a few lawyers played the dominant role—not unlike the father does in many families. As this same informant recalled: "In the old days there were always one or two strong people. And if it was known what they had decided, everybody went along with it without discussion. Frequently, they decided things all by themselves, so that really there was no issue as to who should make a decision."

Patterns of leadership take on a new dimension as partnerships grow and differentiate. The relations between the strata can no longer be rationalized as they might be in a patriarchy. Hence, as the roles of leading partners diverge from the rest of the firm, a new authority system must take its place. Some of the conflicting tendencies that accompany growth were expressed in the same interview:

> [The firm is in] a schizophrenic situation. . . . We have a set of partners who are partners in the firm in a formal sense, but they really are not partners in the firm. They make a hell of a lot less money. They have a hell of a lot less say in how the firm is run. Maybe it would be better if the firm [were] organized so that there was just a chairman of the board and there were offices like there are in a corporation. Maybe that would help to run things more smoothly. The problem is that a lot of partners are not equal anyway.

The remarks illustrate some of the tensions in governance addressed in chapter 2. Even in firms with relatively closed governance systems, leaders are concerned to preserve collegiality, but at the same time equal, even significant, participation in governance becomes next to impossible. In an effort to preserve collegiality, the governing elite tend to minimize the distinctiveness of their leadership role. They see themselves as partners, possibly as a group of first among equals, but not as officials. A long-standing member of a group of partners whom I later learned had virtually unchecked control over the division of profits and general policy-making in a firm would not recognize the leadership role in his firm:

> Q. Are there any regular working groups or departments in the firm?
>
> A. There are departments, but there are no heads of departments. There are also a number of committees in the firm, but there are no chairmen of them. Even on the [governing committee] there is no chairman. . . .
>
> Q. If there are really no leaders, it strikes me that there must be some kind of informal leadership network in the firm. How are decisions made?
>
> A. The committees who are in charge of various matters make preliminary decisions on a course of action, but then the entire firm votes on it. . . .
>
> Q. Have you noticed any opinion leaders in the firm who tend to have greater influence over various subject matters?
>
> A. No, no, I really haven't . . .
>
> Q. What you're telling me suggests that there is hardly any hierarchy in the partnership at this firm.
>
> A. Yes, that is correct. That is how we like to run things here.

"That is how we like to run things here." A wonderful sentence with which to conclude the denial of power. The more typical leader's point of view is to recognize the leadership role but to justify it as a responsibility to other members of the firm. For example, the leader of a medium-sized firm that merged with a larger firm expressed his reasons for seeking a merger as well as his dismay at the reactions of associates and younger partners:

> I mean, that was something that surprised me, how they reacted. . . . I was doing this for them, and at first they didn't realize it. They misread the situation. It was really all for their benefit, to make a more exciting kind of practice, with good people to work with, and a very stable future. But they missed it at first. They thought it was something I was doing to them for my own benefit.

The leaders of law firms, like leaders in other organizations, indeed in whole societies, justify their position of authority as being in the best interest of the group as a whole.

Members of the elite often spoke of the necessity of making policies that unified the partnership. In the words of one lawyer, "Leadership that gets too far from the preferences of the rest of the partners is not good leadership." Hence, even though the leaders of firms increasingly assume an explicitly managerial role in which they dictate the direction of the firm's practice and the internal organization of work, they continue to foster and appeal to bonds of partnership with their colleagues. This approach may result from the internalization of the norms of partnership, from the relative weakness of the elite stratum in a client-oriented structure, or from a purposive strategy to attempt to maintain high levels of commitment and cohesiveness in a potentially volatile organization. Whatever its origins, the principle of consensus affects the style if not the substance of managerial decision making in firms.

THE APPEAL OF PROFESSIONALISM

Professionalism is the binding ideology of the law firm. It is the rationale for the highly specialized role large firms play in the market for corporate services. In various forms it justifies the organization of careers, work, and rewards in firms.

The Appeal to Clients. The large law firm occupies a privileged position in the market for legal services. It charges top-dollar prices to corporations for high-quality, custom service. As inside counsel in corporations have taken over the high-volume, routine aspects of corporate practice, the practice in large firms has become highly specialized. In the face of this increased competition from internal legal staffs, firms have had to justify the extraordinary cost of their services in terms of their unique competence. As a leading member of a large firm suggested, the future of large firms depends on staying "special."

Q. What do you think the future of large firms is, given the development of internal legal departments?

A. The large law firm will survive because it will offer top skills that are not available inside the corporation. I would say there are two major factors. First of all, I think there is the factor of talent. Private firms can still attract the best talent coming out of law schools, and as a result, they will have more sheer brain power than internal corporate departments.... Second, the law firm can keep a stable of experts.... There is no way a corporate legal department can match the performance of a law firm who has a specialist spending virtually all of [his or her] time in certain areas. Essentially, I think the survival of the large law firm will depend on its being good. And I am fairly confident that it will remain so.

The law firm must remain the ultimate professional. It must offer legal services that clients think are nonfungible because the lawyers providing them are so smart, so expert, or so influential.

The Appeal within the Firm. Being special is not only an external image. Large firms rely on professionalism as a culture of motivation within the firm. As an attorney with supervisory responsibility suggested: "We have quite a bit of looseness in the way we let attorneys work. We feel that an attorney will do better if let alone to a certain extent. It helps him to mature. And if he is happy, he will do better work." Autonomy is thought to increase productivity. But is it the same broad-ranging autonomy that we associate with the image of the free professional? Clearly not. There are inescapable tensions because the professional expertise of lawyers must be channeled into the fields a firm needs. The same interviewee continues:

Q. [There] seems like something of a paradox [here]. How can you both maximize freedom and yet move people around in an efficient way to handle specialized matters?

A. I think the paradox is only apparent.... There really is a great deal of personal freedom. It is not the kind of freedom that will allow the person who wants to do everything—both practice in litigation, finance, real estate, securities, public utilities regulation. If someone does that, they won't learn anything, they won't develop skills, they won't mature as persons. It would really be a very destructive kind of general practice.... What generally develops here is that an individual will choose a field to work in, so that he will develop a cluster of specialties or subspecialties. And within the area of related work, he can move around. But if you are talking about a general practice, no. There is no problem of a lack of individual freedom except in the case of the crazy person.

The professionalism of the large firm is structured professionalism. As the argument is presented to the associate entering the large firm, it is only responsible, only "professional," in the modern era to choose a specialty, perhaps even a subspecialty. In this fashion the firm attempts

216   Structure of the Large Law Firm

to resolve the fundamental dilemma of controlling the professional
work process and appealing to a sense of professionalism in motivating
high quality performance. In a highly specialized organization of work,
the client-producers in the firm can encourage the individual initiative
and professional responsibility of lawyers by invoking the image of the
autonomous professional. Hence, as Larson (1977) suggests, the ideal
of individual professional freedom that has proved so attractive to
generations of upwardly mobile Americans can be harnessed to serve
the ends of the organization.

Firms pursue different theories of how best to ensure the desired
exercise of discretion; as a result firms use varying approaches to recruits and young associates. Some firms emphasize quality by recruiting
the top talent; other firms take lawyers of lesser academic standing and
emphasize organization to achieve a high degree of specialization. A
partner at Becker contrasted the approach his firm follows in the recruitment and training of associates from that followed at Duncan:

> I think there is a particular strength in recruiting law students [and] being
> able to say there is not a binding choice of specialty [required in the
> firm]. . . . I've noticed that those who are most aware of the issue, and who
> ask about it, tend to be the most intelligent and the brightest kind of recruits,
> both in terms of academic credentials and in terms of their performance
> once they enter the firm. . . . There are some [entering] people who desire
> more structure and a greater degree of specialty earlier on. And I think it is
> attributable to fear of the firm—that they want to find a niche. Now other
> firms can make use of those people. They tell me that they will take people
> with somewhat lower grade records and will turn them into very useful
> attorneys. [At the Duncan firm] I think they take it almost as a point of
> pride that they will train people with somewhat lower records and turn them
> into good lawyers.

This articulates a particular strategy and a particular ideological appeal.
A recruit's expression of interest in a period of general practice is seen
as a mark of intellectual strength and professional promise. Duncan's
less status-conscious strategy of intensive specialization is dismissed as
déclassé. My interviews at Duncan confirmed the firm's positive promotion of the notion that specialization benefits associates by making
them expert within a shorter time than would be possible in other firms.
They are then said to be able to take on client responsibility sooner.
This ideology inside the firm also shows up as a part of Duncan's
market appeal. Duncan always has stressed the cost effectiveness of its
style of practice. Specialization and departmentalization are presented
as the means of achieving such competitiveness.

The ideology of professionalism has an appeal to clients and associates, but it can also be used to explain differences in the status and earnings of partners. Although partners joke about the determinants of compensation in firms—that the lawyers who make the most are those who are good at cocktail parties or on the golf course—the dominant ideology is that those who are the best get the most. As one young associate expressed it, the governing group in his firm was the "cream who had risen to the top." Consistent with the notion that professionalism provides a choice of work within a structure of specialties is the conception of the law firm as an opportunity structure that can be climbed. The well-worn cliché that captures the essence of this ideology can be heard repeatedly in law school interviewing rooms and read in innumerable firm résumés in law school placement offices: "Individuals are given responsibility at the rate at which they can accept it."

The ideology of professional development rationalizes the domination of the firm by attorneys with client responsibility. The client-responsible elite of firms are quite literally seen as the "strongest lawyers" in the firm. Hence, a leading member of a firm suggested that "a lawyer who is responsible for a number of clients in the firm is thought to be smarter because of it." A former member of a governing group in a firm also suggested that merit was the basis of leadership in the firm.

Q. How do people rise to positions of authority in this firm?

A. How do people rise to become president of the United States? How do people rise to become the president of a corporation or the editor of a law review, or how does someone become the dean of a law school? . . . There's a whole mixture of reasons. But I think one of the distinctive things about this firm is that the leadership of the firm has been chosen on the basis of ability rather than how much business they can control. And that's very important.

Q. But it seems like it's somewhat [more] complicated because those lawyers with the most ability also tend to get a lot of clients.

A. Well, that's correct. And things are different now than they used to be. Now, the firm is bigger, I think there is more concern about getting clients.

Attaining client responsibility is viewed as a professional achievement. I was pursuing the same line of questioning with a partner who had joined a firm laterally, bringing several major clients and associates with him, and who was immediately brought onto the firm's governing committee. When I asked why he was put on the governing group he looked at me quizzically. "It is not something which is done formally at all. But certainly if you have a man who represents [X] or [Y] or [Z] [all major corporations] naturally you are going to listen to what he says. And the odds are much better that he will be a member of the policy committee or will have significant input into firm policy." The power of the client-responsible elite is cloaked in the ideology of professionalism. I do not suggest that this is a facade. Quite the contrary. The image of professional competence is as important to clients who entrust legal work to an attorney as it is to the lawyers who entrust their careers to the authority of a firm's governing group. Seen from outside or from within, professionalism is a critical element of authority in the law firm.

Differences in Professional Values by Firm and Partnership Status. This qualitative evidence portrays the significance of professionalism as an ideology that mediates relationships within firms and between firms and clients. Moreover, it suggests several variations on the central theme: different firms and different groups within firms construct their own models of the professional ideal. Such a finding tends to contradict Smigel's model of the professional bureaucracy, which emphasized the role that universally shared professional values play in the firm. To examine the issue more systematically I presented respondents in the four-firm sample with a series of questions about how law firms should be run. Five items dealing with policies on growth, specialization, assignment to specialties, departmentalization, and business-getting were combined to generate a scale measuring the level of support for the rationalization of the law firm. Individuals could score between 1 and 5, with 5 indicating strong agreement with all efforts to rationalize the firm and 1 indicating strong opposition to all such proposals. Table 24 reports a breakdown of the scale by firm and partnership status and the results of an analysis of variance.

The table indicates that both independent variables have a significant effect. As expected, the members of the Duncan firm have a far more businesslike view of law firm organization. Both partners and associates in Duncan on the average agree with efforts at rationalizing organization policies. If Duncan is dropped from the analysis, firm differences are insignificant. Again we find that despite the emergence of a bureaucratic structure in the Becker firm, it maintains traditional professional values concerning organizational policies. Indeed, its partners express the lowest level of support for rationalizing organization policies. This

TABLE 24. MEAN SCORE ON SCALE OF LAW FIRM RATIONALIZATION BY FIRM AND PARTNERSHIP STATUS[1]

	Partnership Status*	
Firm	Associates	Partners
Aaron	2.70 (21)[2]	3.57 (18)
Becker	2.97 (36)	3.34 (34)
Curran	2.92 (31)	3.64 (18)
Duncan	4.09 (30)	4.47 (38)

[1] The scale consisted of the following items with five response categories ranging from 1 (strongly disagree) to 5 (strongly agree). Mean = 3.49; standard deviation = 1.15; Cronbach's alpha = .86.
  a. Regardless of its ultimate size, this firm should grow at a rate that keeps up with client demand.
  b. The firm should seek to increase the productivity of lawyers by encouraging specialization.
  c. Associates should be directed to choose a specialty soon after joining the firm.
  d. The firm should be formally organized on a departmental basis such that assignments are made, work is coordinated, and developments in the law and with clients are the administrative responsibility of departmental units.
  e. Within the limits of taste, the firm should seek the business of other firms' clients, just as any other business would.

[2] Number of cases in parentheses

* P-value < .001 in a two-way anova of scale by firm and partnership status

further validates the historical analysis in chapter 2 which suggested that there was a sharp divergence between ideology and managerial practice at Becker.

Perhaps the more interesting finding in table 24 is the difference in values between partners and associates. In all firms associates have more traditional attitudes toward law firm organization. We might have expected an opposite result, that older attorneys would have been steeped in the traditions of the organizations whereas novices would favor new styles of management. Instead, the results reflect the tension between partners, who see it in their interest to rationalize the firm, and associates, who see themselves as the parties who bear the brunt of the rationalization. If we examine the specialization index by firm and partnership status, we find an almost perfectly inverted pattern from that for the rationalization scale. With the exception of Becker, associates have more specialized time-allocation patterns than partners. Not surprisingly, then, these are the lawyers who have the most at stake in the redesign of work in the firm. And their opinions diverge from those of their seniors.

The results contradict oversimple models of the law firm as a value-rational organization in which norms act as the invisible glue holding

220   Structure of the Large Law Firm

the firm together. Instead of a common set of professional values about the conduct of these organizations, there are structured differences across firms. At least in the case of partners, we find lawyers adopting the firm's party line. In Duncan there is support for bureaucratic management. In the other three firms there is agreement with the "expressed" managerial ideology. This pattern suggests that in large measure professional values related to organizational policies arise *inside the firm and reflect the managerial ideology of the elite in power.* Moreover, in all the firms there is decidedly less support among associates for policies of rationalization. This may in part reflect incomplete socialization into the norms of the organization. And as associates who disagree with managerial policies leave, we can expect greater convergence of associates' attitudes with those of partners. But it is quite clear that there is not an across-the-board consensus on firm policies. Whether they know it or not, associates enter firms with a conception of how the firm should be run that does not accord with the managerial ideology of the partners who actually run it.

BUREAUCRACY AND COMMITMENT

A classic theme in the professions literature is the antagonism between bureaucracy and professionalism (Davies 1983). Whether the problem is attributed to the personalities of professional workers (Merton 1940), the conflicts between administrative priorities and professional standards (Ben-David 1958; Scott 1965), or fundamental differences in organizing principles between the professions and bureaucracy, researchers have often asserted that professionals in bureaucratic settings are subject to high levels of alienation from the organization. More recent empirical and theoretical analyses have begun to question the presumed antagonism (Hall 1967; Hastings and Hinings 1970; Wilensky 1964; Miller 1968). The reactions of professionals to bureaucratic organization typically have been studied in organizations where professionals are not the dominant group or where there exist dual lines of authority, one professional, one administrative (see, e.g., Kornhauser 1962; Marcson 1960; Freidson 1970a, b). There have been no comparisons between autonomous professional organizations that vary in the degree of bureaucratization. It is not clear, therefore, whether the bureaucratization of professional firms would result in the alienation of the professional work force.

I sought to examine the relationship between bureaucratization and commitment by asking the cross section "What are your future career plans?" This was followed by a probe: "Would your ultimate goal be to spend your career practicing in this firm?" Responses were coded into categories indicating level of commitment to the organization. Those responding that they definitely would stay, would stay until something better came along, or would stay if made partner or a member of the governing committee were all coded as committed to the firm. The remainder of responses were coded as uncommitted. Table 25 reports the breakdown of responses by firm and partnership status.

Table 25 makes evident that levels of commitment vary drastically between partners and associates, with barely half (51 percent) the associates planning to stay with their firms, whereas 85 percent of all partners are committed to staying. Such a difference is hardly surprising, since partners have tenure in the organization. While commitment varies by less than 10 percent among the partners of the four firms, there are significant differences across firms at the associate level. Associates in Aaron and Curran, the least bureaucratic firms, have the lowest levels of commitment (50 percent and 33 percent, respectively, compared to 56 percent and 63 percent for Becker and Duncan, respectively). This pattern turns the expected relationship on its head. Lawyers in the bureaucratic firms are more committed to the organization. Why?

Much of the difference across firms is attributable to the different work demands placed on associates. Recall from chapter 4 that lawyers in Aaron and Curran work substantially more hours than the lawyers

TABLE 25. PERCENTAGE COMMITTED BY FIRM AND PARTNERSHIP STATUS

Partnership Status*	Firm*				
	Aaron	Becker	Curran	Duncan	Total
Associates	50.00%	55.88%	33.33%	63.33%	50.88%
	(20)	(34)	(30)	(30)	(114)
Partners	88.24%	79.41%	88.24%	86.84%	84.91%
	(17)	(34)	(17)	(38)	(106)
Total	67.57%	67.65%	53.19%	76.47%	67.27%
	(37)	(68)	(47)	(68)	(220)

Number of respondents in parentheses.
Four cases were missing information.
* Chi-square p < .01.

222   Structure of the Large Law Firm

in other firms. Table 26 presents in multiple-classification analysis form
the results of an analysis of covariance of the proportion of lawyers
committed by firm and partnership status, with total hours worked
entered as the covariate. After controlling for total hours, differences
by firm are no longer significant. The effect of total hours, however, is
significant. With an unstandardized beta of $-.015$, a difference of four
hundred hours worked is estimated to reduce commitment by six percent. The results indicate that after controlling for total hours worked
and the proportion of associates, differences by firm are reduced considerably. The adjusted differences between Aaron, Becker, and Duncan
are no greater than 6 percent. Curran remains the lowest of the firms,
however, some 9 percent under Aaron and Becker and 15 percent less
than Duncan.

The remaining differences between firms, while not statistically significant, bear some comment. Lower levels of commitment may result

TABLE 26.   MULTIPLE-CLASSIFICATION ANALYSIS:
PERCENTAGE COMMITTED BY FIRM, PARTNERSHIP STATUS
WITH TOTAL HOURS WORKED AS THE COVARIATE

Grand mean = 67.27

Firm	N	Adjusted Deviation
Aaron	37	1.16
Becker	68	−.30
Curran	47	−9.48
Duncan	68	6.22
		Eta = .12
*Partnership Status**		
Associates	114	−15.45
Partners	106	16.41
		Eta = .34
*Total Hours Worked***		Beta = −.015

$R^2 = .148$

N = 224; 4 cases were missing information.

* p < .05
** p < .01

P-values are taken from an analysis of covariance of percentage committed entering firm and
partnership status as main effects and total hours worked as a covariate. No interaction effects were
found to be significant.

from factors inside organizations, such as structure, work demands, and treatment of associates. But it may also result from recruitment practices or field of practice. If Curran recruits lawyers who in general have less fixed notions about their careers, in a sense they tolerate a more diverse orientation on the part of associates. It may also be that the skills associates develop in some firms are in greater general demand; these associates may then have more options for future employment. Skills in litigation fields certainly fall in this category. Perhaps the lawyers at Becker and Duncan develop specialties that are less easily transferred, creating greater dependence on the firm but also greater commitment, as we have measured it here. While I cannot separate these factors, it does appear that Curran recruits a politically more liberal set of associates. Hence, the firm appears to attract associates who for ideological reasons would not otherwise consider large firm practice. Lower levels of commitment are not necessarily a result of alienating conditions inside firms. Clearly additional research is necessary to test the generalizability of the findings.

The results suggest that without taking into consideration the material conditions of work we cannot assume that professionals will be less satisfied in bureaucratic work settings. By making more reasonable work demands, bureaucratically organized professional firms can garner higher levels of career commitment from the professional staff. It is important to remember, however, that the range of variation, even among these maximally different large firms, is not great. If the comparison were between two radically different organizational contexts, for example, between lawyers working in Hyatt Legal Services and solo practitioners, we might well find a greater difference in career satisfaction. But the critical finding remains. Within the category of large firms, the introduction of bureaucratic administrative and work-group structures does not by itself produce the alienation of associates.

A final issue to consider is the double face of commitment. This analysis has focused on career satisfaction, but perhaps the question of work commitment is more important. How hard do lawyers work for the organization? When we consider this dimension the results indicate support of traditional structures. Even though the associates in traditional firms are less certain about spending their career in the firm, they still work considerably more hours for the firm than their counterparts in bureaucratic firms. This is eloquent testimony to the adaptability of authority systems. Traditional firms can convert low levels of career commitment to high levels of work commitment, while bureaucratic

224   Structure of the Large Law Firm

firms generate higher levels of career commitment through stable work
structures and modified work demands.

CLIENT CONTROL AS A CONSTRAINT ON MANAGERIAL AUTHORITY

The meaning of professional values as they affect the organization
of practice now appear subject to reinterpretation by the leaders of law
firms. Moreover, there does not appear to be an inherent conflict between bureaucratization and the career satisfaction of the professional
work force. The limiting factor on the bureaucratization of the law firm
is not so much the professional norms of lawyers as structural constraints. Given the difficulty of centrally controlling the work process,
the leaders of firms necessarily rely on the structured discretion of their
colleagues. More important, a position of managerial authority in the
firm, whether it be membership on the governing committee, a position
at the head of a department, or managing partner, will always be
subordinate to the power of the lawyers controlling the largest bloc of
clients. As a leading partner in one firm concluded:

> Let me tell you that you can set up a law firm that's either run by the
> producers in the firm, or it's run by the nonproducers in the firm. But believe
> me, if you have a firm in which the nonproducers are running things, it's
> going to go [straight downhill]. And, of course, you'd expect that if the
> nonproducers are the ones running the firm, [the producers] will get a
> thousand more a year or two thousand more a year than the nonproducers.
> And believe me, if you have that kind of arrangement, the producers would
> leave and you'd be left with a bunch of nonproducers to pay the rent and
> overhead. . . . [I]f you were a guy bringing in a lot of business, why would
> you pay those guys the money you could be making yourself?

Bureaucratization in the law firm will always be subject to the prerogatives of the client-responsible elite. The historical narratives in
chapter 2 confirm the significance of this fact for the organization of
the firms in this study. The Curran firm experienced several failed
attempts at introducing rational managerial practices because each attempt challenged the baronial prerogatives of some group of lawyers.
Similarly, the Aaron firm's elite resisted departures from the traditional pattern of direct administration because they saw it as potentially
threatening to their interrelationships, even though a majority of the
partnership favored the adoption of a more bureaucratic organizational
structure. Most dramatic of all is the recent history of Duncan. De-

spite strong agreement among partners that the firm should continue to organize its operations bureaucratically, the emerging "finders" demanded control of the bureaucratic apparatus. Even in the most bureaucratic firm, managerial authority ultimately was subject to the power of the client-responsible attorneys.

Despite the tensions between managerial authority and client responsibility, the trend toward bureaucratic organization will continue and probably accelerate. The change of administrations at Duncan, for example, did not displace the bureaucratic managerial policies that had governed the firm from its origins but merely represented the assertion of power by a new group of partners. Indeed, bureaucratization as a means of improving service to clients and increasing partnership profits appears to be in the economic self-interest of the client-responsible elite. As increasing numbers of firms adopt bureaucratic managerial approaches, pressure will increase on other firms to do the same. Moreover, as more firms move toward bureaucratic management, erosion of the traditional meaning of professionalism will continue and new values will emerge to legitimate the new organizational structure of firms. But bureaucratization will not mean greater stability. The intrusion of client relationships into managerial functions, coupled with the growing unpredictability of those relationships, will be a continuing source of instability for partnerships.

The dynamics of social change in the large law firm lead to a redefinition of the tensions between bureaucracy and professionalism in autonomous professional organizations. The cultural history of the legal profession reveals that for decades the elite of the corporate bar have worried that their practice was declining from a profession into a business. In commencement addresses and bar association speeches they have extolled the higher values of professionalism—independence, imagination, public service (Gordon 1984). Only last year the president of the American Bar Association, himself a partner in a major law firm, appointed a special commission on professionalism. Yet these same members of the elite have presided over the transformation of small, traditionally organized offices into the bureaucratic megafirms that now are reshaping the landscape of corporate legal services. The explanation for this seeming paradox is the elite's use of professionalism as an ideology that obscures and justifies the organization of the firm and the elite's role in that structuring. The firm is said to embody the highest professional standards in order to attract clients and recruits, exact high levels of individual commitment to work, and justify differences in the earnings and power of members. The appeal to professionalism thus increasingly legitimates the introduction of bureaucratic managerial, administrative, and work-group structures.

Comparison of the four firms in this study reveals significant variations in the professional ideologies invoked. The appeal that Duncan makes to clients is based on a businesslike approach to law: the delivery of sound legal services for a good price. Similarly, the businesslike approach to law inside the firm, in the shape of departments and specialization, is held to offer Duncan's associates better training and earlier responsibility. In Becker a traditional ideology constitutes the appeal to recruits and is widely shared by partners and associates alike. But this conservative ethic does not conflict with the development of stable, specialized work groups. The appeal to professionalism at Aaron and Curran commands long hours despite uncertain career expectations. Whether professionalism is invoked to rationalize more bureaucracy or more work, whether it informs the firm's organization or blinds lawyers to the firm's functioning, the ideology meets the needs of the organization.

My interpretation of authority relationships in the law firm represents a significant departure from previous conceptions of autonomous professional firms. While this analysis must be tested in other organizational settings, it nevertheless raises critical questions about the nature of social change in professional firms. First, we can posit a greater potential for conflict in professional firms than some organization scholars acknowledge (see, e.g., Satow 1975). An alternative explanation for the relative lack of formal structure in firms is the difficulty of achieving a consensus on organizational policies. The recent history of law firms supports this view. The media covering firms contain innumerable reports of dissension and conflict resulting in defections from firms and managerial shake-ups (see chap. 1).

Second, my interpretation of authority redefines the relationship between professionalism and bureaucracy. As the case of the Duncan firm demonstrates in the extreme, there is no inherent conflict between bureaucratization and professional values. It is possible for firms to tailor the meaning of professionalism to accommodate bureaucratic administrative and work-group structures. Moreover, by providing more stable working relationships and more reasonable time demands, bureaucratic firms are able to command a higher level of career commitment from their associates. Thus we can expect the trend toward the bureaucratization of professional firms to intensify. The more impressive variable in the bureaucratization of the law firms is the power of the managerial elite to develop a cohesive policy-making body and maintain control over the major clients of the firm. The vulnerability of managerial authority to diffuse or shifting patterns of client responsibility remains a distinguishing element of professional organizations like the law firm and a source of uncertainty for the governance of such organizations.

Finally, we can conclude that autonomous professional organizations are not as autonomous of client interests as the term implies. One of the attributes said to distinguish the professions from other occupations is the role professional colleagues play as the major reference group for decision making (see e.g., Hughes 1958). Terence Johnson (1972) roots his analysis of the power of the professions in a typology based on this difference, distinguishing between systems in which professionals are controlled by clients, which he labels patronage systems, and those in which professionals are accountable to peers, which he labels collegial systems. Other scholars have argued that bureaucratization is not a threat to professional autonomy because professionals in bureaucratic settings often work in a sort of organizational enclave that is controlled by professionals and in which principles of collegiality predominate (see, e.g., Marcson 1960; more generally, see Freidson 1986, pp. 158–179). Halliday (1983), for example, celebrates Bosk's (1979) findings that surgeons in a teaching hospital are subject to the social control of the professional group as evidence that bureaucratization does not undercut the ability of professionals to enforce a distinctive moral code in the course of their work. Halliday thus concludes that collegial control is a mechanism through which the modern professions continue to make significant contributions to the normative fabric of society.

My analysis of the authority structure of the firm contradicts the assumption in the professions literature that collegial organization necessarily enhances professional autonomy. We simply cannot equate collegial control with professional autonomy without regard to the context. In the law firm the power of the dominant colleagues derives from their relationships with clients. At the top of the decision-making pyramid on any case or matter is the colleague with the strongest links to clients, and that partner can be expected to have internalized the client's perspective on questions of social and legal policy. In such a collegial hierarchy the interests, indeed, probably the tastes, of clients will be enforced. The resilience of collegial authority in the law firm

will have the opposite effect from that posited in the professions literature. Instead of producing an organization that is more autonomous
from client interests, collegial authority ensures that even as the organization becomes more specialized internally and moves in the direction
of bureaucratic organization, it will remain under the control of clients.[2]

PART III
The Law Firm as a Social Institution

7
Ideology, Practice, and Professional Autonomy: Social Values and Client Relationships

The large law firm is an institution that embodies a paradox of power in the American legal system. Its influence is widely and variously asserted: its lawyers handle the most consequential of economic transactions and litigated disputes (Hurst 1950; J. Stewart 1983), exercise leadership in bar associations and organized efforts at law reform (Halliday 1976; Powell 1982; Grossman 1965), participate in the "political communities" that surround and shape the formal organs of state power (Polsby 1980), and are reputed to be the most effective representatives of the interests of clients in the courts, regulatory agencies, and legislatures (see e.g., Green 1975; Macaulay 1979). Firms boast of their independence from clients and partisan politics, often pointing to the relative lack of autonomy enjoyed by inside corporate counsel and the questionable ethics of lower status lawyers.[1] The dramatic growth in the size of these organizations in recent years demonstrates their ability to command an increasing pool of resources. Yet virtually from its inception the large law firm has been attacked for selling out to big business, for recruiting the best legal talent away from public service careers, for organizing "law factories" that diminish the ability of lawyers to make informed ethical judgments, and for lack of commitment to pro bono projects (Brandeis 1933; Mills 1953, pp. 125–126; Nader 1970). Recent scholarship questions the very foundations of its power, arguing not only that the large law firm is the captive of its clients but

232   The Law Firm as a Social Institution

that it has only a marginal effect on the distribution of scarce resources (Heinz and Laumann 1982, pp. 353–373; Heinz 1983; Gordon 1983).

This chapter examines this paradox by analyzing the relationship between the political, legal, and professional attitudes of lawyers in large firms and their practice. My central thesis is that lawyers in large firms adhere to an ideology of autonomy, both in their perceptions of the role of legal institutions in society and the role of lawyers vis-à-vis clients, but that this ideology has little bearing on their practice. In the realm of practice these lawyers enthusiastically attempt to maximize the interests of clients and rarely experience serious disagreements with clients over the broader implications of a proposed course of conduct. The dominance of client interests in the practical activities of lawyers contradicts the view that large-firm lawyers serve a mediating function in the legal system. The lawyers of elite firms may well take progressive stands on certain issues within the profession, may lead efforts at legal rationalization, and may exhibit a liberal orientation on general political questions, but both the direction of their law reform activities and their approach to the issues that arise in ordinary practice ultimately are determined by the positions of their clients. Although the growth of large law firms reflects the increased demand for legal services by corporations—and thus, by implication, the increasing importance of the expertise and organizational capacity that large firms offer—this growth in power does not represent the emergence of a more autonomous professional organization. In fact, trends in the organization of corporate legal services will widen the gap between the ideology of autonomy and a client-dominated practice.

THE PROBLEM OF PROFESSIONAL
AUTONOMY

The starting point for the empirical analysis that follows is the model of professional autonomy developed in Smigel's study of Wall Street law firms (1969, pp. 311–340). Smigel argued that growing size and diversification of the client base had increased the autonomy of large law firms from their clients and reinforced their ability to act as "a kind of buffer between the illegitimate desires of . . . clients and the social interest" (1969, p. 335, quoting from Parsons 1962). Smigel acknowledged that the main function of the firm was to maintain the status quo in the interest of corporate clients, but he suggested that the large law firm's most valuable contribution to society came from its efforts to restrain clients. Thus, he saw Wall Street lawyers as enlightened professionals struggling to moderate the unreasonable and illegal demands of recalcitrant clients (Smigel 1969, p. 342). This is the conception of lawyers as mediators who interpose their own sense of justice in representing clients (Frank 1965). The model implies that lawyers have different values about the use of the law, or at least a different view of what is possible in a legal context, than the clients they represent. It further suggests that one of the most important functions of lawyers is telling their clients "that they are damned fools and should stop" (Hurst 1950, pp. 344–345, quoting Elihu Root).

The principal theme in Smigel's interpretation of the social role of large firms and in much of the literature on the American legal profession is professional autonomy. This is a problematic concept upon which to base a research tradition. Like the term profession from which it derives, professional autonomy is an ambiguous concept that has been defined in numerous, inconsistent ways[2] and has had a legacy of uncritical use as one of the defining attributes of professional occupations (Johnson 1972). Attempts to operationalize the concept by studying lawyer-client interactions face serious difficulties of access and reactivity (Danet, Hoffman, and Kermish 1980). As a result, we have few empirical studies of the transactions between lawyers and clients (but see Kritzer 1984; Rosenthal 1974; Cain 1983). Yet professional autonomy is a kind of "tar baby" concept. Despite attacks, it remains at the center of debates about the roles of lawyers in society. For example, in the conclusion of their treatise on Chicago lawyers, Heinz and Laumann turn to professional autonomy as the key theoretical issue (1982, pp. 358–373). They reject Smigel's interpretation of the autonomy of large law firms, arguing instead that the prestigious, corporate sector of the profession is more dependent on and constrained by clients than are the congeries of lower status lawyers who represent personal clients. Stewart Macaulay's most recent classic, an analysis of consumer protection lawyers, grants large firms more autonomy from clients than Heinz and Laumann do. But Macaulay, too, confronts the same fundamental question: "Are lawyers agents of social control or are they so tied to their clients as to lack the professional autonomy so often ascribed to them?" (1979, p. 151; see also Rueschemeyer 1983).

The debate over the autonomy of lawyers has undeniable significance. The usual focus has been the extent to which lawyers disregard the best interests of personal clients, who typically have small claims for breach of warranties or personal injury (Rosenthal 1974; Landon

234   The Law Firm as a Social Institution

1983). If lawyers fail to pursue the interests of these clients aggressively, formal legal rights may have little more than symbolic value. The representation of corporate clients poses the opposite problem. The effectiveness of law in the corporate sphere depends on the willingness of lawyers to inform corporate actors of rules and decisions that contradict a proposed course of conduct.[3] This concern prompted proposals from the profession and from government agencies to impose formal obligations on counsel for policing the behavior of clients (Lorne 1978; *New York Times,* December 17, 1978, section 3, p. 1). Given Galanter's supposition that corporations wield sufficient resources to influence the legal process in their favor (1974), the mediating role of counsel becomes all the more important. If lawyers do not moderate their clients' tendency to extract the maximum advantage from the legal system, we can expect legal outcomes to become increasingly skewed in favor of resourceful parties, thus undermining the legitimacy of legal institutions.

Beyond the issue of supervising client behavior, the autonomy of lawyers from clients has implications for law reform. Brandeis reserved his most vigorous criticism of the elite corporate bar for its failure to pursue the public interest in efforts at legislative change (1933, p. 339). Because legislative change often has a broader impact on the distribution of rights and benefits than do particular judicial decisions and therefore involves a wider array of social interests, Brandeis argued that the profession has a greater obligation to serve the public interest in its law reform activities than in the private representation of clients before the courts. Given the continuing prominence of large-firm lawyers in such activities, the orientation of these lawyers will affect the course of legal change.

I will not attempt a comprehensive definition of professional autonomy. Instead, I will analyze empirically two issues relevant to the debate about the autonomy and influence of the large law firm. First, I will examine the ideology of lawyers in large firms—their attitudes about social issues, the law, and the roles lawyers should play in client relationships. Second, I will analyze the behavior of lawyers toward clients, focusing in particular on the incidence of serious conflicts between lawyers and clients. The measures I examine touch only some of the important theoretical issues concerning the autonomy and influence of large law firms. For example, I do not consider how lawyers transform the requests of clients into legal categories, thereby influencing the definition of the situation, even though this is a pervasive aspect of lawyer-client relationships (see, e.g. Cain 1983; Hosticka 1979). What follows is only a step in the direction of a broader inquiry. But by illuminating the relationship between ideology and practice in large firms this analysis has important implications for the autonomy and influence of the large law firm.

Obviously a sample drawn from only four firms is not ideal for making inferences about the entire population of large law firms. The findings presented here must be considered preliminary. Nevertheless, a number of characteristics make this sample worthy of serious attention with respect to the social role of large firms. First, the sample contains lawyers from a range of social backgrounds. More than a quarter of the sample were Jewish (27.6 percent) and more than a quarter were Roman Catholic (28.1 percent). A majority of the sample (52.3 percent) termed themselves political moderates and 29.6 percent said they were liberals; 17.1 percent said they were politically conservative. In terms of national political preference 38.5 percent said they were Democrats, 38.0 percent said they were Independents, and 23.5 percent said they were Republicans. The profile is not terribly dissimilar to that found by Heinz and Laumann (1982) for a random cross section of Chicago lawyers as a whole. Hence, this sample is probably more socially diverse and more politically liberal than is the population of lawyers in large Chicago firms.[4] Biased in this direction, the sample should pose even a more stringent test for Smigel's model of the lawyer as mediator. If we do not find evidence supporting the model in a relatively liberal, heterogeneous sample of large-firm lawyers, we are unlikely to find such evidence among the general population of lawyers in large firms.

Second, concern about the representatives of the sample can be eased somewhat by the consistency in the findings discussed here across firms and groups with different social backgrounds. Although previous chapters have established that the four firms differ significantly in structure, work, and patterns of authority, the attitudes and reported behavior analyzed here do not vary significantly by firm. Nor do social background variables have strong or consistent effects on the dependent variables. For that reason I will report most of the results for the sample as a whole. Third, this analysis is valuable simply because no one else has collected data of such quantity and detail which addresses the relationships between work, values, and client relationships in large law firms.

These data of course display the strengths and weaknesses of survey data. The structured interviews produced a substantial amount of new,

236   The Law Firm as a Social Institution

replicable data about the attitudes and behavior of lawyers in large law firms. The approach is necessarily rather crude. I have not been able to capture all the nuances of meaning and control in client relationships. Nor have I been able to probe in depth the ideology of large-firm practitioners. To more fully accomplish those ends, it would be necessary to observe lawyers at work, ask them about their decision making, and analyze their transactions with clients. While my data are limited, I hope they at least raise questions that will be explored in further research.

GENERAL SOCIAL AND LEGAL VALUES

The longest standing jeremiad directed at the large law firm is that it has "sold out" to big business, abdicated its professional responsibility to act in the public interest (J. Auerbach 1976, p. 41; Mills 1956; Berle 1948; Nader 1970). The two themes implicit but central to this critique are autonomy and inequality: First, to what extent are lawyers in large firms merely the instruments of their clients and to what extent do they attempt to modify clients' behavior? Second, what impact does the advice and advocacy of the large firm have on society's allocation of scarce resources? What is its impact on social inequality? The value orientations of members of large firms are a useful starting point for examining these questions. If lawyers exercise a modifying influence on business clients, we would expect their attitudes to be different from those of business elites. Of particular importance are lawyers' attitudes about social inequality and the role of the legal system in dealing with it. Their attitudes will suggest whether there is a tension in their role as the representatives of parties with large resources or whether they find the current allocation of legal rights appropriate and just. If these practitioners had doubts about the wisdom or justice of the system, we might expect them to attempt to change the allocation of legal resources through law reform and pro bono legal services programs.

For purposes of systematic data collection, I posed a set of standardized agree/disagree questions, many of which had been used in previous surveys. The items were intended primarily to measure the economic liberalism of respondents; to define their positions on the division of power among business, labor, and government; as well as to define the role of law in shaping economic and social conditions. The responses to these items are reported in table 27.

I begin with an item that directly raises the issue of the power

TABLE 27. RESPONSES TO SELECTED VALUES ITEMS (PERCENTAGES)

	Strongly Agree	Agree	Undecided	Disagree	Strongly Disagree	Total
1. There is too much power concentrated in the hands of a few large companies for the good of the country.	16 (7.3)	70 (32.1)	30 (13.8)	86 (39.4)	16 (7.3)	218 (100)
2. Labor unions have become too big for the good of the country.	34 (15.5)	83 (37.9)	43 (19.6)	55 (25.1)	4 (1.8)	219 (100)
3. The protection of consumer interests is best ensured by a vigorous competition between sellers rather than by federal government intervention and regulation on behalf of consumers.	23 (10.6)	71 (32.7)	29 (13.4)	83 (38.2)	11 (5.1)	217 (100)
4. On the whole, society is better off when the government does not attempt to regulate the economy through such legal instruments as the antitrust laws, securities regulation, banking law, and consumer protection.	15 (6.9)	25 (11.5)	29 (13.4)	122 (56.2)	26 (12.0)	217 (100)
5. On the whole, rules governing occupational health and safety impose undue burden on employers.	9 (4.1)	52 (24.0)	49 (22.6)	91 (41.9)	9 (7.4)	217 (100)
6. Economic profits are by and large justly distributed in the U.S. today.	3 (1.4)	63 (28.9)	51 (23.4)	83 (38.1)	18 (8.3)	218 (100)
7. Americans should have equal access to necessary medical care regardless of ability to pay.	53 (24.3)	106 (48.6)	23 (10.6)	30 (13.8)	6 (2.8)	218 (100)
8. The law should be molded always to do the greatest justice and progress for those who have the least.	11 (5.1)	29 (13.4)	29 (13.4)	123 (56.9)	24 (11.1)	216 (100)
9. Doctrines and rules pertaining to class actions should be interpreted to permit liberal use of the class action technique.	11 (5.0)	58 (26.5)	50 (22.8)	91 (41.6)	9 (4.1)	219 (100)
10. Differences in income between occupations should be reduced.	10 (4.6)	27 (12.4)	23 (10.6)	111 (51.2)	46 (21.2)	217 (100)

Number of missing cases varies between 5 and 8 cases for each item.

possessed by the predominant clientele of large firms, the large corporation: "There is too much power concentrated in the hands of a few large companies for the good of the country." When Heinz and Laumann posed the same question in 1974 to a cross section of Chicago lawyers, a majority (52 percent) of their sample agreed and only 31 percent disagreed (1982, p. 139). The pattern of responses they found was thus quite similar to that found among a national sample of the American public, 53 percent of whom agreed with the proposition (Robinson, Rush, and Head 1968, p. 196). In contrast, the plurality of respondents in my large-firm sample (46.7 percent) disagreed and only 39.4 percent agreed. It is nevertheless somewhat surprising that so large a segment of large-firm lawyers, almost 40 percent, think that corporate power is too concentrated. There is no great consensus that corporate power is benign. Still, the responses to this and other questions reveal the alignment of corporate lawyers with their clients. It is not the case that large-firm lawyers are generally more favorably disposed toward the power held by large organizations. When asked if labor unions have become too big for the good of the country, a majority (53.4 percent) agreed. While the majority of the American public and the majority of Chicago lawyers have been found to have a negative perception of organized labor,[5] making them suspicious of the power of both corporations and labor, corporate lawyers are more likely to distinguish between potential clients and opponents.

Although it is hardly surprising that large-firm lawyers support corporate management over organized labor, it is more difficult to predict their attitudes toward government power. Does loyalty to clients lead lawyers to embrace a laissez-faire ideology? Or do the attitudes of large-firm lawyers evince what Parsons (1954) called their "paradoxical position," in which they depend equally as much on the attempts of government to regulate business as on the favor of corporate clients whom they defend against government regulation? I examined this issue through several questions on the merits of various regulatory schemes.

The first item assessing the sample's opinion about government regulation dealt with the extent to which government must police the marketplace in the interest of consumers: "The protection of consumer interests is best ensured by a vigorous competition between sellers rather than by federal government intervention." The sample was evenly split on the question, 43.3 percent agreeing, 43.3 percent disagreeing. Heinz and Laumann (1979, p. 139) found virtually an identical split (46 percent agreeing, 44 percent disagreeing). While these responses do not amount to a ringing endorsement for either government regulation or competition, they diverge sharply from the attitudes of business elites. Three-quarters (74 percent) of Laumann's sample of members of the community elite in a middle-sized midwestern city, most of whom were businessmen, had more faith in competition than regulation (Heinz and Laumann 1982, p. 141, n. 5).[6] Based on this and other research,[7] it appears that businessmen are substantially more optimistic about the capacity of the market than are the legal elite who represent them.

I then pursued the question of government intervention by asking about broad aspects of the legal framework for regulating the national economy: "On the whole, society is better off when the government does not attempt to regulate the economy through such legal instruments as the antitrust laws, securities regulations, banking law, and consumer protection." The item is hardly subtle. To agree would mark a radical departure from the trend toward increased legal regulation which has marked American government in this century. Indeed, only a little less than a fifth (18.4 percent) of our sample agreed, while a solid majority disagreed (68.2 percent). The business elite also are likely to recognize the value of this fundamental regulatory framework for maintaining public confidence in investment and for preventing gross illegality in financial transactions. One would not expect a similar reception for a sweeping regulatory program that was initiated in the early 1970s, which some argue contributed nothing to the integrity of markets—the regulation of occupational safety and health (OSHA) by the Department of Labor. Therefore, I asked the sample: "On the whole, rules governing occupational safety and health impose undue burdens on employers." Only 28.1 percent of the sample agreed with this indictment of OSHA, while almost half (48.2 percent) disagreed. At a time when OSHA regulation was highly controversial, under attack in court, Congress, and national political campaigns, this was a rather remarkable endorsement for the government regulation of business. Large-firm lawyers almost certainly have a more favorable view of federal administrative involvement in the day-to-day activities of employers than do the business clients they represent.

As Parsons suggested, lawyers in large firms embrace both the positions of their business clients and the institutional arrangements by which law regulates economic affairs. In terms of general social values, then, large-firm lawyers may be relatively autonomous from clients and might be expected to influence the course of social change in ways that are sometimes contrary to the narrow self-interest of corporate clients. But what is the extent of disagreement about the conception of society held by this legal elite and the corporate clientele they typically represent? How does the general social orientation of this elite translate into views on the role of legal institutions in shaping legal change? To address this question, I turn to attitudinal data concerning the second major theme in the literature on the social role of law and lawyers, the relationship of legal institutions to social inequality.

Unger (1976, pp. 38–40) suggests that the central contradiction in modern society is the gap between consciousness about social relations and the actual state of social relations. Liberal society's guiding norm— the ideal of formal equality—is said to be under constant, increasing pressure from the continuing and ever more visible lack of substantive equality among various strata. As a result, the central contradiction facing the law in modern society is the divergence "between a dominant ideology that puts impersonal law at the center of society and a day-to-day experience for which such law stands at the periphery of social life" (Unger 1976, p. 44).

To begin a meaningful analysis of the attitudes of lawyers in large firms about inequality in modern society and the appropriate role of legal institutions in redressing inequality, we must measure lawyers' views on the general state of inequality. I put to the sample a proposition concerning the relative justice of our society's system of economic rewards: "Economic profits are by and large justly distributed in the United States today." Not quite a third of the sample (30.3 percent) agreed with the statement, and almost half the sample (46.4 percent) disagreed. The proportion is lower than that reported by Heinz and Laumann for their Chicago sample (55 percent of which disagreed with the item) (1982, p. 139), but my responses nonetheless reveal that a substantial segment of the elite strata of the bar regards the distribution of economic rewards to be unjust. Moreover, the sample agrees that the government should provide for individuals who cannot afford to pay. In response to the item "Americans should have equal access to necessary medical care regardless of ability to pay," 72.9 percent of the sample agreed. These items indicate an awareness of substantive inequality and support for some government efforts to redress the unequal access to the resources necessary to meet some basic human needs. But what do lawyers in large firms see as the appropriate response by government and legal institutions to these recognized inequities?

Although many large-firm lawyers think that economic profits are unjustly distributed, they nevertheless do not countenance a redistribution of income among different occupational groups. Only 16.8 percent agreed with the statement "Differences in income between occupations should be reduced," and 72.2 percent disagreed. Lawyers in large firms are not different from the rest of the profession in this regard. Heinz and Laumann also found little support for a broad-based redistribution of income (only 14 percent agreed, 73 percent disagreed) (1982, p. 139).

Resistance to policies for redistributing advantage through legal institutions was equally firm. To gauge the sample lawyers' general orientation toward such issues, I asked their opinion on the statement "The law should be molded always to do the greatest justice and progress for those who have the least." Less than a fifth of the sample endorsed such a general perspective, while nearly three-quarters (68 percent) disagreed. The item in question is admittedly crude, suggesting an across-the-board preference for parties of lesser status without regard to equities or broader policy implications. The sample may have been responding to this rigidity more than rejecting an ameliorative role for legal institutions. Two additional items that concern the procedures and decision-making priorities of the courts may better indicate how the sample conceives of the proper role of legal institutions.

An issue of recurrent significance since the 1960s has been the scope of rules and doctrines governing the use of class-action litigation. Class actions may significantly increase access to the courts to redress wrongs that otherwise would be too small individually to merit the expense of litigation. Hence, they are an important symbol of access to the courts for individuals. Yet the expansion of class actions during the late 1960s and early 1970s dramatically increased the exposure of corporate clients to litigation. These suits have therefore been a source of business and possibly of consternation for corporate lawyers. Because significant questions remain about the doctrinal scope of class actions, I was able to pose a statement that did not fly in the face of established legal norms: "Doctrines and rules pertaining to class actions should be interpreted to permit liberal use of the class action technique." Somewhat less than one-third (31.5 percent) of the sample agreed and almost half (45.7 percent) disagreed. That even one-third of a sample who presumably oppose class actions in the course of their practice supports the expansion of class actions as a general policy is somewhat surprising. But the overall distribution of views is certainly what we would expect from a segment of the bar representing a predominantly corporate clientele. Large-firm lawyers differ here from the Heinz and Laumann sample, in which there was virtually an even split between the two

242   The Law Firm as a Social Institution

positions, with 42.5 percent favoring liberal interpretations of doctrines
on class actions and standing in court and 45.5 percent disagreeing.[8]
On a question of legal policy that calls for no deviation from traditional
norms of legal interpretation but which may be symbolic of litigation
aimed at redistributing benefits from corporations to individuals, large-
firm lawyers take a more conservative view than the profession as a
whole.[9]

Finally, I attempted to probe general attitudes among respondents
about the relative importance of adhering to precedent versus doing
substantive justice in the course of judicial decision making. Adherence
to precedent is typically viewed as a principle for limiting the purview
of judicial remedies in American law, although the impact of precedent-
based rulings does vary with the context of particular cases, and new
judicial principles are often articulated as mere extensions of past hold-
ings (Cardozo 1924; Levi 1949). Hence, through the limited frame of
a question about the proper role of a judge, I attempted to elicit the
views of our sample on the contradiction that Unger suggests is critical: the tension between procedurally limited definitions of justice and
broader social conceptions of substantive justice. The sample was asked:
"If you were a judge, what do you think would be more important in
your decisions: (1) developing the continuity of law and following
precedent, or (2) doing justice in particular cases?"[10]

Because the question assumed a conflict that the respondents might
not accept, the uncertain were urged to make a choice and responses
were coded to reflect whether they chose one alternative without qualification, whether they objected to the supposed conflict but chose one
alternative after being urged to make a choice, or whether they refused
to make a choice despite our urgings.[11] Almost one in five (18.6 percent)
refused to choose, and another 14.4 percent only did so at the urging of
interviewers. Whereas 29.4 percent gave priority to precedent and continuity, 37.5 percent chose justice in particular cases. When the cases
coded as leaning one direction or the other are combined with those
making a choice, 37.5 percent favor continuity and precedent and 43.9
percent favor justice in particular cases. Thus, among those lawyers
who will make a choice, there is a fairly even split between the two
priorities. Moreover, more than three-quarters of those refusing to
choose a position commented that continuity and substantive justice
are values that must themselves be balanced on a case-by-case basis.
Only a quarter of these respondents indicated in their comments that
there could be no conflict between observing the two values.

The fragmented nature of responses to this question shows the difficulty of characterizing the general philosophy of this relatively homogeneous group of practitioners. Even though they practice in a similar setting, represent the same types of clients, and come from similar educational (if not social) backgrounds, the absence of a monolithic ideology is apparent in their responses. Lawyers in large firms express a considerable difference of opinion over what the law is and what law should attempt to do in resolving disputes.

While the legal values of large-firm lawyers cannot be reduced to general philosophical positions, the overall pattern of responses yields an informative mosaic. This legal elite identifies with both their business clients and the government's regulation of business, but perhaps more than anything else these lawyers identify with the current balance of power between government and private enterprise. They may differ with their clients on the value of government regulation and they may recognize the inequity of the current distribution of economic benefits in society, but they strongly resist fundamental shifts in government policy or in the role of legal institutions that might substantially alter current arrangements. While this segment of the profession may not be a mere extension of its corporate clients, the moderate views of this elite are quite compatible with the maintenance of their clients' favorable position in society. As Larson remarks: "Because the legal profession mediates the institutionalized resolution of conflict, its expertise and its livelihood directly depend on the stability and legitimacy of a given institutional and legal framework. In the wider sense of the word, the legal mind is therefore inherently conservative" (1977, p. 168). In the context of their general commitment to a stable social formation in which law is an important brokering institution, lawyers in large firms exhibit partisan ties to their clients. Their general social values simultaneously express loyalty to the particular types of clients they represent and reaffirm the legitimacy of the law as an institution that transcends conflict between competing groups.

PROPOSED CHANGES IN THE FIELDS IN
WHICH LAWYERS PRACTICE

The general values of large-firm lawyers are a useful means of defining their orientation to broad questions of social policy. But perhaps more important are the attitudes of this group toward the specialized fields in which they actually work, on which they are likely to have a more immediate impact, both in their private role as client advisors and in their public role as participants in organized efforts at changing the law. I turn now to the specific policy preferences of my sample.

To capture the practical orientation of the respondents, I asked them to play king—to say what they would change about the law they practice if they had the necessary legislative and judicial power. Section A of table 28 reports the frequency distribution of responses collapsed into a detailed set of categories. Respondents were allowed to make up to three suggestions, which produced a total of 275 coded responses from 222 respondents. The table reports both the frequency of responses and the percentage of cases giving a particular response.

By far the most frequent responses were those suggesting reduction of the power of the federal government in general or of specific governmental agencies. The most hated organ of government is the Internal Revenue Service, which 18 percent of the sample saw as too powerful or as operating under rules that are too complicated. The next most hated was the Securities and Exchange Commission, an agency whose enforcement policies have been particularly controversial in recent years. The next major source of concern was the courts, both as a system and as a forum for litigation. A substantial segment of the sample (11.3 percent) suggested measures to improve the quality of the judiciary, mostly through the selection of judges by merit. Next came concern with the abuses of the discovery system, with 10.8 percent arguing that procedures need to be streamlined to make discovery more efficient. A dozen lawyers suggested that the cost of litigation should be borne by the losing party, a position frequently urged by the defense bar.

In addition to direct attacks on the IRS, a number of lawyers suggested various changes in the tax laws. Most of these proposals called for reducing taxes, but others involved a value-added tax, taxing on the basis of consumption rather than income, and so forth. A smaller number made suggestions about other areas, mostly favoring the positions that lawyers in large firms must advocate for their clients. Although proposals concerning criminal law were evenly divided between those favoring the defense and the prosecution, all the recommendations concerning labor were pro-management, six of seven recommendations about antitrust favor the defense of antitrust clients, and all suggestions concerning banking law favored creditors and banks, with the exception of three lawyers who recommended that the rights of consumers in credit and contract law should be expanded. Only a little

TABLE 28. PROPOSED CHANGES IN THE FIELDS IN WHICH
LAWYERS PRACTICE BY SUBJECT OF PROPOSED CHANGE,
IMPACT ON CLIENTS, AND IMPACT ON LAWYERS' PRACTICE

A. Changes by Subject of Proposed Change	Number of Responses	% of Responses	% of Cases
No Proposals	25	8.0	11.3
Court Reform			
Improve judges/Merit selection	25	8.0	11.3
Alternative dispute resolution	9	2.9	4.1
Systems, procedural changes	8	2.6	3.6
Law Simplification	4	1.3	1.8
Reduce Government Power or Regulations			
General	25	8.0	11.3
Internal Revenue Service	40	12.8	18.0
Securities and Exchange Commission	16	5.1	7.2
Equal Employment Opportunity Commission	4	1.3	1.8
Department of Energy	2	0.6	0.9
Litigation Reform			
Limit class actions	5	1.6	2.3
Losing party pays fees (English rule)	12	3.8	5.4
Make discovery more efficient	24	7.7	10.8
Criminal Law Reform			
Pro defendant	7	2.2	3.2
Pro government/prosecution	6	1.9	2.7
Labor: Pro-Management	4	1.3	1.8
Antitrust—Pro-defendant	6	1.9	2.7
Antitrust—Pro-plaintiff	1	0.3	0.5
Tax Reform			
General	2	0.6	0.9
Progressive changes to income tax	6	1.9	2.7
Reduce estate and capital gains taxes	13	4.2	5.9
Encourage pension plans	4	1.3	1.8
Cut taxes generally	8	2.6	3.6
Real Estate Reform			
Modernize, make uniform real-estate laws	7	2.2	3.2

TABLE 28.   (continued)

	Number of Responses	% of Responses	% of Cases
Pro-tenant	2	0.6	0.9
Banking—Pro-banks/ creditors	11	3.5	5.0
Pro-small business (tax, regulation)	2	0.6	0.9
Pro-consumer (credit, contracts)	3	1.0	1.4
Pro-liberal social issues (ERA, abortion, civil rights)	9	2.9	4.1
Pro-access to courts/legal services	10	3.2	4.5
Other	12	3.8	5.4
Total	275	99.7	142.5

Responses from 222 cases. 2 cases were missing information.

B. Impact of Proposed Changes on Clients	Number of Responses	% of Responses	% of Cases
Lower legal costs	75	26.7	40.1
Decrease operating expenses	34	12.1	18.2
Allow business to work better	33	11.7	17.6
More certainty	26	9.3	13.9
Expedite cases—win more	25	8.9	13.4
Hurt some clients	23	8.2	12.3
Generally beneficial	20	7.1	10.7
No effect	19	6.8	10.2
Free to operate	12	4.3	6.4
Fewer suits—less liability	11	3.9	5.9
Other	3	1.1	1.6
Total	281	100.1	150.3

Responses from 187 responses. 12 cases were missing information.

C. Impact of Proposed Changes on Lawyer's Practice	Number of Responses	% of Responses	% of Cases
Improve their work	80	36.9	43.5
Reduce work	68	31.3	37.0
Little or no effect	57	26.3	31.0
Expand work	11	5.1	6.0
Other	1	0.5	0.5
Total	217	100.1	117.9

Responses from 184 cases. 15 cases were missing information.

more than 6 percent of the proposals favor liberal social issues, increased access to the courts, or support for legal services to the poor.

Roughly one-third of the responses as a whole concerned the systemic aspects of the legal system: the quality of its judges, the ability of courts to handle disputes, the efficiency of discovery, the simplification or modernization of various fields of law. The remainder of the responses were quite partisan in character, in that they supported one particular side in a contest. Not surprisingly, there was a consistent pro-client cast to the suggestions. Specific recommendations came out against the government, for management, for the defense in litigation, for wealthy taxpayers, and for banks and creditors. The partisan quality of the suggestions becomes even clearer when we examine the respondents' evaluations of the impact of these changes on their clients. Respondents were asked an open-ended question about how the changes they proposed would affect their clients. Section B of table 28 presents the percentage distribution of 281 coded responses by response and case. The response that was twice as common as all others (given by 40.1 percent of the cases and 26.7 percent of the responses) was that the proposed change will lower client legal costs. Other estimated effects ran in a similar vein: The changes would decrease operating expenses, allow business to work better, increase certainty, help clients win more cases or incur less liability. In all, 80.2 percent of the responses suggested that the proposed changes would have salutary effects for clients. In contrast, only 12.3 percent of the respondents (8.2 percent of the responses) saw potential harm to *any* clients, which is only slightly higher than the proportion who thought that the changes would not affect clients much either way.

How do these findings fit with the Parsonian paradigm of the lawyer as mediator, as a buffer between the "illegitimate" desires of clients and the social interest that Smigel (1969, p. 335) adopted? Not well at all. If there is a distance between large-firm lawyers and their corporate clientele over general social and political questions, there is not much disparity between client concerns and the lawyers' agenda for change in the legal fields in which they practice. The proposals made by sample attorneys and their assessments of the consequences of these changes for clients indicate that the closer the examination of values approaches the actual work of lawyers, the less meaningful the concept of mediation becomes. Given an unconstrained power to change the law, the majority would change the law to suit the interests of their clients.

What is the origin of such commitment to client positions? How does it relate to lawyers' self-interest? The cynic might question the claim that these proposals would benefit clients. Certainly some reforms could line lawyers' pockets. With this issue in mind I concluded the questions on proposed changes by asking about the impact of proposed reforms on the lawyers' own practice. Again, the responses fit into a small number of categories, as shown in section C of table 28. The leading response (offered in 43.5 percent of the cases, 36.9 percent of the responses) was that the changes would improve their work, allowing them to take on more important or interesting matters. Another third (31.0 percent of the cases and 26.3 percent of the responses) perceived no great consequences; whatever changes occurred in the law, this group thought that there would always be a market for their services. A final third (37 percent of the cases, 31.3 percent of responses) thought the reforms might substantially reduce their work. Only 6 percent of the cases, a very small minority, reported that their proposed changes might expand their practice.

By these accounts lawyers are not very entrepreneurial in their outlook on law reform. Indeed, more than a third of the respondents proposed changes that would reduce their work. The common thread in the findings is that lawyers in large firms see their role in the system self-assuredly. Their job—however specialized—is to handle the legal problems of large corporations. By proposing changes in the law that facilitate that practice, even if in the short run it would reduce the demand for their work, these lawyers express a principal concern with their clients' long-term interests (Macaulay 1979, p. 163). The realistic assessment underlying these proposals is that the government will continue to regulate the activities of corporate clients, that corporations will continue to rely heavily on various legal instruments in transacting their business, and that the scope of regulation and the use of law is unlikely to change in any fundamental way. Attorneys seek to contribute to their clients' welfare by making the law marginally more useful or less burdensome. These proposals advance the interests of lawyers indirectly by attempting to make the law more "rational" from their clients' point of view.

These findings have three implications. First, these results run counter to what we expect from Smigel's model of the lawyer as mediator. If lawyers perform a mediating function, they do so in subtle fashion, at most proposing changes that are less extreme than those favored by clients. The results show such a strong identification with the interests of clients, even to the point of putting clients' long-term interests above their own short-term interests, that it is unrealistic to think of corporate lawyers as neutral professionals who are detached from the substantive interests of clients.

Second, there is strong evidence here for the supposition made fifty years ago by Llewellyn that the most powerful determinant of the attitudes and social orientation of lawyers is the work they do:

> Now, any man's interests, any man's outlook, are shaped in greatest part by what he *does*. His perspective is in terms of what he knows. His sympathies and ethical judgments are determined essentially by the things and the people he works on and for and with. Individual exceptions there are; rarely indeed do they work deflection of the mass movement. Hence the practice of corporation law not only works for business men toward business ends, but develops within itself a business point of view—toward the work to be done, toward the value of the work to the community, indeed, toward the way in which to do the work. (1933, p. 177)

Since lawyers come to adopt the positions of the corporate clients they represent, it is unlikely that their law reform activities will depart to any significant extent from the positions that they advocate for clients.

Third, the results suggest that corporate practitioners can maintain a relatively liberal political orientation while simultaneously remaining committed to their clients' positions in specific fields of practice. Certainly, my sample is less than politically radical and tends to have a conventional perspective on the role of legal institutions in society, but on general social issues these lawyers are more liberal than the corporate elites they represent. Yet they are staunch advocates of client interests in their professional practice. This pattern is consistent with other research indicating that attitudes requiring concrete choices are often inconsistent with positions taken on more general social values questions (see, e.g., Mann 1970). Erlanger and Klegon (1978), for example, found that although the general social values of law students underwent little change between the first and second years of law school, their professional orientation (ratings of the importance of pro bono work and of the desirability of jobs involving social reform) became significantly more conservative. Lawyers may not need to remake their worldview in order to remake their views about law practice. The nature of a lawyer's practice, however, may affect his or her general social values. Heinz and Laumann (1982, pp. 163–165) report that the longer lawyers practice in certain conservative, wealth-preserving fields, the more conservative they become on economic issues compared to lawyers practicing in other fields.

250   The Law Firm as a Social Institution

Although these findings cast doubt on Smigel's interpretation of the role played by lawyers in large firms, it is possible that in the dyadic relationship between lawyers and clients the lawyers do check the unreasonable demands of clients. To consider that possibility we must examine the relationships between lawyers and clients more directly.

THE LAWYER-CLIENT RELATIONSHIP

TIME DEVOTED TO PRINCIPAL CLIENT

I begin the analysis of lawyer-client relationships by examining the degree to which individual lawyers in large law firms concentrate their work on one client. These data address Smigel's (1969, p. 342) argument that the diversification of law firm client bases "frees" individual lawyers from dependence on particular clients. As we saw in earlier chapters, the large firm continues to be a mixed case of institutional and personal authority. Claims to responsibility for clients continue to be a critical determinant of standing in the firm. Individual lawyers "depend" on the clients they "control," and a loss of clients threatens to reduce economic and political participation in the firm. Although there are qualitative indications of the strength of these ties, there are no systematic data on the phenomenon. In an attempt to generate reasonably objective measures by which to test Smigel's assumption, I asked the sample what proportion of their work time during the last year was spent on their principal client. Table 29 reports the mean response by firm and field of practice.[12]

Table 29 presents a snapshot of lawyer time allocation by client.[13] Lawyers spend a substantial proportion of their time on the client for whom they work the most, averaging more than one-third in the sample as a whole and almost one-half in the corporate field. This pattern tends to contradict Smigel's assumption. Lawyers' time commitments in fact are not dispersed across the gamut of the firm's clientele but instead are clustered around particular clients. As expected, time allocation for clients varies by firm and field of practice. The highest concentrations are found in Becker, where lawyers spend close to half their time working for one client. This pattern reflects Becker's representation of a number of major institutional clients and the firm's organization around those clients. Lawyers working in the two broad fields most closely associated with Becker's institutional clients (the corporate area and other office fields) spend an average of almost 60 percent of their time (58.3 percent and 56.6 percent, respectively) on their principal

Ideology, Practice, and Professional Autonomy 251

TABLE 29. MEAN PERCENTAGE OF TIME SPENT ON PRINCIPAL
CLIENT IN THE LAST YEAR BY FIELD OF PRACTICE AND FIRM

Field	Firm				
	Aaron	Becker	Curran	Duncan	Total
Litigation	47.37	42.04	32.64	35.69	38.58
	(19)	(27)	(36)	(16)	(98)
Corporate	31.33	58.32	28.75	39.80	47.98
	(6)	(25)	(4)	(10)	(45)
Finance	23.75	23.44	25.00	17.00	19.73
	(4)	(9)	(2)	(22)	(37)
Other office	25.38	56.57	18.33	21.32	27.82
	(8)	(7)	(6)	(19)	(40)
Total	38.58	47.98	30.21	26.09	35.38
	(37)	(68)	(48)	(67)	(220)

Number of respondents in parentheses.

client. In the other three firms lawyers in the other office fields represent mostly smaller clients and individuals; they spend an average of less than a quarter of their time on any one client.[14]

Preliminary as these results are, they make two important points. First, despite the overall diversity of a firm's clientele, individual lawyers are likely to spend a considerable portion of their time on particular clients. In making inferences about the degree to which lawyers depend on particular clients, one cannot rely on data about the firm as a whole. Second, to the extent that we make inferences at the level of the firm, we should take account of structural differences in firms in the pattern of lawyer-client relationships. The character of these relationships will be determined not only by differences in the scope of practice but also by the particulars of working relationships in firms. It is necessary to examine the level of diversity of the client relationships of individual partners, the nature of relationships between subunits of the law firm and subunits of clients, and the mechanisms for supervising lawyer-client ties (such as double-audit procedures). What then is the nature of lawyer-client interactions within the four firms?

ROLE PERCEPTIONS AND REPORTS OF
LAWYER-CLIENT CONFLICT

Analysis of lawyer-client interactions poses some severe methodological problems. Lawyers are very sensitive about relationships with clients and are reluctant to discuss the details of these interactions

252   The Law Firm as a Social Institution

frankly, particularly if they involve disagreements between lawyer and client. Such interactions, however, are of considerable sociological interest because they may indicate who controls the professional work process in various contexts. But how can we investigate the nuances of lawyer-client interactions in the course of legal decision making? In the absence of an opportunity to observe the interactions directly (Sarat and Felstiner 1986) or to discuss decisions with lawyer and client in detail (Rosenthal 1974), the subtleties of lawyer-client dealings will be difficult to capture through reliable measures.

After experimenting with various formulations I chose to ask three questions about the lawyer-client relationship. First, I sought to measure the lawyer's perception of the breadth of his or her role. A commonly mentioned concern is that specialization in large firms has narrowed lawyers' view of their normative role, that lawyers may no longer consider it their responsibility to gain an overview of their clients' affairs or to give clients more than technical legal advice (see, e.g., Schwartz 1980). I then posed a second and related question dealing with the lawyer's opportunity to give nonlegal advice in order to ascertain how opportunities arose and whether opportunities were accepted when presented. The opportunity for giving nonlegal advice is a useful measure of how often the division of labor in large firms allows holistic lawyer-client interactions, at least holistic enough to go beyond technical legal advice.[15] And third, I asked whether the lawyer had ever refused an assignment or potential work because it was contrary to his or her personal values. This construction was intended to include matters that violated the code of professional ethics as well as other values not codified. Because the question was limited to rejected assignments, efforts to shape client positions short of all-out refusals are not included. Pretests persuaded me that measuring the incidence of more subtle lawyer-client conflicts would be difficult. I therefore asked about refusals and followed the question with others that would explain the presence or absence of lawyer-client conflict. The responses indicated that respondents went to great lengths to tell interviewers about any problems that had arisen with clients. My formulation, while necessarily somewhat crude, appears to have elicited information on lawyer-client conflict. With this complement of attitudinal and behavioral questions, I was able to generate focused data on the inclination and opportunity to advise clients beyond purely legal considerations as well as construct a clear line to measure lawyer-client conflicts. The results are presented in tables 30 and 31.

TABLE 30. THE OPPORTUNITY TO GIVE NONLEGAL ADVICE BY PARTNERSHIP STATUS, FIELD, AND REASONS AFFECTING SUCH OPPORTUNITIES

A. Percentage Reporting Opportunity to Give Nonlegal Advice by Partnership Status and Field of Practice[a]

	Partnership Status**		
Field*	Associates	Partners	Total
Litigation	53 (64)	83 (36)	64 (100)
Corporate	95 (19)	85 (27)	89 (46)
Finance	65 (17)	85 (24)	88 (41)
Other office	76 (17)	96 (20)	76 (37)
Total	65 (117)	87 (107)	75 (224)

[a] Probability values given are from three-way anova entering effects for field, firm, partnership status, and all possible interactions.
* $F_p < .05$
** $F_p < .01$
Number of respondents in parentheses.

B. How Opportunity for Giving Nonlegal Advice Arises

Responses	Number of Responses	% of Responses	% of Cases
Client asks	24	11.5	14.2
Lawyers' role	10	4.8	5.9
Field requires it	42	20.1	24.9
Business decisions	74	35.4	43.8
Personal investment decisions	19	9.1	11.2
Personal advice	33	15.8	19.5
Public relations concerns	4	1.9	2.4
Msg Dk	3	1.4	1.8
Total	209	100.0	123.7

N = 166; 2 cases were missing information

C. Reasons for No Opportunity to Give Nonlegal Advice

Responses	Number of Responses	% of Responses	% of Cases
Field too technical	9	21.4	22.5
Too late to give advice	7	16.7	17.5
No client contact	20	47.6	50.0
Another lawyer's responsibility	6	14.3	15.0
Total	42	100.0	105.0

N = 40; 6 cases were missing information.

TABLE 31. REFUSALS OF ASSIGNMENTS BY CIRCUMSTANCES
OF REFUSAL AND REASONS FOR NO REFUSALS

A. Percentage Refusing an Assignment or Potential Work as Contrary to Personal Values

	N	%
Refused	36	16.22
Never refused	186	83.78
Total	222	100.0

2 cases were missing information. 12 cases reported 2 refusals.

B. Percentage Distribution of Circumstances of Refusals[a]

	N	%
Against personal values	22	47.83
Violations of ethical code	23	50.00
Ignored lawyer's advice	1	2.17
Total	46	100.0

Reason: Personal Values	N
Did not like client or position	10
Would not defend race discrimination	2
Would not defend age discrimination	1
Would not defend organized crime	1
Civil rights case	2
Would not defend pollution	2
Involved company participating in boycott of Israel	1
Would not represent management against labor	1
Would not defend violent crime	1
Would not defend redlining	1
Total	22

Reason: Ethical Code	N
Client was committing a crime	10
Conflict of interest	5
Client was not being honest	4
Client harassing others through law	2
Client refused to produce documents	1
Convinced client not to proceed for ethical reasons	1
Total	23

[a] Unit of analysis is refusal. Information on 2 refusals is missing.

C. Percentage Distribution of Reasons Why No Refusals

	N	%
No conflicts with personal values	158	91.9
Personal values should not dictate	14	8.1
Total	172	100.0

14 cases were missing information.

Ideology, Practice, and Professional Autonomy

Despite specialization and growth in firms, large-firm lawyers adhere to a broad conception of their role vis-à-vis clients. More than three-quarters of the sample (76 percent) responded that it was appropriate to act as the conscience of a client when the opportunity presented itself—a consensus that did not vary by age, firm, or field of practice. Virtually the same majority (75 percent) responded that they had the opportunity to give nonlegal advice to clients, but as section A of table 30 indicates, there are significant differences by field and partnership status. Litigation presents practitioners with fewer opportunities for giving nonlegal advice. As section C of table 30 suggests, the reasons are that litigation associates have little contact with clients and that by the time a case is in litigation it is too late to give nonlegal advice.

By far the leading reason for giving nonlegal advice (mentioned by 43.8 percent of respondents) is that a business decision is involved. The majority of other responses have a pragmatic ring as well: that the client asked for advice (14.2 percent), that the field of law required it as part of the practice (24.9 percent), that matters required personal investment decisions (11.2 percent), or that the client needed personal advice (19.5 percent). Very few of the responses suggest broader moral or social concerns. Only 2.4 percent of the respondents mentioned giving advice to address "public relations concerns," the category that would seem to come closest to concern for the public interest. These responses make it clear that lawyers and clients typically come together on business, investment, or fairly narrow legal problems, and it is on those kinds of questions that lawyers and clients most often engage in open discussion. Again, a normative model is inappropriate for the majority of lawyer-client interactions. When lawyers advise clients in a practical vein, questions of the greater good seldom arise.

While lawyers may not often be asked to offer advice concerning the commonweal, how often do they have conflicts with clients over the propriety or morality of client positions? Respondents were asked, "Have you ever refused an assignment or potential work because it was contrary to your personal values?" If they answered yes, they were asked "under what circumstances?" If they answered no, we asked whether it was because "your work has never required you to take a position contrary to personal values or because you do not believe personal values should dictate what work a lawyer will do?" Table 31 shows the breakdown of responses.

Only 16.22 percent of the sample had ever refused an assignment or potential work, and one-third of these thirty-six respondents had done so twice. Section B of table 31 groups the circumstances of refusal into three categories. Half of the coded refusals were in response to violations of professional ethics, such as ongoing criminal conduct by clients, conflicts of interest, and the use of the law to harass other parties. To assist clients in these endeavors would have violated professional ethics and clearly went beyond offending personal values. Roughly one-half of the other refusals implicated personal values, with several respondents refusing to defend clients against certain types of accusations. Reflecting their seniority, partners were more than twice as likely as associates (28 percent to 11 percent) to have refused an assignment. Of those respondents who had never refused an assignment, 91.9 percent had never been confronted with an assignment contrary to their personal values. Only 8.1 percent of the subset who had never refused said that personal values should not dictate what a lawyer does. Hence, three-quarters of the respondents for whom I have complete data have never been faced with a conflict between their personal values and the request of a client.

Two questions of interpretation concerning this finding must be addressed. First, it could be argued that this is too crude a measure to be meaningful, for it does not include all instances in which lawyers infused value preferences into advice or made other more subtle efforts to change their clients' positions. Nor does the measure necessarily include occasions when lawyers reported being "too busy" to accept a personally objectionable assignment. The follow-up probes, however, encouraged respondents to report such instances. Moreover, this finding is consistent with other studies of lawyer-client relationships in corporate firms indicating that such instances are exceedingly rare (Kritzer 1984; Macaulay 1979, pp. 143–151). Second, it could be argued that since we do not know how often clients ask lawyers to do something repugnant, we cannot judge the independence of lawyers from such statistics alone. Calling the glass half-full rather than half-empty, we could argue that this level of incidence shows that the corporate bar has an active conscience. It would, of course, be preferable to know how often lawyers receive untoward requests. But the definition of matters that run contrary to "personal values" is so subjective that I doubt one could ever generate a meaningful baseline measure. Moreover, we know from table 31 that 75 percent of the sample report never having confronted such a conflict. Because of the novelty of the question, we lack established standards for judging whether this level of incidence is high or low. It would be shockingly high for cancer rates but dismally low as a batting average. Yet because the question queries the entire span of a lawyer's career, I am prepared to argue that this demonstrates a striking absence of serious conflict between lawyer and client.

What can we infer from the finding that less than a quarter of the practitioners in this sample have encountered a conflict with personal values and that half of the situations in which lawyers refused work did not involve the subtleties of the public interest but were instead rather obvious violations of professional rules? Three broad explanations can be offered for this pattern. First, the majority of tasks of lawyers in these firms turn on technical matters involving parties of roughly equal status and resources. In preparing a securities offering, in arranging a leveraged leasing transaction, or in planning an estate, lawyers are not called on to deal with questions of good and evil (beyond considerations of simple honesty). Even in hotly contested matters, such as the hostile acquisition of another corporation or antitrust litigation, the contest is not between "good guys" and "bad guys." During the course of pretesting the values questions, one associate chuckled at the moral tone of the items. His comment was something like: "Are you kidding? My work [big case litigation] doesn't raise questions of conscience; it's just a fight over which big corporation is going to get a bigger chunk of the pie." The social questions of our time simply do not come up frequently in large-firm practice.

Second, even though the social values of my sample may be somewhat more liberal than those of the business elite, the attitudes of lawyers and clients are not widely divergent. Sharing the same basic values as their clients, these lawyers will often interpret the social implications of a course of action in much the same way that their clients do. The similarity of values between lawyer and client is reinforced by the career choices of lawyers. Clearly there are some types of practice that involve rather explicit choices about which side a lawyer will take, for instance, between labor and management in labor relations and between plaintiff and defendant in several areas of litigation. Most of these choices are made when a lawyer chooses the law firm or other setting in which he or she will practice. Once this choice is made, lawyers are left with a limited set of case-by-case, client-by-client judgments about refusing assignments (Heinz and Laumann 1978).

Third, it may be that professional training and experience teach lawyers to transform potentially troubling questions of values into matters of technique and strategy. Aubert (1963) suggests that this is

258   The Law Firm as a Social Institution

one of the primary functions of lawyers and that it may contribute to
the resolution of disputes between embittered adversaries. But this
tendency also may undercut the ability and inclination of lawyers to
mediate conflicts or act as normative agents. Litigated matters represent
the most frequent example. The list of circumstances in which lawyers
refused assignments (table 31, section B) suggests that conflicts with
personal values most often arise in litigation. Table 30, section A,
indicates, however, that litigators have the least opportunity to provide
nonlegal advice to clients, in part because they do not have direct client
contact (which is especially true of litigation associates) and in part
because the lawyer's task is the defense of a past action, making it too
late to advise the client about how to avoid the controversy. Of course,
even in the context of an ongoing dispute there are different ways of
playing the game. Counsel can facilitate the progress of litigation and
offer various kinds of advice on settlement. More often, however, the
"heat of battle" syndrome will take effect, so that considerations of
public interest will be dwarfed by the effort to win (Frankel 1978;
Simon 1978).

In the course of one of my interviews, one of the firm's leading
litigators dropped in to see the partner I was interviewing. He recounted
the following story:

> [A new associate said during a training session the other night] "You
> know, the only difference between us and the small-time crook and dirty
> litigator is that they try and do the same thing by dishonesty that we try to
> do by cleverness." And, you know, I had to agree with him. At least it's
> something I've been thinking about a lot ever since then, and it is still
> bothering me. . . . . It's something that we do try and do in a certain way. It's
> something that comes up a lot in an area where there is a piece of information
> that is requested through discovery that you don't want to give over. It raises
> some very tough ethical problems. The way we try and teach that is . . . [He
> describes how they try to finesse such requests for critical information].

Norms about acting as an officer of the court, serving the truth-finding
processes of litigation, thus give way to legal technique in order to
minimize the risk to clients.

Whatever the proper balance may be among these explanations, the
facts do not support Smigel's view that lawyers mediate social conflict
by modifying the unreasonable demands of clients. The notion that
lawyers struggle with clients over fundamental questions about the
common good is simply wrong. Occasionally a lawyer will be faced by
the dishonest or crooked client, and I do not mean to suggest that this

presents a trivial problem. But, in general, large-firm lawyers strive to maximize the substantive interests of their clients within the boundaries of legal ethics. It is neither useful nor accurate to attribute to this elite segment of the bar the kind of broad mediating role that Smigel envisioned. The lack of empirical support for Smigel's model of professional autonomy does not necessarily mean that there is something wrong with the social role played by large firms. That is a normative question that data alone cannot answer. What it does suggest, however, is that a new theory of the social role of large law firms needs to be developed.

TOWARD AN INSTITUTIONAL THEORY OF THE ROLE OF THE LARGE FIRM IN LAW AND SOCIETY

I began this chapter with the supposition that the large law firm is a paradoxical institution: It has the trappings of power and prestige but lacks autonomy from clients. The empirical results support that basic proposition. While the findings are preliminary in many respects, they are sufficiently compelling to raise questions about the source and the dimensions of this paradox. How did the divergence between ideology and practice arise and how is it sustained? Given their lack of autonomy from clients, what influence do large firms have in the legal system?

THE DIVERGENCE BETWEEN IDEOLOGY AND PRACTICE

The divergence between the ideology of professional autonomy and the practice of client advocacy is not new to the American legal profession. The legal elite of the late nineteenth century sought to reform law and government in their "public" roles while representing in private practice the most notorious entrepreneurs of the era, men like James Fisk and Jay Gould (J. Auerbach 1976; Gordon 1984). Several of these reform lawyers—Charles O'Conor, David Dudley Field, John Shearman, and John Sterling—were themselves deeply involved in corrupt activities that could have led to disciplinary action (Gordon 1984, pp. 56–57). We can, however, discern some coherence in these divergent roles, even though the actors might not have been conscious of it. The political and legal reforms to which they dedicated so much of their

260   The Law Firm as a Social Institution

time and energy can be seen as an attempt to rescue their practices from
the risk of scandal. By extricating the law from the crass control of
political patronage and corruption, they could establish a more stable
and legitimate social position that would enable them to serve a broader
range of corporate interests. Indeed, two central tenets of the Cravath
system, the paradigm for the successful law firm, were independence
from partisan politics and the rejection of influence peddling (Swaine
1946, pp. 11–12). Early efforts at reform by the corporate bar thus
tended to unify practice and ideology.

This was but a fleeting historical moment. The very success of the
Cravath system for recruiting and organizing legal talent led to a more
fundamental problem, an increase in the level of inequality in American
society. As Louis Brandeis recognized, the alliance between the elite law
firms and big business led to an unequal distribution of representational
resources that could limit progressive change and undermine the legitimacy of the legal order (1933, pp. 337–343). To resolve the conflict,
Brandeis urged the profession's corporate elite to perform a mediating
role in private practice—as "counsel for the situation"—and to avoid
being wedded to their clients' positions in the public sphere of legislative
reform (1933, pp. 340–343, Frank 1965, p. 702).

Although there never has been a coherent response to Brandeis's
challenge and although the social role of the large law firm has been
subject to intermittent criticism throughout this century (see e.g., Mills
1953, Nader 1970, Berle 1948), the ideology of professional autonomy
retains a surprising vitality in large law firms. This is explainable in
part by the rhetoric of law reform. Large law firms have long maintained
programs for the representation of clients *pro bono publico,* which
could be cited as evidence of the firms' attempts to redress the unequal
distribution of legal services. Although some pro bono programs are
substantial,[16] the general level of interest in pro bono work has dropped
significantly since the late 1960s and early 1970s (*Washington Post,*
December 27, 1983, p. C1, col. 2). The lawyers in three of the four
firms in my sample, on the average, spent less than fifteen hours a year
on pro bono projects. Clearly in most firms the investment in pro bono
representation is insignificant.

Other law reform activities of large firms also are cited as proof of
their autonomous role in legal change. The elite corporate bar occasionally appears in the vanguard of the profession, advocating progressive
reforms opposed by the rest of the bar. Elihu Root (1916), for example,
was an early proponent of the need to develop a sound legal theory of

the administrative agency.[17] At roughly the same time, the president of the American Bar Association was proclaiming the bar's stern opposition to the departure from traditional principles of the separation of powers.[18] Later, during the debates on the Administrative Procedure Act, the leading administrative law practitioners in Washington and the Association of the Bar of the City of New York, then a bastion of prestigious Wall Street firms (Powell 1982), broke from the position of the ABA and supported the version of the bill (which eventually passed into law) that allowed more administrative discretion and less judicial procedure than the version advocated by the ABA (Harrington 1983, pp. 19–21).

The debates in the ABA House of Delegates over the proposed Model Rules of Professional Conduct present a more recent example of the divergence between some members of the corporate elite and the rest of the bar, one that pertains directly to the lawyer-client relationship. The most hotly contested issue was the whistle-blowing proposal that would have required lawyers to disclose information necessary to prevent a client from doing serious bodily harm to another person and would have permitted lawyers to disclose information to prevent or rectify the consequences of other deliberately wrongful acts by clients (see American Bar Association, 1980, pp. 21–26). The proponents of the stricter obligation to disclose were members of elite corporate law firms: Robert Kutak, Robert Meserve, Randolph Thrower, and others (*New York Times,* Feb. 7, 1983, p. 1, Feb. 10, 1983, p. 9, cols. 1–6). For these lawyers the critical issue was maintaining the legitimacy of the profession by mandating that lawyers at least avoid contributing to illegal conduct. This was a select minority of corporate practitioners. The Corporation, Banking, and Business Law Section of the ABA had opposed related provisions of the proposed model rules that would have imposed new obligations on corporate practitioners to report to the board of directors or other corporate officials when they perceived that management was acting in disregard of the law or the corporation's best interests.[19] On the whistle-blowing provision itself, the corporate section remained largely silent. The opposition to the stricter provisions was headed by the American College of Trial Lawyers and a group of "small-town, small-firm and lone practitioners" whose interests were more practical (*New York Times,* February 10, 1983, p. 9, cols. 1–6). Practical interests won out, of course. The opposition succeeded in tightening the rules *against* such disclosure.[20]

These examples may not be typical of the involvement of legal elites in legal change. The law reform activities of members of the elite frequently work to benefit lawyers themselves and their clients. When elite practitioners participate in the revision of a civil practice act, the development of a new divorce statute, or the writing of a condominium ordinance,[21] they can exploit the advantages of time and money which they possess over other practitioners. Typically, they stand to gain business as the experts on the changed law. The support of the elite bar for the Administrative Procedure Act, for example, no doubt reflected a corporatist tendency to view regulation as relatively easily controlled and certainly as a lesser evil than unbridled administrative discretion (see Irons 1981, pp. 17–34). Lawyers engaged in high-status corporate practice face less risk from the obligation to blow the whistle on clients than do criminal defense lawyers, who must deal with client indiscretions as the core of their practice. Nonetheless, these examples of attempted reform are revealing in two respects. First, they point up the highly fragmented nature of the leadership of the bar. As Heinz and Laumann (1982) demonstrate, this fragmentation shows up most dramatically in different practice settings and with different types of clients. But there is also enormous variety and potential for conflict between business interests. As a result, members of the corporate legal elite will not necessarily take the same position on important issues (Salisbury 1986). Second, and more important, these tentative efforts at change suggest that the elite of the profession are more likely than other lawyers to consider the long-run, systemic implications of legal change. Absent the direct and overriding interest of a client, the legal elite will take positions on legal and social issues that maintain the legitimacy of the system as a whole. As has sometimes been observed, the one interest members of the elite have in common is their concern for preserving the system in which they are the elite.

Perhaps an even more pervasive influence in maintaining the ideology of autonomy is the continuing assertion that the law and the law firms partake of a different set of cultural meanings, habits of mind, and organizational practices than ordinary business (see chap. 6). "Commitment to a professional calling involves acceptance of high ethical standards, which generally include a dedication to public service for the benefit and protection of society that looks beyond the mere earning of a livelihood. . . . We must not permit the practice of law to become just another business" (Harrell 1983, p. 864).

So it is asserted that lawyers are a breed apart whose practice is based more on ethical principles than on economic relationships. Such a sermon could be found in any number of law school commencement addresses or bar association speeches at the turn of the century (J. Auerbach 1976, pp. 40–41; Gordon 1984, pp. 63–64). Its recent appearance on the "President's Page" of the *ABA Journal* is a testament to the resilience of this ideology of professionalism (see also Shepherd 1984, p. 6).

While the ideology of professional autonomy persists, the changing organization of work in the corporate sector continues to increase the divergence between ideology and practice. In chapter 1, I argued that the role of general counselor has become increasingly internalized within the corporate structure. Often it is the head of the internal corporate legal department who monitors the organization's legal affairs, defines legal problems, and chooses outside legal counsel. As a result, large law firms have lost many of their wide-ranging, continuous client relationships and have come to depend upon specialized fields and ad hoc, "transactional" tasks for a growing proportion of their practice. Hence, the emerging division of labor in the corporate sphere locates the role of the general counselor in the most constrained organizational environment, the corporate legal department, while lawyers in outside firms are relegated to specialized assignments with predetermined ends. In this increasingly competitive market, lawyers are less likely than ever to play a mediating role with respect to client demands. They are more likely to press for the client's maximum advantage as a way of attracting future business.[22] These changes in the work roles of corporate lawyers will further strain the already stretched ideology of autonomy.

THE INFLUENCE OF LARGE FIRMS

The failure of Smigel's model of professional autonomy and the shift to increasingly ad hoc, highly specialized relationships between law firms and corporate clients raise a fundamental question: If large firms are not autonomous from client interests, what is the nature of their power within the legal system and within society?

My colleague John Heinz has recently posed the same question about the legal profession more generally, but his analysis is especially relevant to lawyers in large law firms. Heinz argues that the power of lawyers should be measured principally by "whether they modify their clients' goals or objectives" (1983, p. 897). Citing the findings I have reported here, as well as evidence from his and Edward Laumann's

264   The Law Firm as a Social Institution

study of Chicago lawyers (Heinz and Laumann, 1982, pp. 379–385), Heinz concludes that in both their private and public functions, lawyers do not possess much power: "[I] conclude that the prestige of the legal profession, the influence of lawyers on their clients, and the collective political action of lawyers do not often bring about an allocation of the society's scarce resources that differs in any substantial way from the distribution that would have been willed by the lawyers' clients or by the polity apart from that prestige, influence, or action" (Heinz 1983, p. 911).

I agree with much of this line of argument. The findings of this chapter substantiate the view that lawyers strongly identify with the objectives of their clients. Thus, if one defines power in terms of changing the goals of others, Heinz is right: Corporate lawyers seldom change the goals of their clients. But if our purpose is to examine the impact of the large law firm on society, this definition of power is too narrow. For a broader theoretical purpose we must develop an institutional model of the firm and include in the analysis the firm's relationships not only with clients but also with legal institutions (courts, bar associations, law schools), community power structures, and other cultural and political institutions. Viewed from an institutional perspective, the elite of the profession exert considerable influence. They have an impact not because they bring about an allocation of society's scarce resources which differs from that willed by clients but precisely because they maintain and make legitimate the current system for the allocation of rights and benefits. This influence is exercised through the large law firms' economic resources, control of the production of legal knowledge, and their impact on law as an ideological system.

Economic Resources of the Firm within the Legal System. Any theory of the law firm as a social institution must first confront the implications of political-economic change in the corporate sphere of the legal profession. The large law firm has been highly successful as an economic enterprise, commanding increasingly larger proportions of the revenues paid for private legal services and growing far more rapidly than the legal profession as a whole. Like the leading organizations in accounting, architecture, and medicine, among others (Starr 1982), the large law firm has in recent years attracted a substantially greater proportion of our society's economic resources. What accounts for this tremendous rate of expansion? And what does it suggest about the role of this institution?

The expansion of large firms has not relied on monopolistic practices.

Unlike the personal client sphere of the profession, the corporate bar has not had to rely on minimum fee schedules or prohibitions of advertising, nor has it had to jealously guard the boundaries of practice from nonlawyers. Nor have large law firms been the beneficiaries of corporate largesse. Instead, as government regulation of business has expanded, as litigation involving corporate actors has become more common and more complex, and as the use of law in business dealings has increased (because of economic growth, the development of new legal forms, and new types of legal maneuvers), large law firms have become the leading entrepreneurs in the expanding market for corporate legal services. By exploiting their position of status within the legal profession, they have become the dominant suppliers of the technical expertise and organizational resources through which corporations react to and shape legal change. Their growth thus reflects largely rational choices by corporations for dealing with the legal environment. The economic expansion of large law firms is evidence of their increasing participation in decisions and processes that affect the distribution of society's resources.

Economic growth, by itself, may not be an appropriate measure of influence. Heinz and I jointly have noted the analytic difficulties in attempting to differentiate the influence of lawyers from the other service occupations in high demand.[23] How can we distinguish the corporate lawyer from the computer programmer, for instance? Both have experienced rapid economic growth; both (well, at least programmers) are indispensable to the workings of corporations; both possess esoteric technical knowledge and require intellectual creativity. Yet computer programmers are not seen as possessing the broader influence on the polity and the society which is commonly ascribed to lawyers. Given this difficulty, Heinz's earlier work suggests taking a narrow definition of power. Because computer programmers do not alter organizational goals, but lawyers might, defining power in terms of the impact on goals effectively distinguishes the two groups.

Despite this difficulty, a broader definition of influence which includes economic growth is more useful theoretically. First, even if the touchstone of the analysis is lawyers' impact on the goals of clients, the economic aspects of lawyer-client relationships are critical. Market conditions affect the degree to which professional producers depend on the consumers of their services and vice versa; these conditions are therefore an important determinant of the relative abilities of the two parties to control the relationship. (For a discussion of producer-consumer relationship, see Johnson 1972, pp. 45–46.)

Second, I do not shrink from considering money as a form of power.

266   The Law Firm as a Social Institution

It is the kind of power with which one pays the rent. As Stinchcombe
suggests, a particularly useful measure of the rank of an organization
in society is its ability to borrow money, for at the time of borrowing
money "prestige . . . is turned into that control over resources" (1965,
p. 171). This is clearly relevant in comparing the resources of large law
firms with other actors in the legal system. For although the economic
resources controlled by large law firms are insignificant relative to the
economy as a whole, within the legal profession large firms are by far
the most dominant economic actors. Their material advantages allow
them to recruit the best legal talent, develop highly specialized expertise,
and command superior organizational resources.

Control Over the Production of Knowledge. In assessing the influence
of large firms, however, we must not stop at the economic aspects of
the organization. For what most sharply distinguishes lawyers from
computer programmers is the special nature of the social relationships
involved in law practice. The relationship between lawyer and client
is itself shaped by a particular set of norms entailing mutual trust and
fiduciary obligations (see chap. 6). Moreover, the producers of legal
services are subject to a broader set of normative commitments to act
as officers of the court and keepers of the public trust. Perhaps, most
important, because the very stuff on which lawyers work consists of
social relationships—whether expressed in the form of a contract or a
lawsuit—the work of large firms is necessarily connected to our society's conceptions of justice and rights. To understand the role of the
large firm, we must examine who controls the production of legal
knowledge as well as the ideological implications of such knowledge.

The basis for the market power of the large law firm is its ability
to control the production of expertise, that is, to produce the most effective form of legal representation. The organization of the law firm
is itself testimony to the power of firms to determine their own standards of quality, for firms maintain much of their traditional professional form despite mounting pressure from corporate counsel for the
delivery of services in a more cost-effective fashion. The craftlike division of labor in the large law firm may be dictated in part by the
technical requirements of the work, but in any event it is the professional group inside the law firm which decides what the work requires.
In order for corporate clients to use the legal expertise of the firm,
they must accept the firm as it is organized.

The control of technical expertise enhances the power of the law firm both with respect to clients and the legal system. Although corporate clients seldom hear their lawyers objecting to corporation proposals on general policy grounds, they most certainly listen to their lawyers' evaluations of tactical considerations. Such tactical considerations will shape client behavior by suggesting what can be accomplished legally. Indeed, the very process of consulting a professional can transform the nature of a client's decision-making process.[24]

The technical expertise and organizational resources of the large law firm may well make a difference as to how society allocates scarce resources through the legal system. As Galanter has argued so persuasively (1974, pp. 117–119), the impact is most apparent when there is an imbalance of representational resources among the parties, but it shows up in other contexts as well.[25] Given the increasing significance of decisions made by the courts and regulatory agencies in numerous areas of social, economic, and political life (Friedman 1986; Chayes 1976), style of legal representation will have a broader impact on the distribution of society's resources than ever before. Although this means that large law firms affect more aspects of our society and are in that sense more powerful, it is not because they are more autonomous from client interests. On the contrary, in the private market the most skilled representation is bought by the highest bidder. And because the law firm is stratified according to responsibility for major clients, there is no question about whose ends will be served.

The Ideological Function of the Firm. The last aspect of the firm's institutional power entails a different and more difficult level of analysis. (For a more fully developed analysis of the ideological functions of the corporate bar, see Gordon 1984, pp. 51–74.) The practical activities of lawyers always serve two functions in society. The first and most immediate is the particular service for a specific client, such as writing a will or drafting documents for corporate reorganization. The second and more abstract function is the invocation of a particular regime of rights which orders property claims, for example, among potential heirs or creditors, according to the dominant ideology of the period. Although the analysis of this latter function and its relationship to the details of everyday practice is methodologically vexing, it is undeniably relevant to the study of lawyers. Surely we are interested in more than whether lawyers hoodwink clients in personal injury or consumer fraud cases; we are interested in the vindication of rights.[26] The intellectual activity of the large law firm constantly affects the jurisprudence of our

268   The Law Firm as a Social Institution

age as new questions are raised, new legislation is drafted, and legal scholarship is generated. This activity also enhances the legitimacy of the legal system in the eyes of the business and political elites with which firms interact directly and, to a lesser extent, in the eyes of the general public. The large law firm is only one actor in the ideological system of American law, and its ideological significance should not be exaggerated. Yet we can gain some idea of the ideological impact of the firm by first returning to the findings reported in this chapter concerning the ideology of the law firm and then considering the appeal that such an ideology might have to other elites and the polity as a whole.

The social and legal values of the lawyers in my survey sample are consistent with the present set of relationships between law, government, and private business. That is, while recognizing the necessity for government regulation of business and a significant institutional role for the law, lawyers adhere to the view that there is a coherent boundary between the public and the private spheres that defines the proper role of law in society. It is not immediately clear, however, why corporate clients submit to institutional relationships in which they must cede some of their independence to lawyers. Corporate clients might well prefer forms of decision making that are less complex procedurally and that allow a more direct exercise of power (Abel 1979, pp. 21–22). Yet we may infer that the appeal of the present legal order for corporate clients is essentially pragmatic. Often, even powerful corporate actors recognize that they have little choice but to submit to certain rules given the strength of the political forces supporting a particular kind of government regulation. Indeed, corporate actors may welcome some involvement by public institutions in their affairs in that it shifts some of the responsibility for the results of their conduct to public authorities. Moreover, formal decision-making procedures afford opportunities for the strategic use of superior representational resources, thus allowing a measure of control over outcomes (Galanter 1974, pp. 119–124).

The public's conception of the law is more removed from the daily activities of large-firm practice, but there is still an important similarity between the public's conception and the ideology of large-firm lawyers. The literature on the psychology of justice suggests that the adversary model of decision making has remarkable appeal in American society (Thibaut and Walker 1978; Dolbeare and Hammond 1968; Murphy and Tanenhaus 1968). Even though American legal institutions rarely function in a fashion even remotely approaching full adversary procedures (Alschuler 1976; Galanter 1986), the adversary ideal dominates the image of American law. Corporate elites of the profession can thus rationalize their aggressive pursuit of client interests in terms that are acceptable to the general public, namely that the procedures followed in arriving at decisions are formally fair.

The paradox of power in the large law firm is deeply rooted in the nature of the American legal system. One need not argue that law firms use their resources of expertise and organizational capacity in autonomous fashion to argue that these resources can make a significant difference in the decisions of legal institutions. On the contrary, in the private market for legal services, the only parties who can support such a style of practice are those with the most resources. Indeed, that is the other half of the paradox of power in the large firm. The influence of these organizations in the legal system derives from and can only serve the interests of corporate clients.

The changing division of labor in corporate legal services may strain the ideology of an autonomous professional practice even more in the future. But the ideology of independence has persisted alongside the reality of a client-dominated profession for so long that I doubt that there will be any dramatic changes soon. At the height of the Watergate scandal, the number of applications to law schools was setting new records. The corruptibility of those lawyers holding the most powerful and responsible positions in the national government did little to discourage students from the prospect of interesting and remunerative work in the law. Besides, one could always identify with the role of Dash or Ervin rather than with that of Dean or Ehrlichmann. The continuing growth of social conflict and government regulation will likely contribute to the continued economic success of the large law firm. But the future impact of these organizations on the distribution of justice and the legitimacy of legal institutions is far more problematic.

8
Rationalization and Power

As the leading organization in the private sector for legal services in the United States, the large law firm mirrors the successes and failures of American law. The large firm has been incredibly successful in garnering the rewards of money and status for its members. Unlike so many other professional groups and indeed many of the more marginal segments of the legal profession, its power derives not from a state-licensed monopoly over the market but rather from its preeminent position in the market. By recruiting the top graduates of the most prestigious law schools and by establishing an organizational structure that maximizes specialization and the commitment of professionals to their work, large firms have converted the power of professional status into the power of organized professional knowledge. The large law firm has made itself the leading center for expertise on complexities of law, thus exercising enormous influence on the course of legal change. Experts from large firms are often key figures in the law reform efforts of bar associations and legislatures. They are leading innovators in developing legal forms of action, whether those be the stock holding company, the trust indenture, or the poison pill. The most pervasive impact of such expertise may not be in the creation of law but in the devising of ways for corporate clients to use the law to seek private ends or to minimize the law's effects on their activities.

The influence of the large firm has been based in part on its ability to shape the culture and image of the American legal profession. The large firm captured the imagination of law students by promising the resources and training necessary to achieve the full realization of professional knowledge and skill. It constructed an ideal of professionalism that promised not just strict adherence to the profession's code of ethics but service to the public interest. Occupying the most prestigious segment of the profession, free from economic dependence on any given client, the large firm seemed to be a bastion of professional autonomy. In private practice the large-firm lawyer was deemed to be in a position to exert a positive moral influence on the powerful corporate actors he represented. In public affairs he was motivated not by narrow self-interest but by a commitment to enhancing the fairness and rationality of the law as an instrument for ordering society. The large law firm thus projected an image that was the culmination of the functionalist vision of the modern professional organization in which status and financial success reflected the institution's contribution to society.

As the law firm has achieved unprecedented economic success in recent years, however, the tensions inherent in its organizational structure and in its role in society have become apparent. The market forces that contributed to rapid growth have bred new levels of competition between firms, and between firms and corporate counsel, leading to uncertainties about economic performance. These changes have altered relationships between lawyers within firms. Partners who do not bring in business face reduced earnings and possibly loss of full partnership status. Associates are under pressure to specialize rapidly, and they put in long hours to justify their comparatively high starting salaries. The chances for rising to partnership status have diminished. With increasing frequency questions about the distribution of profits and the governance of the organization break out into open conflict, leading to the departure of important partners and even the dissolution of firms. Despite widespread efforts to achieve efficient managerial and administrative structures, firms continue to experience serious problems of internal organization.

The conception of professionalism which has justified the firm's privileged position in the profession has been challenged by these changes as well. In the newly competitive market for corporate legal services, legal expertise has clearly become a commodity to be bought and sold. Firms must hawk their wares, promising to achieve the greatest gain for clients at the cheapest cost. Firms no longer can (if they ever did) distance themselves from particular clients. They cannot take the posture of neutral experts seeking to achieve a just resolution of

272   The Law Firm as a Social Institution

conflicting positions; they must present themselves as zealous advocates. As the large firm's claim to professional independence has eroded, the legitimacy of the legal system is itself called into question. If the benefits of legal knowledge are sold to the highest bidder, untempered by the profession's commitment to civic values, the distribution of justice will reflect little more than the distribution of economic power in society.

Thus, the contradictions that confront the large law firm in the course of social change parallel the contradictions confronting law in liberal society. Central to both is the conflict between rationalization and power. The organizational rationalization of the law firm is never fully achievable, because managerial authority is always subject to the power of client-responsible lawyers. Similarly, attempts to develop a more rational and just system of law—which attempts are often led by large-firm attorneys—ultimately are constrained by those groups who hold power in society. So long as legal rationalization serves the interests of these powerful groups, they will support it. But the rationalization of law cannot proceed independently of the balance of power among competing groups.

PROSPECTS FOR ECONOMIC CHANGE

The engines of economic growth in law firms so far show a vitality that presages the continued rapid expansion of firms which has marked the years since the mid-sixties. After a brief pause in growth rates in the recession years of 1981 and 1982, firms have recommenced hiring increasingly larger cohorts of new associates, adding branch offices in different cities, and seeking mergers with smaller firms. What is remarkable is that the magnitude of growth has not yet been affected by the growth of internal counsel or the deregulation of an increasing number of industrial sectors. Only a relatively small number of firms that were heavily dependent on the fields most affected, such as those specializing in energy law and antitrust defense, have experienced a sharp drop in demand. What explains this pattern? And how long can it be sustained?

It is possible that large firms will soon reach a plateau at which growth rates will stabilize. The growth of internal counsel has not yet decreased the rate at which corporations turn to outside firms, but it is an open question whether this recourse will continue. It may also be that the expanded presence of internal counsel led to a jump in outside work because lawyers for the first time were monitoring corporate activity and identifying previously undiscovered "problems." Once monitoring systems are established, the incidence of legal problems may diminish. And as internal legal staffs increase in size and sophistication, the rate at which problems are referred to outside firms will decline.

This scenario, however, does not survive scrutiny. When we consider the type of legal problems that have fed the "boom" in large firms, they do not appear to be largely undiscovered operational problems, such as the processing of sales contracts in the purchasing departments. Instead, large law firms have handled cases involving the massive organization-threatening lawsuit, the investment portfolio gone bad, the application of a new regulatory framework, the latest tax shelter, the legal requirements for attracting new capital, the rapid growth of a new technology or industry. In short, the growth of the law firm appears to be a response to a broad pattern of increasingly rapid change, not only in the law but in American society as well. This tumultuous pattern of growth and change is not likely to subside. Even deregulation does not necessarily imply a drop in the demand for legal expertise. The changes in the banking industry, for example, are giving rise to a new set of economic entities that will require legal services. Bell's recent research on the use of lawyers by corporations suggests that firms that frequently employ lawyers use both internal and external counsel rather than choosing one or the other (1984). The overall prospects for economic growth, therefore, remain excellent for the corporate sector of the legal profession.

Rising aggregate demand, however, does not necessarily guarantee the economic success of individual firms. The shift in growth patterns to specialty firms and away from general service firms and the attendant rise in competition between large firms and between internal counsel and firms will increase the level of economic uncertainty for law partnerships. We have already begun to see some clear winners and losers in the changed market, and this trend will no doubt continue. As is characteristic of booming industries in general, there will be rapid shifts in the fortunes of individual organizations, with widening disparities in the size and profitability of the leading firms.

PROSPECTS FOR STRUCTURAL CHANGE: SPECIALIZATION AND BUREAUCRATIZATION

Changes in the environment of firms will tend to produce law firms that are more specialized and more bureaucratic. The trend toward specialty representation is a general phenomenon that is transforming the client base of even the most established general service firms. The prototypical case of a specialty practice is a firm whose reputation is identified with a particular field or function and which attracts business through the specialized market that develops for those services. When the government of India sought to retain legal counsel for its suit against Union Carbide over the Bhopal disaster, it interviewed some twenty different law firms before selecting a Minneapolis firm that specializes in catastrophe litigation (*New York Times*, March 12, 1985). Specialty groups within large firms also more frequently confront a more competitive market. To be successful specialty groups cannot rely solely on referrals from other clients of the firm but instead must tap into the demand for their specialized services. Thus the protean entrepreneurial spirit that has always characterized the American legal profession has been unleashed in the attempt to develop specialized markets, as firms search for new fields and new legal techniques that will generate a flow of business.

The processes of growth and specialization introduce additional pressures for firms to develop bureaucratic managerial, administrative, and work-group structures. At the managerial level, it will become increasingly apparent that some group within the organization must plan strategically for firms to defend their client bases or take advantage of new opportunities. Hence, the role of leading partners in firms will become more distinct from that of the rest of the organization. As the organization becomes larger and more specialized internally, it will also need to develop internal structures to monitor and coordinate the activities of subgroups. To more efficiently utilize the professional staff, firms will begin to formalize work groups, departments, and assignment procedures. Associates will be under increased pressure to find a manageable niche within the ever more specialized division of labor. They are likely to respond by quickly developing specialties and subspecialties within particular fields, thus staking their chances for partnership on the rate of growth in their chosen field.

The process of bureaucratization will work inexorably in firms, whether the course is explicitly adopted as a managerial policy by firm leaders or evolves through changes in practice which are not acknowledged by managerial pronouncements. But certain limits on bureaucratization are inherent in the law firm. First, the composition of work remains subject to ongoing change and typically involves matters that require custom treatment by skilled professionals. The work process is therefore not subject to direct, centralized control. The rationalization of work procedures will involve the assignment of work, the stability and composition of work groups over time, and mechanisms for coordinating the relationships between various groups. Second, managerial policies in the firm are contingent on a consensus among leading partners. In the absence of agreement among factions, rational managerial initiatives cannot be implemented effectively. Third, bureaucratization will be modified or cloaked in traditional professional terms as a means of attracting clients, recruiting law graduates, and maintaining the commitment of the professional staff. Even though the ideal of the independent professional is strikingly inappropriate as a description of large-firm practice and even though this ideal has been reshaped in the image of the modern bureaucratic law firm, it retains sufficient symbolic power to influence the style of law firm organization.

INTERNAL HIERARCHY

Smigel wrote that the trend in New York law firms in the sixties was toward more democratic forms of governance (1969). To the extent that most firms now contain several partners with substantial client responsibility who must be included in the policy-making council of the firm, in contrast to the one- or two-man leadership systems that characterized the earlier eras of firms, his observation is correct. But the more pervasive phenomenon occurring in firms currently is increasing stratification among lawyers. Whether recognized formally by changes in the partnership agreement or not, many firms consist of a dual partnership in which lawyers with substantial client responsibility run the firm and take home a major portion of the profits while other lawyers function as little more than salaried staff. The work life of associates in large firms has never been pleasant. Even in the era of traditional law firm organization, they were subject to the demands of partners. In today's larger firms their experience is perhaps even more alienating, although better paying. Chances of making partner are diminished, work assignments are less flexible, access to clients and to responsible tasks is more limited.

Three distinctive strata of lawyers in firms—"the finders, the minders, and the grinders"—now occupy increasingly different roles. The relationships between these strata have become more volatile in the changed market for law firms. Whereas ten years ago it would have been virtually unthinkable for a firm to recruit a lawyer from another firm, it is commonplace today. Headhunters routinely inquire into the availability of specialists working in established firms. As a result, young partners have an unprecedented degree of independence. The former option of waiting patiently to move up in responsibility within a firm or of choosing a smaller firm no longer holds; young partners now have the prospect of moving to another firm to establish their own client base and work group.

Even more transient are the associates entering firms. A bare majority of the associates in the four-firm sample, and no more than 63 percent of the associates in any one firm, expressed career commitment to the firm. Roughly half the associates in Chicago's largest firms leave the firm within three years. As firms have grown, associates have become so much grist for the mill. While law graduates willingly accept the high starting salaries and long hours, for many this is a temporary experiment, a good place from which to move. The need to recruit large numbers of law graduates has contributed to diversity in incoming classes with respect to gender and law school status, but associates enter firms today on a much different basis than in earlier years. Despite continuing attempts to appeal to traditions, admission to a law firm is no longer like admission to a select club which, after the individual proves his mettle, guarantees success and prosperity. Instead, the majority of associates in the large cohorts entering firms will leave in a short time without ever having been integrated into the organization.

IDEOLOGY, AUTHORITY, AND CONFLICT

A substantial body of literature suggests that autonomous professional organizations, that is, organizations run by members of a professional group, are very different from other organizations. Smigel (1969) and those citing his work (Satow 1975; Scott 1981) argue that such professional firms lack the hierarchy, the rules, and the conflict that characterize other organizational forms because they are organized around a set of commanding professional norms and standards. Perhaps this conception was appropriate to the stable professional community of New York law firms in the late 1950s when Smigel conducted his fieldwork. It is clearly not accurate today. Large firms are the regimes of client-producers, and this stratum of partners dictates the policies of the firm and projects the ideology of professionalism that justifies the structure of the firm and the client-producers' role in it. That there are not more rules results not simply from professional values but from the inherent difficulties of centrally controlling professional work, from the diffusion of power among the elite themselves (which limits the development of a cohesive managerial approach), and from the resistance of associates and junior partners to the bureaucratization of work and career.

My view of the professional law organization has profoundly different implications from the optimistic rendering by Smigel and others. First, I suggest that the professional law firm may not be the most desirable model for organizational design in postindustrial society. It is prone to conflict and instability, it may be inefficient, and its promise of open participation may be illusory. Moreover, this very form, which has been cited as an alternative to bureaucratic organization, is under increasing pressure and shows increasing tendencies to develop bureaucratic structures.

My conception also suggests that the tension between professionalism and bureaucracy is less a conflict between values than it is a conflict between different groups in the professional organization. As the history of the Duncan firm so eloquently demonstrates, there is no inherent inconsistency between professional values and bureaucratic managerial policies. The leadership of firms can develop a version of professional ideology that elevates the importance of specialization and departmentalization as a means of serving clients better and of providing meaningful experience for lawyers at an early stage in their careers. The failure to rationalize most law firms results from a failure of power. In the Becker firm the concentration of power permitted the implementation of bureaucratic structures even while the expressed ideology of the firm remained traditional. In the two traditional firms the elite did not take the steps to introduce rational administrative and workgroup structures because they could not develop a consensus among themselves.

The same problem appears in the relationship between members of the elite and other partners and between partners and associates. For all the economic and political power the elite possess, they depend on the enthusiastic commitment of their colleagues to their work. They must defer in form if not in practice to the traditional organizational patterns that other partners and associates view as integral to the professional organization. Similarly, although partners are led by economic self-interest to favor the rationalization of the firm, they must defer somewhat to the traditionally oriented prerogatives of potential recruits and new associates. Moreover, the power of leading partners is directly affected by changes in the economics of the firm's

278   The Law Firm as a Social Institution

practice, more so than the managerial stratum in other forms of economic enterprise. If they lose a client or if their field dries up, they
will eventually lose their position of leadership to partners with a growing clientele. Thus, while social change may benefit large firms as a
whole, it is a source of vulnerability to particular sets of elites within
firms.

If professional values are not an autonomous source of organizational structure but reflect the interests and power of different groups
within the firm, questions about the autonomy of the professional
organization arise. The leading partners of the law firm are those
lawyers who are personally responsible for major clients. Contrary to
the usual dictum in the professions literature—that systems of collegial
control serve to enhance the autonomy of professionals—the law firm
provides an example in which the dominant colleagues enforce the interests of clients. This need not operate in crude fashion. The structure
of incentives in the organization, norms of client service, similar social
backgrounds, the very act of repeatedly articulating the client's position,
all will reinforce the pursuit of client interests. In such a context lawyers
will seldom pause to think whether what they are doing is right or just;
even less often will they act on their concerns. The resilience of collegial
structures in a professional organization cannot be presumed to ensure
the exercise of professional judgments independent from client interests.

The tensions between groups within the firm and the relationship
between the law firm and its environment (including clients, law students, other community elites) are mediated by the ideology of professionalism. Although work and careers have changed significantly as
firms have grown and become differentiated, the model of the professional continues to be the independent practitioner. According to the
model, individual lawyers choose their roles (the field they work in, the
partners they work for, the hours they work) and are ultimately responsible for their personal success or failure in the organization. Particularly
in recruitment, firms emphasize the autonomy and flexibility available
in a career with them. But individual autonomy in the abstract is very
different from the options that are available practically. Choice is left
to the individual, but the menu from which the selections are made is
highly structured. Soon after the young attorney enters a firm he or she
sees the ideal of the professional role shifting from that of the general
practitioner to that of the technical functionary. The sheer complexity
of the subject matter and the prospect of developing an expertise that
other lawyers rely on are all the justification this new model of pro-

fessionalism requires. To attempt to cover a number of fields or to change fields comes to seem irresponsible, both because the investment in learning a particular area will have been lost and, more important, because the very definition of competence becomes specialized expertise.

One paradox of this revised ideal of the professional role is that the partners at the top of the organization are precisely those lawyers who have broken out of a narrow technical function to achieve responsibility for clients and earn a position of supervisory authority over the work of technical specialists. The clearest evidence of this pattern was presented in the analysis of the organization of work (chap. 4) where we found that client-responsible lawyers occupied positions that spanned boundaries between groups of specialists and that the partners in client-intake fields were less specialized by substantive field than their counterparts in other specialties. Hence, while it is necessary to establish competence as a specialist, to achieve the greatest power and rewards in the organization, it is also necessary to move beyond such specialized skills. This is a source of considerable frustration for the middle-level partners working in the "service" specialties in firms. Although they are well paid and respected and occasionally they may strike up an innovative strategy for building their own client base, they play a relatively narrow role in the organization and are dependent on the client-producers to bring them work.

The reformulation of the model of professional practice is the principal means by which firms have attempted to accommodate the conflicting needs for bureaucratization and the maintenance of commitment to professional work. While the strategy has been remarkably successful thus far, the strains on the ideology of professionalism are apparent and increasing. No longer is pride in "the firm" sufficient to maintain organizational cohesiveness. With increasing frequency partners at all levels of seniority are defecting from firms in which they have spent their careers. Associates now are less likely to think of the firm as the place where they will spend their careers, and increasingly they evaluate firms on entirely pragmatic grounds. Hence, firms may encounter greater difficulties in obtaining the enthusiastic devotion of associates to their work. Perhaps most revealing are the expressions of concern and disillusionment among firm leaders. The oldest generation of the elites, who are now approaching retirement, speaks of the fear of becoming too big, of losing the esprit de corps. An elderly named partner confided that he wasn't sure he would enter the practice of law today (personal interview, 1979). Still among the most popular speeches on the stump in bar associations is the cry against the deprofessionalization of practice. The speeches will continue, but with little effect. They will serve primarily to bolster the symbols of traditional professional practice while the growth and bureaucratization of firms proceeds quietly and persistently to put greater distance between symbolism and reality.

RATIONALIZATION AND POWER

The rise of the large law firm poses a central problem for sociological analyses of the professions, organizations, and law. Can the structure of the law firm and its position in society be explained by the knowledge it produces or by the power of legal elites and the clients they serve? The orthodox conception of the professions, which is rooted in functionalist social theory, suggests that knowledge is the source of the firm's influence. Accordingly, the expansion of the law firm represents the increasing need for the rational application of legal knowledge. The growth of the firm thus becomes evidence for the progression of law toward greater intellectual consistency and moral force, both of which will enable legal institutions to contribute to the formation of a society that is more rational and just. Opposing theories in the professions literature argue that in an important sense power precedes knowledge. So it is the monopoly of the professional group that allows it to define what constitutes knowledge, how such knowledge is to be produced and consumed, and by whom. From this perspective the standing of the large firm is based on its links to powerful groups in society. While the law firm may produce knowledge, whether the knowledge it produces will serve the interests of society or only of particular groups is far more problematic.

My perspective, developed throughout this book, is a synthesis of these two conflicting positions. I have argued that monopoly theories and related notions of professional dominance fail to explain the rise of the large firm. For while these theories may explain how professional groups gain control over the market for their services, they do not explain changes in the growth or contours of the market itself or the relationship between the nature of the market and the structure of the professional organization that produces services for the market. The strength of functionalist theory is that it provides an explanation for the increasing demand for professional services: the growing need for professional expertise in the increasingly complex systems of social and productive relationships of modern society. But functionalism fails to recognize the historical and political contingencies that affect the production and use of knowledge. The theory overstates the power of professional knowledge in its own right and understates the potential for the arbitrary definition of knowledge or for the abuse of sources of knowledge by powerful groups in society.

I have pursued the problem of social change in the large law firm as a problem of organizational dominance. In this conception the market for professional services is a critical determinant of patterns of growth and structural change in the professional organization. While the nature of both supply and demand is heavily influenced by the professional status of the producers and the distinctive expectations of consumers concerning professional services, the market forces affecting large firms today quite clearly have not been controlled either by the profession as a collectivity or by that segment of the profession practicing in large firms. In this book I have sought to explain how large firms have attempted to maintain their predominant position in the changing market as well as how the leaders of firms have attempted to maintain their position of dominance within the firm. In an argument similar to the functionalist one, I concur that the power of the law firm depends on its capacity to produce usable knowledge. But I depart from the functionalist conception of the origins and ultimate effects of such knowledge. The large firm is not an agent of rationality and justice in the law. Rather, it is the agent of private corporate power. The firm's attempts at rationalization of law must therefore be understood as attempts at refining and legitimating the use of private power. Let us review the evidence for and against these interpretations, both generally and on the basis of the findings in this study.

Functionalist theory would explain the growth of large law firms as a response to the increasing need for specialized expertise in modern society. An integral aspect of the functionalist view of the professions, however, is the relationship between social values and professional work. Durkheim (1964) and Parsons (1951) saw the professions and their collective institutions not merely as sources of knowledge but also as mechanisms for integrating industrial society. In the functionalist conception the modern professions—steeped in the importance of core societal values (justice, health, religion) and trained to develop the knowledge and institutional frameworks with which to pursue these values—are an autonomous elite contributing to the realization of a more advanced social order (see also Shils 1975; Halliday 1987). Certainly it would appear that the law is a critical integrating institution in American society. It was apparent even to Tocqueville that law and lawyers served an important function in the American system by providing the link between the propertied classes and the masses (1863, pp. 348–358). This role has been transformed and intensified during the course of urbanization and industrialization. Not only are legal institutions centrally involved in the articulation of core social values and their optimum implementation, but they have become directly implicated in the operation of a wide range of social institutions, from the family to schools, to prisons, and to welfare agencies among others (Friedman 1986).

The expansion of the large law firm reflects the expanding functions of law as it affects corporations, whether that expansion results from the initiatives of private parties (in the form of litigation, new types of transactions or economic enterprises) or the government (in the form of direct regulation or the creation of new rights that individuals may enforce against corporations, such as antidiscrimination laws). Smigel concluded that large firms executed their expanding role in a socially responsible fashion (1969). Although acknowledging that they served the interests of corporate clients, he suggested that because corporations relied on the firms' expertise, the firms could effectively mediate the demands of clients and the public interest. The continuing growth of firms was thus interpreted as evidence that firms were becoming even more independent of particular corporate interests. Smigel's analysis supported the basic functionalist proposition that autonomous professional expertise played an increasingly important role in social change.

In chapter 7, I disputed Smigel's assertion that large-firm lawyers perform such a mediating function. First, the diversification of the client base of firms has not necessarily made individual lawyers autonomous from client interests. Second, although large-firm lawyers embrace the ideology of professional autonomy in the abstract, when it comes to questions of legal policy that pertain to their practice they strongly identify with their clients' positions and interests. Practice thus determines lawyers' specific conceptions of law and justice. Third, the reported incidence of disagreements between lawyers and clients is extremely rare, never occurring in the careers of three of four lawyers in my four-firm sample. The evidence indicates that the legal elite functions as an enthusiastic advocate of clients, not as an autonomous professional class.

In addition to the failure of Smigel's specific conception of the law firm, there are other fundamental difficulties with functionalist explanations of the firm. The functionalist model accurately links modernization and the rise of professional occupations. That there has been a dramatic increase in the demand for professional services is undeniable. But the model fails to establish the connection between core values and the forms professional organizations take. What is there about the American conception of justice that leads to the emergence of big law firms? Is it at all useful to attribute the rise of these organizations to a set of totemic values? Implicit in the consistent public anguish over the commercialization of practice is the recognition that the success of the law firm derives not from service to particular values but from its success as an economic enterprise.

An alternative explanation for the transformation of the law firm is the power of large-firm attorneys to establish a monopoly over the delivery of their services (Wilensky 1964; Freidson 1970b; Larson 1977). As Larson herself recognizes, theories of monopoly do not fit the legal profession comfortably (1977, pp. 166–176). The difficulty with this explanation, particularly when focusing on the role of elite lawyers, is the relationship between the efforts of the professional group *as a collectivity* and their social position. First, American lawyers are not a unified profession but are instead fragmented in terms of social status and client interests (Heinz and Laumann 1982). They do not often act as a collectivity, and quite frequently different segments of the bar take conflicting positions on issues of professional regulation (see Powell 1985). The power of the profession's collective institutions is very much in doubt. In the last decade bar associations have been stripped of their powers to control the market for legal services by setting fees and limiting advertising. Given the steady expansion in the number of new lawyers throughout this century, it is doubtful whether the profession has been effective at controlling entry. These efforts at market control are not directly relevant to the practice of large firms anyway but primarily affect the market for services to individual clients.

Second, although a number of scholars have argued that the corporate elite of the profession have controlled its collective institutions, the evidence is not clear-cut. Jerald Auerbach suggests that the elite of the bar were principal actors in tightening entrance requirements as a means of preventing the admission of immigrants and other "undesirable" groups to the bar (1976). Carlin found that ethics rules imposed on New York lawyers reflect the power of the corporate elite to define as improper those activities that lower status lawyers are likely to be handling but that seldom arise in the course of corporate practice

284   The Law Firm as a Social Institution

(1966). Given the position of the elite on the bar's ethical boards, disciplinary action can be interpreted as control of lower status practitioners by the corporate elite. Citing Auerbach and Carlin, one might well argue that large firms can control the critical boundaries of the legal profession, thus ensuring their own monopoly (see also Heinz and Laumann 1982, pp. 389–392).

We should note, however, that Auerbach's thesis on the control of bar associations by the corporate elite has been contradicted by other recent research. Halliday and Cappell's study of recruitment to the board of governors of the Chicago Bar Association (CBA) since the 1950s disclosed no evidence of the systematic exclusion of lawyers with a lower status class background or a lower status legal education (1979). In a later study the same researchers found that no one group has controlled the CBA in the modern era; instead, different status groups have asserted greater influence at different times and on different policy issues (Cappell and Halliday 1983). Even granting for the sake of argument that the corporate elite do control the bar, where is the link between the bar's monopoly position and the practice of large firms? If anything, the path of influence runs from the large firm to the bar association. The time and resources of large-firm practitioners allow them to act as a category of modern *honoratiores* in the profession (Weber 1978). Although large firms may use bar association committees to legitimate the positions of clients the firms represent, and although partners may attempt to build referral networks through bar associations, large-firm practice does not depend on the functions performed by the organized bar. The managing partner of one of Chicago's leading firms was quick to point out that bar association activities were not important to standing in his firm (personal interview, 1982). He boasted that there were partners in the firm who were highly visible in bar associations who earned less than half his salary.

A variant on the monopoly thesis is that the source of the large firm's social position is the status-class characteristics of its lawyers. Alexis de Tocqueville claimed that lawyers were the American aristocracy, that they served to protect the legitimacy of private property against the dangers of majority rule (1868, pp. 348–358). Several scholars have used the same argument, focusing in particular on lawyers representing corporations. Corporate lawyers are said to function as a patrician elite who, by dint of common social background and training in law and administration, coordinate the activities of numerous segments of the capitalist class (Bryce 1912; Barlow 1979). In these conceptions what elite lawyers do is less important than who they are. As a distinctive, relatively cohesive class, they could act as intermediaries between highly decentralized commercial enterprises. Jerald Auerbach suggests that in their efforts to control admission to the bar the corporate elite were attempting to maintain the ethnic and class purity on which their position depended (1976, pp. 32–37). Faced with the impossibility of achieving this goal for the bar as a whole, they did so in recruitment to the firm by selecting only from certain law schools and social groups (J. Auerbach 1976, pp. 32–37).

It is undeniable that many large firms discriminated against Jews and other groups through the 1950s. But the critical issue is whether social selectivity explains the large firms' dominance of the profession. The status of firms may have been important to their practice in the nineteenth century, when they operated as intermediaries between emerging capitalist enterprises and the relatively closed social circles of financial interests concentrated in the Northeast. But by 1900 the financial markets had developed a broad capital base in which the personal reputation of lawyers was not necessary to gain financing (see Navin and Sears 1955). This class alliance thesis becomes even less appropriate in the modern era. As Auerbach (1976, p. 184) himself recognizes in his analysis of the impact of the New Deal on the career opportunities of Jewish lawyers, the increasing formalization and complexity of dealings between commercial interests and between government and corporations made the social characteristics of large-firm lawyers less important to what they did in practice. The status-class characteristics of lawyers may remain important corollaries of corporate practice in the modern era, reflecting the preferences of some clients for lawyers of a particular social background as well as the continuing ability of higher status social groups to achieve high professional status through better education and social connections. But the point is that without a demand for *what they do,* the practice of elite firms would not have expanded as it has.

The organizational dominance perspective I have pursued attempts to explain both the material success of the law firm and the tensions that have become increasingly apparent in the organization. The rise of the law firm is in a direct sense the product of organizational rationalization. The dominant centers of economic and political power in modern society are bureaucratic organizations, the corporation and government. Modern corporate power is the result of the rationalization of economic activity brought about through the managerial revolution (Chandler 1977). Similarly the enlargement of government in the modern welfare state reflects not only the growth of welfare functions but the creation of regulatory and fiscal mechanisms that attempt to control the vagaries of economic cycles (see, e.g., Mandel 1975; Habermas 1975). As I argued in chapter 1, the growth of the large law firm has reflected and reinforced these developments. Its expertise and social status have been committed to facilitating the accumulation of capital and responding to changes in the relationship between government and business. In short, the heart of the large law firm's practice has been the process of changing law.

In three distinct senses the law firm embodies the relationship between rationalization and power in American law. First, as an organizational form the large firm expresses the attempt to combine status, expertise, and efficiency in order to provide business with the highest quality legal representation. The genius of Cravath was to recruit and motivate lawyers on the basis of professional status while also developing a coordinated staff of specialists. In its idealized version the Cravath system rewarded technical competence without requiring lawyers to bring in business themselves. The model was highly successful. It capitalized on the emerging ideology of professionalism in law schools that depicted law as a rational and politically pure instrument whose proper functions could be ascertained through scholarly analysis. Rather than rely on personal reputation or crass political connections, corporate practice relied on technical expertise. The Cravath system thus offered the corporation an efficiently organized professional apparatus whose instrumental conception of the law accommodated the needs of business for rapid economic expansion.

Second, in both their public and private roles, large-firm lawyers have been centrally involved in the rationalization of law or in the progressive application of legal doctrine and knowledge to the affairs of corporate clients. Hurst (1970) and other historians (see, e.g., Noble 1977; Dean 1957; Chandler 1977) provide numerous examples of legal innovations involving forms of corporate organization and corporate financing. In a tradition traceable to David Dudley Field, the outspoken proponent of codification (see Friedman 1973, pp. 340–358), the corporate elite have often led efforts for law reform. As draftsmen of changes in state constitutions, federal and state law, and local ordinances, large-firm attorneys not only influenced the form and substance of law but reinforced their position as leading experts in fields of law undergoing change.

In their role as interpreters of law for corporate clients large-firm attorneys have often become the agents of rationalization within the corporation. The advice of corporate lawyers concerning antitrust laws has been credited with encouraging the trend away from horizontal mergers toward the integrated operating company after 1890 (see Chandler 1977, pp. 315–339, 375–376; Kocka 1980, p. 106). Macaulay (1979) describes the impact of counsel in getting banks and consumer finance companies to revise their procedures to conform to truth-in-lending legislation. As a result of equal employment opportunity laws and changes in the contractual relations between unions and management, numerous aspects of employment relationships within organizations have been structured and monitored by lawyers or legally assisted personnel managers (see Selznick 1968; Burawoy 1979, pp. 109–120). By encouraging the development of formal, rule-bound systems in legally sensitive areas of the corporation's operations, corporate lawyers promote the further bureaucratization of the corporation.

Third, there is another sense in which we can speak of corporate lawyers as agents of rationalization. The large law firm "rationalizes" power in the sense that its intellectual labors legitimate the current system of legal rights (see chap. 7). Only in a political system that separates public and private power could an organization like the large law firm develop. Although it performs manifestly public functions by interpreting the law and shaping the course of legal development, and although it embraces a code of ethics that implies an obligation to public service, the large firm is a creature of private market forces. Its services are for sale to the highest bidder. But only major corporate actors can afford the price. The private market for legal services thus creates the bond between large firms and corporate clients and a shared commitment to the institution of private property. In this sense the lawyers in large firms are organic intellectuals (Gramsci 1971, pp. 5–23). The product of their intellectual labors can only be appropriated by a particular class in a particular type of social system. Such lawyers will always resist efforts to fundamentally remake the social structure.

In this conception the large law firm is an important source of ideology supporting the social system. Gordon's work on the role of corporate lawyers early in this century presents the fullest account of this ideological function (1983). Gordon argues that the legal elite have contributed to a particular vision of American society, occasionally by the articulation of values in highly visible arenas but more pervasively through their day-to-day practical activities. It is precisely through the development of new legal forms and doctrines that large firms have played their most significant ideological role. Through these activities large firms have clothed private interests with the mantle of legitimate authority. The corporate legal elite created the legal fiction of the corporation, transformed it from an instrument limited to specific, public functions to a private entity endowed with the constitutional rights enjoyed by real persons, and enshrined the autonomy of corporate management through the business judgment rule (Hurst 1970, Berle and Means 1932). They delayed the intrusion of government regulation into the affairs of business on the constitutional grounds of freedom of contract until the political and economic realities of the Depression forced a retreat from such a separation between public and private spheres (Irons 1981). In the modern era they have pragmatically served the ends of corporate clients, through increased regulation or deregulation. But despite acceptance of the regulatory state, this elite has continued to provide the intellectual underpinnings for the distinction between public power and private property. By recruiting the graduates of the best law schools, the elite in large law firms continue to socialize new generations of practitioners into this conception of society and the role law should play in it. As the leading consumer of law school graduates, as an important source of alumni contributions, and as a source of members of university boards of trustees, the large law firm is an important constituency of the law school. Directly or indirectly the dominant mode of teaching law students and doing legal research reflects their ideology and interests.

But the rationalization of law and the rationalization of the law firm are inherently partial and conflictual processes in the American legal system. The law firm is a product of its labors. Reflecting the elaboration of legal rules and legal maneuvers and the expansion of modern law in which it has played a central role, the large law firm has inexorably become a large-scale bureaucratic organization consisting of groups of highly specialized practitioners and a differentiated hierarchy of client-producers, managers, and workers. The traditional form of law firm organization has fallen victim to the success of the enterprise and the efforts of corporations to control rising legal costs. Yet the ultimate limits on rationalization in the law firm are the sources of power in the organization. Given their dependence on the enthusiastic commitment of partners and associates to their work, the leaders of firms must defer to some traditional professional norms. More important, managerial authority will never become autonomous from the leading client-producers. The ideal of the Cravath system, in which lawyers are rewarded based on legal competence rather than client-getting, has never been attained. Bureaucratization is thus contingent on the ideology and interests of leading partners.

The role of large firms as advocates of the rationalization of law is similarly circumscribed by client interests. For all the law firm's apparent power and despite its invocation of the ideology of professional autonomy, its commitment to the rationalization of law extends only insofar as it does not intrude on client interests. This may seldom be apparent. As Weber notes in his sociology of law, support for formally rational systems of law typically comes from those groups in society that already are in power, for it is often a means of securing their advantages through apparently neutral procedures (1978, pp. 729–730). Efforts toward legal change by large-firm practitioners do not necessarily reflect a steady march toward more rational and just systems of rules but instead reflect the firms' particular ideologies and the interests of their clients.

Despite the economic and political power of the corporations they represent and their own success in influencing the law, large law firms cannot control legal change. They themselves are not a unified group; they reflect divisions among business interests along industry and regional lines. Nor can they resist broad-based political movements such as that which realigned government and business during the New Deal. Although the ideology of professional independence and high competence continues to attract clients and law graduates, that too appears increasingly vulnerable. Rather than rely on professional mystique or personal relationships in choosing law firms, clients have begun to critically examine the results they get from outside firms. Law students have become increasingly wary of the career prospects offered by firms. While the graduates of prestigious schools still almost routinely start out in large firms, their commitment is often tentative and short-lived. Even within the ranks of partners, firms can no longer maintain cohesiveness. From the junior specialist to the most senior client-producer, partners are finding that other firms are willing to bid for their services. With increasing frequency lawyers are trading institutional loyalty for the opportunities offered elsewhere.

The erosion of institutional stability and the ideal of professionalism within the large law firm may be the manifestation of a growing malaise in the most powerful segment of the legal profession. It is ironic that in the period of its most dramatic success the large law firm faces the greatest doubts about its unifying principles and its role in society. The uncertainty inside firms may be rooted in the broader contradictions in American society, a society that aspires to the ideals of a rational and just legal order, but in which the realization of those ideals depends on the economic resources and political power of private interests.

Appendix A

OPEN-ENDED INTERVIEW: TOPICAL OUTLINE

I. Statement of Purpose

Two kinds of interviews, one with leaders and senior members asking about the direction of the organization and one with a random cross section asking about personal practice and attitudes. Someone will contact you later about the cross-sectional i.v.

II. Confidentiality

III. Personal Career

IV. Description of Position/Role in Firm

A. Field

1. Future developments affecting growth of practice in firm

   a. House counsel
   b. Specialty firms
   c. Changes in law
   d. Changes in economy
   e. Policies of firm in area: conflicts, staffing, etc.
   f. Trends in specialization
      1. Will it increase?
      2. What subspecialties are emerging?

2. How certain is the growth?

3. How do you or the firm monitor growth?

4. What attracts clients to firm in this area?

   a. Established vs. specialty clients
   b. Importance of individual vs. firm reputation
   c. Referral systems
   d. Types of clients

B. Work group/Department/Personal Working Style

   1. Do you administer a section of the firm?

      a. Formally or Informally
      b. Composition of group
      c. What responsibilities?/What does group do as a group?/
         Personal work style.

         1. Assignment

         2. Division of labor

            a) How detailed?
            b) Routine training
            c) Size of actual work group
            d) Continuity of work groups
            e) Mixture of specialties or within one specialty
            f) Coordination among groups
            g) Supervision and quality control:
               How intensive? Rules about review?

         3. Group meetings, lunches, etc.

         4. Developments in law: how keep current?

         5. Personnel requirements

            a) How get lawyers within firm? Requests for recruitment
            b) Rate of specialization in area: from beginning,
               gradually, or how?
            c) Use of paralegals

         6. Equipment: use of computer research, word processing

7. Accounting information

    a. Personal hours:
        1. Administration
        2. Supervision
        3. Personal practice
    b. For work group
    c. For firm
    d. What are important concerns? Is there any indication of profitability from different kinds of practice?

8. Succession within group or to your clients

    a. Do you groom heirs, formally or informally?

C. Firm as a Whole

1. Formal Structure

    a. Committees
    b. Offices: chairman, managing partner, etc.
    c. Selection procedures: basis for selection
    d. Terms, turnover, stability
    e. Changes in formal structure over the years
    f. Partnership agreement
        1. Exist?
        2. How inclusive?
    g. Decision making: how does it work?
        1. Voting?
        2. Voting powers?

2. Policies

    a. Specialization: rate, choice, guidance
    b. Compensation
        1. New business/old business/other factors
        2. Decision process
    c. Admissions to partnership
        1. Ingredients of success/failure
        2. Decision process
    d. Growth
        1. Sheer size
        2. New fields
        3. Lateral hiring
        4. Branch offices
        5. Plans for future
        6. Partner-associate ratios

e. Structure
   1. Departmentalization
   2. Assignments
   3. Rules
f. Comparison to New York
   1. Why different?
   2. Any trend in that direction?

3. Organizational Domain

   a. What is unique about firm?

   b. Future directions of firm's practice within context of trends in profession as a whole
      1. House counsel
      2. Competition with other firms
      3. Firm's market

4. Organizational Success

   a. What is most important for a successful operation?
   b. How handle increasing size?
   c. Esprit de corps
      1. Impact of size
      2. Impact of other policies

Appendix B

STRUCTURED INTERVIEW SCHEDULE

Interview Schedule
Large Law Firm Study
Robert L. Nelson
2/25/80

Key: — Conditions for asking certain questions are put in parentheses preceding the question, such as, '(IF YES) What specialty is that?'; or immediately following the response that is the condition, such as, '1. Yes (ASK A) 2. No (GO TO 2).'

— Instructions to interviewers are capitalized, such as, RECORD ABOVE.

— Simple probes to get an answer started are indicated by 'PROBES:'

— Probes to be asked regarding open-ended questions if the information covered in the probe has not been volunteered are underlined, such as, Did law school courses affect your decision?

— Questions to be answered from listings prior to the interview, if possible, are indicated by 3 asterisks in the left margin.

— Aides to interviewers concerning potential inquiries are in brackets beginning with '??:' immediately after the question.

296   Appendixes

Introduction
READ TO RESPONDENT PRIOR TO THE INTERVIEW

Before beginning this interview, I would like to tell you about this project.
The American Bar Foundation is sponsoring a study of the history and current
organization of large law firms in Chicago which we hope to expand to other
cities later. Your responses are completely confidential. No member of the firm
will see your responses. The name of this firm, its clients, and its attorneys will
be kept strictly confidential.

I am not a lawyer and therefore am not familiar with all legal terminology,
but I have been trained in this material. So I may ask you to explain some of
the things you tell me. For convenience sake, because some of our questions
call for fairly complicated descriptions of your career and your attitudes, I
would like to tape the interview. As you will see, none of our questions ask
about confidential or privileged information. And, of course, you can tell me
to turn off the tape recorder at any time.

$$\boxed{0}\boxed{1}$$
1–2

I. Work History

$$\boxed{}\boxed{}\boxed{}$$
3–5

1. I would like to begin by asking you some questions about your
   work history.

   A. What jobs have you held since graduating from law school?

      1. Current firm only (SKIP TO PAGE 3)
      2. Other jobs $$\boxed{}$$
                                                                          6

      FOR EACH POSITION ESTABLISH THE FOLLOWING
      AND RECORD BELOW.

JOB 1: Name Employer: _____ $$\boxed{}\boxed{}\boxed{}$$
        Former Name: _____   7–9
        No Longer Exists: __96__
        DK   __98__ $$\boxed{}\boxed{}\boxed{}$$
                                                            10–12

        A. Type Employer

           1. Law firm
           2. Court (spec. _____) $$\boxed{}$$
           3. Govt. (spec. _____)   13
           4. Armed forces
           5. Other (spec. _____)

        B. Period: From _____ To _____ $$\boxed{}\boxed{}$$
                                                            14–15

Appendixes 297

    C. Location: □□ 16–17

      1. Chicago
      2. New York
      3. Washington
      4. Other _____ □ 18

JOB 2: Name Employer: _____ □□□ 19–21
      Former Name: _____
      No Longer Exists: 96
      DK   98 □□□ 22–24

    A. Type Employer

      1. Law firm
      2. Court (spec. _____)
      3. Govt. (spec. _____) □ 25
      4. Armed forces
      5. Other (spec. _____)

    B. Period: From _____ To _____ □□ 26–27

    C. Location: □□ 28–29

      1. Chicago
      2. New York
      3. Washington
      4. Other _____ □ 30

JOB 3: Name Employer: _____ □□□ 31–33
      Former Name: _____
      No Longer Exists: 96
      DK   98 □□□ 34–36

    A. Type Employer

      1. Law firm
      2. Court (spec. _____)
      3. Govt. (spec. _____) □ 37
      4. Armed forces
      5. Other (spec. _____)

    B. Period: From _____ To _____ □□ 38–39

    C. Location: □□ 40–41

      1. Chicago
      2. New York

3. Washington
4. Other _____   □
                                                     42

IF THERE ARE OTHER JOBS, RECORD SAME INFOR-
MATION ON THE BACK OF THE PAGE.

2. When were you first employed with this firm?

   _____   ☐☐☐☐
                  (month/year)   55–58

   A. What was your status with the firm then? USE AS PROBES
      OR RECORD

      ┌ 1. Paralegal
      ┌─ 2. Summer clerk—1st year
      └ 3. Summer clerk—2nd year
        4. Associate
        5. Partner
        6. Other (Specify) _____   □
      │   59
      └────────▶ So when did you start on a regular basis as a
                 lawyer with the firm? _____   ☐☐☐☐
                          (month/year)   60–63

   B. Currently you are a _____ , is that right?   □
                        1. Partner 2. Associate   64

                 (FROM PREVIOUS INFORMATION)
           (IF THEY DID NOT START AS A PARTNER BUT
                   CURRENTLY ARE, ASK C)

   C. When were you made partner? _____   ☐☐
                                (Year)   65–66

3. How did you happen to join this firm?   ☐0☐2☐☐☐
   RECORD VERBATIM.   1–5
   PROBES: How did you first learn about the firm?
           Why did you join the firm?   ☐☐☐☐☐☐
                                                     6–11

   A. Did you have friends with the firm when you joined it: [??:   □
      Include acquaintances]   12

      1. Yes   2. No

   B. Have members of your family ever been employees of the firm?   □
                                                                     13

      1. Yes   2. No

      └▶ Who? _____
         What relation to you? _____   ☐☐☐
                                                           14–16

II. Career in Firm

4. Now I would like to ask you some questions about your career within the firm. The careers of lawyers in firms follow many different patterns, but are frequently marked by a few events or developments that are important to their individual careers. These developments may include becoming specialized in a field or type of work, working on a big case, working closely with an important partner, assuming responsibility for a client or a piece of litigation, making partner, etc. To the extent possible, could you please give me a brief chronological profile of your career within the firm, including any developments you see as important to your career here. ACCOUNT FOR ENTIRE PERIOD WITH FIRM.

PROBE: What kind of work did you do when you first started here?

|⃞|⃞|⃞|⃞|
17–20

Phase/Event 1—Begin Date: _____
(month/year)

End Date: _____
(month/year)

|⃞|⃞|⃞|⃞|
21–24

        Specialty 1. _____
        Case   2. _____
        Lawyer   3. _____
        Client   4. _____
        Autonomy 5. _____

|⃞|⃞|
25–26

|⃞|⃞|
27–28

PROBE: When and how did that change?

|⃞|⃞|⃞|⃞|
29–32

Phase/Event 2—Begin Date: _____
(month/year)

End Date: _____
(month/year)

|⃞|⃞|⃞|⃞|
33–36

        Specialty 1. _____
        Case   2. _____
        Lawyer   3. _____
        Client   4. _____
        Autonomy 5. _____

|⃞|⃞|
37–38

|⃞|⃞|
39–40

PROBE: When and how did that change?

|⃞|⃞|⃞|⃞|
41–44

Phase/Event 3—Begin Date: _____
(month/year)

End Date: _____
(month/year)

|⃞|⃞|⃞|⃞|
45–48

Specialty 1. _____
Case   2. _____
Lawyer   3. _____   □□
Client   4. _____   49–50
Autonomy   5. _____

                              □□
                              51–52

- -

PROBE: When and how did that change?   □□□□
                                          53–56

Phase/Event 4—Begin Date: _____
                              (month/year)
End Date: _____   □□□□
                              (month/year)   57–60

Specialty 1. _____
Case   2. _____
Lawyer   3. _____   □□
Client   4. _____   61–62
Autonomy   5. _____

                              □□
                              63–64

- -

PROBE: When and how did that change?   □□□□
                                          65–68

Phase/Event 5—Begin Date: _____
                              (month/year)
End Date: _____   □□□□
                              (month/year)   69–72

Specialty 1. _____
Case   2. _____
Lawyer   3. _____   □□
Client   4. _____   73–74
Autonomy   5. _____

                              □□
                              75–76

- -

PROBE: When and how did that change?   [0][3]□□□
                                          1–5

Phase/Event 6—Begin Date: _____
                              (month/year)
End Date: _____   □□□□
                              (month/year)   6–9

Specialty 1. _____
Case   2. _____   □□□□
Lawyer   3. _____   10–13
Client   4. _____
Autonomy   5. _____   □□
                              14–15

                              □□
-   16–17

Appendixes

Let me review a few things we are especially interested in.

A. First of all, let's examine to what extent changes in your career in the firm have been changes in the fields of law you have worked in or the type of work you have done.

   1. What was the first type of work you concentrated on? _____
                                                    18–19

     (a) When did you begin to concentrate on that? _____
                                          (Year)   20–21

     (b) How did you come to concentrate on that? What were your reasons? _____
                                                  22–23

     (c) Did other lawyers advise you to specialize in that?

        1. Yes 2. No RECORD COMMENTS VERBATIM   24

        ↳On what grounds?   25–26

   2. What, if any, was the next type of work you concentrated on? _____
                                                27–28

     (a) When did you begin to concentrate on that? _____
                                          (Year)   29–30

     (b) How did you come to concentrate on that? What were your reasons? _____
                                    31–32

     (c) Did other lawyers advise you to specialize in that?

        1. Yes 2. No RECORD VERBATIM   33

        ↳On what grounds: 34–35

   3. What, if any, was the next type of work you concentrated on? _____
                                                36–37

     (a) When did you begin to concentrate on that? _____
                                          (Year)   38–39

     (b) How did you come to concentrate on that? What were your reasons? _____
                                    40–41

     (c) Did other lawyers advise you to specialize in that?

        1. Yes 2. No RECORD VERBATIM   42

        ↳On what grounds?   43–44

302   Appendixes

4. Are there any other fields of law in which you have worked
   enough that we should know about in order to have a good
   profile of your specialization? What is that? _____
                                                                    45–46

   (a) When did you begin to concentrate on that? _____
                                            (Year)   47–48

   (b) How did you come to concentrate on that? What were
       your reasons? _____
                                                                    49–50

   (c) Did other lawyers advise you to specialize in that?
                                                                     51
       1. Yes   2. No   RECORD VERBATIM
       └   52–53

       └▸On what grounds? RECORD VERBATIM
                                                                    54–55

B. Another aspect we might explore is responsibility for clients.

   1. Have you brought any new clients or matters to the firm?

      1. Yes   2. No (SKIP TO C)
      ↓   56
      2. About how many?_____
      ↓   57–58
      3. How would you describe the amount of legal work they
         have brought to the firm? RECORD VERBATIM

         PROBE: Are they big clients to the firm, minor
                clients, or something in between?
                                                                    59–60

   4. When did you first bring a new client or matter to
      the firm? _____
                           (Year)   61–62

      (IF THEY BROUGHT MORE THAN ONE NEW
      CLIENT TO THE FIRM, ASK 5, OTHERWISE
      SKIP TO C)

   5. Have there been any major increases in the amount
      of new business you have brought to the firm that
      stand out in your mind as substantial additions to
      your client responsibility, or has the amount of
      business you have brought in increased rather
      steadily over the years?

      1. Substantial additions   2. Steady increases
      ↓   (SKIP TO C)   63

Appendixes

      6. Without actually naming the clients, could you please tell me what the major increases were and about when they occurred?

C. Have you ever sent a bill to a client?

      1. Yes   2. No (SKIP TO D)

      1. Within the last twelve months, would you say you have sent out bills 1. Once or twice 2. Occasionally 3. Regularly?

      2. Do you have authority to send out bills to clients without having the bill reviewed by another lawyer in the firm?

          1. Yes   2. No (SKIP TO D)

      3. For how many clients? _____

      4. How would you describe the amount of legal work these clients have brought to the firm?
RECORD VERBATIM

         PROBE: Are they big clients to the firm, minor clients, or something in between?

      5. When did you first get the authority to send a bill directly to a client, without it being reviewed by another attorney here? _____
                                     (Year)

      6. Was that a new client you had brought to the firm?

         1. Yes   2. No

      (IF THEY HAVE AUTHORITY TO SEND BILLS TO MORE THAN ONE CLIENT, ASK 7)

      7. (Other than any clients you brought to the firm as new clients) Have there been any major developments that stand out in your mind as substantial increases in your responsibility for sending bills to clients or has that responsibility increased rather steadily over the years?

         1. Substantial increases   2. Steady increases
            (ASK 8)   (SKIP TO D)

      8. Without actually naming clients, could you tell me what the major increases were and roughly what year they occurred? _____
                                     (Year)

304   Appendixes

D. Finally, we would like to know if you act as a primary contact between any clients and the firm, in the sense that the client or its personnel frequently contact you directly about new matters, etc. (IF SUBJECT HAD BROUGHT NEW BUSINESS TO THE FIRM OR HAD FINAL BILLING AUTHORITY FOR ANY CLIENTS, SAY: Please do not include the clients you brought to the firm or for whom you have final billing authority.

Are you a primary contact with any clients or for any matters?

1. Yes   2. No (SKIP TO E)

☐
24

1. For how many clients? _____

☐☐
25–26

2. How would you describe the amount of legal work they have brought to the firm? RECORD VERBATIM

☐☐
27–28

   PROBE: Are they big clients to the firm, minor clients, or something in between?

3. When did you first become a primary contact with a client? _____
                           (Year)

☐☐
29–30

   (IF THEY ARE PRIMARY CONTACT FOR MORE THAN ONE CLIENT)

4. Have there been major developments that stand out in your mind as substantial additions to your responsibilities as a primary client contact or has your responsibility increased rather steadily?

   1. Substantial additions   2. Steady increases
                                   (SKIP TO E)

☐
31

5. Without naming any clients, could you please tell 32–35 ☐☐☐☐
   me what these major developments were and
   roughly when they occurred?   36–39 ☐☐☐☐

                                                        40–43 ☐☐☐☐

E. 1. Throughout your career here have there been one or two partners who stand out in your mind as ones you have worked with very closely?

                                                        44 ☐

   1. Yes   2. No

   └─►Who? 1. _____ 2. _____   ☐☐☐☐☐☐
                                                        45–50

Would you say you worked with him/them on:

1. one or two cases
2. a particular client
3. or a variety of things?

☐☐ 51–52

Other Comments: (RECORD VERBATIM)

☐☐ 53–54

2. Have you ever belonged to a relatively well identified group of lawyers in the firm, such as a department, a case team, etc.?

1. Yes   2. No (SKIP TO E)

☐ 55

↳ What was the first group: _____

☐☐ 56–57

When would you say you joined them?
_____
          (Year)

☐☐☐☐ 58–61

When did that end? <u>1. It continues</u>
                      (Year)

What was the second group? _____

☐☐ 62–63

When did you join them? _____
                  (Year)

☐☐☐☐ 64–67

When did that end? <u>1. It continues</u>
                      (Year)

What was the third group? _____

☐☐ 68–69

When did that end? <u>1. It continues</u>
                      (Year)

☐☐☐☐ 70–73

F. (ASK ASSOCIATES ONLY) Most associates begin working in a firm with fairly close guidance and do not handle many matters on their own, without supervision. After a while, they begin to work more autonomously. Would you say that you now practice with substantial autonomy?

1. Yes   2. No (SKIP TO NEXT SECTION)

☐ 74

↳ 1. About when did you begin to obtain such autonomy? _____

☐☐☐☐ 75–78

306   Appendixes

III. Current Practice—Time Expenditures

5. I would like to ask you a series of questions about how you have
   spent your working time in the last twelve months. We are trying
   to develop a good general profile of your current practice, so
   please don't worry about giving precise answers, and please bear
   with us if this seems tiresome. HAND CARD A

   A. First of all, for comparative purposes, please briefly
      review the standardized list of fields of law on Hand
      Card A. I am going to ask you to tell me roughly what
      percent of your time you spent in these fields during
      the last 12 months (or since you started working at the
      firm if that was less than 12 months ago).

      $\boxed{0\,|\,5\,|\,|\,|\,}$
      1–5

      You will note that civil litigation is one of the fields. Did
      you spend any time in civil litigation in the last 12 months?

      > 1. Yes   2. No (SKIP TO 2) $\boxed{}$
      >   6
      > └▶Then please include all the time you spent on litigated
      >   matters in the civil litigation category, and we will
      >   break that time down after you describe the rest of your
      >   time.

      └▶2. Without worrying too much about the percentages
           adding to 100% could you tell me how much of your
           time you spent in these fields?

LEGAL SPECIALTIES

_____ Admiralty	13–15	$\boxed{}$
_____ Antitrust—Plaintiffs	16–18	$\boxed{}$
_____ Antitrust—Defendants	19–21	$\boxed{}$
_____ Banking—Regulatory	22–24	$\boxed{}$
_____ Banking—Other	25–27	$\boxed{}$
_____ Civil Litigation	28–30	$\boxed{}$
_____ Civil Rights/Liberties	31–33	$\boxed{}$
_____ Commercial Law (Contracts, UCC, etc.)	34–36	$\boxed{}$
_____ Condemnations	37–39	$\boxed{}$
_____ Consumer Law and Debtor/Creditor— Consumer/Debtor	40–42	$\boxed{}$
_____ Consumer Law and Debtor/Creditor—Seller/Bank/ Creditor	43–45	$\boxed{}$
_____ Criminal Law—Defense	46–48	$\boxed{}$
_____ Divorce (including family law, adoption, etc.)	49–51	$\boxed{}$

Appendixes 307

_____ Environmental Law—Plaintiffs   52–54
_____ Environmental Law—Defendants   55–57
_____ General Corporate   58–60
_____ General Family Practice   61–63
_____ Labor Law—Unions   64–66
_____ Labor Law—Management   67–69
_____ Landlord-Tenant   70–72
_____ Municipal Law (including Bond issues)   73–75
_____ Patent, Trademarks and Copyright   76–78
_____ Personal Injury—Plaintiffs
_____ Personal Injury—Defendants
_____ Probate (Wills and Trusts)/Estate Planning
_____ Public Utilities, Administrative Law and
       Regulated Industries
_____ Real Estate—Personal Residential (pursuant to
       sale of individual residences)   1–8 | 0 | 6 |
_____ Real Estate—Commercial   9–11
_____ Securities   12–14
_____ Tax—Corporate   15–17
_____ Tax—Personal (Income, Estate, etc.)   18–20
_____ Other (specify) _____

(IF THEY SPENT TIME IN CIVIL LITIGATION) Of your
time in civil litigation, roughly what percent fell
into the other categories?   21–23   24–26

PERCENT OF TIME SPENT IN CIVIL LITIGATION

_____ Admiralty   27–29
_____ Antitrust—Plaintiffs   30–32
_____ Antitrust—Defendants   33–35
_____ Banking—Regulatory   36–38
_____ Banking—Other   39–41
_____ Civil Rights/Liberties   42–44
_____ Commercial Law (Contracts, UCC, etc.)   45–47
_____ Condemnations   48–50
_____ Consumer Law and Debtor/Creditor—Consumer/Debtor 51–53
_____ Consumer Law and Debtor/Creditor—Seller/Bank/Creditor

308   Appendixes

_____ Divorce (including family law, adoption, etc.)   54–56 [| |]
_____ Environmental Law—Plaintiffs   57–59 [| |]
_____ Environmental Law—Defendants   60–62 [| |]
_____ General Corporate   63–65 [| |]
_____ General Family Practice
_____ Labor Law—Unions   66–68 [| |]
_____ Labor Law—Management   69–71 [| |]
_____ Landlord-Tenant
_____ Municipal Law (including Bond issues)   72–74 [| |]
_____ Patent, Trademarks and Copyright   75–77 [| |]
_____ Personal Injury—Plaintiffs   78–80 [| |]
_____ Personal Injury—Defendants   1–11 [0|7| | | |] [| |] [| |]
_____ Probate (Wills and Trusts)/Estate Planning
_____ Public Utilities, Administrative Law and
         Regulated Industries   12–14 [| |]
_____ Real Estate—Personal Residential (pursuant to
         sale of individual residences)   15–17 [| |]
_____ Real Estate—Commercial   18–20 [| |]
_____ Securities   21–23 [| |]
_____ Tax—Corporate   24–26 [| |]
_____ Tax—Personal (Income, Estate, etc.)   27–29 [| |]
_____ Other (specify) _____   30–32 [| |]
                                                              33–41 [| |]

1. Do you consider yourself a specialist in any of these
   fields?

   1. Yes   2. No (SKIP TO b)   [ ]
   | 42
   └➤ What specialty is that? RECORD VERBATIM
      1. _____ 2. _____   [| | | | | | |]
      3. _____ 4. _____   43–50

   a. Is there a particular type of work within
      1. _____ that is a special skill   [| |]
               (specialty)   51–53
      or subspecialty of yours? _____
      _____

How about 2. _____ ? _____   [| |]
            _____   54–56

How about 3. _____ ? _____   [| |]
            _____   57–59

Appendixes

How about 4. _____ ? _____
_____ 60–62

    b. Would you say that other members of the firm regard you as a specialist?

       1. Yes   2. No   63

       ↳ In what fields?

       1. _____ 2. _____
       3. _____ 4. _____   64–71

(IF THEY SPENT TIME IN CIVIL LITIGATION, ASK 2–5, OTHERWISE SKIP TO B)

    2. What proportion of your time in civil litigation during the last twelve months was spent in what is commonly referred to as "big case" litigation, that is, cases involving extended discovery, voluminous documents, and extensive preparation for trial? _____   72–74

    3. Did you represent any plaintiffs last year?

       1. Yes   2. No   75
       ↓
       What proportion of your time in civil litigation was for plaintiffs? _____   76–78

    4. How many trials or evidentiary hearings did you participate in during the last twelve months? _____   79–80

       [??: Include attendance where subject did not say anything] | 0 | 8 | | | |
                                                                   1–5

       a. (IF ANY) In how many were you first chair? _____   6–8

    5. How many appellate cases did you personally argue in the last twelve months? _____   9–11

B. I would also like to get an idea of roughly how frequently you engaged in other activities that practice typically involves. Hand Card 1, in the packet before you lists some common activities. Please indicate how frequently you performed these during the past twelve months (or since starting with firm if that was less than 12 months ago) by circling the appropriate number. HAND CARD 1.

	Never	Seldom	Sometimes	Frequently	Very Frequently
1. Taking depositions (Includes defending depositions)	1	2	3	4	5
2. Appearing in court	1	2	3	4	5
3. Doing legal research	1	2	3	4	5
4. Administering a particular function in the firm (such as recruitment, assignments, etc.)	1	2	3	4	5
a. What aspect of the firm was that?					
5. Writing letters	1	2	3	4	5
6. Negotiating with lawyers not in the firm	1	2	3	4	5
7. Conferring with lawyers belonging to the firm	1	2	3	4	5
8. Supervising and reviewing the work of other lawyers in the firm	1	2	3	4	5
9. Writing briefs and legal memoranda	1	2	3	4	5
10. Preparing motions, complaints, answers, requests, etc., connected with litigation	1	2	3	4	5
11. Preparing for trial, interviewing witnesses, etc.	1	2	3	4	5
12. Reviewing documents	1	2	3	4	5
13. Drafting legal documents, such as contracts, settlement papers, wills, etc.	1	2	3	4	5
14. Talking to clients or other lawyers in person or on the telephone	1	2	3	4	5

Appendixes

	Never	Seldom	Sometimes	Frequently	Very Frequently
15. Participating in continuing legal education of some kind	1	2	3	4	5
16. Professional activities, such as bar association work.	1	2	3	4	5

Other—Please specify what other activities we need to know about to have a good grasp of what your practice entails.

	Never	Seldom	Sometimes	Frequently	Very Frequently
17. _____	1	2	3	4	5
18. _____	1	2	3	4	5
19. _____	1	2	3	4	5
20. _____	1	2	3	4	5
21. _____	1	2	3	4	5
22. _____	1	2	3	4	5

6. How many hours do you estimate you billed in 1979? [??: Include matters of professional development billed to the firm, nonpaying clients, etc.]

   ☐☐☐☐ 12–15

   _____ (ASK A)
   DK ____98____ (GO TO B)

   A. Approximately how many non-billed hours did you work? [??: Include all time spent practicing within firm that was not billed in some way.]

   _____ (GO TO C) DK __98__ (GO TO C) ☐☐☐☐ 16–19

   B. About how many hours did you work in a typical week last year? _____ ☐☐ 20–21

   C. Do you have a goal for the number of hours you would like to bill?

   1. Yes   2. No (SKIP TO D)   22 ☐

   ↳ 1. What is it?   ☐☐☐☐☐ 23–27

   ↓ 2. How did you arrive at that goal?   ☐☐ 28–29

312   Appendixes

   D. Is there pressure to bill a certain number of hours?

     1. Yes   2. No (SKIP TO 7)

     └▶a. Where does it come from?

7. How often did you go to court during the last twelve months?
   For example, did you go once a month, for two days, etc.?
   RECORD NUMBER AND RELEVANT UNIT OF TIME.

         Frequency   Time Interval

        _____   _____

   IF THEY WENT AT ALL, ASK A, B. OTHERWISE GO TO 8.

   A. Did you go to other kinds of formal hearings, such as arbi-
      trations? [??: Do not include depositions]

     1. Yes   2. No

     └▶How often? _____

   B. In what types of courts, agencies, or other forums did
     you appear?

     1. Federal district
     2. Federal appellate level (e.g., court of appeals)
     3. State trial level (circuit)
     4. State appellate level (court of appeals)
     5. Municipal
     6. Chancellory
     7. Probate
     8. Other (specify) _____

Now we would like to ask you some questions about where you get
your work or your assignments within the firm.

8. During the last 12 months what proportion of your time was
   spent on assignments or work that came directly from clients
   rather than other lawyers in the firm? [??: Directly from clients
   includes any work arising directly from client contact, even if a
   lawyer had originally been assigned to the matter by another
   lawyer.]

     _____ %   1. Less than 10%   2. Less than 5%

   (IF 100%, SKIP TO 9)

Appendixes

A. What proportion of your time during the last twelve months did you spend on assignments made by an assignments partner; that is, through a formal assignments system?

_____ %   1. Less than 10%   2. Less than 5%   ☐☐☐
                                                 45–47

(IF 100%, SKIP TO 9)

1. Where does the remainder of your work come from? RECORD VERBATIM. PROBES: Do you get it from informal contacts or from a group of lawyers?   ☐☐☐
                                                                                                                                                 48–50

   (a) So would you say you get the remainder primarily from (1) a wide variety of informal contacts or from (2) a fairly stable group of lawyers? (IF A STABLE GROUP) Which group? _____   ☐☐☐
                                                                                                                                                                                                       51–53

9. About what proportion of your time during the last 12 months was spent on spot assignments for which you are called on to handle a specific task or a discrete aspect of a matter, as opposed to some kind of continuing involvement in a matter?

   _____ %   1. Less than 10%   2. Less than 5%   ☐☐☐
                                                    54–56

IV. Organization of Practice Within the Organization of the Firm

Now that we have described your activities in some detail, I would like to put that into the context of how the firm as a whole is organized.

10. Because most law firms are organized very informally, it is difficult to get a clear idea of how lawyers work together. For that reason, we are simply giving you a list of partners and associates in the firm, and are asking you to indicate about how much time you worked with someone during the last twelve months. HAND CARD 2. Please include all kinds of working contacts in which you had some kind of direct working relationship with other lawyers in the firm during the last twelve months.

   > RESPONSES TO POTENTIAL INQUIRIES:
   >
   > 1. Base answer on amount of time spent rather than number of cases or matters alone.
   > 2. Closeness of working relationship: direct enough that you know they read your work product or that you read or used their work product.
   > 3. Include professional work done within the firm, such as bar association work, writing, firm administration.

314   Appendixes

11. The next few questions ask for some general information
    about the clients you represent.

    A. Roughly what proportion of your working time last year
       did you spend representing individuals on personal
       matters (such as wills, divorces, etc.). _____ %   ☐☐☐
                                                                        57–59

       So you spent the remaining _____ % on business
       clients and other entities?   ☐☐☐
                                                                        60–62

    B. About what proportion of your time did you spend on the
       client you worked the most for during the last 12 months?

       _____ %   ☐☐☐
                                                                        63–65

       1. Was last year typical in that respect?

          1. Yes   2. No   8. Don't Know   ☐
                       | 66
                       ↳Why not? _____   ☐☐
                                                                        67–68

    C. About what proportion of your time did you spend on
       clients who bring business to the firm on a one-case or one-
       transaction basis, as opposed to regular or longstanding
       clients of the firm? [??: Even if the case is very long and
       drawn out, that is a one-time client if the firm doesn't do
       other work for it.]

       _____ %   1. Less than 10%   2. Less than 5%   ☐☐☐
                                                                        69–71

12. Did you spend any time on pro bono law last year?

    1. Yes   2. No (SKIP TO 13)   ☐
     | 72
     ↳1. About how many hours? _____   ☐☐☐
     ↓   73–75
      2. What kinds of projects did this work involve?   ☐☐
                                                                        76–77
                                                          ┌──┬──┬──┬──┬──┐
                                                          │0 │9 │ │ │ │
                                                          └──┴──┴──┴──┴──┘
                                                            1–5

13. What do you see as the attitude of the firm toward pro bono
    work?   ☐☐
                                                                        6–7
    A. Is it actively encouraged?   ☐
                                                                        8
       1. Yes   2. No—Why not? RECORD VERBATIM   ☐☐
        | 9–10
        ↳How? RECORD VERBATIM

Appendixes

B. Would you like to do more pro bono work than you do?

    1. Yes   2. No RECORD COMMENTS

14. Lawyers sometimes are in a position to give advice beyond the purely legal questions surrounding a case or transaction, whether it be on matters of business judgment, policy issues, or matters of ethics. Do you have much opportunity to provide such non-legal advice?

    1. Yes   2. No—Why not? (THEN SKIP TO 15)

    ↳1. How does the opportunity arise?
    ↓
    2. Do you take the opportunity when it is presented?

       1. Yes   2. No

15. In general, do you think it is proper for lawyers to try and act as the conscience of their clients in situations where that opportunity presents itself? RECORD VERBATIM [??: Is it proper to tell clients what they should do in addition to what the law permits them to do?]

V. Professional and Community Activities

The next set of questions deals with your activities in professional and community organizations.

16. What bar associations do you belong to?

    1. ABA
    2. CBA
    3. ISBA
    4. CCL
    5. Am. College of Trial Lawyers
    6. 7th Circuit B.A.
       Other (specify)
    7. _____
    8. _____
    9. _____

    A. Have you held any offices or chaired any committees in these organizations?

       1. Yes   2. No (SKIP TO B)
       ↓
       Please give me up to five of the most important positions you have held, or hold, as well as the years you held them.

Org. Code (From above)	Office/Chair	Period From	To	
_____	_____	____	____	⬜⬜⬜⬜⬜⬜⬜⬜ 36–43
_____	_____	____	____	⬜⬜⬜⬜⬜⬜⬜⬜ 44–51
_____	_____	____	____	⬜⬜⬜⬜⬜⬜⬜⬜ 52–59
_____	_____	____	____	⬜⬜⬜⬜⬜⬜⬜⬜ 60–67
_____	_____	____	____	⬜⬜⬜⬜⬜⬜⬜⬜ 68–75

B. Have you served on any committees in these organizations?

1. Yes 2. No (SKIP TO C) ⬜ 76

Please give me up to five of the <u>most important</u> you are on, or have been on, and what years you were on them. $\boxed{1}\boxed{0}$ ⬜⬜⬜ 1–5

Org. Code (From above)	Committee Name	Period From	To	
_____	_____	____	____	⬜⬜⬜⬜⬜⬜⬜⬜ 6–13
_____	_____	____	____	⬜⬜⬜⬜⬜⬜⬜⬜ 14–21
_____	_____	____	____	⬜⬜⬜⬜⬜⬜⬜⬜ 22–29
_____	_____	____	____	⬜⬜⬜⬜⬜⬜⬜⬜ 30–37
_____	_____	____	____	⬜⬜⬜⬜⬜⬜⬜⬜ 38–45

C. About how many hours did you spend on bar association activities in the last twelve months? _____ ⬜⬜⬜ 46–48

1. Has your involvement advanced your professional career?

    1. Yes 2. Only slightly (SKIP TO 2)

    3. No (SKIP TO 2) ⬜ 49

    ↳How? ⬜⬜ 50–51

2. Has it benefited the firm?

    1. Yes 2. Only Slightly (SKIP TO D)

    3. No (SKIP TO D) ⬜ 52

    ↳How? ⬜⬜ 53–54

Appendixes 317

D. 1. Have you held a government office or served on professional or government committees, such as counsel to a government body, or on a law reform commission, etc., since joining the firm?

    1. Yes   2. No (SKIP TO 2)   ☐
    ↓   55

    a. What were those and roughly when was that?
                                                   56–59
                                                   60–63
                                                   64–67
                                                   68–71

  2. Have you ever participated in the legislative or rule-making process, either by drafting legislation, testifying in hearings, lobbying, or in any other way since joining the firm?

    1. Yes   2. No (SKIP TO 3)   ☐
    ↓   72

    a. Can you very briefly give me the three most important occasions and tell me when they happened?

        1. _____
                                                73–75

           Date _____
                                                76–77

           Were you representing paying clients in this matter?

           1. Paying clients
                                                78–79

           2. Other (specify) _____

        2. _____ | 1 | 1 | | | |
                                                 1–5

           Date _____
                                                6–8

           Were you representing paying clients in this matter?

           1. Paying clients
                                                9–12

           2. Other (specify)

3. _____   ☐☐☐
                                          13–15

    Date _____

    Were you representing paying clients in this
    matter?   ☐☐
                                               16–17

    1. Paying clients   ☐☐
                                               18–19

    2. Other (specify) _____

3. Have you published any writing in professional journals,
   law reviews, or elsewhere since joining the firm?

   1. Yes   2. No (GO TO 4)   ☐
                                               20

   a. Would it be convenient for you to give me some
      citations? If not someone will contact you later
      about them.

      RECORD NAME OF PUBLICATION, VOLUME,
      PAGE NOs., YEAR. PUBLICATION AND YEAR
      WILL SUFFICE IF THEY DON'T KNOW THE
      OTHERS.

      _____ Contact further

4. Have you participated in brief writing or arguments
   leading to written decisions by the U.S. Supreme
   Court since joining the firm?

   1. Yes   2. No (ASK a)   ☐
                                               21

   How many? _____   ☐☐
                                               22–23

   (a) How about U.S. Court of Appeals decisions?

   1. Yes   2. No (ASK b)   ☐
                                               24

   How many? _____   ☐☐
                                               25–26

   (b) How about state supreme court decisions?

   1. Yes   2. No   ☐
                                               27

   How many? _____   ☐☐
                                               28–29

17. A. Here is a list of the kinds of organizations that many people belong to. Please look over this list (HAND CARD B) and for each heading *give the names* of the organizations you belong to. READ EACH HEADING AND RECORD NAMES THEY GIVE YOU.

   B. (ASK FOR EACH ORGANIZATION LISTED:) How actively involved are you in (NAME OF ORGANIZATION)? Have you held a leadership position in the organization, have you been actively involved, or have you been inactive?

   (IF THEY HAVE BEEN ACTIVE IN ANY OF THESE, ASK C)

   C. Has your involvement in any of these advanced your professional career? Which one(s)? How?

   RECORD VERBATIM, USING LETTERS AND NUMBERS TO INDICATE WHICH ORGANIZATION THEY ARE REFERRING TO.

   [ ][ ][ ][ ] 30–33

   1. Has your involvement in any of these benefited the firm? Which one(s)? RECORD VERBATIM, USING LETTERS AND NUMBERS TO INDICATE WHICH ORGANIZATION THEY ARE REFERRING TO.

   [ ][ ][ ][ ] 34–37

	A.	B.		
		Involvement		
		Leader	Active	Inactive

a. On Boards of Directors, Boards of Trustees, etc. RECORD NAMES OF PUBLICLY HELD CORPS.

	Leader	Active	Inactive		
1. _____	3	2	1	38–42	▢▢▢▢▢
2. _____	3	2	1	43–47	▢▢▢▢▢
3. _____	3	2	1	48–52	▢▢▢▢▢
4. _____	3	2	1	53–57	▢▢▢▢▢
5. _____	3	2	1	58–62	▢▢▢▢▢

b. Religious Connected Groups

	Leader	Active	Inactive		
1. _____	3	2	1	63–67	▢▢▢▢▢
2. _____	3	2	1	68–72	▢▢▢▢▢

c. Business Groups; such as Chamber of Commerce, Rotary

	Leader	Active	Inactive		
				1–5	1 2 ▢▢▢
1. _____	3	2	1	6–10	▢▢▢▢▢
2. _____	3	2	1	11–15	▢▢▢▢▢
3. _____	3	2	1	16–20	▢▢▢▢▢

d. Political Groups or Organizations

	Leader	Active	Inactive		
1. _____	3	2	1	21–25	▢▢▢▢▢
2. _____	3	2	1	26–30	▢▢▢▢▢
3. _____	3	2	1	31–35	▢▢▢▢▢

e. Legal Clubs (not Bar Associations)

	Leader	Active	Inactive		
1. _____	3	2	1	36–40	▢▢▢▢▢
2. _____	3	2	1	41–45	▢▢▢▢▢

f. Civic, Charity or Welfare Organizations

	Leader	Active	Inactive		
1. _____	3	2	1	46–50	▢▢▢▢▢
2. _____	3	2	1	51–55	▢▢▢▢▢

VI. Integration into Firm

The next few questions deal with your plans for the future and your attitudes about the organization of the firm. Let me remind you at this point that your answers will not be made available to other persons in the firm.

18. What are your future career plans?

    A. Would your ultimate goal be to spend your career practicing in the firm?

    (IF THEY EXPRESS ANY DOUBTS ABOUT STAYING, ASK 1)

    1. What alternatives to staying here would you consider? RECORD VERBATIM

    (IF THEY MENTION GOING TO OTHER FIRMS ASK) How large a firm would that be?

    B. What things currently attract you to this firm? USE CATEGORIES IF CONVENIENT, OTHERWISE RECORD VERBATIM.

        1. Job security
        2. Money
        3. Opportunity for advancement w/i firm
        4. Personal friendships
        5. Intellectual challenge
        6. Firm as a resource for practice
        7. Tradition/feeling for firm
        8. Prestige of firm
        9. Quality of work done

    C. What things, if any, bother you about the firm? RECORD VERBATIM

322   Appendixes

D. (IF THEY ARE A PARTNER) Do you aspire to a position of leadership within the firm, such as membership on the governing committee of the firm?

1 | 4 | | |
1-5

1. Yes   2. No

6

19. If you had your choice, what things, if any, would you change about your practice? RECORD VERBATIM

7-8

9-10

11-12

A. Would you change your fields of law?

13-14

1. Yes   2. No

15-16

17

B. Would you change the extent of your specialization?

18

1. Yes   2. No

20. If you had your choice, what things, if any, would you change about this firm?

19-20

21-22

23-24

25-26

A. Would you introduce more structure, or would you reduce structure?

27-28

1. Yes—Why? RECORD VERBATIM
2. No—Why not?

29

30-31

B. Should policymaking be democratic? Why or why not?

32

1. Yes—Why? RECORD VERBATIM
2. No—Why not?

33-34

21. Of your five best friends, how many are with the firm?

35-36

Appendixes

    A. How many lawyers at the firm do you consider good friends of yours? _____

37–38

22. Have you ever refused an assignment or potential work because it was contrary to your personal values?

39

    1. Yes   2. No (ASK B)

    A. Under what circumstances? (THEN SKIP TO 23)

40–41

    B. Is that because (1) your work has never required you to take a position contrary to your personal values or (2) because you do not believe personal values should dictate what work a lawyer will do?

42

43–44

    (CIRCLE NUMBER AND RECORD VERBATIM)

23. The following questions are about your position on how various aspects of this firm should be run. Would you please answer the questions on Hand Card 3 by circling the appropriate response code for each statement. HAND CARD 3

VII. Socio-Legal Values

The next set of questions deals with your attitudes about certain legal and social issues. I will begin with some very general questions, which we use to see what different individuals volunteer in response to a general question.

24. If you were a judge, what do you think would be more important in your decisions: 1. developing the continuity of law and following precedent, or 2. doing justice in particular cases? CIRCLE NUMBER AND RECORD VERBATIM

45

46–47

    A. Could you briefly discuss why you chose that as more important?

48–49

50–51

324   Appendixes

25. If you possessed the necessary legislative and judicial power,
    what are the one or two most important changes, if any, that
    you would make in the law you practice? RECORD
    VERBATIM

                                                                    52–53

    1. _____
                                                                    54–55

    2. _____
                                                                    56–57

    3. _____

    A. How would those changes affect your clients? PROBES:
       For example, would it lower their legal costs, or would it
       decrease their operating expenses, etc? RECORD   58–59
       VERBATIM

       1. _____
                                                                    60–61

       2. _____
                                                                    62–63

       3. _____
                                                                    64–65

    B. How would those changes affect your personal practice?
       PROBES: For example, would it decrease the demand for
       your services, or would it make your job simpler?
       RECORD VERBATIM   66–67

       1. _____
                                                                    68–69

       2. _____
                                                                    70–71

       3. _____
                                                                    72–73

26. The following questions deal with your position on certain
    legal and social matters. Would you please answer the ques-
    tions on Hand Card 4 by circling the appropriate response
    code for each statement. Please answer based on your per-   1 5
    sonal values rather than on your interpretation of any   1–5
    law. HAND CARD 4

                    VIII. Background Questions

I would like to conclude this interview with a few questions about
your personal background.

27. What year were you born? _____
                                                                     6–7

Appendixes 325

28. Which of the following comes closest to the type of place you were living in during most of the time you were at high school? READ EACH CATEGORY UNTIL THEY RESPOND.

   1. In a large city (over 250,000)
   2. In a suburb near a large city
   3. In a medium-sized city (50,000–250,000)
   4. In a small city or town (under 50,000)
   5. In open country or on a farm
   8. Don't know

   ☐
   8

29. Which of the categories on Hand Card C best describes the kind of work your father (father substitute) usually did while you were growing up? Could you please give me the letter?
   _____

   ☐☐
   9–10

   A. Which of the categories best describes the kind of work your mother (mother substitute) usually did while you were growing up? Could you please give me the letter?
   _____

   ☐☐
   11–12

30. Was your father self-employed or did he work for someone else?

   1. Self-employed
   2. Some one else
   8. Don't know

   ☐
   13

   A. (IF THE MOTHER WAS EMPLOYED) Was she self-employed or did she work for someone else?

   ☐
   14

   1. Self-employed
   2. Someone else
   8. Don't know

31. Was your father a lawyer?

   ☐
   15

   1. Yes   2. No (GO TO 32)
   ↓
   A. What law school did he graduate from?

0. None	1. Chicago	7. Loyola
	2. Columbia	8. Marshall
	3. DePaul	9. Michigan
	4. Harvard	10. Northwestern
	5. Illinois	11. Yale
	6. Kent	___ Other (specify)

   ☐☐
   16–17

32. Where did you go to college? _____

   ☐☐☐
   18–20

33. What was your major? _____

   ☐☐☐
   21–23

326   Appendixes

34. Where did you go to law school?

    0. None   1. Chicago   7. Loyola
               2. Columbia   8. Marshall
               3. DePaul   9. Michigan
               4. Harvard   10. Northwestern
               5. Illinois   11. Yale
               6. Kent   ___ Other (specify)
               _____
                                                              24–25

35. Approximately what was your class standing in law school;
    that is, approximately what percentage of your class ranked
    higher than you upon graduation? _____
                                                              26–27

36. Were you a member of a student publication in law school?
                                                              28
    1. Yes   2. No (SKIP TO 37)

    A. Did you hold an editorial position?
                                                              29
       1. Yes   2. No

       ↳What was that? _____
                                                              30–31

37. Do you hold any other degrees or certifications?

    1. Yes   2. No   32

    ↳What? _____
                                                              33–34

38. In political terms, do you consider yourself a conservative, a
    moderate, a liberal, or what?

    1. Conservative
    2. Moderate
    3. Liberal
    ___Other (Specify) _____
                                                              35–36

39. With respect to national politics do you consider yourself a
    Republican, Democrat, an Independent, or what?

    1. Republican   3. Independent
    2. Democrat   ___Other (specify) _____   37

40. With respect to Chicago politics do you consider yourself a
    Republican, a Democrat, an Independent, or what? [??:
    ANSWER AS IF SUBJECT LIVED IN CHICAGO.]

    1. Republican   3. Independent
    2. Democrat   ___Other (specify) _____   38

41. Do you have a religious preference? That is, are you either Protestant, Roman Catholic, Jewish, or something else?

   1. Roman Catholic
   2. Protestant (specify) _____
   ___ Jewish (would that be:)
   3. Orthodox
   4. Conservative
   5. Reform
   6. Other
   7. None

   39–40

42. How often do you attend religious services? USE CATEGORIES AS PROBES IF NECESSARY.

   1. Never
   2. Less than once a year
   3. About once or twice a year
   4. Several times a year
   5. About once a month
   6. 2–3 times a month
   7. Nearly every week
   8. Every week
   9. Several times a week

   41

43. Are you currently married, widowed, divorced, separated, or single?

   1. Married
      Is this your first marriage? (IF NO) Which marriage is this for you? _____
   2. Widowed
   3. Divorced
   4. Separated
   5. Single

   42

44. What nationality background do you think of yourself as having—that is, besides being American? RECORD EXACT ANSWER.

   43–45

   46–48

   (IF THEY DO NOT GIVE YOU A NATIONALITY OTHER THAN AMERICAN OR MIXED, ASK:)

   What nationality background was your father? _____
   What nationality background was your mother? _____

   49–51

328   Appendixes

45. (CODE RESPONDENT'S SEX)

    1. Male   ☐
    2. Female   52

46. (CODE RESPONDENT'S RACE, ONLY IF YOU HAVE NO
    DOUBT. OTHERWISE ASK) What race do you consider
    yourself?

    1. White   ☐
    2. Black   53
    3. Asian
    4. Indian

47. In which of these groups did your personal earnings from the
    practice of law, for last year—1979—fall? That is, before
    taxes and other deductions. Just tell me the letter. HAND
    THEM CARD D.

    _____ a. Under $10,000
    _____ b. $10,000 to 14,999
    _____ c. $15,000 to 19,999
    _____ d. $20,000 to 29,999
    _____ e. $30,000 to 39,999
    _____ f. $40,000 to 49,999
    _____ g. $50,000 to 59,999
    _____ h. $60,000 to 69,999
    _____ i. $70,000 to 79,999
    _____ j. $80,000 to 89,999
    _____ k. $90,000 to 99,999
    _____ l. $100,000 to 124,999
    _____ m. $125,000 to 149,999
    _____ n. $150,000 to 174,999
    _____ o. $175,000 to 199,999
    _____ p. $200,000 to 249,999
    _____ q. $250,000 to 299,999
    _____ r. $300,000 to 399,999
    _____ s. $400,000 to 499,999
    _____ t. Over $500,000   ☐☐
                                                           54–55

I would like to close with a final statement about confidentiality. In
order to better preserve the confidentiality of your own responses
and to minimize the possibility that the responses of those we interview in the future will be biased, we would appreciate it if you
would not discuss the details of the interview with your colleagues.
Thank you.

INTERVIEWER REMARKS

(TO BE FILLED OUT AS SOON AS POSSIBLE AFTER LEAVING RESPONDENT)

48. Length of interview _____ Minutes
    56–58

49. Date of interview _____ _____
    Month   Day
    59–61

50. In general, what was the respondent's attitude during the interview?

    Friendly and interested 1

    Cooperative but not particularly interested 2

    Impatient and restless 3

    Hostile 4

    62

51. INTERVIEWER'S INITIALS _____
    63–64

330   Appendixes

Hand Card 1

Frequency of Activities during the Last Twelve Months

CARD 16

$\dfrac{16}{1-2}$

▢▢▢ 3–5

	Never	Seldom	Sometimes	Frequently	Very Frequently	
1. Taking depositions	1	2	3	4	5	6
2. Appearing in court	1	2	3	4	5	7
3. Doing legal research	1	2	3	4	5	8
4. Administering a particular function in the firm (such as recruitment, assignments, etc.)	1	2	3	4	5	9
a. What aspect of the firm was that?						10–11
5. Writing letters	1	2	3	4	5	12
6. Negotiating with lawyers not in the firm .	1	2	3	4	5	13
7. Conferring with lawyers belonging to the firm	1	2	3	4	5	14
8. Supervising and reviewing the work of other lawyers in the firm	1	2	3	4	5	15
9. Writing briefs and legal memoranda	1	2	3	4	5	16
10. Preparing motions, complaints, answers, requests, etc., connected with litigation ...	1	2	3	4	5	17
11. Preparing for trial, interviewing witnesses, etc.	1	2	3	4	5	18
12. Reviewing documents	1	2	3	4	5	19
13. Drafting legal documents, such as contracts, settlement papers, wills, etc.	1	2	3	4	5	20
14. Talking to clients or other lawyers in person or on the telephone	1	2	3	4	5	21
15. Participating in continuing legal education of some kind	1	2	3	4	5	22
16. Professional activities, such as bar association work	1	2	3	4	5	23

Other—Please specify what other activities we need to know about to have a good grasp of what your practice entails.

17. _____	1	2	3	4	5	24–26
18. _____	1	2	3	4	5	27–29
19. _____	1	2	3	4	5	30–32
20. _____	1	2	3	4	5	33–35
21. _____	1	2	3	4	5	36–38
22. _____	1	2	3	4	5	39–41

Appendixes

CARD 20   20 / 1–2

☐☐☐   3–5

Hand Card 2
Who You Worked with during the Last Twelve Months

Partners	Once or Twice	On Several Occasions	Regularly
Partner A	_____	_____	_____
•			
•			
•			
•			
Partner Z	_____	_____	_____

Who You Worked with during the Last Twelve Months

Associates	Once or Twice	On Several Occasions	Regularly
Associate A	_____	_____	_____
•			
•			
•			
•			
Associate Z	_____	_____	_____

Appendixes

Hand Card 3

CARD 23

Please indicate how strongly you agree or disagree with each of the following statements by circling the appropriate response.

	Strongly Agree	Agree	Undecided	Disagree	Strongly Disagree	
a. Regardless of its ultimate size, this firm should grow at a rate that keeps up with client demand	5	4	3	2	1	
b. This firm should begin to revise its policy on making partnership offers so that the proportion of lawyers in the firm who are partners is reduced	5	4	3	2	1	
c. The incomes of lawyers in the firm should directly reflect the amount of new business they have brought to the firm	5	4	3	2	1	
d. The firm should have a positive policy encouraging pro bono work, such as allowing lawyers to devote working time to pro bono activities...........................	5	4	3	2	1	
e. The firm should seek to increase the productivity of lawyers by encouraging specialization	5	4	3	2	1	1
f. The income of lawyers in the firm should directly reflect the number of hours they bill .	5	4	3	2	1	1
g. The firm should open branch offices in other cities	5	4	3	2	1	1
h. The firm should formalize assignment procedures to eliminate informally made and ad hoc assignments	5	4	3	2	1	1
i. Associates should be directed to choose a specialty soon after joining the firm	5	4	3	2	1	1
j. The firm should be formally organized on a departmental basis, such that assignments are made, work is coordinated, and developments in the law and with clients are the administrative responsibility of departmental units..............................	5	4	3	2	1	1
k. Within the limits of taste, the firm should seek the business of others firms' clients, just as any other business would	5	4	3	2	1	1
l. The firm should not accept contingent fee cases under any circumstances	5	4	3	2	1	1
m. The firm should have a system for tight control over the quality of work	5	4	3	2	1	1

Appendixes

Hand Card 4

	Strongly Agree	Agree	Undecided	Disagree	Strongly Disagree	
a. In the *Bakke* case, the Supreme Court ruled that medical schools could not reserve a fixed number of admissions for minorities. Without accepting *in toto* any of the different opinions of the Court, the result in the *Bakke* case is correct	5	4	3	2	1	19
b. The exclusionary rule should be applied to suppress evidence seized in violation of the Fourth Amendment regardless of the possible consequence that persons who would otherwise be found guilty will go free	5	4	3	2	1	20
c. When possible, law should be made simpler and legal procedure should be made more efficient, even if it results in the displacement of some lawyers' work	5	4	3	2	1	21
d. By and large the complexity of law is a necessary consequence of the complexity of activities the law governs rather than the artificial creation of lawyers, legislators, and judges	5	4	3	2	1	22
e. On the whole, society is better off when the government does not attempt to regulate the economy through such legal instruments as the antitrust laws, securities regulation, banking law, and consumer protection	5	4	3	2	1	23
f. The law should be molded always to do the greatest justice and progress for those who have the least	5	4	3	2	1	24
g. On the whole, rules governing occupational health and safety impose undue burdens on employers	5	4	3	2	1	25
h. Whenever possible, aspects of the traditional tort system based on negligence should be replaced by systems of no-fault and strict liability that give priority to considerations of cost avoidance	5	4	3	2	1	26
i. Doctrines and rules pertaining to class actions should be interpreted to permit liberal use of the class action technique	5	4	3	2	1	27
j. The protection of consumer interests is best insured by a vigorous competition among sellers rather than by federal government intervention and regulation on behalf of consumers.	5	4	3	2	1	28
k. Labor unions have become too big for the good of the country.	5	4	3	2	1	29
l. Differences in income among occupations should be reduced	5	4	3	2	1	30
m. There is too much power concentrated in the hands of a few large companies for the good of the country	5	4	3	2	1	31
n. Americans should have equal access to necessary medical care regardless of ability to pay	5	4	3	2	1	32
o. Economic profits are by and large justly distributed in the U.S. today	5	4	3	2	1	33
p. The gains that labor unions make for their members help make the country more prosperous	5	4	3	2	1	34

Notes

INTRODUCTION

1. Rationalization is used in three different senses in this book. The first, and the sense used here, is the set of processes aimed at increasing the efficiency of various organizational operations, such as specialization by substantive field or task, the formalization of work groups, record-keeping practices, centralized assignment systems, and so forth. Second is the popular meaning of the term: to provide a justification for a particular behavior, practice, or circumstance. Third is legal rationalization, which, as developed by Weber (1978, pp. 654–658), refers to changes in the form and content of legal rules and legal institutions that make the decisions of legal actors more consistent internally and therefore more predictable. For example, Weber saw code-based legal systems as more rational than common law systems, in that they specified clear, prospective rules in contrast to the gradual articulation of principles on a case-by-case basis. How the word is used in various parts of the book should be clear from the context.

1: SOCIAL CHANGE AND STRUCTURE

1. In 1968 the largest firm nationally, Shearman & Sterling, contained 169 lawyers. In 1984 the largest firm, Baker & McKenzie, employed 697 lawyers; Shearman & Sterling has grown to 409 lawyers currently. In 1968 there were only 20 firms with 100 or more lawyers (Smigel 1969, p. 359), compared to 201 firms in 1984, 60 of which have more than 200 lawyers (*Legal Times* 1984). A recent survey found 500 law firms in the United States with 50 or more lawyers (*Legal Times* 1984).

2. The total population of lawyers increased by 112 percent between 1970 and 1980 (Curran 1982). The fifty largest firms grew by an average of 240 percent during the same period (*Legal Times* 1984; *American Lawyer* 1979; *Martindale-Hubbell Directory* 1970).

336   Notes to Pages 37–82

3. The 1972 census on legal services reported that firms with receipts of $1 million or more contained some 22 percent of the lawyers working in partnerships but 33 percent of gross receipts (U.S. Bureau of Census 1975, pp. 4–32). By the 1977 census such firms contained 30 percent of the lawyers working in partnerships but 49 percent of all receipts paid to partnerships (U.S. Bureau of Census 1981, pp. 5–45). As a result, partners in the largest firms make substantially more than those in smaller firms. According to the Price-Waterhouse survey, the results of which are shown in the table at the end of this note, net income increases steadily with firm size. Lawyers in firms of 150 lawyers or more make almost 50 percent more than their counterparts in smaller firms.

Firm Size (no. of lawyers)	N	Median Net Income to Partners
Over 150	64	$203,610
101–125	44	$167,740
31–50	117	$139,610

SOURCE: *Legal Times of Washington,* August 6, 1984, pp. 1, 4.

(NOTE: Not all major firms participate in the survey, and this is not a random sample. Nonetheless, given the large number of participating firms and the size of the differences, the results certainly are meaningful.)

4. A similar analysis was attempted for New York City firms. Because of inconsistent practices for listing associates, however, no satisfactory tables could be assembled.

5. Some of my interviews have suggested that the real "shakers and movers" of firms occasionally are not on the formal governing committee. This appears to be the exception rather than the rule.

6. As Smigel has pointed out, however, the early hiring policies of many large firms discriminated against Jews (1969, pp. 65–67). Cravath's merit system may have been similarly circumscribed.

7. For an extended discussion of large-firm recruitment patterns see chapter 3.

8. For a display of a wide variety of disclaimers, see firms' résumés contained in the *Directory of Legal Employers,* published by National Association for Law Placement (1984).

9. Heinz and Laumann (1982) find that high-prestige specialists tend to favor the merit selection of judges and no-fault insurance, value positions that are rational by Weber's standards.

10. It should be noted that Weber (1978) seems to be inconsistent in his analysis of the relationship between law and economic development, arguing in some passages that conditions of commerce in large part determine the character of law and the legal profession (pp. 334, 775) and concluding elsewhere that economic factors are less important in shaping law than politics and traditions of legal technique (pp. 654–655). This has given rise to an exegetical argument over the correct interpretation (see Trubek 1972).

Notes to Pages 98–137   337

2: BUREAUCRACY AND PARTICIPATION

1. Numbers are multiplied or divided by a constant.

3: CHANGING STRUCTURE OF OPPORTUNITY

1. The ethnicity and religious backgrounds of lawyers were divided into four groups: Jewish, Roman Catholic, non-Jewish and non-Catholic Northern and Western Europeans, non-Jewish and non-Catholic Others. The chi-square for the cross-tabulation with firms was 32.582, p = .0002.

2. The law schools were selected according to rankings given by the Gourman report (1982). They were Harvard, Michigan, Yale, Chicago, Berkeley, Stanford, Columbia, Cornell, Duke, Pennsylvania, Vanderbilt, Northwestern, NYU, UCLA, Boston University, Virginia, SUNY at Buffalo, Hastings, Wisconsin, University of Washington at Seattle. It should be noted that the composition of the top twenty schools in the Gourman rankings are controversial but that the substitution of some schools would not alter these proportions significantly.

3. The law school status categories developed by Heinz and Laumann (1982) are as follows. Six schools are included in the elite category: Chicago, Columbia, Harvard, Michigan, Stanford, and Yale. Prestige schools include Northwestern, Georgetown, Wisconsin, Virginia, California, Pennsylvania, and New York University among others. The regional category includes the University of Illinois and other Big Ten schools, plus Notre Dame and George Washington University. The local law schools are Chicago Kent, DePaul, Loyola, and John Marshall. I use the same categories throughout this book.

4. Longitudinal inferences from cohort data must be made with caution because we do not know anything about members of the original cohort who may have left the organization prior to the survey.

5. I do not possess complete data on the relative proportion of the lawyer population from the different categories of law schools, which leaves open the question of whether the rise in the proportion of regional and local law school graduates hired by firms from before 1970 through 1980 merely reflects a change in the composition of the recruitment pool and not a change in the hiring policies of firms. We can confidently rule out such a "base-line fallacy," however. The graduates of local and regional law schools in the Chicago area have constituted a much larger proportion of the total population of potential recruits than of the group hired by large firms for any period. It is clear, therefore, that firms could have hired a greater proportion of lower status graduates in earlier years, if they had chosen to.

6. The difference is not an artifact of comparing older males with younger females. The difference in social background is also statistically significant (chi-square p = .0028) for the youngest cohort, those lawyers hired since 1974.

7. Baker and McKenzie, technically the largest firm in Chicago with over five hundred lawyers, was not included because an inordinate number of the lawyers are located in different cities and countries, posing difficulties of tracking entry and exit through the directory.

338   Notes to Pages 139–155

8. This finding contradicts some speculations offered in an earlier article based on less complete data (see Nelson 1983).

9. I have treated nonequity partners as partners throughout analyses involving partnership status.

10. Although there are no hard data on the differential rates of listing in lawyers' directories, lawyers in nonlegal positions, corporate law departments, teaching, and government are generally thought less likely to list.

11. Strictly speaking, the use of the chi-square statistic is inappropriate here. Because individuals could report more than one event, the observations are not independent as is assumed in chi-square tests. The statistic is reported merely to provide some indication of whether differences of this magnitude might be expected by chance alone.

12. Analysis of variance is a statistical technique for determining whether for a given variable (such as the incidence of a particular career event) there is more variance between different groups than within the groups. Main effects are the variables that define the groups being compared, in this case law firms and cohorts of lawyers hired in different periods. It also is possible to test for the presence of an interaction between the variables, that is, to determine whether the effect of one variable on another varies depending on the level or category of a third variable. For instance, it is possible to test whether cohort affects the incidence of career events differently depending on the firm involved. Although the number of events in different periods was too small to allow meaningful statistical comparisons of firms during different periods, inspection revealed that many differences across firms existed in earlier periods. This pattern indicates that differences in bureaucratization have historical roots in organizations and do not emerge merely as a result of growth. It also underscores the fact that the general bureaucratization of large firms has taken place in specific, organizationally mediated fashion. Hence, the general nature of change in firms must be analyzed in a comparative organizational framework.

13. The incidence of these events did not vary significantly by cohort with the exception of gains in client responsibility. Almost one-fifth of the respondents hired before 1970 (18.6 percent) reported such gains compared to only 4.1 percent of the cohort joining in 1970–1974 and only 1.8 percent of those joining after 1975. $p < .01$, F-statistic. None of the interaction effects between firm and period joined were statistically significant.

14. Reasons for choosing a type of work which were not considered to be channeled by the firm were: interest prior to law school, interest from law school, liked it after exposure, liked people in the field, chose that department or type of work, related degree (CPA, MBA, etc.), happenstance, improved chances for advancement, appropriate work for a woman, thrust of firm's practice, provided broader practice. Reasons that were considered to be channeled by the firm were: assigned to it, firm asked me to, need for that work in firm, department or person in department asked me to, hired for a specialty or already specialized in field.

15. A three-way analysis of variance of the proportion of respondents who considered themselves specialists, entering firm, field, and years of practice, did not yield statistically significant effects for field or for the interactions with

field. While this result means that lower levels of self-perceived specialization by litigation associates can be explained statistically—based on their lack of seniority—their status as the leading category of unskilled labor in firms should not be dismissed. Lack of seniority, lack of specialization, and work in litigation are too highly correlated for there to be a significant difference between fields when controlling the other variables. It is impossible and inappropriate to decompose the effects of the variables.

4: ORGANIZATION OF WORK

1. The choices given were "not at all," "once or twice," "on several occasions," or "regularly." After reviewing the pattern of responses and recognizing that the distinction between the latter two categories was too subjective, I chose to define a working "tie" as one in which the lawyers had worked on several occasions or more. Respondents were instructed to answer based on the frequency with which they worked with each attorney rather than merely counting numbers of cases or matters. They were to include all types of professional working collaborations done within the firm (including firm administration, pro bono work, and so forth). But they were to limit their responses to direct relationships in which there was at least some exchange of work product that was read or used. The broad definition of work has the disadvantage of lumping different types of work together, which limits the ability to distinguish the practicing ties of the elite from the relationships they develop in governing the firm. Given the limits of time, however, there was no alternative. Moreover, pretests proved it was difficult for respondents to separate different kinds of administrative, supervisory, and practicing ties. I therefore opted for a more holistic definition of relationships.

2. For a general discussion see McFarland and Brown 1973; Berkowitz 1982; Knoke and Kuklinski 1982. The measure of distance input to the smallest space program was based on the minimum number of "steps" a pair of lawyers had to make before they were linked, either directly or indirectly. Lawyers with a direct link, meaning they had worked together on several occasions or more in the last year, were only one step apart. If they had a mutual contact, they were two steps apart, and so forth. The matrix of distances was computed by a digraph program written by Peter V. Marsden, based on the directed graphing techniques developed by Harary, Norman, and Cartwright (1965). The program drops isolates, those points with no links to any points.

Figures 3 through 6 are two-dimensional models. They achieve only moderately good to mediocre fit according to the rules of thumb suggested by Guttman (1968) and Kruskal (1964). According to Guttman, models are useful when the Guttman-Lingoes coefficient of alienation is lower than .15 (1968). Kruskal suggests that values of Kruskal's stress over .15 are "poor"; values from .1 to .15 indicate a "fair" fit; and values under .1 represent a good fit (1964). Nonetheless, the fit we obtain for our models is comparable to that reported by networks scholars (see Heinz and Laumann 1982). Because the models are quite interpretable and are consistent with the blockmodeling results reported below, the two-dimensional models are defensible.

340   Notes to Pages 162–174

3. The labels are largely self-explanatory (see chap. 2). Practitioners are assigned to the field in which they reported spending a majority of their time.
Lawyers not spending a majority of their time in any field were assigned to
"mixed office" if they spent less than 25 percent in litigation and to "mixed
office–litigation" if they spent 25 to 49 percent of their time in litigation.

4. The centroid is the point in the plane on which it would balance if all
plotted points were weighted equally.

5. It should be noted that three of the groups in the final models did not
have a single modal specialty but instead consisted of a mixture of specialties.
These groups were simply defined as mixed groups, and those lawyers whose
specialty did not fall within the broader definition were counted as errors.

6. The results of the blockmodeling are available from the author.

7. Respondents were asked to further divide time spent on civil litigation
into subject areas in which litigation took place. I had considered the possibility
that it would be appropriate to lump time spent on litigation in some substantive
areas with other time spent in that substantive field. An examination of copractice among fields persuaded me to leave civil litigation as an independent
category. Only 20 percent of the practitioners who spent any time in a field—in
a litigating or nonlitigating capacity—spent time doing both substantive work
in the field and litigating in the field.

For general discussions of time-budget methodology see Szalai (1972),
Robinson and Converse (1972), and Young and Willmott (1973). To minimize
problems with response bias arising from the tendency to assign more time to
the first fields encountered in the list, respondents were instructed not to worry
about making the percentages add to 100. Because three-quarters of respondents spent time in three fields or fewer, this was an uncomplicated task. I
received very few aberrant time allocation profiles. All totals fell within 75
percent and 140 percent; 87.1 percent fell between 95 percent and 100 percent;
96 percent between 90 percent and 110 percent.

8. The general form of the index is:

$$SI = 1 - \frac{\hat{H}}{H_{max}}$$

where $\hat{H} = \sum_{i=1}^{C} P_i \ln \frac{1}{P_i}$ for all $P_i > 0$; and $H_{max} = C \ln C$.

P_i is estimated by the proportion time allocated to category C_i. H will take a
value zero when all activity is allocated to one category, i.e., when some one
$P_i = 1$. $\hat{H}$ reaches maximum value (H_{max}) when time is allocated equally among
all categories P_i through P_c.

9. Cappell (1979) derived the specialization index from measures of the
entropy of distributions (see Theil 1972). He asserts it is superior for time allocation analysis to more familiar measures of distributions, such as the Gini
index.

10. A four-category field of practice variable was constructed which clas-

sified lawyers as practicing in litigation, corporate-commercial, finance, or "other office" fields. The litigation category (N = 100) included all attorneys who spent 25 percent or more of their time in a litigation field, which was defined to include administrative law, antitrust, civil litigation, labor law, utilities regulation, and bankruptcy. Most "litigators" (93 of 100) spent more than half their time in a litigation field. The corporate-commercial field (N = 46) included those attorneys who spent a majority of their time on banking, commercial, corporate, and securities law. The finance category (N = 39) included lawyers spending a majority of time in the finance field and corporate and personal tax. The "other office" category (N = 40) consisted mainly of lawyers spending a majority of their time on real estate (both commercial and personal), probate, or special finance, but also included all other attorneys who did not devote a majority of their time to the previously mentioned sets of fields and spent less than 25 percent of their time in litigation. Constructing the variable in this fashion preserved a strong distinction between those who worked in litigation fields and those who did not; and the office practice fields were divided consistent with the results of my analysis of patterns of copractice among fields.

11. As above, I define litigators as all lawyers spending 25 percent or more time in any of the litigation fields, including administrative law, utilities regulation, labor law, bankruptcies, and litigation.

12. For a general discussion of multiple classification analysis, which is a variant of analysis of variance, see Morgan et al. 1964; Laumann 1973. The assumption of additive effects is violated by a three-way interaction effect between independent variables for percentage of time spent on spot assignments. While this creates the potential that the additive effects model is misspecified, intensive inspection of the three-way breakdown among the variables convinced me that the presentation of a simpler model was appropriate. I will note in the text some of the complexities in the three-way relationship between these variables for the spot assignments variable.

The first row of the three columns for the dependent variables represents the grand mean for the sample overall. The asterisks indicate whether the main effect for the particular variable was significant when entered in a three-way analysis of variance for each dependent variable. The effect parameters express the difference between the grand mean on the dependent variable and the mean of the category of the independent variable, after controlling for the effects of the other two independent variables entered in the model. The betas are a standardized coefficient measuring the explanatory power of changing categories within the independent variables, while controlling for the effects of the two other independent variables. The R^2 value indicates the proportion of variance in the dependent variable explained by the model.

13. Pretests indicated that respondents generally felt more comfortable answering for the year as a whole. Respondents who could not give a total for the year were asked how many hours they worked in an average week, which was multiplied by fifty to produce total hours worked. The hours of lawyers who had worked only part of the year were adjusted to produce a total based on fifty weeks. In retrospect, it was a mistake to use Duncan's records rather than ask the questions as in the other firms. Duncan has the lowest average

342   Notes to Pages 192–233

total hours worked of the four firms, raising the possibility that the difference is an artifact of how the data were collected. Yet I was informed that Duncan's rules require lawyers to record all time, billed and unbilled. In the course of interviewing I learned that Duncan's lawyers were aware that the numbers of hours recorded were circulated weekly among partners to determine who might be available for additional assignments. This "computer round-robin," as one respondent characterized it, presumably accentuates the importance of complete time recording.

5: ECONOMIC REWARDS

1. The log transformation increased the total variance explained by the final model by 4.4 percent from 79.26 percent to 83.66 percent. The betas for two lesser variables changed so that they were no longer significantly different from zero.

2. In all equations that follow, an individual's income is predicted as a function of the constant and the values they achieve on the independent variables weighted by the betas of the independent variables. The prediction in a simple one-variant case is:

$$\hat{Y} = a + bX$$

where $\hat{Y}$ is estimated income, a is the constant, and b is the beta for the variable X.

6: PROFESSIONALISM, BUREAUCRACY, AND COMMITMENT

1. It is now quite common for individual partners in firms to establish themselves as professional corporations. Corporate status has certain advantages for tax purposes but does not fundamentally alter the "individual" character of partners. Nor does it affect norms concerning relationships between the partners of a firm.

2. This interpretation adds further evidence to Heinz and Laumann's assertion that corporate clients dominate their relationships with corporate lawyers (1982).

7: IDEOLOGY, PRACTICE, AND PROFESSIONAL AUTONOMY

1. See, e.g., Swaine (1965, pp. 11, 12). Several members of the elite asserted their autonomy from clients. A colleague informs me that the leader of one large New York firm claimed that his firm never allowed any one client to contribute more than 5 percent of the firm's revenues. For a discussion of the role of corporate elites in defining and enforcing professional ethics, see Carlin (1966, pp. 66–83).

2. See Freidson (1983). Professional autonomy can be and has been defined as control over how work is done and evaluated (Becker 1970, pp. 96–97); the

ability to choose a particular field of practice or career line (Hughes 1960, pp. 60–61); freedom from extra-professional pressures imposed by the broader community (Landon 1982); or, even more broadly, the ability to influence the authoritative allocation of scarce values (see Heinz 1983, p. 892). The range of definitions makes clear that autonomy is a multidimensional concept. Kritzer (1984) suggests that lawyer-client relationships have professional, business, and social aspects and that each of these dimensions can be divided in various ways as well.

Scholars of professional ethics sometimes argue that different ethical standards apply in adversary versus nonadversary situations or in the context of civil versus criminal litigation (see, e.g., Schwartz 1980). I will not dwell on this distinction in this analysis. Whatever the situation, adversary or not, lawyers can mediate between the demands of clients and broader considerations of what legal strategy will serve the public interest. For a marvelously rich discussion of theoretical questions concerning models of advocacy, see Simon (1978).

3. For a general discussion of corporate compliance and its breakdown, see Stone (1975). A similar set of issues arises for the lawyers of government agencies (Horowitz 1977).

4. One notable difference that may affect social values is the relatively high proportion of Jewish lawyers in my sample. Heinz and Laumann found that 16 percent of the lawyers in firms of 30 or more lawyers were Jewish, compared to 27.6 percent in my sample (Heinz, Laumann, et al. 1976, p. 780). Jewish lawyers tend to have politically more liberal attitudes than lawyers of other ethnoreligious backgrounds (Heinz and Laumann 1982, p. 157).

5. Fifty-five percent of a national opinion sample agreed that labor unions have become too big (Robinson, Rush, and Head 1968, p. 197). Heinz and Laumann found that 53 percent of Chicago lawyers agreed that labor unions had become too big (1982, p. 159).

6. This difference might be attributed to differences in education and urbanization, quite apart from differences in occupation.

7. Barton, Denitch, et al. (1978) posed a roughly comparable question to a set of positionally defined elites: "The pricing system in American industry is basically a competitive, free-market system, not 'administered' or 'monopolistic.'" The business elites in the sample, drawn from Fortune 500 corporations, overwhelmingly agreed with the proposition, with only 11 percent disagreeing. In contrast, 63 percent of the elite members from organized labor disagreed. While no separate results were reported for lawyers, the respondents who might most closely resemble lawyers in their orientations due to similar educational background and involvement in public policy—career civil servants—were halfway between business and labor. One-third of that group disagreed with the item. Given the rather extreme faith in competition held by the national business elite, it is likely that there is a considerable difference between the attitudes of corporate management and corporate lawyers about free enterprise.

8. Heinz & Laumann data on file with the author. The formulation by Heinz and Laumann probably tended to bias the results against favoring the class action technique. "Access to the court should be carefully limited—

through strict application of such requirements as 'standing,' 'economic interest,' and 'exhaustion of remedies,' and through dismissal of all cases that are 'moot' or not 'ripe' for decision—because it is more important to preserve the *quality* of justice than it is to increase the *quantity* of cases dealt with by our courts" (Heinz and Laumann 1982, p. 413).

9. Policy preferences about class actions may involve rather complicated sets of attitudes regarding their potential for abuse, their impact on the courts, and their allocation of rewards to plaintiffs or attorneys. Also, class actions in securities and antitrust do not raise the classic issues of social inequality that civil rights actions raise. Nonetheless, because respondents presumably take competing considerations into account, the question remains a useful gauge of the importance lawyers attach to individuals' access to the courts.

10. The question is adapted from an item Casper used (1972, p. 202).

11. Interviewers were instructed to record initial reactions to the question and to urge those who would not choose one of the fixed responses to indicate a preference. All respondents were asked a follow-up question probing the reasons for their answers. Responses to the closed-ended question and the ensuing comments were evaluated in coding the position of the respondent on the question.

12. The field-of-practice variable classified lawyers according to their reported allocation of time across fields. To protect the identities of the firms, the fields cannot be defined specifically. The litigation category includes all attorneys who spent 25 percent or more of their time in a litigation field, which was defined to include administrative law, antitrust, civil litigation, labor law, utilities regulation, and bankruptcies. Most "litigators" (93 of 100) spent more than half their time in a litigation field. The corporate-commercial field included those attorneys who spent a majority of their time on banking, commercial, corporate, and securities law. The finance category included lawyers spending a majority of time in a financial specialty and corporate and personal tax. The "other office" category consisted mainly of lawyers spending a majority of their time on real estate (both commercial and personal), probate, or special finance but also included all other attorneys who did not devote a majority of their time to the previously mentioned sets of fields and spent less than 25 percent of their time in litigation. Constructing the variable in this fashion preserved a strong distinction between those who worked in litigation fields and those who did not; and the office practice fields were divided consistent with the results on copractice among fields.

13. As with any time estimate the estimates in table 28 are subject to periodicity, that is, change from year to year. To control for periodic effects, we asked the sample whether the amount of time devoted to their principal client in the last year was typical or atypical and if atypical, why. Fifty-six and three tenths percent of the sample reported it was a typical year. Thirteen and four tenths percent, mostly new associates, reported they did not know because they had nothing to compare it to. Less than a quarter (24 percent) reported it was an atypical year for various reasons. These figures indicate that the pattern in table 28 is reasonably typical across years. Unfortunately, the follow-up question on typicality did not specifically ask whether respondents devoted

the same amount of time to the same clients across years. Therefore, we cannot be completely confident that table 28 reflects the concentration of time for a stable array of clients.

14. Lawyers in the two specialty firms, Curran and Duncan, spend substantially less time on their principal client. This reflects the case-by-case or functionally specific nature of client relationships characteristic of special representation firms. The two exceptions to this general pattern are worth noting. Duncan's corporate practitioners spend a greater proportion of their time on particular clients, indicating the development of continuous client relationships in that field. The most concentrated client commitments in Aaron fall in the litigation field, representing the prevalence of large-case litigation in which lawyers devote a major portion of their time to one case.

A regression analysis of firm and field effects indicates that the differences between firms are not statistically significant, although the time concentrations in the other office field at Becker are statistically significantly higher than in other firms.

15. The question was not limited to any particular kind of nonlegal advice, even though some kinds of nonlegal advice-giving may be irrelevant to the mediating role that I was seeking to analyze. Instead, I asked for a description of the context in which advice was given. From the responses I was able to draw inferences about the relationship of advice-giving to mediation while still preserving data on the general extent of nonlegal advice giving.

16. Since the 1960s and early 1970s the opportunity for pro bono work has remained as a staple in the self-presentation of firms in their recruiting efforts, as witnessed by the standard entry in firm résumés concerning "pro bono policy." See, e.g., the listings by firms in *Directory of Legal Employers* (National Association of Law Placement 1984). Thirty of New York City's largest law firms recently pledged themselves to a minimum number of hours on nonpaying cases (*New York Times,* May 2, 1984, section A, at p. 1, col. 5). Lawyers in one Chicago firm devote an average of more than three hundred hours annually to pro bono representation (personal interview, 1979). Other firms, such as the Washington, D.C., law firm of Hogan and Hartson, maintain full-time public interest departments (personal interview, 1981).

17. Root's public activities were not always so progressive, as witnessed by the Root Committee's efforts to increase the education requirements for bar admission as a means of limiting the number of foreign-born and Jewish lawyers. See J. Auerbach 1976, pp. 112–117.

18. "There can be no doubt that the bar of the country is unalterably opposed to this departure. It follows that liberals in political and social theory, both in and out of the government who advocate an extension of such policy, consider the men of the law as enemies of progress" (Lashly 1939, p. 654).

19. Personal communication with Professor Theodore Schneyer, University of Arizona, who is analyzing the papers of the Kutak Commission.

20. The rule adopted by the House of Delegates, Rule 1.6 of the *Model Rules of Professional Conduct,* allows but does not require disclosure of information to prevent serious bodily harm to another (Model Rules of Professional Conduct 1983, p. 7).

346   Notes to Pages 262–267

21. Lawyers in large firms were in fact the leading participants in such revisions in Illinois and Chicago at the time I began my research.

22. A similar assertion is made concerning the impact of competition on the independence of audits done by major accounting firms. See *New York Times*, May 13, 1984, section 3, p. 1, col. 2.

23. Memorandum by John P. Heinz and Robert L. Nelson, circulated among the participants of the Symposium on the Law Firm as a Social Institution, March 1984 (on file with the author).

24. Adherents to the model of lawyers as mediators might argue that this process infuses the client's decisions with society's core values. See, e.g., T. Halliday (1987). A number of theorists argue that the opposite takes place: that the introduction of specialized, technical knowledge shifts the basis for decision away from normative factors toward the instrumental considerations of what can be accomplished. See, e.g., J. Ellul 1964; M. Foucault 1979.

25. See, e.g., Galanter 1983a. The idealized version of how legal maneuvering affects case outcomes is provided in *The Partners* (Stewart 1983), where large firm litigators are portrayed much like frontier heroes: The smart, tough ones win; the slow, soft ones lose. The dominant message of *The Partners* is that the guile and cunning of lawyers determine the result of litigation, almost without regard to the underlying law or facts. One need not accept so grandiose an interpretation to credit the basic point that how lawyers represent clients will affect the course of events.

26. For this argument, it is not necessary to consider the debate about the desirability or meaning of a rights-based system. See, e.g., Tushnet 1984.

References

Abel, Richard. 1979. "Socializing the Legal Profession: Can Redistributing Lawyers' Services Achieve Social Justice?" *Law & Policy Quarterly* 1: 5–51.
———. 1982. "Toward a Political Economy of Lawyers." *Wisconsin Law Review* 1982: 1117–1187.
Abramson, Jill, and Barbara Franklin. 1986. *Where They Are Now: The Story of the Women of Harvard Law 1974.* New York: Doubleday.
Alchian, Armen A., and Harold Demsetz. 1972. "Production, Information Costs, and Economic Organization." *American Economic Review* 62: 777–795.
Alschuler, Albert. 1976. "Plea Bargaining and Its History." *Columbia Law Review.* 76: 1059–1154.
Althauser, Robert P. 1971. "Multicollinearity and Non-additive Regression Models." In *Causal Models in the Social Sciences,* edited by H. M. Blalock, pp. 453–472. Chicago: Aldine.
American Bar Association. 1972–1983. *Review of Legal Education in the United States.* Chicago: American Bar Association.
———. 1980. *Discussion Draft of the Proposed Model Rules of Professional Conduct.* Chicago: American Bar Association.
———. 1983. *Model Rules of Professional Conduct.* Chicago: American Bar Association.
———. 1986. ". . . In the Spirit of Public Service." A Blueprint for the Rekindling of Lawyer Professionalism. Report by the Commission on Professionalism.
American Bar Association Journal. 1983. "Muting the Whistle: ABA Debates Kutak Ethics Rules." 69: 421–423.
———. October 1985. "Law Poll: Lawyers' Workweek Averages 50 hours." 71: 42–43.

American Lawyer. August 11, 1978. "Reuben Fights Kirkland & Ellis for Lawyers, Clients." Pp. 1, 13–16.
———. 1979–1984. Bar Talk Column. (Page locations vary by issue.)
———. September 1979. "Kutak's Conversion Factor." P. 6.
———. September 15, 1981. "Erisa Quarry." P. 15.
———. 1982. *American Lawyer's Guide to Law Firms 1981–1982.* New York: Am-Law Publishing.
———. 1983. *American Lawyer's Guide to Law Firms 1982–1983.* New York: Am-Law Publishing.
———. June 1984. "K and E Loses out to Skadden." P. 30.
———. July/August 1986. "The Am Law 75." Pp. 35–74.
Aubert, Wilhelm. 1963. "Competition and Dissensus: Two Types of Conflict and Conflict Resolution." *Journal of Conflict Resolution* 7:26–42.
Auerbach, Carl A. Forthcoming. *Historical Statistics on Legal Education.* Chicago: American Bar Foundation.
Auerbach, Jerold S. 1976. *Unequal Justice.* New York: Oxford University Press.
Barber, Bernard; John J. Lally; Julia Louglin Makarushka; and Daniel Sullivan. 1973. *Research on Human Subjects: Problems of Social Control in Medical Experimentation.* New York: Russell Sage.
Barlow, Andrew. 1979. "Coordination and Control: The Rise of Harvard University: 1825–1910." Ph.D. dissertation, Harvard University.
Barton, Allen, Bogdan Denitch, et al. 1978. "Background, Attitudes and Activities of American Elites—A Report of the American Leadership Survey." Center for the Social Sciences. Columbia University.
Bates and O'Steen v. Arizona State Bar. 1977. 433 U.S. 350.
Becker, Gary S. 1975. *Human Capital.* New York: Columbia University Press.
Bell, Daniel. 1976. *The Coming of Post-industrial Society.* New York: Basic Books.
Bell, Robert. 1984. "How Corporations Use Lawyers." Paper presented at the Annual Meetings of the Law & Society Association, Boston, June 9, 1984.
Ben-David, Joseph. 1958. "The Professional Role of the Physician in Bureaucratized Medicine." *Human Relations* 2: 901–911.
Bendix, Reinhard. 1974. *Work and Authority in Industry.* Berkeley, Los Angeles, London: University of California Press.
———. 1977. *Max Weber: An Intellectual Portrait.* Berkeley, Los Angeles, London: University of California Press.
Berkowitz, Steven D. 1982. *An Introduction to Structural Analysis.* Toronto: Butterworth.
Berle, Jr., Adolph A. 1948. *Encyclopedia of the Social Sciences* 9: 340–345. New York: Macmillan.
———, and Gardiner C. Means. 1932. *The Modern Corporation and Private Property.* New York: W. S. Hein.
Beyer, Janice M. 1982. "Power Dependencies and the Distribution of Influence in Universities." In *Research in Sociology of Organizations,* edited by Samuel Bachrach, pp. 167–208. Greenwich, Conn.: JAI Press, Inc.
Bibby, John F.; Thomas E. Mann; and Norman J. Ornstein. 1982. *Vital Statis-*

tics on Congress. Washington: American Enterprise Institute for Public Policy Research.

Bidwell, Charles E., and Rebecca S. Vreeland. 1963. "Authority and Control in Client-serving Organizations." *Sociological Quarterly* 4: 231–241.

Blau, Peter M. 1956. *Bureaucracy in Modern Society.* New York: Random House.

———. 1963. *The Dynamics of Bureaucracy: A Study of Interpersonal Relations in Two Government Agencies.* 2d ed. Chicago and London: University of Chicago Press.

———. 1968. "The Hierarchy of Authority in Organizations." *American Journal of Sociology* 73: 553–567.

———. 1973. *The Organization of Academic Work.* New York: John Wiley & Sons.

Bledstein, Burton J. 1976. *The Culture of Professionalism: The Middle Class and the Development of Higher Education in America.* New York: W. W. Norton & Company, Inc.

Bodine, Larry. August 13, 1979. "Mammoth Firm Keeps Steamrolling." *National Law Journal.* Pp. 1, 64–65.

Bok, Derek. 1983. "A Flawed System." *Harvard Magazine* 85: 35–40.

Boorman, Scott A., and Harrison C. White. 1976. "Social Structure from Multiple Networks. II. Role Interlock." *American Journal of Sociology* 81: 1384–1446.

Bosk, Charles L. 1979. *Forgive & Remember.* Chicago/London: University of Chicago Press.

Brandeis, Louis D. 1933. *Business—A Profession.* Boston: Hale, Cushman & Flint.

Breiger, Ronald L.; Scott A. Boorman; and Phipps Arabie. 1975. *An Algorithm for Blocking Relational Data with Applications to Social Network: Analysis and Comparison with Multidimensional Scaling.* Stanford: Institute for Mathematical Studies in the Social Sciences.

Bryce, James. 1912. *American Commonwealth.* New York: Macmillan.

Bucher, Rue. 1970. "Status in the Medical School." In *Power in Organizations,* edited by Mayer Zald, pp. 151–179. Nashville: Vanderbilt University Press.

Bucher, Rue, and Joan Stelling. 1969. "Characteristics of Professional Organizations." *Journal of Health and Social Behavior* 10: 3–15.

Burawoy, Michael. 1979. *Manufacturing Consent: Changes in the Labor Process under Monopoly Capitalism.* Chicago: University of Chicago Press.

Burstein, Paul. 1986. *Discrimination, Jobs, & Politics: The Struggle for Equal Opportunity in the U.S. since the New Deal.* Chicago: University of Chicago Press.

Business Lawyer. 1975. Panel Discussion on the Securities Laws and the Code of Professional Responsibility. *Business Lawyer* 30: special issue (March).

Cain, Maureen. 1983. "The General Practice Lawyer and the Client: Towards a Radical Conception." In *The Sociology of the Professions,* edited by Robert Dingwall and Philip Lewis, pp. 106–130. New York: St. Martin's Press.

Cantor, David J. 1978. "Law Firms are Getting Bigger . . . and More Complex." *American Bar Association Journal* 64: 215–219.

Caplow, Theodore, and Reece McGee. 1958. *The Academic Marketplace.* New York: Basic Books.

Cappell, Charles L. 1979. "Organization and Specialization of Legal Activity." Working Draft, American Bar Foundation.

————. 1980. "A Perspective on Law School Achievement and the Reproduction of Status." Paper presented at the annual meeting of the Law and Society Association, Madison, Wisconsin.

Cardozo, Benjamin N. 1924. *The Growth of the Law.* New Haven: Yale University Press.

Carlin, Jerome E. 1962. *Lawyers on Their Own: A Study of Individual Practitioners in Chicago.* New Brunswick, N.J.: Rutgers University Press.

————. 1966. *Lawyer's Ethics: A Survey of the New York City Bar.* New York: Russell Sage Foundation.

Carr-Saunders, A. M., and P. A. Wilson. 1933. *The Professions.* Oxford: Oxford University Press.

Casper, Jonathan D. 1972. *Lawyers before the Warren Court: Civil Liberties and Civil Rights, 1957–66.* Urbana: University of Illinois Press.

Chamberlayne, Charles F. 1906. "The Soul of the Profession." *Green Bag* 18: 397.

Chandler, Alfred D., Jr. 1962. *Strategy & Structure: Chapters in the History of the American Industrial Enterprise.* Cambridge: M.I.T. Press.

————. 1977. *The Visible Hand: The Managerial Revolution in American Business.* Cambridge: Harvard University Press.

Chayes, Abram. 1976. "The Role of the Judge in Public Law Litigation." *Harvard Law Review* 89: 1281–1316.

Chicago Lawyer. June 1980. "One in Three Associates Left Firms in 70's." P. 7.

Chicago Sun-Times. "Law Memo: Sharing the Wealth." January 19, 1981. P. 52.

Christensen, Barlow F. 1967. *Specialization.* Chicago: American Bar Foundation.

Cole, Robert E. 1979. *Work, Mobility, & Participation: A Comparative Study of American and Japanese Industry.* Berkeley, Los Angeles, London: University of California Press.

Crain's Chicago Business. July 30, 1979. "Shakeup at Winston Typifies Changes Here." Pp. 1, 28.

————. November 14–20, 1983. "Attorneys' Fast Tracks Leaves Loyalty Behind." P. 29.

Curran, Barbara A. 1985. *The Lawyer Statistical Report: A Statistical Profile of the U.S. Legal Profession in the 1980s.* Chicago: American Bar Foundation.

————. 1982. "Lawyers' Demographics." Paper presented at the annual meetings of the American Bar Association, New Orleans, Louisiana.

Danet, Brenda; K. B. Hoffman; and N. C. Kermish. 1980. "Obstacles to the Study of Lawyer Client Interactions: The Biography of a Failure." *Law & Society Review* 14: 905–922.

Darby, D. Weston, Jr. December, 1985. "Are You Keeping Up Financially?" *American Bar Association Journal* 71: 66–68.

Davies, Celia. 1983. "Professionals in Bureaucracies: The Conflict Thesis Revisited." In *The Sociology of the Professions*, edited by Robert Dingwall and Philip Lewis, pp. 177–194. New York: St. Martin's Press.

Dean, Arthur H. 1957. *William Nelson Cromwell, 1854–1948: An American Pioneer in Corporation, Comparative, and International Law.* New York: Ad Press.

DeAngelo, Linda A. 1981. "Auditor Size and Audit Quality." *Journal of Accounting and Economics* 3: 183–199.

Derber, Charles. 1982. *Professionals as Workers: Mental Labor in Advanced Capitalism.* Boston: G. K. Hall and Co.

Dolbeare, Kenneth M., and Phillip E. Hammond. 1968. "The Political Party Basis of Attitudes toward the Supreme Court." *Public Opinion* 32: 16–30.

Donnell, John D. 1970. *The Corporate Counsel: A Role Study.* Bloomington: Bureau Business Research, Graduate School of Business, Indiana University.

Durkheim, Émile. 1958. *Professional Ethics and Civic Morals.* Glencoe, Ill.: The Free Press.

———. 1964. *The Division of Labor in Society.* Translated by George Simpson. New York: The Free Press.

Dworkin, R. M. 1977. *Taking Rights Seriously.* Cambridge: Harvard University Press.

Earle, Walter. 1963. *Mr. Shearman and Mr. Sterling and How They Grew: Being Annals of Their Law Firms.* New Haven: Yale University.

Ellul, Jacques. 1964. *The Technological Society.* New York: Vintage Books.

Epstein, Cynthia Fuchs. 1981. *Women in Law.* New York: Basic Books, Inc.

Erlanger, Howard S., and Douglas A. Klegon. 1978. "Socialization Effects in Professional School." *Law & Society Review* 13: 11–35.

Foucault, Michel. 1979. *Discipline and Punish: The Birth of the Prison.* New York: Vintage Books.

Frank, John P. 1965. "The Legal Ethics of Louis D. Brandeis." *Stanford Law Review* 17: 683–709.

Frankel, Marvin E. 1978. *Partisan Justice.* New York: Hill & Wang.

Freidson, Eliot, ed. 1963. *The Hospital in Modern Society.* New York: The Free Press.

———. 1970a. *Profession of Medicine: A Study of the Sociology of Applied Knowledge.* New York: Dodd-Mead.

———. 1970b. *Professional Dominance: The Social Structure of Medical Care.* Chicago: Aldine.

———. 1984. "The Changing Nature of Professional Control." *Annual Review of Sociology* 10: 1–20.

———. 1986. *Professional Powers: A Study of the Institutionalization of Formal Knowledge.* Chicago: University of Chicago Press.

———. and Buford Rhea. 1972. "Knowledge and Judgement in Professional Evaluation." *Administrative Science Quarterly* 1: 107–124.

———. and Judith Lorber, eds. 1973. *Medical Men and Their Work.* Chicago: Aldine-Atherton.

Friedman, Lawrence M. 1973. *A History of American Law*. New York: Simon & Schuster.

———. 1985. *Total Justice*. New York: Russell Sage.

Galanter, Marc. 1974. "Why the Haves Come Out Ahead: Speculations on the Limits of Legal Change." *Law & Society Review* 9: 95–160.

———. 1983a. "Mega-Law and Mega-Lawyering in the Contemporary United States." In *The Sociology of the Professions*, edited by Robert Dingwall and Philip Lewis, pp. 152–176. New York: St. Martin's Press.

———. 1983b. "Reading the Landscape of Disputes: What We Know and Don't Know (and Think We Know) about Our Allegedly Contentious and Litigious Society." *U.C.L.A. Law Review* 31: 4–71.

Gilb, Corinne L. 1967. *Hidden Hierarchies: The Professions & Government*. New York: Harper Row.

Gilboy, Janet. 1975. *Perspectives & Practices of Defense Lawyers in Criminal Cases*. Ph.D. dissertation, Northwestern University.

Gilson, Ronald J., and Robert H. Mnookin. 1985. "Sharing among the Human Capitalists: An Economic Inquiry into the Corporate Law Firm and How Partners Split Profits." *Stanford Law Review* 37: 313–392.

Goldberg, Victor P. 1985. "Price Adjustments in Long-term Contracts." *Wisconsin Law Review*. 1985: 527–543.

Goldfarb v. Virginia State Bar. 1975. 421 U.S. 773.

Gordon, Robert W. 1975. "Introduction: J. Willard Hurst and the Common Law Tradition in American Legal Historiography." *Law & Society Review* 10: 9–55.

———. 1983. "Legal Thought and Legal Practice in the Age of American Enterprise 1870–1920." In *Professions and Professional Ideologies in America*, edited by Gerald Geison, pp. 70–110. Chapel Hill: University of North Carolina Press.

———. 1984. "The Ideal and the Actual." In *The New High Priests; Lawyers in Post-Civil War America*, edited by Gerard Gawalt, pp. 51–74. Westport Connecticut Press.

Goss, Mary. 1961. "Influence and Authority among Physicians in an Out-patient Clinic." *American Sociological Review* 26: 39–50.

———. 1963. "Patterns of Bureaucracy among Hospital Staff Physicians." In *The Hospital in Modern Society*, edited by E. Freidson, pp. 170–194. New York: The Free Press.

Gouldner, Alvin W. 1954. *Patterns of Industrial Bureaucracy*. New York: The Free Press.

Gourman, Jack. 1982. *The Gourman Report: Ratings of Graduate and Professional Programs*. Los Angeles: National Education Standard, 1982.

Gramsci, Antonio. 1971. *Selections from the Prison Notebooks of Antonio Gramsci*. New York: International.

Green, Mark. 1975. *The Other Government*. New York: Grossman.

Greenwood, Glenn, and Robert Frederickson. 1964. *Specialization and the Legal Profession*. Mundelein, Illinois: Callaghan & Company.

Grossman, Joel B. 1965. *Lawyers and Judges: The ABA and the Politics of Judicial Selection*. New York: John Wiley & Sons.

Guttman, Louis. 1968. "A General Nonmetric Technique for Finding the Smallest Coordinate Space for a Configuration of Points." *Psychometrika* 33: 469–506.
Habermas, Jurgen. 1975. *Legitimation Crisis.* Boston: Beacon Press.
Hall, Oswalt. 1948. "The Stages of Medical Careers." *American Journal of Sociology* 53: 327–336.
Hall, Richard. 1967. "Some Organizational Considerations in the Professional-Organizational Relationship." *Administrative Sciences Quarterly* 12: 461–478.
———. 1968. "Professionalization and Bureaucratization." *American Sociological Review* 32: 92–104.
Halliday, Terence C. 1976. "Inns, Courts and Honoratiores: Legal Associations and the Rationalization of the Judiciary." Paper presented at the annual meetings of the American Sociological Association, New York.
———. 1983. "Professions, Class, and Capitalism. *European Journal of Sociology* 224: 321–346.
———. 1987. *Beyond Monopoly: Lawyers, State Crises, and Professional Empowerment.* Chicago: University of Chicago Press.
———, and Charles L. Cappell. 1979. "Indicators of Democracy in Professional Associations: Elite Recruitment, Turnover, and Decisionmaking in a Metropolitan Bar Association." *American Bar Foundation Research Journal* 1979: 697–767.
Hannan, Michael T.; Nancy Brandon Tuma; and Lyle P. Groenveld. 1978. "Income and Independence Effects on Marital Dissolution: Results from the Seattle and Denver Income Maintenance Experiments." *American Journal of Sociology* 84: 611–633.
Hannan, Michael T., and Nancy Brandon Tuma. 1979. "Methods for Temporal Analysis." *Annual Review of Sociology* 5: 303–328.
Harary, Frank; Robert Z. Norman; and Darwin Cartwright. 1965. *Structural Models: An Introduction to the Theory of Directed Graphs.* New York: John Wiley & Sons.
Harrell, Morris. 1983. "Preserving Professionalism." *American Bar Association Journal* 69: 864.
Harrington, Christine. 1983. "Political Economy of Administrative Law Practice." Paper presented at the annual meetings of the Law & Society Association, June 2–5, 1983, Denver.
Harvard Law School Placement Office. 1978. *Employer Directory.* Cambridge: Harvard Law School.
Hastings, A., and C. R. Hinings. 1970. "Role Relations and Value Adaption: A Study of the Professional Accountant in Industry." *Sociology* 4: 353–366.
Haug, D. M. 1973a. "Deprofessionalization: An Alternative Hypothesis for the Future." *Sociological Review Monograph,* No. 20: 195–211.
———. 1973b. "The Deprofessionalization of Everyone?" *Sociological Focus,* August, pp. 197–213.
Heintz, Bruce D. 1981. "New Trends in Partner Profit Distribution." *Legal Economics* 7: 9–14.
———. 1983. "Elements of Law Firm Competition." *National Law Journal,*

December 26, 1983, p. 19, col. 2.

Heinz, John P. 1983. "The Power of Lawyers." *Georgia Law Review* 17: 891–911.

———, and Edward O. Laumann. 1978. "The Legal Profession: Client Interests, Professional Roles and Social Hierarchies." *Michigan Law Review* 76: 1111–1142.

———. 1982. *Chicago Lawyers: The Social Structure of the Bar.* New York: Russell Sage Foundation and American Bar Foundation.

Heinz, John P.; Edward O. Laumann; Charles L. Cappell; Terence C. Halliday; and Michael H. Schaalman. 1976. "Diversity, Representation, and Leadership in an Urban Bar: A First Report on a Survey of the Chicago Bar." *American Bar Foundation Research Journal* 1976: 717–785.

Heinz, John P., and Robert L. Nelson. 1984. Memorandum to the Stanford Conference on the Law Firm as a Social Institution. On file at the American Bar Foundation, Chicago, Illinois.

Heydebrand, Wolf V. 1973. *Hospital Bureaucracy: A Comparative Study of Organizations.* New York: Dunellen.

Hinings, C. R.; D. J. Hickson; J. M. Pennings; and R. E. Schneck. 1974. "Structural Conditions of Intraorganizational Power." *Administrative Sciences Quarterly* 19: 22–44.

Hirschman, Albert O. 1970. *Exit, Voice and Loyalty: Responses to Decline in Firms, Organizations and States.* Cambridge: Harvard University Press.

Hobson, Wayne K. 1984. "Symbol of the New Profession: Emergence of the Large Law Firm, 1870–1915." In *The New High Priests: Lawyers in Post-Civil War America,* edited by Gerald Gawalt, pp. 3–27. Westport, Conn.: Greenwood Press.

Homans, George C. 1950. *The Human Group.* New York: Harcourt, Brace.

Horowitz, Donald. 1977. *Jurocracy: Government Lawyers, Agency Programs, and Judicial Decisions.* Lexington, Mass.: Lexington Books.

Horwitz, Morton J. 1977. *The Transformation of American Law, 1780–1860.* Cambridge: Harvard University Press.

Hosticka, Carl. 1979. "We Don't Care about What Happened, We Only Care About What Is Going to Happen: Lawyer-Client Negotiations of Reality." *Social Problems* 26: 599–610.

Hughes, Everett. 1958. *Men and Their Work.* Glencoe, Ill.: The Free Press.

Hurst, James W. 1950. *The Growth of American Law: The Lawmakers.* Boston: Little, Brown & Company.

———. 1970. *The Legitimacy of the Business Corporation in the Law of the United States, 1780–1970.* Charlottesville: University of Virginia Press.

Illinois State Bar Association. 1975. "Economics of Legal Services in Illinois—A 1975 Special Bar Survey." *Illinois Bar Journal* 64: 73–134.

Irons, Peter. 1981. *The New Deal Lawyers.* Princeton, N.J.: Princeton University Press.

Janowitz, Morris. 1960. *The Professional Soldier.* New York: The Free Press.

Johnson, Terence J. 1972. *Professions and Power.* London: Macmillan.

Johnstone, Quintin, and Dan Hopson, Jr. 1967. *Lawyers and Their Work: An Analysis of the Legal Profession in the United States and England.* In-

dianapolis: Bobbs-Merrill.
Kagan, Robert. 1978. *Regulatory Justice.* New York: Russell Sage.
Kairys, David, ed. 1982. *The Politics of Law: A Progressive Critique.* New York: Pantheon Books.
Kanter, Rosabeth M. 1977. "Some Effects of Proportions on Group Life: Skewed Sex Ratios and Responses to Token Women." *American Journal of Sociology* 82: 965–990.
Katz, Jack. 1982. *Poor People's Lawyers in Transition.* New Brunswick, N.J.: Rutgers University Press.
Knoke, David, and James H. Kuklinski. 1982. *Network Analysis.* Beverly Hills, Calif.: Sage.
Kocka, Kurgen. 1980. "The Rise of the Modern Industrial Enterprise in Germany." In *Managerial Hierarchies: Comparative Perspectives on the Rise of the Modern Industrial Enterprise,* edited by Alfred D. Chandler, Jr., and Herman Daems, pp. 77–116. Cambridge: Harvard University Press.
Kornhauser, William. 1962. *Scientists in Industry.* Berkeley, Los Angeles: University of California Press.
Kritzer, Herbert. 1984. "The Dimensions of Lawyer-Client Relations: Notes toward a Theory and a Field Study." *American Bar Foundation Research Journal* 1984: 409–425.
Kruskal, J. B. 1964. "Multidimensional Scaling by Optimizing Goodness of Fit to a Nonmetric Hypothesis." *Psychometrika* 29: 1–27.
Ladinsky, Jack. 1963. "Careers of Lawyers, Law Practice, and Legal Institutions." *American Sociological Review* 27: 47–54.
Landon, Donald. 1983. "Clients, Colleagues, and Community: The Shaping of Zealous Advocacy in Country Law Practice." Paper presented at the annual meetings of the Law & Society Association, June 3–5, 1983, Denver.
Larson, Magali S. 1977. *The Rise of Professionalism: A Sociological Analysis.* Berkeley, Los Angeles, London: University of California Press.
Lashly, Jacob M. 1939. "Administrative Law and the Bar." *Virginia Law Review* 25: 641–658.
Laumann, Edward O. 1973. *Bonds of Pluralism: The Form and Substance of Urban Social Networks.* New York: Wiley Interscience.
———, and John P. Heinz. 1977. "Specialization and Prestige in the Legal Profession: The Structure of Deference." *American Bar Foundation Research Journal* 1977: 155–216.
———. 1979. "The Organization of Lawyers' Work: Size, Intensity, and Copractice of Fields of Law." *American Bar Foundation Research Journal* 1979: 217–246.
Laumann, Edward O., and Peter V. Marsden. 1982. "Models of Integration and Microstructural Analysis." Paper presented at the Sun Belt Social Network Conference, Tampa, Florida.
Legal Times of Washington. May 28, 1979. "Crowell & Moring Debuts Friday." P. 7.
———. September 21, 1981. "Annual Law Firm Survey." Pp. 29–43.
———. February 28, 1983. "New 'Senior Attorney' Program Draws Attention at Davis Polk." P. 3.

———. September 24, 1984. "Legal Times 500." Supplement, A1–40.

———. June 30, 1986. "D.C. Firms Adjust and Grow in Deregulatory Era." P. 12.

Leibowitz, Arleen, and Robert Tollison. 1978. "Learning and Earning in Law Firms." *Journal of Legal Studies* 7: 65–81.

———. 1980. "Free Riding, Shirking, and Team Production in Legal Partnerships." *Economic Inquiry* 18: 380–394.

Levi, Edward H. 1949. *An Introduction to Legal Reasoning.* Chicago: University of Chicago Press.

Llewellyn, Karl. 1933. "The Bar Specializes—With What Results?" *Annals* 167: 177.

Lorne, Simon M. 1978. "The Corporate Securities Adviser, the Public Interest, and Professional Ethics." *Michigan Law Review* 75: 423–496.

Lukes, Steven. 1974. *Power: A Radical View.* London: Humanities.

McBarnett, Doreen. 1986. "The Use and Avoidance of Law." Paper presented at the annual meetings of the Law & Society Association, May 31, 1986, Chicago.

Macaulay, Stewart. 1979. "Lawyers and Consumer Protection Laws." *Law & Society Review* 14: 115–171.

McChesney, Fred S. 1982. "Team Production, Monitoring, and Profit Sharing in Law Firms: An Alternative Hypothesis." *Journal of Legal Studies* 11: 379–393.

McClosky, Herbert, and Alida Brill. 1983. *Dimensions of Tolerance: What Americans Believe about Civil Liberties.* New York: Russell Sage.

McCurdy, Charles. 1984. Presentation given at the annual meetings of the Law & Society Association, June 9, 1984, Boston.

McFarland, David, and David Brown. 1973. "Social Distance as a Metric: A Systematic Introduction to Smallest Space Analysis." In *Bonds of Pluralism, the Form and Substance of Urban Social Networks,* by Edward O. Laumann, pp. 213–253. New York: Wiley Interscience.

McHugh, Carol. 1983. "Many Firms Slow to Hire Minority Lawyers." *Chicago Daily Law Bulletin,* April 23, 1983, p. 13.

Mandel, Ernest. 1975. *Late Capitalism.* London: NLB.

Mann, Michael. 1970. "The Social Cohesion of Liberal Democracy." *American Sociological Review* 35: 423–439.

Marcson, Simon. 1960. *The Scientist in American Industry.* Princeton, N.J.: Industrial Relations Section, Department of Economics, Princeton University.

Martindale-Hubbell Law Directory. 1935, 1950, 1965, 1970–1985. Summit, N. J.: Martindale-Hubbell, Inc.

Marx, Karl. 1967. *Capital.* Translated by Samuel Moore and Edward Aveling. New York: International Publishers.

Masters, Edgar L. 1927. *Levy Mayer and the New Industrial Era.* New Haven: Yale University Press.

Menkel-Meadow, Carrie. Forthcoming. "The Comparative Sociology of Women Lawyers: The 'Feminization' of the Legal Profession." In *Lawyers and Society: A Comparative Approach,* edited by Richard Abel and Philip

Lewis. Berkeley, Los Angeles, London: University of California Press.
———, and Robert G. Meadow. 1983. "Resource Allocation in Legal Services: Individual Attorney Decisions in Work Priorities." *Law & Policy Quarterly* 5: 237–256.
Mensch, Elizabeth. 1982. "The History of Mainstream Legal Thought." In *The Politics of Law: A Progressive Critique,* edited by David Kairys, pp. 18–39. New York: Pantheon Books.
Merton, Robert K. 1940. "Bureaucratic Structure and Personality." *Social Forces* 17: 560–568.
Meyer, Marshall W. 1972. "Size and the Structure of Organizations: A Causal Analysis." *American Sociological Review* 37: 434–441.
Miller, George A. 1968. "Professionals in Bureaucracy: Alienation among Industrial Scientists and Engineers." *American Sociological Review* 32: 755–768.
Mills, C. Wright. 1953. *White Collar.* New York: Oxford University Press.
———. 1956. *The Power Elite.* New York: Oxford University Press.
Mincer, Jacob. 1974. *Schooling, Experience, and Earnings.* New York: National Bureau of Economic Research, Columbia University Press.
Mindes, Marvin W., with Alan Acock. 1982. "Trickster, Hero, Helper: A Report on the Lawyer Image." *American Bar Foundation Research Journal* 1982: 177–234.
Moldenhauer, Howard H. 1972. "Formula and Nonformula Systems for Distributing Partnership Net Income." *Law Office Economics and Management* 13: 21–52.
Montagna, Paul. 1966. *Bureaucracy and Change in Large Professional Organizations.* Ph.D. dissertation, New York University.
———. 1968. "Professionalization and Bureaucratization in Large Professional Organizations." *American Journal of Sociology* 74: 138–145.
———. 1971. "The Public Accounting Professional." *American Behavioral Scientist* 14: 475–481.
Morgan, James, et al. 1964. *Income and Welfare in the United States.* New York: McGraw-Hill.
Murphy, Walter F., and Joseph Tanenhaus. 1968. "Public Opinion and the United States Supreme Court." *Law & Society Review* 2: 357–384.
Nader, Ralph. 1970. "Law Schools and Law Firms." *Minnesota Law Review* 54: 493–501.
National Association for Law Placement. 1984. *Directory of Legal Employers.* 6th ed. New Orleans: National Association for Law Placement.
National Law Journal. August 13, 1979. "National Law Firm Survey." Pp. 64, 65.
———. October 1, 1979. "It's Harder to Make Partner." P. 1.
———. September 13, 1982. "National Law Firm Survey." Pp. 14–19.
———. May 26, 1986. "Shakeout Begins over Pay Hikes." Pp. 1, 8.
———. September 20, 1982. "National Law Firm Survey." Pp. 13–16.
Navin, Thomas R., and Marian V. Sears. 1955. "The Rise of a Market for Industrial Securities, 1887–1902." *Business History Review* 19: 105–138.
Nelson, Robert L. 1981. "Practice and Privilege: Social Change and the Struc-

ture of Large Law Firms." *American Bar Foundation Research Journal* 1981: 95–140.

———. 1983. "The Changing Structure of Opportunity: Recruitment and Careers in Large Law Firms." *American Bar Foundation Research Journal* 1983: 109–142.

New York Times. December 17, 1978. "A.B.A., S.E.C. Study Change in Corporate Law Standards." Section 3, p. 1.

———. May 19, 1981. "Nader Conference Airs Complaints on Law Fees." P. 29.

———. January 18, 1982. "For Cravath, Life after I.B.M." Pp. 23, 26.

———. April 2, 1982. "Putting Litigation on a Budget." Pp. 32–33.

———. January 16, 1983. "A Gentlemanly Profession Enters a Tough New Era." Pp. 1F, 10F.

———. February 7, 1983. "Lawyers Vote Against Disclosure of Fraudulent Activity by Clients." Pp. 1, 21.

———. February 10, 1983. "A.B.A.'s Decision: Lawyer Confidentiality over Disclosure of Crimes-to-Be." P. 9.

———. March 12, 1985. "The Lawyers Chosen by India." Pp. 25, 30.

———. May 2, 1984. "Big Firms Setting Up Volunteer Services in the City." Section A, p. 1.

———. May 13, 1984. "Auditors Feel the Heat of a New Scrutiny." Section 3, pp. 1, 26.

———. May 29, 1984. "Retaining Valued Attorneys." Pp. 27, 29.

Noble, David. 1977. *America by Design: Science, Technology, and the Rise of Corporate Capitalism.* New York: Knopf.

O'Gorman, Hubert J. 1963. *Lawyers and Matrimonial Cases: A Study of Informal Pressures in Private Professional Practice.* New York: Free Press of Glencoe.

Oppenheimer, M. 1973. "The Proletarianization of the Professional." Sociological Review monograph, no. 20: 213–227.

Ouchi, William G. 1980. "Markets, Bureaucracies, and Clans." *Administrative Sciences Quarterly* 25: 129–141.

———, and Jerry B. Johnson. 1978. "Types of Organizational Control and Their Relationship to Emotional Well-being." *Administrative Sciences Quarterly* 23: 293–317.

Parsons, Talcott. 1951. *The Social System.* Glencoe: Free Press.

———. 1954. "A Sociologist Looks at the Legal Profession." In *Essays on Sociological Theory,* edited by Talcott Parsons, pp. 370–385. New York: Free Press of Glencoe.

———. 1960. *Structure and Process in Modern Societies.* New York: Free Press of Glencoe.

———. 1962. "The Law and Social Control." In *Law and Sociology,* edited by William M. Evan, pp. 65–78. New York: The Free Press.

Perrow, Charles. 1961. "The Analysis of Goals in Complex Organizations." *American Sociological Review* 26: 854–865.

———. 1970. *Organizational Analysis: A Sociological View.* Belmont, Calif.: Wadsworth.

Peters, Thomas J., and Robert H. Waterman, Jr. 1982. *In Search of Excellence: Lessons from America's Best-Run Companies.* New York: Warner Books.

Pfeffer, J., and G. R. Salancik. 1978. *External Control of Organizations: A Resource Dependence Perspective.* New York: Harper and Row.

Platt, Gerald M., and Talcott Parsons. 1968. "Decision-making in the Academic System: Influence and Power Exchange." In *The State of the University,* edited by Carlos E. Kruytbosch and Sheldon L. Messinger, pp. 133–180. Beverly Hills, Calif.: Sage.

Polsby, Nelson. 1980. "The Washington Community, 1960–1980." In *The New Congress,* edited by Thomas E. Mann and Norman J. Ornstein, pp. 7–31. American Enterprise Institute for Public Policy Research.

Powell, Michael. 1982. "Social Change and an Elite Professional Association: The Politics of Inclusion." Ph.D. dissertation, University of Chicago.

———. 1985. "Developments in the Regulation of Lawyers." *Social Forces* 64: 281–305.

Punnett, Spencer. 1986. Law Firm Mergers: An Empirical Study. Chicago: Northwestern University School of Law.

Rehnquist, William H. September 12, 1986. Law School Dedication Speech. Indiana University, Bloomington.

Reich, Charles. 1964. "The New Property." Yale Law Journal 73: 733–787.

Robinson, John P.; Jerrold G. Rush; and Kendon B. Head. 1968. *Measures of Political Attitudes.* Ann Arbor: University of Michigan, Survey Research Center.

Robinson, John P., and Philip E. Converse. 1972. "Social Change Reflected in the Use of Time." In *The Human Meaning of Social Change,* edited by Angus Campbell and Philip Converse, pp. 17–86. New York: Russell Sage.

Root, Elihu. 1916. "Public Service by the Bar." *American Bar Association Journal* 41: 736–750.

Rosen, Robert Eli. 1984. Lawyers in Corporate Decision-Making. Ph.D. dissertation, Department of Sociology, University of California, Berkeley.

Rosenberg, Sheli. 1978. Remarks at the Chicago Council of Lawyers' Conference on Law Firms.

Rosenthal, Douglas. 1974. *Lawyer and Client: Who's in Charge.* New York: Russell Sage.

Ross, H. Laurence. 1970. *Settled out of Court: The Social Process of Insurance Claims Adjustments.* Chicago: Aldine.

Rothman, Robert A. 1984. "Deprofessionalization: The Case of Law in America." *Work and Occupations* 11: 183–206.

Rueschemeyer, Dietrich. 1973. *Lawyers and Their Society.* Cambridge: Harvard University Press.

———. 1983. "Professional Autonomy and the Social Control of Expertise." In *The Sociology of the Professions,* edited by Robert Dingwall and Philip Lewis, pp. 38–58. New York: St. Martin's Press.

Salancik, Gerald R., and Jeffrey Pfeffer. 1974. "The Basis and Use of Power in Organizational Decision Making: The Case of a University." *Administrative Sciences Quarterly* 19: 453–473.

Salisbury, Robert H. 1986. "Towards a New Understanding of Interest

Groups." In *Interest Group Politics,* edited by A. Cigler and B. Loomis, pp. 146–161. Washington: Congressional Quarterly Press.

Sarat, Austin, and William L. F. Felstiner. 1986. "Law and Strategy in the Divorce Lawyer's Office." *Law & Society Review* 20: 93–134.

Satow, Roberta L. 1975. "Value Rational Authority and Professional Organizations: Weber's Missing Type." *Administrative Science Quarterly* 20: 526–531.

Schwartz, Murray L. 1980. "The Reorganization of the Legal Profession." *Texas Law Review* 58: 1269–1304.

Scott, William R. 1961. A Case Study of Professional Workers in a Bureaucratic Setting. Ph.D. dissertation, Department of Sociology, University of Chicago.

———. 1965. "Reactions to Supervision in a Heteronomous Professional Organization." *Administrative Sciences Quarterly* 10: 65–81.

———. 1981. *Organizations: Rational, Natural, and Open Systems.* Englewood Cliffs, N.J.: Prentice-Hall.

Selznick, Philip. 1949. *TVA and the Grass Roots.* Berkeley: University of California Press.

———. 1968. *Law, Society, and Industrial Justice.* New Brunswick, N.J.: Transaction Books.

Shepherd, John. 1984. "Professionalism and Public Service: The Age of Renewal." *American Bar Association Journal* 70: 6.

Shils, Edward. 1975. *Center and Periphery.* Chicago: University of Chicago Press.

Sikes, Bette H.; Clara N. Carson; and Patricia Gorai, eds. 1971. *The 1971 Lawyer Statistical Report.* Chicago: American Bar Foundation.

Simon, William. 1978. "The Ideology of Advocacy: Procedural Justice and Professional Ethics." *Wisconsin Law Review* 1978: 29–144.

———. 1985. "Comment: Babbitt vs. Brandeis: The Decline of the Professional Ideal." *Stanford Law Review* 37: 565–587.

Smigel, Erwin. 1969. *The Wall Street Lawyer: Professional Organizational Man?* 2d ed. Bloomington: Indiana University Press.

Spangler, Eva. 1986. *Lawyers for Hire.* New Haven and London: Yale University Press.

———; Marsha A. Gordon; and Ronald M. Pipkin. 1978. "Token Women: An Empirical Test of Kanter's Hypothesis." *American Journal of Sociology* 84: 160–170.

Spangler, Eva, and P. M. Lehman. 1982. "Lawyering as Work." In *Professionals as Workers,* edited by C. Derber, pp. 63–99. Boston: G. K. Hall.

Spector, Malcolm B. 1971. Legal Careers and Government Service: A Study in the Social Psychology of Occupations. Ph.D. dissertation, Northwestern University.

Spilerman, Seymour. 1978. "Careers, Labor Market Structure, and Socioeconomic Achievement." *American Journal of Sociology* 83: 551–593.

Stanford Law Review. 1982. Project: "Law Firms and Lawyers with Children: An Empirical Analysis of Family/Work Conflict." *Stanford Law Review* 34: 1263–1308.

Starr, Paul. 1982. *The Social Transformation of American Medicine*. New York: Basic Books, Inc.
Stevens, Robert. 1971. "Two Cheers for 1870: The American Law School." In *Perspective in American History (Vol. 5)*, edited by Donald Fleming and Bernard Bailyn, pp. 405–511. Cambridge: Harvard University Press.
Stewart, James. 1983. *The Partners*. New York: Simon and Schuster.
Stewart, Richard. 1975. The Reformation of American Administrative Law." *Harvard Law Review* 88: 1669–1837.
Stinchcombe, Arthur L. 1959. "Bureaucratic and Craft Administration of Production." *Administrative Science Quarterly* 4: 168–187.
———. 1965. "Social Structure and Organizations." In *Handbook of Organizations*, edited by James March, pp. 142–169. Chicago: Rand McNally.
———. 1980. "Norms of Exchange." Unpublished manuscript.
Stone, Christopher D. 1975. *Where the Law Ends: The Social Control of Corporate Behavior*. New York: Harper and Row.
Sullivan's Law Directory. 1982. Barrington, Ill.: Sullivan's Law Directory, Inc.
Swaine, Robert T. 1946. *The Cravath Firm and Its Predecessors, 1819–1947*. New York: Ad Press, private printing.
Swanson, Guy. 1980. "A Basis of Authority and Identity in Post-industrial Society." In *Identity and Authority*, edited by Burkhart Holzner and Roland Robertson, pp. 190–217. Oxford: Blackwell's.
Szalai, Alexander, et al. 1972. *The Use of Time*. The Hague: Mouton.
Theil, Henri. 1972. *Statistical Decomposition Analysis*. Amsterdam/London: North-Holland.
Thibaut, John, and Laurens Walker. 1978. "A Theory of Procedure." *California Law Review* 66: 541–566.
Thompson, J. D. 1967. *Organizations in Action*. New York: McGraw-Hill.
Tocqueville, Alexis de. 1863. *Democracy in America*. Cambridge: Sever & Francis.
Trubek, David. 1972. "Max Weber on Law and the Rise of Capitalism." *Wisconsin Law Review* 1972: 720–753.
Tuma, Nancy B.; Michael T. Hannan; and Lyle P. Groenveld. 1979. "Dynamic Analysis of Event Histories." *American Journal of Sociology* 84: 820–854.
Tushnet, Mark. 1984. "An Essay on Rights." *Texas Law Review* 62: 1363–1403.
Unger, Roberto M. 1976. *Law in Modern Society*. New York: The Free Press.
U.S. Bureau of Census, 1975. *1972 Census of Selected Service Industries: Legal Services*. Washington, D.C.: Government Printing Office.
———. 1981. *1977 Census of Service Industries: Legal Services*. Washington, D.C.: U.S. Government Printing Office.
Wall Street Journal. March 23, 1981. "In-House Legal Staffs Grow 10 Percent at Top Firms." P. 19.
———. November 18, 1983. "A Blue-Chip Law Firm Comes on Hard Times After a Coup d'Etat." Pp. 1, 16.
Washington Post. December 27, 1983. "Critics See Lawyers Losing Interest in Public-Service Cases." Pp. C1, C2.

Weber, Max. 1978. *Economy and Society,* edited by Guenther Roth and Claus Wittich. Berkeley, Los Angeles, London: University of California Press.

White, H. C.; S. A. Boorman; and R. L. Brieger. 1976. "Social Structure from Multiple Networks. I. Blockmodels of Roles and Positions." *American Journal of Sociology* 81: 730–780.

Wilensky, Harold. 1964. "The Professionalization of Everyone." *American Journal of Sociology* 70: 137–158.

Williamson, Oliver. 1975. *Markets and Hierarchies: Analysis and Antitrust Implications.* New York: The Free Press.

Wrong, Dennis H. 1968. "Some Problems in Defining Social Power." *American Journal of Sociology* 73: 673–681.

Young, Michael, and Peter Willmott. 1973. *The Symmetrical Family.* New York: Pantheon Books.

Zald, Mayer N., ed. 1970. *Power in Organizations.* Nashville: Vanderbilt University Press.

Zehnle, Richard. 1975. *Specializations in the Legal Profession: An Analysis of Current Proposals.* Chicago: American Bar Foundation.

Zemans, Frances K. 1982. "Legal Structure and Access to Justice: The Case of the American Rule." Paper presented at the annual meetings of the Law & Society Association, June 5, 1982, Toronto, Canada.

Index

Note:

Tables are indicated by numerals in italics. Figures are indicated by numerals in boldface type.

Aaron, Smith & Kimball, 93–101
  characteristics of, 92, 93
  difficulties in internal governance, 98, 99
  firm size by year, 87
  frequency distribution of specialization index, *173*
  gender, year hired, *135*
  governance decisions, 100
  historical development, 93–101
  income regressed on sets of independent variables, *196–197*
  law school representation, year hired, *132*
  lawyers, percentage of, reporting on given types of events, *148*
  percentage committed by partnership status, *221*
  percentage committed by partnership status with total hours worked, *222*
  percentage of time spent on principal client in last year, by field of practice, *251*
  rates of change from first field of specialty, *154*
  reason for choice of field, *156*
  smallest space model of, **164**
  specialization index by firm and field of law, *174*
  structural characteristics, major, *94–95*
  total hours worked per year, by partnership status and field of practice, *186*
Abel, Richard, 7, 268
Abramson, Jill, 140
Addington, Ames & Seibold, 40
Administrative Procedure Act, 262
Alchian, Armen A., 64, 190
Alschuler, Albert, 269
Althauser, Robert P., 198
American Bar Association (ABA), 127
  Commission on Professionalism, 3
  enrollment in twenty leading law schools, 133
  House of Delegates, debates, 261
  1980, 261
  past presidents, recent, 3
  racial composition of leading law schools, 131
  special commission on professionalism, 225
American Bar Association Journal 1985, 202

363

American College of Trial Lawyers, 261
American Lawyer, 38
    August 11, 1978, 74
    1979, 2
    1979–1984, 60
    September 15, 1981, 60
    1983, 49
    July/August 1986, 66
American Lawyer's Guide to Law Firms
    1981–1982, 137
    1984, 60
American legal profession, set of practitioners of, 22
American Telephone & Telegraph. *See* AT&T
Antitrust, 244
Arabie, Phipps, 169
Associate(s)
    economic role of, 77
    and firms, conflict between, 26
    hiring and turnover in, nineteen firms in Chicago, *138*
    and partners, divergence between, 28
    skills, 202
    turnover rate, 143
AT&T (American Telephone & Telegraph), 57
Attorneys-at-law. *See* Lawyers
Aubert, Wilhelm, 257
Auchincloss, Louis, 185
Auerbach, Carl A., 37, 134
Auerbach, Jerold S.
    corporate elite and efforts to control admission to bar, 283, 284, 285
    effects of social background vs. individual achievement, 127
    elite corporate bar, 11
    jeremiad directed at large law firm, 236
    lawyers at turn of century, 262, 263
    legal elite, dual role of, 259
    nativism, 66
    significance of large law firm, 1
Authority, in large law firm, 205–228
    appeal of professionalism, 214–220; to clients, 214, 215; differences in professional values by firm and partnership status, 218, 220; and professional values, 220; within, 215–218
    bureaucracy and commitment, 220–224
    client control, as constraint on managerial authority, 224–228; conclusions, 227–228; interpretation of, 226, 227
    ideology of professionalism, 208, 209
    law firm rationalization by firm and partnership status, *219*

organizational dominance perspective, 206
partnership, collegial form, 211–214
percentage committed by firm and partnership status, *221*
percentage committed by firm, partnership status with total hours worked, *222*
power, exchange and, 207–209
prior literature and authority in professional organizations, 209–211; and assumption of authority, 211; model of professional firm, 210, 211; value-rational, 210
role of professionalism in, 206
Authority system, of firm, 28
Autonomy, professional,
    baronial, 114
    ideology and practice, divergence between, 259–263
    of management, 90
    proposed changes in fields in which lawyers practice, 245–246
    technical, of professional subordinates, 20

Baker-Hostetler, 48
Baker & McKenzie, 42, 61, 121
Banking law, 244
Barlow, Andrew, 284
Baronial autonomy. *See* Autonomy, professional
Bates v. State Bar 1977, 22
Becker, Gary S., 193
Becker, Solomon, & Jones, 101–107
    characteristics of, 92, 93
    firm size by year, 87
    frequency distribution of specialization index, *173*
    gender, year hired, *135*
    historical development, 101–107
    income regressed on sets of independent variables, *196–197*
    law school representation, year hired, *132*
    lawyers, percentage of, reporting on given types of events, *148*
    percentage committed by partnership status, *221*
    percentage committed by partnership status with total hours worked, *222*
    percentage of time spent on principal client in last year, by field of practice, *251*
    rates of change from first field of specialty, *154*

Index 365

reason for choice of field, *156*
smallest space model of, 165
specialization index by firm and field of law, *174*
structural characteristics, major, *94–95*
total hours worked per year, by partnership status and field of practice, *186*
Bell, Daniel, 18
Bell, Robert, 273
Ben-David, Joseph, 220
Bendix, Reinhard, 24, 210
Berkowitz, Steven D., 161
Berle, Adolph A., Jr., 12, 236, 260, 288
Bibby, John F., 7
Bidwell, Charles E., 210
Big Eight accounting firms, 66–67
Blatchford, Richard, 72
Blau, Peter M., 24, 30, 159
Bledstein, Burton J., 18
Boorman, Scott A., 169
Bosk, Charles L., 18, 25, 78, 159, 227
Branch office(s)
 consequence of, 59, 60
 as indicator, 59
 and Washington, D.C., 59
Brandeis, Louis D., 231
 on alliance between elite law firms and big business, 260
 on obligation of legal profession, 234
 statement on Progressive ideal, 11
Breiger, R. L., 169
Bryce, James, 284
Bucher, Rue, 18, 30, 208, 209
Burawoy, Michael, 159, 210, 287
Bureaucracy
 and commitment, 220–224
 and professionalism, conflict between, 4
 rules and, 13
Bureaucracy and participation, 86–124
 historical analysis on conflict between, 88–90
 structural differences, overview, 91–93
Bureaucratic management, 91
 advantages, 10
 characteristics, 91
Bureaucratization
 and client-responsible elite, 225
 in firms, and advocacy of client interests, 17
 in law firm, 17
 limiting factor on, 224
 process of, 10
 process and limits, 274, 275
 and professionalism, conflict between, 10
 of professional organization, structural changes, 4
Burstein, Paul, 7

CBA. *See* Chicago Bar Association
Cain, Maureen, 17, 233, 235
Cappell, Charles L., 1, 134, 172, 284
Cardozo, Benjamin N., 242
Carlin, Jerome E., 1
 and elite corporate bar, 11
 ethics rules imposed on New York lawyers, 283
 impact of professional style of large firms, 27
 large firms' control of legal profession, possibility, 284
 legal profession's status hierarchy, 37, 130
Carr-Saunders, A. M., 20
Carson, Clara N., 57
Chamberlayne, Charles F., 170
Chandler, Alfred D., Jr., 24
 Alfred Sloan, Jr. and multidivisional corporation, 71
 American business enterprise, 70
 analysis of structural change in major industrial enterprises, 120
 integrated operating company after 1890, 287
 management as autonomous stratum, 90
 modern corporate power, 285, 286
 relationship between entrepreneurs and managers, 73
Channeling, 151–156
 and percentage of choices, by field of practice, *153*
 and percentage of lawyers, into field of practice, *152*
Chapman & Cutler, 42
Chayes, Abram, 267
Chicago Bar Association (CBA)
 board of governors recruitment, 284
Chicago Kent College of Law of Illinois Institute of Technology, 137
Chicago law firm(s)
 associate hiring and turnover, *138*
 and development of new legal doctrines, 81
 relative standings and nature, 40
 salaries, starting, 75
 ten largest, *41*
 turnover rates, 137
Chicago Sun-Times, January 19, 1981, 203
Christensen, Barlow F., 81
Civil Aeronautics Board, 57

Class-action litigation, use of, 241, 242
Cleary-Gottlieb, 65
Client base, 91
  of Becker, 101
  expansion of, 121
Client responsibility, 91
Client-responsible elite
  and bureaucratization, 225
  and organizational rationalization of firm, 5
Cole, Robert E., 25
Collegial domination, system of, 16
Collegial hierarchy, defined, 4
Collegiality
  attitude of, 70
  and leaders of firms, 4
Comed (Commonwealth Edison)
  internal legal unit of, 42
  and Isham, Lincoln & Beale, 40
Commission on Professionalism (ABA), 3
Commonwealth Edison. See Comed
CONCOR algorithm, 169
Continental Bank, and Mayer, Brown & Platt, 42
Corporate bar
  and law reform, 11
  professional obligations, 11
Corporate law firm(s), new function for, 8
Corporate lawyer(s), autonomy of, 4
Corporate legal department(s), growth of, 57
Corporation(s)
  general counsel of, 57
  relationship with law firms, 22
Coudert Brothers, 49
Counsel. See Lawyer(s)
Covington & Burling, 49, 65
Crain's Chicago Business
  July 30, 1979, 203
  November 20, 1983, 75
Cravath, Paul D., 65, 73
  genius of, 286
  and jump in starting salaries, 143
  system, 71
  up or out rule, 72
Cravath, Swaine, & Moore, 39, 75
Cravath system, 71–73, 180
  career patterns and, 136
  and corporation, 286
  ideal of, 289
  tenets of, two, 260
Curran, Barbara A., 57
Curran, Geller & Heinz, 107–114, 134
  characteristics of, 92, 93
  firm size by year, 87
  frequency distribution of specialization index, 173

gender, year hired, 135
governance of firm, 108, 111
historical development, 107–114
law school representation, year hired, 132
lawyers, percentage of, reporting on given types of events, 148
percentage committed by partnership status, 221
percentage committed by partnership status with total hours worked, 222
percentage of time spent on principal client in last year, by field of practice, 251
rates of change from first field of specialty, 154
reason for choice of field, 156
smallest space model of, 167
specialization index by firm and field of law, 174
structural characteristics, major, 94–95
total hours worked per year, by partnership status and field of practice, 186

Danet, Brenda, 233
Davies, Celia, 220
Dean, Arthur H., 286
DeAngelo, Linda A., 62
Defection(s), types, 60, 61
Demsetz, Harold, 64, 190
Departmental system(s), 4
DePaul University—College of Law, 137
Derber, Charles, 20, 171, 189
Dewey-Ballantine, 49
Discrimination, 130, 131
Dishonorable work, 27
  and attitudes of firm leaders, 53
Dissension, 49
  between finders and minders, 74, 75
  precipitation of, 203
  types of, 60, 61
Diversification, 64, 65
Division of labor, status-based, 26
Dolbeare, Kenneth M., 268
Domination, 16, 17
Donovan-Leisure, 49, 74, 109, 203
Duncan, Martin & Levy, 114–124
  characteristics of, 92, 93
  firm by year, 87
  frequency distribution of specialization index, 173
  gender, year hired, 135
  governance of firm, 118
  historical development, 114–124
  law school representation, year hired, 132
  lawyers, percentage of, reporting on

given types of events, *148*
percentage committed by partnership status, *221*
percentage committed by partnership status with total hours worked, *222*
percentage of time spent on principal client in last year, by field of practice, *251*
rates of change from first field of specialty, *154*
reason for choice of field, *156*
smallest space model of, **168**
specialization index by firm and field of law, *174*
structural characteristics, major, *94–95*
total hours worked per year, by partnership status and field of practice, *186*
Durkheim, Emile, 24, 159, 281

Earle, Walter, 39, 50
Earnings. *See* Income
Economic rewards, 190–204
  equations for variables, 195
  full model, of income determination, 198–204; seniority explaining variance, 201; significance of seniority, 200
  income, 190
  income distribution, 191
  measures and preliminary models, general patterns, 192–198; income regressed on sets of independent variables, *196–197*; income by years in practice, *193*
Economy and Society, 23
Elite. *See* Managerial elite
Entrepreneurial approach, to practice, 8
Epstein, Cynthia Fuchs, 127, 133, 134, 135, 140
Equal Employment Opportunity Commission, 7
Erlanger, Howard S., 249
Ethical standards, 11
Ethnic segmentation, result of, 130
Ethnoreligious divisions, 130, 131
Ex ante contract, 64

Federal Register, 7
Federal regulatory activity
  Equal Employment Opportunity Commission, 7
  and *Federal Register*, 7
Felstiner, William L. F., 252
Field, David Dudley, 39, 259, 286
Field Codes, 39
Finders, 9
  different role of, 275, 276

entrepreneurial role of, 70–73
Finley-Kumble, 43, 48, 61, 121
Firm-specific capital, 64
First National Bank of Chicago, 42
Forces of practice and privilege, 25
  tensions of, 86
Frank, John P., on lawyers as mediators, 233
Frankel, Marvin E., 258
Franklin, Barbara, 140
Frederickson, Robert, 172
Free choice, in careers, 151, 152
Freidson, Eliot, 4
  bureaucratization and professional autonomy, 227
  and character of power, 19
  characterizations of professional organizations, 30
  control of organizational context of work, 210
  dual lines of authority, 220
  double meaning of profession, 18
  organization of work, in professional organizations, 159
  on professional power, 20, 21
  theory of professional dominance, 21
Friedman, Lawrence M., 7, 39, 267, 282, 286
Functionalist model, of Talcott Parsons, 11

Galanter, Marc, 37
  American legal institutions and adversary procedures, 269
  corporations and legal process, 234
  expansion of private law functions, 8
  functioning of formal legal institutions, 7
  impact of large law firms, 267
  strategic use of superior representational resources, *268*
General Motors, 57
General service fields, 52
General service firm
  factors favoring growth, *58*
  growth in, 51
  and lateral recruitment, 55
  prototypical cases of, 52
  typical role of, 54
Gibson-Dunn, 48
Gilb, Corinne L., 18
Gilson, Ronald J., 62, 64, 65, 191
Goldberg, Victor P., 65
Goldfarb v. Virginia State Bar 1975, 22
Gorai, Patricia, 57
Gordon, Robert W., 3
  contributions of legal elite, 287

elite corporate bar, 11
elite of corporate bar and values of professionalism, 225
on elite of legal profession, views of, 9
ideological functions of corporate bar, 267
law firms prior to regulated financial markets, 56
legal elite of late nineteenth century, 259, 263
power of large firms, 231, 232
promotion of growth of law schools, large firms, 66
Goss, Mary, 18, 30, 209
Gouldner, Alvin W., 13
Governance
decisions, Aaron, 100
of firm, Curran, 108
of firm, Duncan, 118
internal, difficulties in Aaron, 98, 99
limited democratization of, 120
tensions in, 212, 213
Gramsci, Antonio, 287
Great Depression, 40, 228
Great World and Timothy Colt, The (Auchincloss), 185
Green, Mark, 12, 231
Greenwood, Glenn, 172
Grinders, 9, 75–77
different role of, 275, 276
Groenveld, Lyle P., 145
Grossman, Joel B., 1, 231

Habermas, Jurgen, 286
Hall, Richard, 18, 220
Halliday, Terence C.
autonomous elite, 281
collegial control as mechanism, 227
drafting new laws and experts of large law firms, 81
large law firms, recruitment, 1
lawyers in large firms and leadership in bar associations, 231
origination of professional values, 79
role of professions in politics, 18
study on recruitment to board of governors of CBA, 284
Hammond, Phillip E., 268
Hannan, Michael T., 145
Harrell, Morris, 262
Harrington, Christine, 261
Hastings, A., 220
Haug, D. M., 26, 171
Head, Kendon B., 238
Heintz, Bruce D., 190
Heinz, John P.
analytic difficulties, 265

careers of lawyers, 128
corporate lawyers vs. lawyers representing individuals, 4
development of new legal doctrines, large firms, 81
ethnic and class groups, 130
foundations of power, large firms, 232
fragmentation of leadership of bar, 262
fragmentation within legal profession, 283, 284
general state of inequality, perceptions by lawyers, 240
government regulation, 239
highest levels of specialization, large firms, 84
key theoretical issue, 233
law practice, specialized, 172
law school status, 131
lawyers' social values, 249
measurement of power of lawyers, large firms, 263, 264
power of large companies, 238
profile of Chicago lawyers, 235
redistribution of income, 241
refusing assignments, relationship to work setting, 257
status hierarchy of fields of practice, 27
status of firms, 37
Hierarchy(ies)
collegial, 4; structure, 16
professional, discretion of subordinates in, 20
status, 9, 10; large firms and, 37
Hills, Charles W. and Jones, 40
Hinings, C. R., 220
Hirschman, Albert O., 84
Historical construction, of large law firm, 39–80
general patterns, 39–49; changed market, 58–62; economic theories of growth, 62–69; entrepreneurial role, finders, 70–73; of fifty largest, size and rank, 44–47; grinders, 75–77; historical literature, 39; managerial role, minders, 73–75; number of firms with fifty or more lawyers, by city, 48; rise of internal counsel, 56–58; structure of firm, 69–77; theory of law firm growth, general service and special representation, 49–69; value rationality, collegial domination and bureaucracy, 77–80
sociology of firm to sociology of law, 81–85
Hobson, Wayne K., 39, 56
Hoffman, K. B., 233
Hogan & Hartson, 49

Index

Homans, George C., 159, 161
Homogeneity, 13, 14
Hopkins-Sutter, 52
Hopson, Dan, Jr., 57, 159, 172
Horwitz, Morton J., 82
Hosticka, Carl, 235
House Counsel, 56
 expansion of, threat from, 83
 growth of, 57
Howrey & Simon, 49, 52, 109
Hubbell Legal Directory, 39
Hughes, Everett, 129, 150, 227
Human capital theory, 193
Hurst, James W.
 examples of legal innovations, 286
 functions of lawyers, 233
 influence of large law firms, 231
 legal fiction of corporation, 288
 money and status in large law firms, 56
 surveys of American legal history, 39
Hyatt Legal Services, 63, 223

IBM (International Business Machines, Inc.), 57, 73
Ideology
 bureaucratic managerial, 80
 of independence, 269
 managerial, 38
 professional, 78–80
 of professional autonomy, 12, 260
 of professional development, 217
 of professionalism, appeal of, 217
Image of professionalism, 38
Income, 190
 distribution, 191
 measures and preliminary models, general patterns, 192–198
Independent counsel, 56
Internal counsel
 and changes in content of work, 61
 expanded role of, 59
 growth of, 272
 inside corporation, 5
 practice of, 57
 rise of, 56–58
Internal Revenue Service, 244
International Business Machines, Inc. *See* IBM
Irons, Peter, 262, 288
Isham, Lincoln & Beale, 40

Jenner and Block, 52
Johnson, Jerry B., 78, 210
Johnson, Terrence, 15, 17, 227, 233, 265
Johnstone, Quintin, 57, 159, 172
Jones-Day, 48
Judges by merit, 244

Kagan, Robert, 28
Kanter, Rosabeth M., 139
Katz, Jack
 involvement of legal authorities in affairs of public and private organizations, 7
 lawyers in different stages of career, 128
 legal problems of poor vs. legal problems of corporations, 26
 legal service organizations, different functions in legal system, 25
 professional ideology, and effects on law firm, 78
Katzenbach, Nicholas, 57
Keck, Cushman, Mahin, & Cate, 40
Kermish, N. C., 233
Kirkland & Ellis, 42, 60, 203
Klegon, Douglas A., 249
Knowledge
 imbalance of, 22
 professions' control of formal, 19
Kocka, Kurgen, 287
Kornhauser, William, 18, 220
Kritzer, Herbert, 26, 233, 256
Kutak, Robert, 261
Kutak, Rock & Campbell, 49, 121

Ladinsky, Jack, 1, 37, 130
Landon, Donald, 233
Large law firm(s)
 analysis of social organization of, and sociology of law, 6
 and associates, conflict, between, 26
 authority system of, 28
 and autonomous managerial stratum, 15
 bureaucratization in, 17
 changes in organization of, 2, 3
 contradictions of, 2
 divergence between practice and ideology, 11, 12
 entrepreneurial approach to practice, 8
 and ethic of professionalism, 3
 factors favoring, 62
 and forces of practice and privilege, 25
 growth of, 2
 and ideology of professionalism, 3
 and image, 59
 increase in demand for specialized knowledge of, 8
 lack of autonomy from clients, 5
 model of, 12
 and modern business corporation, 17
 need for analysis, 37
 and nonadoption of managerial policies, 10
 organization of, 25, 26

patterns of social change in, 7
practice of law in, 82, 83
pro bono work of, 12
professional culture of, 27
relationships with corporate clients, 8
significance, 1
social change in, practice and privilege, 25–29
social organization of, aspects, 27
in society, and Progressive ideal, 11
specialization in, 26
status-based division of labor, 26
status hierarchy of, 9, 10
traditional to bureaucratic, 7
transformation of, 7–12
as voice for interests of clients, 6
Larson, Magali S.
conditions for achieving professional status, 18
division of labor, 171
engineering professionals, 56
ideal of individual professional freedom, 216
institutionalized resolution of conflict, 243
the professional project, 22
professionals' ability to control careers, 129
theory of rise of professionalism, 23
Lateral entry, to partnerships, 55
Laumann, Edward O.
careers of lawyers, 128
development of new legal doctrines, large firms, 81
ethnic and class groups, 130
foundations of power, large firms, 232
fragmentation of leadership of bar, 262
fragmentation within legal profession, 283, 284
general state of inequality, 240
government regulation, 239
highest levels of specialization, large firms, 84
key theoretical issue, 233
law practice, specialized, 172
law school status, 131
lawyers' social values, 249
measurement of power of lawyers, large firms, 263, 264
power of large companies, 238
profile of Chicago lawyers, 235
redistribution of income, 241
refusing assignments, relationship to work setting, 257
status hierarchy of fields of practice, 27
status of firms, 37
Law firm(s), corporate. *See* Corporate law firm(s)

Law school(s)
large law firm as constituency of, 288
local and regional graduates, rise in, 133
representation by firm, year hired, *132*
on specialization, 76
status of, position of large law firms, 66
Lawyer-client relationship(s), 250–259
Lawyer(s)
as agents of rationalization, 287
characteristics of, 283
dealings of, 82, 83
managerial authority of, 28
mediating role of, 234
and professional autonomy, debate over, 233, 234
professional status of, 3
and proposed changes in fields of practice, 243–250
on questions of law and policy, 12
self-view, 12
serving as special representatives, 55
traditional view of, 11
tripartite relationship of, 11
Leadership
and client base, 27
and collegiality, 4
and dishonorable work, 53
and long-term strategic issues, 70
as managerial elite, 27
and norms of collegiality, 28
LeBoeuf-Lamb, 48
Legal Times 1983, 59
February 28, 1983, 143
1984, 2
September 24, 1984, 59
June 30, 1986, 109
Legal Times Advertising Letter, August 1984, 59
Legal Times of Washington, May 28, 1979, 2, 74
Leibowitz, Arleen, 64, 190, 193, 201
Levi, Edward H., 242
Literature. *See* Organizations literature; Professions literature
Litigation, defined, 107
Llewellyn, Karl, 249
Lockstep income systems, 65
Lorber, Judith, 159
Lorne, Simon M., 234
Loyola University School of Law, 137
Lukes, Steven, 207

Macaulay, Stewart
analysis of consumer protection lawyers, 233
functioning of formal legal institutions, 7

large law firms as effective representatives of interests of clients, 231
lawyer-client relationships in corporate firms, 256
lawyers' expression of concern of clients' long-term interests, 248
truth-in-lending legislation, impact of counsel, 287
McBarnett, Doreen, 2
McChesney, Fred S., 64, 190, 193
McCurdy, Charles, 9
McDermott, Will & Emery, 42, 52, 60
McHugh, Carol, 131
Managerial authority, 28
Managerial elite
 challenges to, 27
 emergence of, 38
 manner of governance, 27
Managerial order, emerging, 9
Managerial policy(ies)
 without autonomous managerial stratum, 15
 defined, 91
 nonadoption of, large law firms, 10
Mandel, Ernest, 286
Mann, Michael, 7, 249
Marcson, Simon, 18, 220, 227
Marshall, John Law School, 137
Martindale-Hubbell Law Directory 1965, 59
 1979–1984, 49
 1984, 135
Marx, Karl, 159
Masters, Edgar L., 39
Mayer, Brown & Platt, 39, 42, 52, 60
Mayer, Levy, 39
Meadow, Robert G., 159
Means, Gardiner C., 288
Memmel-Jacobs, 61
Menkel-Meadow, Carrie, 140, 159
Merger(s)
 consequence of, 60
 as indicator, 59
 Punnett's research on, 65
Merton, Robert K., 220
Meserve, Robert, 261
Meyer, Marshall W., 88
Miller, George A., 18, 230
Mills, C. Wright
 attacks on large law firms, 231
 division of labor, large law firm, 159
 ideology of professional autonomy, 12
 jeremiad directed at large law firm, 236
 large firms as law factories, 170
 social role of large law firm, twentieth century, 260
Mincer, Jacob, 201
Minders, 9

different role of, 275–276
managerial role of, 73–75
Mnookin, Robert H., 62, 64, 65, 191
Model, of organizational dominance, 6
Model Rules of Professional Conduct, proposed, 261
Moldenhauer, Howard H., 190
Monopoly perspective, 22
Montagna, Paul
 autonomous professional organization, 13, 15
 Big Eight accounting firms, 66, 209
 professional organizations, 30
 professional values, 79
Moral authority, 21
Murphy, Walter F., 268

Nader, Ralph, 12, 231, 236, 260
National Law Journal, 38
 1982, 2
 May 26, 1986, 75, 143
National rankings, 49
Navin, Thomas R., 285
Network analysis, defined, 161
New Deal, impact of, 285
New York City law firm(s)
 early predominance of, 66
 predominance of, 43
 salaries, starting, 75
 signing bonuses of, 76
 Smigel's interpretation of, 6
 strategies for growth, 71
 turnover rates, 137
New York system, of partnership, 9
New York Times
 December 17, 1978, 234
 May 19, 1981, 57
 January 18, 1982, 73
 April 2, 1982, 57
 January 16, 1983, 59
 February 7, 1983, 261
 February 10, 1983, 261
 May 29, 1984, 143
 March 12, 1985, 274
Noble, David, 286
Nonbureaucratic structures, 15
 large law firm as, 82
Nonlegal advice, 252, 253

Occupational Safety and Health Administration (OSHA), 239
O'Conor, Charles, 259
Oppenheimer, M., 26, 171
Organization(s)
 professional; derivation of structure of, 20; dualism in, 18; and political-economic analysis, need for, 19; and processes of social change, 24

social, aspects, 27
structure of, considerations, 25
value-rational, 210
Organizational dimensions, characteristics, 13
Organizational dominance
emphasis on, for comprehensive view, 24
model of, 6
perspective of, 23, 38
Organization of work, 159–189
assignments, percentage of time spent on, summary table, *182*
core of, 188, 189
division of labor in law firm, 170–172
hours, total worked, 184–189
social structure of work, network's approach, 161–170; blockmodeling, 162, 169; smallest space analysis, 162–169
specialization by field of law, 172–177; specialization index (SI), frequency distribution of, *173*
task differentiation, 176–180; assignments, sources and types of, 181–184; legal tasks, analysis of frequency of performing, *179*; legal tasks by field of law, scaled frequency of performing, *178*; total hours worked per year, by firm, partnership status, and field of practice, *186*
Organizations literature
focus on professionals in organizations, 18
on nature of commitment, 16
on significance of client interests to stratification of firm, 16
on social structure of professional firm, 15
theories, 23
value rational organizations, 78
variations in organizations, 23, 24
Ornstein, Norman J., 7
Ouchi, William G., 6, 15, 78, 205, 210

Paradigm, of professional dominance, 21
Parsonian paradigm, 247
Parsons, Talcott
attitudes of large firm lawyers, 238, 239
axiomatic conception of organizations, 89
functionalist model, 11
functionalist theories, 20
illegitimate desires of clients and social interest, 232
social values and professional work, relationship between, 281

Partner(s)
and associates, divergence between, 28
finders, minders, and grinders, 9
nonequity and super, 9
strained relationships between, 8
turnover among, 141
Partner-managers, in firms, 74
Partnership(s), 4
closed or open, 77
collegial form, 211–214
dual, aspects, 141, 275
fundamental principle of, 8, 9
lateral entry into, 55
New York system, 9
policies, 140, 141
policies on admission of associates to, 76, 77
as system of collegial domination, 16
traditional conceptions of, 4
Patent firm(s), nature, 40
Patterns of participation, 91
Pepper, Hamilton & Scheetz, 49
Perrow, Charles, 26, 88, 210
Peters, Thomas J., 120
Pipkin, Ronald M., 140
Political-economic analysis, 6
and domination, 17
implications of, 38
of organizational change, 91
of professional organization, 19
Polsby, Nelson, 231
Pope & Ballard, 42
Powell, Michael, 231, 283
Power
denial of, 213, 214
in firm, 5
in management, 19
money as form of, 265, 266
relationships, within professional group, 20
Primus inter pares, 79
group of, Curran, 111
Pro bono work, 186
large law firms commitment to, 12
pro bono publico, 260
Professional bureaucracy. *See* Bureaucracy
Professional firm(s)
as exemplars of nonbureaucratic organizations, 15
social structure, 15
Professionalism
appeal of, 214–220
and bureaucratization, conflict between, 4, 10
erosion of meaning of, 225
ideology of, and large law firm, 3

Index   373

Professional Powers (Freidson), 19
Professions literature
  and lack of political-economic analysis
    of professional organizations, 6
  limitations of, 20
  orthodox conceptions of professions,
    21
  power precedes knowledge, arguments,
    280
  theories, 23
  treatment of bureaucratization, 17
Profit sharing, seniority-based, 65
Progressive ideal
  Brandeis on, 11
  and large law firm in society, 11
Proletarianization
  argument, Freidson on, 20
  of professional labor, 171
  of professionals, 20
Punnett, Spencer, research on mergers, 65

Racial diversity, 131
Rationalization and power, 270–290
  Chicago Bar Association, 284
  economic change, prospects for, 272–
    273
  functionalist theory, 280–282
  ideology, authority, and conflict, 276–
    280
  internal hierarchy, 275–276
  lawyers, as agents of rationalization,
    286
  lawyers, characteristics of, 283
  orthodox conception of professions,
    280
  structural change, prospects for, specialization and bureaucratization,
    273–275
Rationalization of law, 81
  as defined by Weber, 82
Reagan administration, 49
Recruitment
  and approach to departmentalization
    and specialization, 76
  and large law firms, 75
Recruitment and careers, 127–158
  entry, exit, and promotion, 136–144;
    associate hiring and turnover, nineteen firms in Chicago, *138*; lawyers
    leaving firms, current practice setting,
    142; partnership policies, 140, 141;
    replacement and expansion, of associates, 143; turnover rates, 137–
    140
  job change and job choice in firm, 150–
    158; percentage of channeled choices
    by field of practice, *153*; percentage

  of lawyers channeled into field of
    practice, *152*; rates of change from
    first field of specialty, *154*; reason for
    choice of field, by firm, *156*
  patterns of recruitment, 129–136;
    Catholics, 134; discrimination,
    Jewish, 130, 131; gender by firm,
    year hired, *135*; law school representation by firm, year hired, *132*;
    women, 133–136
  work histories in firm, 144–158; career
    events by period, *146*; careers, major
    events in, 144–150
Reich, Charles, 7
Research design, 29–34
  data collected, 31, 32
  generalizability of results, 32–34
  typology and sampling frame, 29–31
Reuben, Don, 42
Rhea, Buford, 4
Risk-avoidance, 64, 65
  and theories of law firm expansion, 66
Robinson, John P., 238
Root, Elihu, 233, 260
Rosen, Robert Eli, 26
Rosenberg, Sheli, 76
Rosenthal, Douglas, 18, 233, 252
Ross & Hardies, 42, 75, 203
Rothman, Robert A., 20, 26
Rueschemeyer, Dietrich, 233
Rule by committee, 111
Rush, Jerrold G., 238

Salisbury, Robert H., 262
Sarat, Austin, 252
Satow, Roberta L., 15, 78, 205, 210, 276
Schwartz, Murray L., 252
Scott, MacLeish, & Falk, 40
Scott, William R.
  administrative priorities and professional standards, conflict between,
    220
  autonomous professional organizations, 276
  professional organizations, 30
  professionals in organizations, 18
  speculation in organization theory, 210
  study of social agencies, 209
Sears, Marian V., 285
Securities and Exchange Commission, 244
Selznick, Philip, 287
Seward, Guthrie & Steele, 71
Seward, William, 39
Seyfarth, Shaw, Fairweather & Geraldson, 42, 52, 61
Shearman, John, 259
Shearman & Sterling, 39, 43, 52

Shepherd, John, 263
Shils, Edward, 20, 281
Sidley & Austin, 42, 57, 61
Sikes, Bette H., 57
Simon, William, 258
Sims, Stransky & Brewer, 40
Skadden-Arps, 42, 43, 48, 60, 61, 121
Skipped-generation cohort structure, 96
Sloan, Alfred P., Jr., 71
Smallest space analysis, 162–169
Smigel, Erwin
  autonomy, 232, 233, 276
  canons of professional ethics, 14
  democratic forms of governance, New
    York law firms, 275
  division of labor, large firms, 159
  ethnic and class groups, New York
    firms, 130
  ethnic and gender segmentation, 127
  large firms, expanding role of, 282
  large firms, professional cultures, 27
  long hours, 185
  and Parsonian paradigm, 247
  powers in partnership agreement, 70
  premise of study, 209
  professional bureaucracy, 205, 206
  professional values, universally shared,
    218
  professional values originating outside
    of firm, 79
  selecting-out process, 139
  and small number of interviews, 29
  study of Wall Street firms and lawyers,
    6, 12–17
  womens' work roles, 135
  work groups organized around fields of
    law, 172
Social change
  in large law firm, practice and privilege,
    25–29
  in law firm, considerations, 24
Social values and client relationships,
    231–269
  influence of large firms, 263–269; con-
    trol of technical expertise, 266, 267;
    economic resources of firm, within
    legal system, 264–266; ideological
    function of firm, 267–269; produc-
    tion of knowledge, control over,
    266–267
  institutional theory of role of large law
    firm in; law and society, toward,
    259–269
  lawyer-client relationship, 250–259;
    opportunity to give nonlegal advice
    by partnership status, field and rea-
    sons affecting opportunities, 253;

percentage of time spent on principal
    client in last year, by field of practice
    and firm, 251; refusals of assign-
    ments by circumstances of refusal
    and reasons for no refusals, 254; role
    perceptions and reports of lawyer-
    client conflict, 251–259; time de-
    voted to principal client, 250, 251
  problem of professional autonomy,
    232–236; debate over autonomy of
    lawyers, 233, 234; ideology and be-
    havior of lawyers, 234; sample, of
    four firms, aspects of, 235–236
  proposed changes in fields of practice,
    lawyers, 243–250; impact of pro-
    posed reforms, 248; implications of
    findings, 248–250; Parsonian para-
    digm, 247
  rationalization and power, 280–290
  social and legal values, general, 236–
    243; autonomy and inequality, as-
    pects of, 236; class-action litigation,
    241, 242; differences in income be-
    tween occupations, 241; government
    regulation, 238, 239; judge, proper
    role of, 242; lawyers' views on gen-
    eral state of inequality, 240; selected
    values items, responses to, 237; sys-
    tematic data collection, 236–238
Sociology of law
  and political-economic analysis, 38
  and sociology of firm, convergence be-
    tween, 82
Sonnenschein, Levinson, Carlin, Nath &
    Rosenthal, 40
Spangler, Eve, 26, 139, 189
Specialization
  and efficiency, 26
  by field of law, 172–177
  and growth, processes of, 275
  highest levels of, in large law firms, 84
Specialization index (SI), 172–175
Special representation fields, 52
  freer development of, 53
  typical role of, 54
Special representatives, careers of, 55
Specialty firm(s)
  growth by special representation, 51
  prototypical cases of, 52
Spector, Malcolm B., 128
Stanford Law Review, 1982, 140
Starr, Paul, 90
Status hierarchy, 9, 10
Stelling, Joan, 30, 208, 209
Sterling, John, 259
Stevens, Robert, 76
Stewart, James, 185, 231

Stewart, Richard R., 7
Stinchcombe, Arthur L., 52, 82, 266
Structure(s)
  nonbureaucratic, 15
  organizational; considerations on variations in, 25; and professional values, relationship between, 15; revelations of, 25
  skipped-generation cohort, 96
  social, of professional firms, professional literature on, 15
Sullivan & Cromwell, 49, 65
Swaine, Robert T., 71, 72
Swanson, Guy, 15, 210

Tanenhaus, Joseph, 268
Technical authority, 21. *See also* Autonomy
Theoretical perspective, 18–29
  organizational dominance and market for professional services, 18–24; formal knowledge, professions' control of, 19; power of management, 19; power relationships, 20; proletarianization argument, 20; scholarship of professions, examples, 18; theories, 23
  practice and privilege, social change in large law firm, 25–29; managerial authority, 28; and managerial elite, 27
Theory(ies)
  of authority, 208
  of domination, 20
  economic, of law firm growth, 62–69
  functionalist, 20; difficulty with and rejection of, 21; and growth of large law firms, 281, 282; strength of, 280, 281
  institutional, of role of large firm in law and society, toward, 259–269
  of law firm growth, 49–69
  of legitimate domination, 23
  of professional bureaucracy, Smigel's, 15
  of professional dominance, 21, 22
  of professional monopoly, 22
  of rise of professionalism, 23
  of structural change, 19
Thibaut, John, 268
Thompson, J. D., 89
Thrower, Randolph, 261
Tocqueville, Alexix de, 282, 284
Tollison, Robert, 64, 190, 193, 201
Traditional management, characteristics, 91
Transaction-costs framework, 67–69

Transformation
  alternate explanation for, 283
  of large law firm, 7–12
  of work process, 171
Treinens, Howard, 57
Tribal customs, firms, 120
Tripartite relationship, 11
Tuma, Nancy Brandon, 145

Unger, Roberto M., 240, 242
U.S. Supreme Court, 22
Up or out rule, 72

Value-added tax, 244
Value-rational organization, defined, 210
Vedder-Price, 52
Vreeland, Rebecca S., 210

Wald-Harkrader, 49, 109
Walker, Laurens, 268
Wall Street Journal
  November 11, 1983, 75
  November 18, 1983, 49, 109
Wall Street law firm(s)
  as professional bureaucracy, 13
  Smigel's interpretation of, 14
  Smigel's study of, 12–17
Wall Street lawyer(s)
  as enlightened professionals, 233
  Smigel's study of, 12–17
Washington law firms, 66
  turnover rates, 137
Washington Post, December 27, 1983, 260
Waterman, Robert H., Jr., 120
Weber, Max
  client-responsible partners acting as *primus inter pares*, 79
  governance decisions via collegial consensus, 100
  large firm lawyers as modern *honoratiores*, 284
  legal *honoratiore*, 1
  rationalization of law, 81, 82
  support for formally rational systems, 289
  theory of legitimate domination, typology of forms, 23
  variables to theories of social hierarchy, 207
Whistle-blowing proposal, 261
White, Harrison C., 169
White & Case, 49
Whyte, William H., Jr., 13
Wilensky, Harold, 18, 220
Wiley, Richard, 42
Willer, David E., 78

Williamson, Oliver, 63, 67, 207
Wilson, P. A., 20
Winston & Strawn, 42, 203
Women
 in law firms, 133–136

turnover rates, 139, 140
Wrong, Dennis H., 207

Zald, Mayer N., 88, 91
Zehnle, Richard, 81, 172

Designer: U.C. Press Staff
Compositor: Prestige Typography
Text: 10/13 Sabon
Display: Sabon
Printer: Braun-Brumfield, Inc.
Binder: Braun-Brumfield, Inc.